CRITICAL INSIGHTS

Slaughterhouse-Five

by Kurt Vonnegut

CRITICAL INSIGHTS

Slaughterhouse-Five

by Kurt Vonnegut

Editor
Leonard Mustazza
Penn State Abington

Salem Press
Pasadena, California   Hackensack, New Jersey

Cover photo: © Bernd Guessbacher/Dreamstime.com

Published by Salem Press

© 2011 by EBSCO Publishing
Editor's text © 2011 by Leonard Mustazza
"The *Paris Review* Perspective" © 2011 by Sarah Fay for *The Paris Review*

∞ The paper used in these volumes conforms to the American National Standard for Permanence of Paper for Printed Library Materials, Z39.48-1992 (R1997).

Library of Congress Cataloging-in-Publication Data
Slaughterhouse-five, by Kurt Vonnegut / editor, Leonard Mustazza.
    p. cm. — (Critical insights)
Includes bibliographical references and index.
ISBN 978-1-58765-721-4 (alk. paper)
1. Vonnegut, Kurt. Slaughterhouse-five. I. Mustazza, Leonard, 1952-
PS3572.O5S638 2011
813'.54—dc22

                                                        2010030222

PRINTED IN CANADA

Contents

Resources

About This Volume

Leonard Mustazza

In 1950, Kurt Vonnegut quit his day job as a publicist for General Electric to become a full-time writer. Soon he was able to make a respectable living by selling short stories to popular magazines and publishing novels, beginning with *Player Piano* in 1952. Despite his early success, however, he did not receive any critical attention for more than fifteen years, apart from a few early book reviews. The first mass-media article devoted to his work was a review essay by C. D. B. Bryan, which was published in the *New Republic* in 1966; that same year the first academic criticism appeared: Robert Scholes's analysis of Vonnegut's use of black humor, which was published in *Hollins Critic* and revised for his 1967 book *The Fabulators*. Everything changed, however, with the publication of *Slaughterhouse-Five* in 1969. The following year marked the beginning of a steady stream of criticism that has so far run for more than four decades, making Vonnegut among the most "documented" of contemporary writers.

Of course, that a great deal of this criticism is devoted entirely or in part to *Slaughterhouse-Five* signals its importance within the vast canon Vonnegut produced during his nearly sixty years as a professional writer. This volume brings together fifteen of the best pieces on the novel that have appeared since 1973. They are arranged chronologically in order to provide a sense of the range of critical responses to the novel over the years. In addition, this volume also includes four introductory essays assessing the novel's literary and cultural significance over more than four decades.

Among the very first and most influential scholars writing on Vonnegut is Jerome Klinkowitz, whose book with John Somer, *The Vonnegut Statement* (1973), virtually launched Vonnegut studies. This volume contains a previously published chapter on *Slaughterhouse-Five* from Klinkowitz's 2004 book *The Vonnegut Effect* and a new, original piece in which Klinkowitz examines the book's critical reception from its earliest 1969 reviews through the numerous journal articles and book chapters that have followed in subsequent decades. Especially interesting in Klinkowitz's incisive analyses of the many attempts to categorize Vonnegut over the years—some critics regard him as a science-fiction writer (and a poor one at that), while others see him as an insightful mainstream writer who uses the trappings of science fiction in the service of moral issues.

In another new essay, "Temporal Cohesion and Disorientation in *Slaughterhouse-Five*," Kevin Alexander Boon offers a close reading of the novel from a provocative perspective. Considering Vonnegut's disjointed narrative technique, Boon examines the ways in which the author manages to construct a cohesive story from disparate fragments of memory, experience, perception, and imagination. The effect, he concludes, is ironic: we come away from this story about hapless, childlike Billy Pilgrim, who believes there is nothing he can do to change the world, with a sense that we need to try to effect change if we are to consider ourselves truly human.

A third essay, David Simmons's "'The War Parts, Anyway, Are Pretty Much True,'" compares *Slaughterhouse-Five* to that other great ironic World War II novel of the 1960s, Joseph Heller's *Catch-22*. Noting the close friendship between the writers and their shared views of war (both generally and with respect to the specific war in which they fought), Simmons offers an analysis that is long overdue—namely, a clear and convincing comparison of the satiric impulses behind and the narrative techniques employed in these unique war novels. Both texts, Simmons concludes, use innovative narrative devices to demonstrate the horrible effects of war on the individual, and both authors deftly employ comedy to suggest the humanist alternatives to armed conflict.

Finally, in her essay "The Vietnamization of World War II in *Slaughterhouse-Five* and *Gravity's Rainbow*," Christina Jarvis offers a cultural and historical perspective on Vonnegut's role in the transformation of popular perceptions about World War II. Even before World

War II came to an end, it had already become the subject of novels and films in which the role of America and its Allies was generally represented in quasi-allegorical terms, the forces of good battling selflessly to make the world safe from the evil clutches of fascism. Before long, this image of World War II as the "Good War" became universally etched in the popular imagination, and it is well reflected in the novels appearing in the fifteen years following the war. Jarvis aptly proposes that Vietnam-era writers such as Vonnegut and Thomas Pynchon overturned this cultural image, offering revisionist views of World War II and its "privileged space" in the American imagination. Following the lead of Heller's *Catch-22*, *Slaughterhouse-Five* and *Gravity's Rainbow* used satire, fragmented postmodern narratives, and hapless, nonheroic characters to reimagine and reconfigure our cultural narratives about the "Good War" in light of the divisive attitudes and bad feelings evoked by the Vietnam conflict.

In addition to these fine essays and the fifteen previously published articles, the volume also contains Peter J. Reed's brief biography of the author and Sarah Fay's assessment of *Slaughterhouse-Five* on behalf of *The Paris Review*. Taken together, these articles provide a comprehensive appreciation of a novel that most literary commentators agree is among the most influential books of the twentieth century.

THE BOOK
AND
AUTHOR

On *Slaughterhouse-Five*

Leonard Mustazza

They say that timing is everything in comedy. In fact, that old show-business adage can well be applied to all artistic productions, fiction not the least of them. Take Harper Lee's *To Kill a Mockingbird*, for instance. Published in the summer of 1960, the novel, a fictional amalgam of racially charged events that took place in Lee's native Alabama in the 1930s, quickly became a runaway best seller and its author a literary celebrity. One can safely conclude that its instant widespread appeal in 1960 had much to do with the divisive events that shook the nation that year. There were the protests at the segregated Woolworth's lunch counter in Greensboro, North Carolina, on February 1—the latest chapter in the roiling national unrest in these early days of the civil rights movement—and, of course, the close presidential election in which a young liberal idealist campaigned on progressive ideas about race in a racially divided nation. It was at this special moment in American history that *To Kill a Mockingbird* made its auspicious debut. Would it have made the same impression and been as successful had it appeared ten years earlier or later? Perhaps, but somehow it seems doubtful.

Much the same can be said of Kurt Vonnegut's classic novel *Slaughterhouse-Five*, a work that, like Harper Lee's opus, is set during one historical era but speaks to the political concerns of its contemporary audience. Published in March 1969, during the height of the antiwar protests over America's involvement in Vietnam, *Slaughterhouse-Five* turned Vonnegut into an instant celebrity. The young were particularly attracted to his fragmented style, absurdist theme, and antiwar stance. (The novel's subtitles, "The Children's Crusade" and "A Duty-Dance with Death" also struck a perfect thematic balance between innocence and war-related macabre that appealed to the imagination of youthful protesters.) Hence, at a time when youth admonished one another not to trust anyone over thirty, Vonnegut crossed over a barrier that purportedly separated the carefree young from the conservatively mature, the liberal progressive dreamer from the knee-jerk defender of the establishment. The title of a *Newsweek* piece about Vonnegut that month said it all: "Forty-six and Trusted."

In many ways, his status as a pop-culture celebrity and hero of the young must have struck Vonnegut as surprising and ironic. To begin with, this "instant fame" actually came nearly two decades after the publication of his first novel, *Player Piano* (1952). Despite his promising start, he would remain a relatively obscure novelist and short-story writer until *Cat's Cradle* made its modest appearance in 1963. None of what came before could betoken the explosive success of *Slaughterhouse-Five*.

Second, there is the matter of timing. Many writers who had seen the horrors of armed conflict during World War II firsthand used their experiences as bases for novels that made them household names. Among the most successful were Norman Mailer's *The Naked and the Dead* (1948), James Jones's *From Here to Eternity* (1951), and Cornelius Ryan's *The Longest Day* (1959), all of them published in the decade and a half after the war, and all of them enormous best sellers that were made into successful films. By contrast, Vonnegut did not get around to turning his wartime memories into fiction for nearly twenty-five years. By the time he did manage to say something about his experiences during the Allied bombing of Dresden in February 1945, the window of opportunity for war novelists had essentially closed. By 1969, the pride in and gratitude toward the veterans of World War II (the "Greatest Generation," as Tom Brokaw would later call them) had dissipated, replaced by divisive antiwar fervor and denunciations of the American military's purposes and tactics in Vietnam. If, as Vonnegut's narrator suggests, the author had hoped to produce a serious conventional war story in the manner of Mailer, Jones, or Ryan, it was too late for that. The horror that he had seen was simply too overwhelming. "Not many words about Dresden came from my mind then," the Vonnegut-like metafictional narrator asserts in the introduction, and so "this lousy little book" ended up costing him decades of anxiety.

Ironically, however, by waiting nearly twenty-five years before finally telling his particular war story, Vonnegut managed, like his fictional predecessors, to produce a masterpiece as well as earn fame and fortune. Unlike them, though, the greatness of this particular masterpiece came not from the glorification of war and the nobility of its warriors but from the opposite. When the narrator meets Mary O'Hare in the novel's first chapter, she expresses her disdain for the typical war stories that get turned into films starring the likes of John Wayne and Frank Sinatra and that make "war look just wonderful." Mary warms to the narrator, however, when he promises not to write this kind of story and even suggests that his book might be called "the Children's Crusade." Ironic in tone, innovative in narrative technique, antiwar in its theme, *Slaughterhouse-Five* was a war novel for a new generation.

Like his friend and fellow veteran Joseph Heller, whose *Catch-22* (1961) used bitter comic irony to portray the purposelessness of war, Vonnegut employs the war generally and his own experiences specifically to create the stuff of black comedy. He takes as his central character a fragile, naïvely innocent young man named Billy Pilgrim, who comes "unstuck in time" as a means of coping with the horrors of war. Helpless and hopeless, Billy is dragged by his time travels not only into his own horrific past and present but also to an imagined future replete with space aliens from the planet Tralfamadore, who offer reassuring insights into the purpose of life (or the lack thereof), the random nature of time, and the uniquely human illusion of free will. "So it goes," the narrator casually declares every time someone or something dies, thus rendering the horrors that the childlike Billy sees at once commonplace and terrible.

Despite, or perhaps because of, its unique approach to war fiction, the novel became an international hit, rising to the top of the *New York Times* best-seller list and garnering mostly positive reviews from major national newspapers and magazines. Not surprisingly, given that Vonnegut was at the time labeled a science-fiction writer (a dubious tag at best), the book was nominated for major science-fiction prizes, including Hugo and Nebula Awards. Its innovative narrative style, quirky presentation of its antiwar theme, and deft postmodern approach to storytelling also appealed to high school and college students, and the book established itself as a staple in English classes, remaining to this day Vonnegut's most widely taught novel. Curiously, however, that very appeal to youth brought with it a good bit of controversy. In 1976, a Long Island conservative community group named Parents of New York United demanded that the Island Trees School District remove a number of books that they found morally objectionable from its library shelves, among them *Slaughterhouse-Five*. The school board agreed that Vonnegut's book was unacceptable because of the author's use of profanity, depiction of sexual scenes, and irreverent comments about God and country and had the book removed from all of its libraries, prompting a First Amendment challenge by a group of students. The case went all the way to the U.S. Supreme Court, which ruled in the students' favor in 1982, asserting that local school boards that remove books simply because they do not like the ideas expressed in them are indeed violating the First Amendment to the Constitution. It was a great victory for Vonnegut and for free-speech advocates everywhere, but the ruling did not stop other school districts from trying to suppress the novel. Indeed, the American Library Association lists the book as one of the 100 Most Frequently Challenged Books of 1990-1999.

Such controversy aside, *Slaughterhouse-Five* remains one of Vonnegut's most relevant and enjoyable books and one of the most influential American novels of our time. In 2005, *Time* magazine named it one of the 100 all-time English language novels, and its influence has extended well beyond the pages of literature. In 1972, George Roy Hill's innovative film adaptation won the Jury Prize at the Cannes Film Festival and the Hugo Award for Best Dramatic Presentation. In 1996, the Steppenwolf Theatre Company staged a theatrical presentation in Chicago, and a revival of the play by the Godlight Theatre Company took place in January 2006, less than a year after Vonnegut's death. There is even a German operatic adaptation, staged by the Bavarian State Opera in Munich in 1996, and a 2009 English radio play by the British Broadcasting Corporation.

This continuing interest in Vonnegut's masterpiece is hardly surprising, for the issues he raises about war and the people who fight have remained relevant since the book's appearance more than four decades ago. As noted at the outset, timing is everything in comedy, particularly satiric black comedy, and few works have proven this better than *Slaughterhouse-Five*.

Biography of Kurt Vonnegut_____

Peter J. Reed

Kurt Vonnegut was born in Indianapolis, Indiana, on November 11, 1922, the son of Kurt and Edith Vonnegut. He was the youngest of three children. His ancestors had come from Germany in 1855. They were prosperous, originally as brewers and merchants, down to Kurt's grandfather and father, who were both architects, and they were prominent in the heavily German Indianapolis society. Then World War I left a residue of anti-German feeling in the United States and prohibitions on the use of the German language, dimming the family's pride and its cultural heritage. Prohibition brought an end to the brewing business, and the Great Depression of the 1930's left Vonnegut's father without work for essentially the rest of his life. Vonnegut wrote frequently of the Depression and repeatedly portrayed people who, like his father, are left feeling purposeless by loss of occupation.

At Shortridge High School, Vonnegut wrote for the *Shortridge Daily Echo*. The rigor of writing daily to deadlines helped shape his habits as a writer. In 1940, he went to Cornell University in Ithaca, New York, where he majored in biochemistry and wrote for the *Cornell Sun*. By January, 1943, Vonnegut was a private in the U.S. Army. In May of that year, his mother committed suicide, an event of which he would write as having left him a "legacy of suicide." Soon thereafter, the Army sent him to Europe, where he was captured and held as a prisoner of war in Dresden, Germany. There he experienced the event that forms the basis of his novel *Slaughterhouse-Five* (1969), the firebombing that virtually destroyed Dresden on the night of February 13, 1945.

After discharge from the Army, Vonnegut undertook graduate studies in anthropology at the University of Chicago. He also married his former high school sweetheart, Jane Cox. While a student, he worked as a police reporter for the Chicago City News Bureau. Vonnegut left Chicago without a degree, although in 1971 his novel *Cat's*

Cradle (1963) was accepted in lieu of a thesis, and he was awarded an M.A.

In 1947, Vonnegut moved to Schenectady, New York, where he worked as a public relations writer at the General Electric Research Laboratory. There he began writing fiction, and his first published short story, "Report on the Barnhouse Effect," appeared in *Collier's* in February, 1950. Encouraged by his success as a short-story writer, he resigned from General Electric and moved to Provincetown, Massachusetts, to devote himself full time to writing. He continued to publish in popular magazines such as the *Saturday Evening Post*, *Ladies' Home Journal*, *Collier's*, and *Cosmopolitan*, but he also placed stories in science-fiction journals such as *Galaxy* and *Fantasy and Science Fiction Magazine*. His first novel, *Player Piano* (1952), was reissued by Bantam in 1954 with the title *Utopia 14*. Largely because of his success with short stories, which often paid well, Vonnegut did not produce his second novel, *The Sirens of Titan* (1959), until seven years after *Player Piano*. Those first two novels, together with a number of the short stories, earned for Vonnegut identification as a science-fiction writer, a label with which he was not always happy, because the genre was disdained in many quarters. During this time, Vonnegut faced personal hardships. In October, 1957, his father died, and in 1958, his sister Alice was stricken with cancer. Days before her death, her husband, James Adams, was killed when his commuter train crashed from a bridge. After this double tragedy, Vonnegut adopted three of their four orphaned children, doubling the size of his family.

The 1960's began as difficult times for Vonnegut but then saw his gradual emergence to fame. Television dried up the magazine market for short stories, and he turned to the paperback book market, first publishing a collection of short stories called *Canary in a Cat House* (1961), then the novel *Mother Night* (1961). Neither achieved great sales. The next two novels, *Cat's Cradle* and *God Bless You, Mr. Rosewater* (1965), appeared in hardcover. In 1965, he went to teach at the Writers' Workshop at the University of Iowa, where he met other writers and critics who influenced him, particularly in encouraging him to enter his fiction more personally. This led to his adding a new and highly personal preface to the 1966 hardcover edition of *Mother Night*; in many of his subsequent works, such autobiographical introductions would become a popular feature.

In 1966 and 1967, Avon and Dell reissued all of his novels in paperback, and *Player Piano* and *Mother Night* were reprinted in hardcover. The coincidence of these events brought greater public attention to his work, and his fame began to build. A new collection of his short stories, *Welcome to the Monkey House*, appeared in 1968. Meanwhile, Vonnegut had won a Guggenheim Fellowship to revisit Dresden and research the event he had struggled to write about for years, the great air raid he had experienced. This led to *Slaughterhouse-Five*. The novel, and the film that followed it, brought Vonnegut broad popularity and financial security.

Success, however, brought its own difficulties. Having faced in fiction the event that had motivated so much of his writing, Vonnegut now struggled. He even considered abandoning the novel for other forms, writing the play *Happy Birthday, Wanda June* (1970). A compilation from his works appeared as a teleplay called *Between Time and Timbuktu* (1972). His marriage to Jane foundered, and he moved alone to New York City. At last, in 1973, he published another novel, *Breakfast of Champions*, different in form from his previous work and illustrated with his own drawings. It drew mixed reviews but achieved excellent sales, with a first printing of one hundred thousand copies.

In 1974 came the publication of a collection of Vonnegut's essays, speeches, stories, and biography called *Wampeters, Foma, and Granfalloons (Opinions)*. Two more novels, *Slapstick* (1976) and *Jailbird* (1979), followed, in what Vonnegut has asserted was a difficult decade for him as a writer. He achieved a feeling of completion with *Slaughterhouse-Five*, he said, and found little that provided stimulation in the society of that period. By 1979, however, Vonnegut had remarried, to the photographer Jill Krementz, and adopted a baby daughter, Lily.

Also in 1979, he had a return to the stage when his daughter Edith produced a musical adaptation of *God Bless You, Mr. Rosewater* in New York. He wrote the text of a children's Christmas story, *Sun Moon Star* (1980), illustrated by Ivan Chermayeff. *Palm Sunday: An Autobiographical Collage* (1981) was another collection, and it was followed by the novels *Deadeye Dick* (1982), *Galápagos* (1985), *Bluebeard* (1987), *Hocus Pocus* (1990), and *Timequake* (1997). Also, *Bagombo Snuff Box*, a collection of Vonnegut's early stories, was published in 1999, as was *God Bless You, Dr. Kevorkian*, a collection of fictional interviews, and *Like Shaking Hands with God: A Conversation About Writing*. Finally, a collection of essays, *A Man Without a Country*, was published in 2005.

Having become a major figure in the American literary establishment, Vonnegut was much in demand as a speaker, frequently using the title "How to Get a Job Like Mine" to embark upon a rambling and highly entertaining evening somewhat in the manner of Mark Twain. He was also much in demand for articles in magazines and even for advertisements—an ironic echo of his beginnings as a public relations writer for General Electric. Vonnegut died in New York on April 11, 2007, after a fall two weeks earlier that resulted in irreversible brain damage.

From *Magill's Survey of American Literature* (Pasadena, CA: Salem Press, 2007). Copyright © 2007 by Salem Press, Inc.

Bibliography

Allen, William Rodney. *Understanding Kurt Vonnegut*. Columbia: University of South Carolina Press, 1991. Allen's study, part of the Understanding Contemporary American Literature series, places Vonnegut, and especially *Slaughterhouse-Five*, in the literary canon. Contains an annotated bibliography and an index.
Boon, Kevin Alexander, ed. *At Millennium's End: New Essays on the Work of Kurt Vonnegut*. Albany: State University of New York Press, 2001. A collection of eleven essays examining the novelist's moral vision.
Broer, Lawrence R. *Sanity Plea: Schizophrenia in the Novels of Kurt Vonnegut*.

Ann Arbor, Mich.: UMI Research Press, 1988. This volume focuses on the theme of social neurosis, with emphasis on schizophrenic behavior in the main characters of the novels through *Bluebeard*. The thesis has relevance to a number of the short stories and gives insight into the evolution of Vonnegut's fiction.

Giannone, Richard. *Vonnegut: A Preface to His Novels*. Port Washington, N.Y.: Kennikat, 1977. Treats the novels up to *Slapstick* and the play *Happy Birthday, Wanda June* in the context of Vonnegut's life and times. Emphasizes developing themes and techniques connecting the novels, with chapters devoted to individual novels.

Klinkowitz, Jerome. *"Slaughterhouse-Five": Reforming the Novel and the World*. Boston: Twayne, 1990. This book contains the most thorough and most modern treatment available of *Slaughterhouse-Five*. With care and insight, Klinkowitz debunks earlier, fatalistic interpretations of the novel. Features a comprehensive chronology, a thorough bibliography, and an index.

_____. *Vonnegut in Fact: The Public Spokesmanship of Personal Fiction*. Columbia: University of South Carolina Press, 1998. Makes a case for Vonnegut as a sort of redeemer of the novelistic form, after writers such as Philip Roth declared it dead. He traces Vonnegut's successful integration of autobiography and fiction in his body of work. Provides an extensive bibliography and an index.

Klinkowitz, Jerome, and David L. Lawler, eds. *Vonnegut in America: An Introduction to the Life and Work of Kurt Vonnegut*. New York: Delacorte Press, 1977. A collection of essays ranging from biography and an "album" of family photographs to Vonnegut as satirist, science-fiction writer, and short-story writer. Discusses his reputation in the Soviet Union and Europe. Contains an authoritative bibliography.

Klinkowitz, Jerome, and John Somer, eds. *The Vonnegut Statement*. New York: Delacorte Press, 1973. A collection of essays by various authors, which establishes the nature and sources of Vonnegut's reputation at this important juncture. Analyzes his career from his college writing to the short fiction, and through the novels to *Slaughterhouse-Five*. Includes an interview and a bibliography. The most important accounting of his career through its first two decades.

Leeds, Marc. *The Vonnegut Encyclopedia: An Authorized Compendium*. Westport, Conn.: Greenwood Press, 1995. A concordance and encyclopedia identifying Vonnegut's most frequently recurring images and all his characters; indispensable for serious students of Vonnegut.

Merrill, Robert, ed. *Critical Essays on Kurt Vonnegut*. Boston: G. K. Hall, 1990. A comprehensive collection of essays on Vonnegut's works and career, which includes reviews, previously published essays, and articles commissioned for this work. The extensive introduction traces in detail Vonnegut's career and critical reception from the beginnings to 1990.

Morse, Donald E. *The Novels of Kurt Vonnegut: Imagining Being an American*. Westport, Conn.: Praeger, 2003. This analysis examines Vonnegut's novels against the framework of American history and literature of the twentieth century.

Mustazza, Leonard, ed. *The Critical Response to Kurt Vonnegut*. Westport, Conn.: Greenwood Press, 1994. Presents a brief history of the critical response to Vonnegut and critical reviews.

Nuwer, Hank. "Kurt Vonnegut Close Up." *Saturday Evening Post* 258 (May/June, 1986): 38-39. A biographical sketch which discusses Vonnegut's writing career, noting that his work often deals with the subject of man's inability to cope with technology.

Pieratt, Asa B., Jr., Julie Huffman-Klinkowitz, and Jerome Klinkowitz. *Kurt Vonnegut: A Comprehensive Bibliography*. Hamden, Conn.: Archon Books, 1987. An authoritative bibliography of works by and about Vonnegut. Lists Vonnegut's works in all their editions, including the short stories in their original places of publication, dramatic and cinematic adaptations, interviews, reviews, secondary sources, and dissertations.

Reed, Peter J. *The Short Fiction of Kurt Vonnegut*. Westport, Conn.: Greenwood Press, 1997. A critical study of the author's short fiction. Includes a bibliography and an index.

Reed, Peter J., and Marc Leeds, eds. *The Vonnegut Chronicles: Interviews and Essays*. Westport, Conn.: Greenwood Press, 1996. Vonnegut discusses, among other topics, postmodernism and experimental fiction. Includes a bibliography and an index.

Schatt, Stanley. *Kurt Vonnegut, Jr*. Boston: Twayne, 1976. Discusses the first eight novels, with separate chapters on the short stories and on the plays. Includes a chronology, a biography, and a bibliography up to 1975.

Stone, Brad. "Vonnegut's Last Stand." *Newsweek* 130 (September 29, 1997): 78. A biographical sketch that focuses on *Timequake*, which Vonnegut has called his last book.

Vonnegut, Kurt, Jr. Interview by Wendy Smith. *Publishers Weekly* 228 (October 25, 1985): 68-69. Vonnegut discusses his writing career, censorship, and his work; notes that he is an ardent foe of book censorship and has strong words for those who seek to limit the free speech of others.

The *Paris Review* Perspective

Sarah Fay for *The Paris Review*

When *Slaughterhouse-Five* was first published in 1969, hippies protesting the Vietnam War walked around with it tucked in their back pockets. The novel's stark portrayal of the firebombing of Dresden spoke to their disgust with lying governments that target civilians in battle. But instead of merely presenting the unadorned misery of war, Vonnegut uses wit, sarcasm, and fantasy—in the guise of illustrations, song lyrics, and aliens called the Tralfamadorians—to show the absurdity of it. *Slaughterhouse-Five* is a war novel, but it is steeped in a kind of humor so distinct that it has taken the name of its creator—Vonnegutian satire.

To write the novel, Vonnegut drew on his own experiences as an infantry scout in World War II: "I saw the destruction of Dresden," he wrote in his memoir *A Man Without a Country*, "and certainly one response was laughter. . . . God knows, that's the soul seeking some relief." By Vonnegut's own account, he wasn't much of a soldier. In an interview with *The Paris Review*, he described how he reacted in battle: "I imitated various war movies I'd seen." After he was captured by the Germans, he and the other soldiers were transported in the same boxcars used to move the Jews to the extermination camps. "Rolling stock is rolling stock," he said. On February 13, 1945, a siren went off and Vonnegut and the other men took refuge in a meat locker two stories underground. "It was cool there," Vonnegut said, "with cadavers hanging all around. When we came up the city was gone."

It would take twenty-five years for Vonnegut to figure out how to write about what happened in Dresden. The air raid killed 135,000 ci-

14

Critical Insights

vilians in a single night, but for a long time the American government denied it ever happened. As Vonnegut told the interviewer for *The Paris Review*, he didn't believe he had a story to tell:

> When I got home . . . I thought of writing my war story, too. All my friends were home; they'd had wonderful adventures, too. I went down to the newspaper office, the *Indianapolis News*, and looked to find out what they had about Dresden. There was an item about half an inch long, which said our planes had been over Dresden and two had been lost. And so I figured, well, this really was the most minor sort of detail in World War II.

But soon he could no longer deny what he had seen: "Every so often I would meet a European and we would be talking about the war and I would say I was in Dresden; he'd be astonished that I'd been there, and he'd always want to know more." After reading David Irving's *The Dresden Raids*, which said the bombing was the largest in European history, Vonnegut resolved to write the novel: "I said, By God, I saw something after all! I would try to write my war story, whether it was interesting or not, and try to make something out of it."

What Vonnegut made is a novel that defies categorization. He said that his purpose was not "to argue with people who thought Dresden should have been bombed to hell," but simply to show that "Dresden, willy-nilly, was bombed to hell." In the opening pages of the novel, the narrator pays a visit to his friend and fellow soldier Bernard V. O'Hare to relive old war stories. But O'Hare's wife won't let the two men glorify the war: "You were just babies!" she cries. To appease her, the narrator vows to tell a real war story—not some macho, John Wayne shoot-'em-up—and to call it "The Children's Crusade." From there, the novel shifts to focus on Billy Pilgrim, the narrator's alter ego, who serves as a chaplain's assistant in World War II. Billy witnesses the bombing of Dresden, returns home safely but emotionally numb, marries a woman he does not love, has two children, and eventually becomes "unstuck in time."

The linear plot is abandoned as Billy zips into the past or whips ahead to the future without warning. Reading it feels like being inside a pinball machine. And if time travel weren't enough, Vonnegut throws aliens into the mix. On the night of his daughter's wedding, Billy is kidnapped by a flying saucer from the planet of Tralfamadore. The Tralfamadorians are "two feet high and green" and shaped like a plunger with a hand for a head and a single eye in the palm. They can see in four dimensions and pity humans for only seeing three. They don't believe that time is linear; instead, they see it like "a stretch of the Rocky Mountains. . . . It does not lend itself to warnings or expectations. It simply *is*." And they don't accept the concept of free will, the notion that we can determine or even affect the course of our lives.

Why use aliens to tell a war story? Before he published *Slaughterhouse-Five*, Vonnegut was known as a science-fiction writer. But he wasn't just falling back on the genre he was most familiar with. The Tralfamadorians let the reader question the way events are ordered and perceived, and Vonnegut can comment on the absurdity of war without overtly moralizing. The Tralfamadorians are the voice of reason: their attitudes toward right and wrong, time and space, and free will are more radical, and yet somehow more credible, than anything Billy Pilgrim, or any other human character, could offer.

Although Vonnegut was willing to test the limits of what readers were willing to accept in a war novel, not everyone, it seems, got the joke. *Slaughterhouse-Five* was banned in schools throughout the country for being unpatriotic or, as a judge in Michigan put it, a "degradation of the person of Christ." As late as 2000, it ranked in the top one hundred of the American Library Association's list of the most frequently banned novels. Vonnegut, characteristically, maintained a sense of humor about the book's reception, both positive and negative. "If you make people laugh or cry about little black marks on sheets of white paper," he said, "what is that but a practical joke?"

Bibliography

Edwards, June. *Opposing Censorship in the Public Schools: Religion, Morality, and Literature.* Mahwah, NJ: Lawrence Erlbaum, 1998.

Vonnegut, Kurt. "The Art of Fiction No. 64: Kurt Vonnegut." Interview by David Hayman, David Michaelis, George Plimpton, and Richard Rhodes. *The Paris Review* 69 (Spring 1977): 56-103.

_____. *A Man Without a Country.* New York: Seven Stories Press, 2005.

_____. *Slaughterhouse-Five.* New York: Dell, 1969.

CRITICAL CONTEXTS

The Critical Reception of *Slaughterhouse-Five*_____

Jerome Klinkowitz

In 1969, when *Slaughterhouse-Five* was published, Kurt Vonnegut had been toiling in obscurity for twenty years as a writer of workmanlike short stories for weekly family magazines such as *Collier's* and the *Saturday Evening Post*. He had authored five novels as well, two as paperback originals, but none had sold well or attracted much critical attention. Therefore it was quite a surprise when his new work rocketed to the best-seller lists and stayed there for more than half the year. Laudatory reviews abounded, followed by thoughtful essays that sought to explain the book's wide appeal. But most impressive was the lead item of *Time* magazine's June 29, 1970, issue: an article devoted to Kurt Vonnegut himself as a cultural phenomenon. Titled "Vonnegut's Gospel," it hailed the author as a guru to disaffected youth and as a messiah for more humane values. This news report indicates one source for the author's sudden popularity. Students at Bennington College had chosen him as their commencement speaker, and to the budding graduates he had offered counsel much different than the usual fare. He advised that, instead of using their freshly acquired knowledge to go out and change the world, they should take some time off to enjoy themselves. They would be more productive in the end, for this way they would learn to value what life is supposed to be about: the appreciation of happy moments apart from the agendas of larger powers that would shape human effort for specific purposes. Above all, they should not feel obliged to resist the Vietnam War by mounting challenges to the military, as protesting students at Kent State University had just done at the cost of their lives. The only person who ever beat a tank was John Wayne, Vonnegut reminded his listeners—and Wayne was in another tank.

Time's lead story captures two key points about Vonnegut's success with *Slaughterhouse-Five* and its great appeal to readers. The first was that a war story, in this case a story about World War II that was couched in terms familiar to readers of the Vietnam War era, could be told without the trappings of Hollywood theatrics and unaccountable heroism. The second was that a proper description of war could be presented in an unaffected, conversational manner, with a simple speaking voice providing authenticity. At Bennington College, as in *Slaughterhouse-Five*, Vonnegut did just this.

Early reviewers were quick to spot these two features and identify them as keys to the novel's success. In the March 29, 1969, issue of the *Saturday Review*, veteran critic Granville Hicks rehearsed the experience of confronting this novel and taking time to discover how it works. As a proponent of socially responsible and factually realistic fiction since the Great Depression era, Hicks was predictably surprised by the novel's rejection of nearly every convention of the traditional novel. Its story was not told chronologically, but rather skipped back and forth in time in a fragmentary, almost schizophrenic manner. Its chief character, Billy Pilgrim, was not a rounded whole, but rather a collection of fragments from disparate times and places that refused to fit together comfortably. Billy seemed to be on a quest for understanding—yet his quest would be anything but a rewarding pattern of fulfillment. Rather much was left incomplete and the reader left to appreciate what the author did not want to seal as conclusive. Yet the result is successful, Hicks concludes, thanks to Vonnegut's candor in chapter 1, in which he abandons all pretension of asking his readers to suspend disbelief and speaks to them directly about the difficulties of writing the book and the strategies that allowed him to complete the task. The manner of this first chapter, which in a more traditional novel would be called a preface, continues throughout the next eight narrative chapters until a final chapter has the reader rejoin Kurt Vonnegut at his writer's desk, where, at an identifiable point in real time (two nights after the assassination of presidential candidate Robert Kennedy), the novel about Billy Pilgrim and his experiences in World War II concludes. It was in this manner of presentation that Hicks recognized a voice he had heard a year before, at the University of Notre Dame's Literary Festival, where, he recalled, Vonnegut delivered "as funny a lecture as I had ever listened to" (25). It is this personal manner that Hicks related to the sardonic humor and satire of Mark Twain and Jonathan Swift, a good combination for recasting a tale of World War II in a manner appropriate to the cultural transformations of the 1960s.

Reminded of the Hicks review many years later, a more comfortably famous Kurt Vonnegut remarked in a January 3, 1990, letter to me, "It really makes a difference, I find, if people hear me speak." In appraising the success of his own work, he had already judged in his essay "How to Write with Style" that "I myself find that I trust my own writing most, and others seem to trust it most, too, when I sound like a person from Indianapolis, which I am" (*Palm Sunday* 79). In a front-page *New York Times Book Review* response to *Slaughterhouse-Five* published on April 6, 1970, critic Robert Scholes took advantage of his familiarity with the writer's earlier work, which he had gained during the two years (1965-67) he and Vonnegut taught at the University of Iowa Writers' Workshop, and drew as well on his appreciation of the man's speaking style, having conducted a lengthy interview with him for Iowa Public Radio in 1966 (reprinted in *The Vonnegut Statement* 90-118). Vonnegut commands a very personal presence in the novel, Scholes notes. Having waited a quarter of a century to publish a work based on the most traumatic event in his life—the firebombing of Dresden, of which he was one of the few epicenter survivors—Vonnegut identifies himself with a biblical figure, Lot's wife, who was turned into a pillar of salt when she looked back at the destruction of Sodom. Scholes takes this professed fixation and shows how it motivates Vonnegut's writing of the novel's radically unconventional first chapter, in which many of the most important rules for traditional novels are broken. Here, distinctions between art and life are erased, along with the suspension of disbelief usually considered essential for fiction to succeed in creating a credible world for the reader. Instead, the writer speaks frankly about his own involvement with the events depicted and—more important—about the difficulties he has encountered in writing this book. These difficulties, Scholes suggests, not only are apparent in the author's first five novels but also are the reasons for their success. By turning the conventions of storytelling back upon themselves, Vonnegut presents his work in a fabulative manner that makes his way of handling the material as interesting as the material itself. Informed by Vonnegut's own intriguing and appealing character, the book inspires readers, as Scholes says, to be kind rather than hurtful. "Death is coming for all of us anyway," the critic hears this novel saying, "and it is better to be Lot's wife looking back through salty eyes than the Deity that destroyed those cities of the plain in order to save them" (1).

For Robert Scholes this "quietistic voice" (1) is appealing. Another reviewer, the famous science-fiction author Michael Crichton, notes this same quality but finds it cause for objection. Writing in the April 26, 1969, issue of the *New Republic*, Crichton objects to a presumed evasion of judgment taken by Vonnegut, several of whose earlier works had employed science-fiction themes and techniques, albeit as satire. "He becomes an offensive writer, because he will not choose sides, ascribing blame and penalty, identifying good guys and bad," Crichton complains.

> The ultimate difficulty with Vonnegut is precisely this: that he refuses to say who is wrong. The simplest way out of such a predicament is to say that everybody is wrong but the author. Any number of writers have done it, with good success. But Vonnegut refuses. He ascribes no blame, sets no penalties. His commentary on the assassinations of Robert Kennedy and Martin Luther King is the same as his comment on all other deaths: "So it goes," he says, and nothing more. (35)

In subsequent years *Slaughterhouse-Five* would continue to fare poorly with science-fiction novelists and readers. The subgenre itself traditionally values thematic content over writerly style, and Vonnegut (as Hicks and Scholes noted) was inverting this principle. Indeed, in his novel *God Bless You, Mr. Rosewater* (1965) the protagonist mocks science-fiction writers for their stylistic weaknesses, just as his second novel, *The Sirens of Titan* (1959), brutally parodies the subgenre's excesses.

Beyond the realm of science fiction, other critics with a vested interest in content would object to *Slaughterhouse-Five*'s apparent lack of seriousness. For Josephine Hendin, writing in *Harper's* July 1974 issue, the novel spoke only for a general nihilism induced by the era's cultural turmoil. Billy Pilgrim offers just a "pessimistic and humiliating passivity" (82) that indicates a mental illness the novel does nothing to cure. More interested in psychoanalysis than literary art, Hendin treats *Slaughterhouse-Five* as an unresolved case study. When critics' orientations were not only psychological but also moral, Vonnegut would be even more harshly condemned. In the pages of *Dissent*, Pearl Kazin Bell views him and his contemporaries as "celebrants of unreason, chaos, and inexorable decay," little more than "a horde of mini-Jeremiahs crying havoc in the Western World" (26), while Nathan A. Scott, Jr., for the *Journal of Religion*, describes the readership of books such as *Slaughterhouse-Five* as "hordes of those long-haired, jean-clad, pot-smoking bohemians who have entered the world of psychedelia" (12-13). This combination of disinterest in literary form and privileging of ethical standards would climax in book-length studies of the era's fiction by Gerald Graff (*Literature Against Itself*, 1977) and John Gardner (*On Moral Fiction*, 1978). Neither work had much praise for Kurt Vonnegut and his most famous novel. Gardner's orientation toward literature was adapted from Leo Tolstoy's belief that God instructs, heroes enact, and writers record. Better sense of *Slaughterhouse-Five* would be made by critics who understood its author's firm rejection of this formula.

One of the first to understand this novel's challenge to assumptions of authority (whether godly or otherwise) was John Somer. As coeditor of *The Vonnegut Statement* (1973), he contributed "Geodesic Vonnegut; Or, If Buckminster Fuller Wrote Novels," the first major essay devoted entirely to *Slaughterhouse-Five*'s spatial dimensions as statements of theme. Somer sees Vonnegut's need to reinvent the novel's form as an outgrowth of his life experience; he found it "difficult to write about the bombing of Dresden because it contradicted everything he was brought up to believe in; and it happened at an age, twenty-two, when a man's beliefs are most vulnerable" (222). He could not write conventionally about the event "because his real subject was the destruction of Kurt Vonnegut" (223) and his ideals of order, stability, and justice—ideals that were also reflected in the form of the traditional novel, with its chronology of time and coherence of character; *Slaughterhouse-Five* would not so much shatter these ideals (the bombing had done that) as discard them in favor of a narrative based on spatial form. In this structure, elements of Billy Pilgrim's identity and experience would not be seen as hopelessly fragmentary but rather as a collage of moments comprehended all at once in a way that would seem "beautiful and surprising and deep" (Somer 247). The critic is specific about how this spatial structure is achieved. Vonnegut first surrounds his novel, a subjective creation, with events from the objective world. He then interjects the narrator of these objective events, which is himself, into the novel's subjective world, creating a "dynamic tension" between fiction and reality. This tension allows Vonnegut to at once identify himself with and distinguish himself from his protagonist, Billy Pilgrim, letting them "create an illusionary, imaginative, and artificial equilibrium" (Somer 248) that gives the novel an objective presence in the world, an artifact understandable as it is made.

When Vonnegut's subsequent novels became best sellers and reissues of his earlier books (including a short-story collection) persevered as strong backlist items, critics could integrate *Slaughterhouse-Five* into this larger canon. Robert Scholes and John Somer had anticipated this, Somer making much of the fact that the firebombing of Dresden was anticipated in the figurative apocalypses that conclude the author's first five novels. For Peter J. Reed, Vonnegut's struggle was to keep these endings comic. *Slaughterhouse-Five*'s physical (as opposed to metaphoric) apocalypse challenges the ethic of comedy, but Reed sees how not just the reality of Dresden's destruction but the inevitability of death itself prompts the protagonist to transcend moment-to-moment living in favor of a more holistic experience. Reed's *Kurt Vonnegut, Jr.* (Vonnegut dropped the "Jr." from his name in 1976) appeared in 1972, when the writer was maintaining his popularity with a play (*Happy Birthday, Wanda June*) and a public television special (*Between Time and Timbuktu*) while complaining about how hard it was (in the face of such great fame) to finish his next novel. With its ending rewritten at the behest of an office courier, *Breakfast of Champions* finally came out in 1973, followed by *Slapstick* in 1976, giving scholars a ten-book canon to work with, sufficient for a mature appraisal. In 1977 James Lundquist and Richard Giannone published their respective studies *Kurt Vonnegut* and *Vonnegut: A Preface to His Novels*, setting the tone for discussing the author of *Slaughterhouse-Five* as a major author in American literature. Lundquist sees Vonnegut's challenge lying in the difficulty of responding to the "new reality" of World War II atrocities that surpass the imagination's ability to comprehend (69). Vonnegut's solution is a dramatic one:

> Through the constant movement back and forth in time that constitutes Vonnegut's narrative, we see Billy becoming his history, existing all at once, as if he is an electron. And this gives the novel a structure that is, to directly state the analogy, atomic. Billy whirls around the central fact of Dresden, the planes of his orbits constantly intersecting, and where he has been, he will be. (74)

Giannone's understanding of *Slaughterhouse-Five* is based on the author's strategy of relating the problems of comprehending the Dresden event to the nature of fiction itself. The narrative's fragmentary nature is appropriate as "an exploration of our moment in relation to death through the broken forms defining the dimensions of our presentness" (86). Vonnegut's manner emulates that of the four Gospels in the New

Testament, specifically in how the author casts himself as witness. "The novel's narrator permits the events of Billy's life to act upon him finally so that he discovers the necessity for a here and now amid the history and foretellings of doom around us," the critic concludes. "The witness in turn invites the reader's consciousness to interact with his. The rhythm of this moral interpenetration of consciousness is the form of *Slaughterhouse-Five*. The revelation that we have a present full awareness is its good tidings" (96).

By 1991 Vonnegut was considered so sufficiently established as a major literary figure to merit coverage in a volume for general editor Matthew J. Bruccoli's Understanding Contemporary Literature Series with the University of South Carolina Press. Chosen for the task was William Rodney Allen. Familiar with Vonnegut's personal voice from editing *Conversations with Kurt Vonnegut* three years earlier, Allen brought an appreciation of both the man and his controversial reputation to his study. *Understanding Kurt Vonnegut* takes into account not just Vonnegut's critical successes but the sometimes distracting nature of his popularity, particularly when propagated by readers who might be comprehending only superficial aspects of his humor. "Vonnegut has experienced a virtual roller coaster ride of literary reputation," Allen attests, citing a weakness in his novels of the mid-1970s and "a backlash against his enormous popularity . . . at least among serious readers" (1). That his academic standing was regained with a series of strong novels published between 1979 (*Jailbird*) and 1987 (*Bluebeard*), encourages Allen to read *Slaughterhouse-Five* as a foundation for Vonnegut's assured presence in literary and cultural history. Allen draws on the author's own commentaries about the difficulties of writing about Dresden and analyzes how he melds them into the confessional nature of the novel's first chapter as a way of integrating the impossibility of saying anything coherent about a massacre with the absolute necessity of doing so if the work were to succeed. Allen perceives the author's spatial solution a bit differently than do other critics. For him, it is "more like an ascending, widening spiral that circles over the same territory yet does so from an ever higher and wider perspective," with the goal of pushing the reader's perspective "as far as he can toward infinity—toward the union of all time and space" (85). To his credit, Vonnegut does not accept the smug satisfaction of having written an antiwar book, but instead "accepts war and death as inevitable" with life always "coming out of death" (97-98).

At about this same time, book-length studies devoted to certain aspects of Vonnegut's work began to appear, all of them throwing different light on the author's achievement in *Slaughterhouse-Five*. Lawrence R. Broer's *Sanity Plea: Schizophrenia in the Novels of Kurt Vonnegut* appeared in 1989 and was revised in 1994. It begins by noticing how "probably no characters in contemporary fiction are more traumatized and emotionally damaged than those of Kurt Vonnegut" (3). Vonnegut sees himself as a shaman devoted to exposing this madness, Broer writes, "dispelling the evil spirits of irresponsible mechanization and aggression while encouraging reflectiveness and the will to positive social change" (4). In *Slaughterhouse-Five* psychic and social trauma are perfectly fused. But rather than praising Billy Pilgrim for his holistic acceptance, Broer prefers to see the character as a tendency Vonnegut has first externalized and then excised from himself, making his writing of the novel a form of self-therapy. "Billy in his tranquilized existence becomes the very embodiment of what Vonnegut has warned against for years," Broer argues. "Insulated from pain, Billy has simply abdicated his humanity, trading his dignity and self-integrity for an illusion of comfort and security, and becoming himself a machine." As for the author, "Kurt Vonnegut may have saved his own sanity through the therapeutic processes of art, climaxed by an act of symbolic amputation: the severing of the Billy Pilgrim within himself, poisoned with existential gangrene" (95-96).

The biblical myth of the Fall is a theme Leonard Mustazza traces through the author's work in *Forever Pursuing Genesis: The Myth of Eden in the Novels of Kurt Vonnegut* (1990). In *Slaughterhouse-Five*, Eden is linked with the planet Tralfamadore, the place where, after becoming "unstuck in time," Billy Pilgrim "tries to construct for himself an Edenic experience out of materials he garners over the course of some twenty years" (102). This quest involves reinventing his world, much as a writer would do when crafting a novel. His fantasies are creative, such as using his liberation from chronological time to view a war movie backward and watching the planes take off in reverse from an airfield to fly backward over their target, using tremendous force to shrink the fires below them into small canisters that are then lifted up into their bomb bays and taken back to base. Billy understands perfectly what he is doing and so can readers, Mustazza infers, because the process doesn't stop just there. Instead, the reverse action continues as the bombs are disassembled, their parts separated into minerals to be shipped to remote areas where they are buried so deep as to never be harmful again. Billy even takes the story beyond the movie, as everyone grows backward into infancy while the human race devolves "to produce two perfect people named Adam and Eve" (Mustazza 105). Most important is what he learns from his Tralfamadorian captors, that time is not linear but omnipresent, that there is no free will, and that the end of the universe already exists as a ridiculous accident. Yet these revelations are a cause not for pessimism but for hope, because within such understanding exists the possibility of living only in good times rather than bad—the essence of Eden itself. Like Broer, Mustazza sees Vonnegut as distancing himself from Billy, but to more positive effect. "This duality of vision is what allows *Slaughterhouse-Five* to be more than the lurid and ludicrous tale of a lone madman and his obsessive behaviors," Mustazza avers. "Rather, its subtext, like that of all of Vonnegut's novels, is a plea for responsible action, for change, for the pursuit of Genesis not as a lost mythic ideal but as an attainable state of innocence" (115).

That Vonnegut's work can withstand and even profit from the most rigorous application of complex theories is demonstrated by Kevin Alexander Boon in *Chaos Theory and the Interpretation of Literary Texts: The Case of Kurt Vonnegut* (1997). "Chaos and disorder on a monumental scale wait silently inside every tiny atom," Boon notes, and he goes on to relate this point to the first use of atomic weapons in 1945. "The realization that situations could unpredictably explode into chaos at any instant became part of our quotidian angst" (8). For Kurt Vonnegut, this knowledge led to his disillusionment with science but also to his belief that a better grounding for optimism about human life must be found. "It is hard to adapt to chaos," Boon quotes Vonnegut as saying, "but it can be done. I am living proof of that. It can be done" (23). The Dresden bombing described in *Slaughterhouse-Five* yields a "fractalean remains of chaos" (86) that Billy as character and Vonnegut as author have to negotiate. Yet fractal images are common to nearly all of Vonnegut's work, from the Ilium of *Player Piano* to the ruins of a future New York City in *Slapstick*. "Fractal shapes offer us a new way of looking at the universe," Boon believes, one that provides "a new way of seeing that limits human suffering and increases our civility toward one another. The presence of human beings in the dynamic system of life keeps Vonnegut from the mere playful description of a universe continually shifting from chaos to order." Instead, he searches beyond the "rigid systems" of interpretation that "are often presented as stagnant, systems of uncreative, flat, dull, constrictive, narrow-minded, and often fascistic" (88).

The author's place in the larger tradition of American literature is explored by Donald E. Morse in *The Novels of Kurt Vonnegut: Imagining Being an American* (2003). In this context, the major issue addressed in *Slaughterhouse-Five* is the need to answer the question of why people suffer. Beyond all anthropological differences, "a touch of suffering makes the whole world kin," Morse acknowledges, adding that "this 'authority of suffering' underlies all of *Slaughterhouse-Five*" (21). Accepting the fact that "suffering is a necessary part of life" marks an important turning point in Vonnegut's career, letting him "satirize particular evils in the world rather than, as earlier, wrestle with the question of evil itself" (22). Alone among major critics, Morse privileges science fiction as a key element in the author's work, where this subgenre "becomes an effective method for asking the truly important questions about the nature of humans and their universe" (24). The science-fiction viewpoint can enable reinventions of the universe, a practical case being the conversion of the slaughterhouse in Dresden that housed the American prisoners into a place that ensures their safety and survival.

A much broader but also more intellectually penetrating view of the issues informing the author's work is provided by Todd F. Davis in *Kurt Vonnegut's Crusade: Or, How a Postmodern Harlequin Preached a New Kind of Humanism* (2006). Davis sees it as his first duty to counter the argument that he is dealing with the work of a nihilist, a common assumption dating back to the hostile comments of critics such as Bell and Scott. "I contend that Vonnegut's ethical position constitutes his main theme," Davis asserts, "that he is more concerned with our response to existence than with the philosophical nature of that existence" (10). That life on earth may be absurd does not mean that all hope disappears in darkness. Instead, Vonnegut makes a "call to common decency" with the hope that "we will learn to respect one another before we destroy ourselves and the planet" (11). Just because the conditions of life are ludicrous, people themselves don't have to be. Instead, as Vonnegut learned in his anthropological studies at the University of Chicago, individuals have the natural ability to form themselves into groups, usually of a hundred or two, devoted to satisfying common needs and improving conditions so that life can become more tolerable. That better circumstances are indeed possible explains how "*Slaughterhouse-Five* remains essentially a testament to one man's battle with the demons of war" (76). Disillusioned with both science and militarism, Vonnegut looks beyond the paradigms of modernism in both thought and literary form in order to confront the reality that such traditional "metanarratives" efface (77).

My own scholarship of Kurt Vonnegut and his works began with essays published in 1971, in the immediate aftermath of *Slaughterhouse-Five* and the onset of his great fame. These initial views, complemented by bibliographical research into the author's earlier works, including fugitive stories and essays, form a chapter on Vonnegut's career in my *Literary Disruptions: The Making of a Post-contemporary American Fiction*. My purpose here was twofold. First, I sought to draw a coherent picture of Vonnegut's development from a writer of family-magazine stories to the author of formally innovative novels. Second, I wanted to integrate this development with the emergence of a new style of American fiction that discarded the conventions of realism in favor of an anti-illusionistic form in which the novel would not depict reality but be its own reality. That *Slaughterhouse-Five* is more appealing than black humor works such as *Catch-22* and *Dr. Strangelove* with which it was initially associated and also more accessible than the intellectually obtuse novels of John Barth and Thomas Pynchon is due in part to Vonnegut's use of the patiently instructive manner that he developed in dozens of *Collier's* and *Saturday Evening Post* stories. He teaches his readers how to comprehend his new form of fiction, giving the example of the Tralfamadorian novel as a demonstration of this aesthetic. My *Kurt Vonnegut* (1982) locates *Slaughterhouse-Five* as the first complete example of the author's transformation of writing method from metaphor to discourse, a process that had become evident in the years just before as he prepared a new edition of his earlier novel *Mother Night* and collected his short stories from the 1950s as *Welcome to the Monkey House* (1968), both volumes of which incorporate autobiographical materials as key elements in the workings of these fictions. In 1998, I looked at the author's personal journalism and presence as a lecturer for *Vonnegut in Fact*, exploring how the closing of markets for short stories prompted the author to begin writing essays that integrated his own life and thoughts with the presentation of materials, the key device that resolved a twenty-year problem he had been having with the thematics of *Slaughterhouse-Five*. *The Vonnegut Effect* (2004) let me deal directly with the unique nature of *Slaughterhouse-Five*'s success in becoming the only genuinely postmodern novel to find a wide readership. With *Slaughterhouse-Five*, Vonnegut's strategy is to challenge narrative authority, expose previously un-questioned assumptions, and discard the conventional illusions of fic-tion writing by speaking to the reader honestly and directly in a voice redolent of the American vernacular characteristic of such beloved fig-ures as Abraham Lincoln, Mark Twain, and Will Rogers.

Unlike most other critics, I do not suggest that Vonnegut is an ab-surdist. Instead, his belief that there is no absolutely verifiable meaning to existence allows us to create our own meaning, which in practice becomes more beneficial to the quality of life than appeals to an abstract, unverifiable authority. My *Kurt Vonnegut's America* relates *Slaughterhouse-Five* to its moment in history, the telling of a World War II story in the cultural manner representative of the American 1960s and the radical transformation of cultural values occurring at the time. This study also addresses the novel's controversial status among social leaders and literary critics. Since its publication, various school boards and religious groups had banned it from classroom and library shelves. While the novel's few instances of vulgar language were cited as cause, the real issue is likely the author's rewriting of the Christian liturgy, recasting the crucifixion not as the murder of the Son of God but as the hideous treatment of a simple human being. I also discuss Loree Rackstraw's complaint in *Love as Always, Kurt: Vonnegut as I Knew Him* (2009) that some critics' hostility borders on the irrational. This hostility is prompted by the fear that postmodern innovations, with their challenges to conventional order, could be made available to the masses.

Works Cited

Allen, William Rodney. *Understanding Kurt Vonnegut*. Columbia: U of South Carolina P, 1991.

Bell, Pearl Kazin. "American Fiction: Forgetting Ordinary Truths." *Dissent* 20 (Winter 1973): 26-34.

Boon, Kevin Alexander. *Chaos Theory and the Interpretation of Literary Texts: The Case of Kurt Vonnegut*. Lewiston, NY: Edwin Mellen Press, 1997.

Broer, Lawrence R. *Sanity Plea: Schizophrenia in the Novels of Kurt Vonnegut.* Rev. ed. Tuscaloosa: U of Alabama P, 1994.

Crichton, Michael. "Sci-Fi and Vonnegut." *New Republic* 26 Apr. 1969: 33-35.

Davis, Todd F. *Kurt Vonnegut's Crusade: Or, How a Postmodern Harlequin Preached a New Kind of Humanism.* Albany: State U of New York P, 2006.

Gardner, John. *On Moral Fiction.* New York: Basic Books, 1978.

Giannone, Richard. *Vonnegut: A Preface to His Novels.* Port Washington, NY: Kennikat Press, 1977.

Graff, Gerald. *Literature Against Itself.* Chicago: U of Chicago P, 1977.

Hendin, Josephine. "The Writer as Culture Hero, the Father as Son." *Harper's* July 1974: 82-87.

Hicks, Granville. "Literary Horizons." *Saturday Review* 29 Mar. 1969: 25.

Klinkowitz, Jerome. *Kurt Vonnegut.* London: Methuen, 1982.

_____. *Kurt Vonnegut's America.* Columbia: U of South Carolina P, 2009.

_____. *Literary Disruptions: The Making of a Post-contemporary American Fiction.* Urbana: U of Illinois P, 1975.

_____. *The Vonnegut Effect.* Columbia: U of South Carolina P, 2004.

_____. *Vonnegut in Fact: The Public Spokesmanship of Personal Fiction.* Columbia: U of South Carolina P, 1998.

Lundquist, James. *Kurt Vonnegut.* New York: Frederick Ungar, 1977.

Morse, Donald E. *The Novels of Kurt Vonnegut: Imagining Being an American.* Westport, CT: Praeger, 2003.

Mustazza, Leonard. *Forever Pursuing Genesis: The Myth of Eden in the Novels of Kurt Vonnegut.* Lewisburg, PA: Bucknell UP, 1990.

Rackstraw, Loree. *Love as Always, Kurt: Vonnegut as I Knew Him.* Cambridge, MA: Da Capo Press, 2009.

Reed, Peter J. *Kurt Vonnegut, Jr.* New York: Warner Books, 1972.

Scholes, Robert. "*Slaughterhouse-Five.*" *New York Times Book Review* 6 Apr. 1970: 1, 23.

Scott, Nathan A., Jr. "'New Heav'ns, New Earths'—the Landscape of Contemporary Apocalypse." *Journal of Religion* 53 (January 1973): 3-13.

Somer, John. "Geodesic Vonnegut: Or, If Buckminster Fuller Wrote Novels." *The Vonnegut Statement.* Ed. Jerome Klinkowitz and John Somer. New York: Delacorte Press/Seymour Lawrence, 1973. 221-54.

Vonnegut, Kurt. *Palm Sunday.* New York: Delacorte Press/Seymour Lawrence, 1981.

"Vonnegut's Gospel." *Time* 95 (29 June 1970): 8.

Temporal Cohesion and Disorientation in *Slaughterhouse-Five*:
A Chronicle of Form Cuts and Transitional Devices in the Novel

Kevin Alexander Boon

Stephen Pinker, in discussing the computational theory of mind, compares the "content of brain activity" to the "content of a book," the latter of which, he points out, "lies in the *pattern* of ink marks" (25). Because content is inseparable from its structure, to understand a work, we must understand its structure. Structure is particularly important in *Slaughterhouse-Five*, a work that abandons conventional linear narrative in favor of nonlinear narrative in order to mirror the experiences of Billy Pilgrim, who has come "unstuck in time" and leaps back and forth through various moments of his life. Traditional narratives tend to present time as we imagine it to be, as a sequence of experiences proceeding chronologically one after the other, but the structure of Pilgrim's story reflects the way time is experienced in the mind—as individual moments reconstituted in our memory or constructed in our imagination. Careful examination of transitional devices in *Slaughterhouse-Five* reveals how the novel constructs a cohesive story from fragments of experience and disorients readers by modeling memory and its relation to time.

The story of Billy Pilgrim is framed by the first and last chapters of the novel. In chapter 1, Vonnegut establishes time as the primary organizational principle of the novel. It took him more than twenty years to finally write about the firebombing of Dresden, time he spent organizing "his own personal mythology before dealing with the biggest event in it" (Klinkowitz and Lawler 28), and by the time the story began to coalesce into *Slaughterhouse-Five*, Vonnegut was, as he admits at the opening, "an old fart with his memories" (2, 7). Memories, Vonnegut illustrates in the novel, are all we have of the past, imagination is all we have of the future, and both exist only in the present—

the *now* of the novel. His protagonist, Billy Pilgrim, like Vonnegut in writing the novel, experiences all events as occurring *now;*[1] thus *Slaughterhouse-Five* not only tells the story of the Dresden firebombing and the tribulations of Pilgrim but also reflects the state of mind of the author during the novel's creation, beginning with the marker "Listen:" (23) at the start of chapter 2, which identifies the beginning of the story proper and which is followed by a statement that influences the structure of chapters 2 through 9: "Billy Pilgrim has come unstuck in time" (23).

Because Pilgrim "pays random visits to all the events in between" (23) the moments of his life, the novel proper (chapters 2 through 9) is structured as a series of seemingly random leaps in time. This "rather complex formal structure" (Edelstein 129) led some early scholars of the work to reorganize the moments of the novel into a linear timeline in order to make sense of the narrative. Arnold Edelstein performed such a "chronological reconstruction" (129) when he wrote about the work in 1974; but reordering the events subverts Vonnegut's authority. More is to be gained by taking the work as we find it—examining the sequence of time leaps as Vonnegut ordered them. When we scrutinize the structure of the novel, we note a number of techniques that Vonnegut employs to maintain a sense of temporal cohesion for readers, to smooth transitions between moments in Pilgrim's life, and to render the text more accessible. Furthermore, we are able to mark when these techniques are eschewed and the effect that has on our understanding of Billy Pilgrim's (and Vonnegut's) recollection of the main subject of the novel: the firebombing of Dresden.

The first and most prominent strategy that Vonnegut uses to make *Slaughterhouse-Five* more accessible is to preface the nonlinear scenes of Pilgrim's life with a four-page linear summary of the entire novel. He starts with Billy's birth in 1922 (23) and ends when Pilgrim is forty-six and is confronted by his daughter, who complains of the letters about aliens that he is writing to the local newspaper and suspects that he has gone senile as a result of an airplane accident (30). This section is followed by a conventional literary elaboration on Pilgrim's experience in the war leading up to the moment when he first became "unstuck in time" (43). Once Billy Pilgrim becomes unstuck in time, the story is organized as a series of leaps in time spanning the entire sweep of Billy's life, from before his birth to after his death. This series of leaps can be divided into forty parts that comprise two sections: parts 1 through 31, which track Billy's leaps in time, occur in an orderly fashion and are facilitated by form cuts and other filmic transitional devices; in parts 32 through 40, which take us to the end of chapter 9, Vonnegut's use of transitional devices unravels as he begins to confront more directly the atrocities of the Dresden firebombing. Parts 1 through 36 and 38 through 40 are structured around Billy's leaps in time, like the previous thirty-one parts, but part 37 is structured around Billy's experiences in the coma, which contains several time leaps in itself. Significantly, it is here that the description of the firebombing occurs. The entire novel is organized as follows:

Chapter 1:
> Opening frame wherein Vonnegut discusses the writing of his Dresden book and his war buddy, Bernard V. O'Hare.

Chapters 2 through 5:
> "Listen:"
> A summary of Billy Pilgrim's entire life.
> Recounting of events in war leading up to when Billy becomes unstuck in time.
> Thirty-one leaps (parts 1-31) in time structured with clear transitional devices for most leaps.

Chapters 6 through 8:
> "Listen:"
> Four leaps in time (parts 32-36) *without* clear transitional devices.
> **Billy in a coma (part 37).**

Chapter 9:
> Three leaps in time (parts 38-40) ending with Billy in alien zoo.

Chapter 10:

> Closing frame wherein Vonnegut reasserts his presence and blends his discussion of Dresden and Bernard V. O'Hare with references to Billy Pilgrim, thus fusing the nonfiction narrative of his experiences with the fictional narrative of Billy's experiences.

The structure of Billy's leaps in time illuminates Vonnegut's psychic gravitation toward the subject of the Dresden firebombing and how survivors of traumatic events often repress their memories of them. Vonnegut refers to *Slaughterhouse-Five* as a "found object" (Allen 94), but one that is incomplete. In a 1973 interview with David Standish for *Playboy* magazine, he explained:

> There was a complete blank where the bombing of Dresden took place, because I don't remember. And I looked up several of my war buddies and they didn't remember, either. They didn't want to talk about it. There was a complete forgetting of what it was like. There were all kinds of information surrounding the event, but as far as my memory bank was concerned, the center had been pulled right out of the story. There was nothing up there to be recovered—or in the heads of my friends, either. (94)

This gap in Vonnegut's memory is articulated in the pattern of Billy's leaps.

The First Thirty-one Leaps in Time and Transitional Devices, from "Listen:" (23) to "Listen:" (136)

One of the difficulties Vonnegut faced in writing this section was how to produce a sense of random jumps in time while still maintaining narrative continuity. Despite his avowed dislike for film, Vonnegut achieves narrative continuity by employing techniques more commonly seen in film editing than in literature.

During the first thirty-one jumps in time, Vonnegut primarily uses the "form cut," a film editing technique in which visual elements are used to smooth the transition from one scene to the next. Form cuts in film are largely associated with visual images: a shot of a pencil in one scene might cut to a shot of a sword in another; a shot of a round birthday cake could cut to a shot of a round wall clock, and so on. Some of the most iconic edits in American film history are form cuts: among them Stanley Kubrick's transition in *2001: A Space Odyssey* (1968) from a primitive man throwing a bone into the air to a shot of a space station spinning in space, which implies the evolution of humans from animals into technologically advanced beings, and Alfred Hitchcock's transition in *Psycho* (1960) from a round shower drain to the dead eye of Marion Crane.

Roy Huss and Norman Silverstein define the form cut as a transitional device that frames "in a successive shot an object which has the shape or contour similar to an image in the shot immediately preceding" (67). The similarity between the two film elements led Brian Gallagher to compare form cuts in film to literary similes. Gallagher argues, "Film's closest approach to the simile is the form cut" (161). But there is a difference between the simile in literature and the form cut in film, as Gallagher notes. Film is limited to "formal similes" (161), visual objects transitioning to similar visual objects, whereas literature has no such restriction and can set up transitional devices on concepts. In film, we can cut from a round object to another round object. In literature, we can also set up a conceptual comparison, such as moving from a deathbed to a gravestone. The form cut in film smoothes transitions between static images—from scene to scene—thus improving an audience's sense of continuity. In *Slaughterhouse-Five*, Vonnegut extensively uses literary form cuts as transitional devices to smooth the movement between Billy's random leaps in time.

Chronicle of the First Thirty-one Leaps

Leap 1: From amniotic fluid to pool water
(1922 to 1932)

Billy Pilgrim's adventure with time begins at the close of the conventional narrative opening chapter 2, which first summarizes Billy's life and then recounts events leading up to when Billy became "unstuck in time" (43). Vonnegut writes that Billy first swung "through the full arc of his life," beyond death and then back to when he was in the womb, which Vonnegut describes as "a red light and bubbling sounds" (43). The first defined time leap occurs when Billy swings from the womb to the shower at the YMCA, where Billy is taking a shower with his father. Billy's father is going to "throw Billy into the deep end" (43) in a misconceived attempt to teach Billy to swim.

TD (transitional device): liquid womb to liquid tomb

Leap 2: From drowning in pool to nursing home with pneumonic mother
(1932-1965)

After his father throws him into the pool, Billy sinks to the bottom and nearly drowns. From there he leaps to "an old people's home" (44) where his mother is nearly dying from pneumonia, a disorder commonly referred to as "water in the lungs."

TD: Billy dying of water in lungs to Billy's mother dying of water in lungs

Leap 3: From reading about Private Slovik to Little League banquet (1965-1958)

Water appears again in Billy's third leap in time. Billy is in the waiting room of the nursing home, reading the "opinion of the staff judge advocate" who reviewed the case of Eddie D. Slovik, the only soldier "shot for cowardice since the Civil War" (45), when he time travels to a banquet for his son's Little League team. The team's coach is praising the players, saying, "I'd consider it an honor just to be *water* boy for these kids" (46). Vonnegut italicizes "water" to accentuate a link between the two scenes. Less obvious, but equally present, is a conceptual contrast cut from an authority figure condemning to an authority figure praising.

TD: Authority figure to authority figure, condemnation to praise, and italicized "water"

Leap 4: From Little League banquet to New Year's Eve party (1958-1961)

Liquid continues to thread Billy's trips in time together. At the New Year's Eve party, Billy is "disgracefully drunk," but more significant is the more conventional cut from one party to another party—from the banquet to the New Year's Eve party.

TD: Party to party

Leap 5: From New Year's Eve party to World War II (1961-1944)

The New Year's Eve party ends with Billy passing out drunk in the backseat of his car, searching for the steering wheel. When somebody shakes him awake, Billy is back in the war and still feeling drunk.

TD: Feeling drunk to feeling drunk, asleep to awake

Leap 6: From World War II to Lions Club speech in Ilium, New York
(1944-1957)

Billy is lost behind enemy lines with Roland Weary and Weary's two reluctant companions when Billy has a "delightful hallucination" (49). He hallucinates that he is "skating on a ballroom floor" (49) to cheering crowds. Vonnegut uses the sound of the cheering crowd to transition to the next leap in time: "The cheering went on, but its tone was altered as the hallucination gave way to time-travel" (49). The cheering in his hallucination in the war is replaced by a "standing ovation" (50) he is receiving at the Lions Club.

TD: Cheering crowd

Leap 7: From Lions Club to World War II
(1957-1944)

Another conceptual contrast cut moves readers from the Lions Club back to the war. At the Lions Club, Billy delivers an eloquent speech. His voice is described as "a gorgeous instrument" (50). Billy leaps in time back to the war where Weary is pummeling him and barking "unintelligibly" (50).

TD: Speaking well to speaking poorly

Leap 8: From stone cottage during war to optometrist's office
(1944-1967)

Billy is captured by the Germans and eventually taken to a "stone cottage" (55) where he falls asleep. When he opens his eyes again, he is in his optometrist's office in Ilium, where he had "fallen asleep while examining a . . . patient" (56).

TD: Falling asleep

Leap 9: From optometrist's office to World War II
(1967-1944)

Billy is in his office reading *The Review of Optometry* when a siren goes off. He is frightened by the sound, which makes him expect that "World War Three" (57) could begin at any time. He closes his eyes while imagining war and reopens them back in "World War Two" (58).

TD: Expecting war to being in war

Leap 10: From World War II to Cadillac on way to Lions Club luncheon
(1944-1967)

Billy is back in the war being photographed by menacing German soldiers who are reenacting his capture for the camera, when that moment overlaps onto Billy in 1967 driving to the Lions Club luncheon. Here Vonnegut constructs the literary equivalent of a film dissolve, fading one image out while fading another image in: "He was simultaneously on foot in Germany in 1944 and riding his Cadillac in 1967. Germany dropped away, and 1967 became bright and clear, free of interference from any other time" (58). Vonnegut further facilitates the time shift by placing Billy in a blighted urban neighborhood that had, like Dresden, been "burned down" (59) a month earlier. This scene is particularly significant as the citizens of the neighborhood were responsible for burning it down; thus it echoes Vonnegut's view of war as self-destructive. Vonnegut strengthens this connection by pointing out, "The neighborhood reminded Billy of some of the towns he had seen in the war" (59).

TD: A dissolve from photo session in Germany to interior of Cadillac

---

Leap 11: From home in Ilium to Luxembourg in World War II (1967-1944)

The sequence closes with Billy back at home, where he has gone to take a nap. He lies down and begins weeping. A cripple, who is being used to con people into buying magazine subscriptions, comes to his door. From his upstairs window, Billy watches the cripples working the neighborhood and continues "weeping as he . . . [contemplates] the cripples and their boss" (63). He closes his eyes and reopens them in the war where he is marching with other prisoners; the winter wind "bringing tears to his eyes" (63).

TD: Tears

Leap 12: From Christmas night in World War II to his daughter's wedding night when he is kidnapped by aliens (1944-1967)

At the close of the war sequence, Billy is a prisoner being transported on a train where he "nestled like a spoon with the hobo . . . and fell asleep" (71). Billy travels to his daughter's wedding night. He and his wife are "nestled like spoons in their big double bed" (72). There is a moment during this sequence when Billy becomes "slightly unstuck in time" (73) and watches a movie backward, but the scene does not change time or location, so from a filmic standpoint, the scene is the same.

TD: Nestling like spoons

Leap 13: From the alien spacecraft to World War II (1967-1944)

Billy is given an anesthetic by the Tralfamadorians and falls asleep. When he wakes up, he is back on the train during the war.

TD: Sleeping

Leap 14: From prisoner delousing station to baby's bath (1944-1922)

The train of prisoners is unloaded and Billy is eventually taken to a delousing station where he is showered. From there, he leaps "back in time to his infancy" (84), where he had just been given a bath by his mother.

TD: Bathing

Leap 15: From baby's bath to golf course (1922-middle age)

The room where Billy is being bathed is described as "filled with sunshine" (84). He leaps from there to a golf course "on a blazing summer Sunday morning" (85).

TD: Sunlight

Leap 16: From golf course to alien spacecraft (middle age-1967)

Billy sinks a putt, the sun moves behind a cloud, he gets dizzy, and then he is back on the alien spacecraft. There is no clear form cut or other transitional device here. The only strong connection is with the reference to bugs trapped in amber. When Billy asks the Tralfamadorians where he is, they say, "Trapped in another blob of amber" (85). When Billy was last on the spaceship (see leap 13), the Tralfamadorians mentioned that each moment in life was like being a "bug trapped in amber" (77). Billy time travels away from the ship for leaps 14 and 15 and returns in leap 16, but the shift from the golf course to the spacecraft does not use transitional devices like the other leaps in this section.

TD: None

Leaps 17 and 18: From alien spacecraft to family vacation (two locations)
(1967-1934)

The Tralfamadorians explain to Billy how Tralfamadorian books are structured:

> Each clump of symbols is a brief, urgent message—describing a situation, a scene. . . . There isn't any particular relationship between all the messages, except that the author has chosen them carefully, so that, when seen all at once, they produce an image of life that is beautiful and surprising and deep. There is no beginning, no middle, no end, no suspense, no moral, no causes, no effects. What we love in our books are the depths of many marvelous moments seen all at one time. (88)

This description of Tralfamadorian books reflects Vonnegut's implied organizational strategy in arranging *Slaughterhouse-Five* as a series of scenes that seemingly occur in random order, and it sets up the next two leaps in time, both of which occur while Billy is on vacation with his parents and both of which present scenes that are experienced as marvelous moments rather than linear narratives. The first leap (17) is to the Grand Canyon. The second leap (18) is from the Grand Canyon to Carlsbad Caverns. Instead of finding these natural wonders inspiring, as his parents expect, Billy is horrified by them. Both natural wonders are vast empty spaces—a canyon and a cavern. They are like the empty space in Vonnegut's memory about the actual bombing of Dresden.

TD: Catalog of two "marvelous moments" that are "beautiful and surprising and deep"

Leap 19: From Carlsbad Caverns to World War II
(1934-1944)

While in Carlsbad Caverns, Billy focuses on the only available light—
the radium dial on his father's watch (90). Billy then time travels from
"total dark to total light" (90) back to the war where he sees "starving
Russians with faces like radium dials" (91).

TD: Radium dials (and conceptual contrast) cut from dark to light

Leap 20: From prison hospital to veterans' hospital
(1944-1948)

Billy and the other prisoners are taken to the Czechoslovakian border
where they are encamped with British prisoners. During a performance
of *Cinderella*, Billy falls into a fit of laughter and is taken to the prison
hospital and dosed with morphine. While asleep, Billy dreams. When
he wakes up, he has time traveled to the mental ward of a veterans' hospital in Lake Placid, New York.

TD: Sleeping in a hospital bed to sleeping in a hospital bed

Leap 21: From veterans' hospital to prison hospital
(1948-1944)

Billy has voluntarily committed himself to a mental hospital during his
final year of optometry school. He is placed in a bed next to Eliot
Rosewater, who introduces him to the science-fiction novels of Kilgore
Trout. While Billy's mother chats with Rosewater, Billy falls asleep and
wakes up back at the prison hospital.

TD: Sleeping in a hospital bed to sleeping in a hospital bed

Leap 22: From prison hospital to veterans' hospital
(1944-1948)

Billy is back in the prison hospital. Edgar Derby is telling the colonel how he was captured, noting that the Germans told them to come "out of the woods with their hands on top of their heads," at which point Billy leaps back to the veterans' hospital, where "the blanket was over his head" (107).

TD: Things over heads, from hospital to hospital

Leap 23: From veterans' hospital to alien zoo
(1948-1967)

Billy is being visited by his fiancée Valencia Merble. The relationship is not ideal. Billy admits that he "didn't want to marry ugly Valencia" and claims that she is "one of the symptoms of his disease" (107). As Valencia is discussing silver patterns, Billy travels to the zoo on Tralfamadore where he looks at an idealized picture of a "Gay Nineties couple on a bicycle built for two" (113) that has been painted on the refrigerator door. Like Billy and Valencia, the couple appear together, but no emotional bond exists beneath those appearances. Billy tries "to think of something about the couple" (113) but nothing comes to him. "There didn't seem to be *anything* to think about those two people," Vonnegut writes, inviting a parallel between the depiction of a couple on the refrigerator and the depiction of Billy and Valencia's engagement.

TD: Superficial image of a couple

Leap 24: From alien zoo to Billy and Valencia's wedding night
(1967-circa 1948)

The Tralfamadorians explain the deterministic nature of the universe to Billy and the impossibility of averting tragedies and that "the idea of preventing war on Earth is stupid" (117). The Tralfamadorians deal with unpleasant moments by simply not looking at them. "We spend eternity looking at pleasant moments," they tell him—"nice moments" (117). Then Billy time travels to his wedding night, which is a "moment which was quite nice" (118). This section also foreshadows the end of the novel where Vonnegut recounts the moment in springtime when Billy (and Vonnegut) discovers that the war is over and he is free.

TD: Nice moment to nice moment

Leap 25: From wedding night to World War II (circa 1948-1944)

On his wedding night, Billy goes "into the darkness of the bathroom to take a leak" (123). As he gropes the wall for the light switch, he travels back to the prison hospital where the candle has "gone out" leaving the room in darkness. Billy gets up and gropes the wall because he also needs to "take a leak . . . badly" (123) in 1944.

TD: Groping a wall in darkness on the way to take a leak

Leap 26: From prison hospital to Billy and Valencia's wedding night (1944-circa 1948)

After relieving himself in the prison latrine, Billy passes through the door to the prison hospital and out of the bathroom door back on his wedding night.

TD: Passing through door after going to the bathroom

Leap 27: From Billy and Valencia's wedding night to train to father's funeral
(circa 1948-1944)

This transition is more implied than explicit. Billy and Valencia go "to sleep nestled like spoons" (126), as was mentioned in leap 12 when prisoners nestling like spoons on the train during the war was used as a transition to Billy and Valencia nestling like spoons on their daughter's wedding night. Leap 12 establishes a relationship between spooning and trains that is replayed here as Billy leaps from spooning with his wife on *his* wedding night to another train. On both the prisoner train and the train to Ilium in this transition, Billy has trouble sleeping.

TD: Parallel between spooning and trains established in leap 12

Leap 28: From train to father's funeral to prison hospital
(1944-1944)

Billy is standing on the train platform in Ilium, trying to "wake up" (126) when he leaps forward in time to Billy's "morphine night in the prison hospital" (127). It is 3:00 A.M. and Paul Lazzaro is being brought in with a broken arm. Presumably, Billy has to wake up for this moment as well.

TD: Waking up

Leap 29: From prison hospital to home in Ilium
(1944-1968)

Billy goes to sleep in the war and wakes up at his home in Ilium where his daughter is scolding him for writing to the newspapers about aliens. In addition to the form cut on sleeping, Vonnegut connects the two moments with the idea of childish behavior. Right before he falls asleep in the war, Billy hears Howard W. Campbell, Jr., describe American soldiers by saying, "Each will be a sulky child" (130). After Billy travels to his home in 1968, his daughter says to him, "If you're going to act like a child, maybe we'll just have to *treat* you like a child" (131).

TD: Sleep, defining adults as children

Leap 30: From home in Ilium to alien zoo (1968-unknown)

The furnace in Billy's house is broken, so Billy's daughter places an electric blanket over Billy. She sets the controls "at the highest notch, which soon made Billy's bed hot enough to bake bread in" (132). From there, Billy travels to Tralfamadore where the actress Montana Wildhack has "just been brought to him" (132). She is naked, as is Billy, and in time she asks Billy to "sleep with her" (133); thus the heat in Billy's bed in Ilium transitions to sexual heat in Billy's bed on Tralfamadore.

TD: Hot bed to hot bed

Leap 31: From alien zoo to home in Ilium (unknown-1968)

Billy travels from "that delightful bed" (134) on Tralfamadore back to his hot bed in Ilium. The next day, Billy goes into the office but is taken home by his daughter after he talks to a boy about aliens and time. The scene and chapter 5 end with Billy's daughter asking Billy, "What *are* we going to *do* with you?" (135).

In relying on filmic transitions during time leaps in this first section (in all but leap 16), Vonnegut interrelates the scenes without subverting the sense of randomness. Each part preceding and following one of Billy's leaps in time during this first section of thirty-one leaps represents a scene or a sequence in Billy's life. These "moments," as Billy,

Vonnegut, and the Tralfamadorians all refer to them, are comparable to shots in a film. Film editing, which involves the ordering of autonomous shots, creates meaning through the piecing together of "moments" of film. Classic Hollywood filmmaking tended to rely on seamless editing to create the illusion that one shot logically followed from a preceding shot. Classic Hollywood films labored to construct the illusion of linear reality. The techniques employed by these early editors (cutting on movement, cutting on eye line, and so on) serve a purpose similar to that of traditional narrative—to create a sense of cause and effect, one event creating the next event in a domino line that falls as a result of natural forces.

All early film editing did not strive for linear narratives, however. Early Russian filmmakers influenced by Lev Kuleshov and the Kuleshov workshop, notably Sergei Eisenstein and Vsevolod Pudovkin, experimented with the juxtaposing of different images in their development of montage. Eisenstein argues in *Film Form* that "the fragment and its relationships" are "specific" (4) to film. He does acknowledge that the process of combining fragments "is to be found in other art mediums" but claims that "the immutable fragment of actual reality in these cases is narrower and more neutral in meaning, and therefore more flexible in combination, so that when they are put together they lose all visible signs of being combined, appearing as one organic unit" (4). However, Eisenstein was writing about film at the height of American literary modernism, a period when unity of vision in a literary work was highly regarded. The singular "organic unit" was often the goal for writers in the first half of the twentieth century. However, during the second half, the period Vonnegut occupies, the boundaries of traditional modernist narrative were challenged. Fragmentation and disorientation ceased to be considered flaws by writers who had discarded—or, in Vonnegut's case, become disillusioned by—notions of unified visions, both in literature and culture.

Lawrence R. Broer credits "the bedlam of violence and social chaos" with inducing "the personal dissolution and incipient madness of Vonnegut's . . . heroes" (5). It is precisely this social chaos that spurred an awareness, in writers who, like Vonnegut, formed the vanguard of postmodern literature, of the universe's reluctance to fit into tidy frames. One of the strengths of *Slaughterhouse-Five* is its refusal to collate the horrors of World War II and the incomprehensibility of the Dresden firebombing into a traditional linear narrative. To illuminate the fragments of history and to accommodate the parlor tricks that time plays on human memory,[2] Vonnegut resorted to the temporal fragmentation of Billy Pilgrim. The transitional devices that Vonnegut uses to suture these fragments together are more properly associated with film editing techniques than literary ones. Form cuts (conceptual or visual) provide this first section of time leaps with a sense of cohesion without sacrificing the theme of fragmentation and disorder central to the novel. The second section, however, radically alters this structure.

Rebooting the Narrative: From Crash to Coma

Chapter 6 begins as chapter 5 began, with the imperative "Listen:" (136), and marks a departure from the previous section. Here Vonnegut has abandoned the use of form cuts. Leap 32 occurs between the end of chapter 5 and the beginning of chapter 6 when the story moves from Billy's home in Ilium back to World War II, but this shift in time is handled in a traditional literary manner, by simply starting a new chapter in a new place and time, a technique that Vonnegut eschewed during the previous four chapters.

In this reboot of the narrative, Vonnegut abandons the transitional devices that he employed during the first part of the novel, thus increasing our sense of temporal distortion and disorientation as the novel moves toward Vonnegut's inevitable confrontation with the firebombing of Dresden. Chapter 6 begins with Billy back in the prison hospital during his "morphine night" (136), but the movement from the war to Billy's death in Chicago is not facilitated by any filmic transitions.

The temporal shift occurs just after Paul Lazzaro tells Billy that he is going to kill him. Immediately after Lazzaro says to Billy, "Whenever the doorbell rings, have somebody else answer the door," Vonnegut writes:

> Billy Pilgrim says now that this really is the way he *is* going to die, too. As a time-traveler he has seen his own death many times, has described it to a tape recorder. The tape is locked up with his will and some other valuables in his safe-deposit box at the Ilium Merchants National Bank and Trust, he says. (141)

This passage is followed with a section that first appears to be recounting what is on the tape, but eventually abandons that orientation and assumes Billy is in Chicago. Several unanswered questions are raised during the time leap (33). Among them, when is the "now" that is referred to in the previous passage that leads us eventually to find ourselves in Chicago at the end of Billy's life? Up to this point, Vonnegut has been careful to mark time. Only one instance in the first thirty-one leaps cannot be clearly attributed to a year in Billy's life (see leap 31), when Montana Wildhack arrives at the zoo on Tralfamadore, but at this juncture we not only do not know *when* we are, but we also do not know to *whom* Billy is saying this. Nevertheless, we are unquestionably in Chicago when leap 34 occurs. Vonnegut writes that after Billy is shot by Lazzaro, "Billy experiences death for a while" and then "he swings back into life again, all the way back to an hour after his life was threatened by Lazzaro—in 1945" (143).

This shift in transitional methodology represents a significant rupture in the narrative. Time is not only nebulous and unpredictable for Billy, it has become nebulous and unpredictable for the reader as well. The narrative continues to avoid the system of transitions formerly in place, instead making its next temporal leap on a chapter break. Like the beginning of chapter 6, chapter 7 begins in a time and place different from where chapter 6 ends. At the end of chapter 6, Billy has been taken to Dresden and housed in a slaughterhouse. Chapter 7 begins with Billy boarding a chartered plane to a Montreal conference for optometrists (leap 34). Only a chapter break is used to move Billy from one time and location to another.

Leaps 35 and 36 represent a unique leap in time that Billy makes: the only leap that Billy intentionally takes. The plane Billy boards at the beginning of chapter 7 is destined to crash, and right before the plane crashes we are told, "Billy, knowing the plane was going to crash pretty soon, closed his eyes, [and] traveled in time back to 1944" (158). At no other place in the novel does Billy choose to time travel or select when and to where he will travel; but at this point he chooses to travel right before the plane crashes, traveling to a point in the war when he is telling Weary and the others to "go on without me" (156). The *center* of the story about the plane crash—the crash itself—has been excised from Billy's experience, which parallels what Vonnegut has said about his memory of the actual firebombing of Dresden, that "the center had been pulled right out of the story" (Allen 94). In a single paragraph, Billy travels back to the war to avoid the crash, then leaps right back to after the crash, when he is rescued by "Austrian ski instructors" (156). This marks the beginning of what is structurally the most significant part of the forty-part structure I am proposing: part 37 (which is more properly a part than a leap, as everything here occurs while Billy is dreaming).

Part 37: The Coma and the Dream

In leaps 32 through 36, the careful control of time and space that Vonnegut exhibited during the first thirty-one time-travel transitions disappears, leaving readers disoriented. Part 37 begins with Billy's plane crash, after which he is "taken to a small private hospital" (157) where he undergoes brain surgery. Billy is "unconscious for two days" (157). During that time, events are cataloged rather than ordered, and Vonnegut finally confronts the Dresden firebombing but only by burying it deep within Billy's states of mind. Part 37 ends when Billy opens "his eyes in the hospital in Vermont" (189).

We are told that during the two days he is unconscious, Billy "dreamed millions of things" and that "the true things were time-travel" (157), so that even when we are told that Billy time travels, we are aware that these trips in time are occurring while Billy is dreaming in a comatose state. Though we are told that the time-travel segments that occur while Billy is unconscious are "true" (157), we have no way of understanding the nature of that truth, in what sense they might be true, or how they correlate with the previous time-travel segments. We cannot know with certainty if Billy is actually traveling in time (as we can in leaps 1-31) or if he is dreaming about travels he has already made in time. Where and when Billy is remains uncertain until he re-opens his eyes. Here the time travel that Billy experiences is aligned with human memory.

One of the "true things" Billy experiences in the coma is "his first evening in the slaughterhouse" (157), when he, Edgar Derby, and a young German guard make their way to the slaughterhouse's kitchen. Without transition or mention of time travel, the next presumed time-travel event is introduced with the statement, "Another true thing that Billy saw while he was unconscious in Vermont" (159), followed by a recounting of Billy's experience working in the malt syrup factory a month before the bombing. This places the time of the event in January 1945, but the introductory statement places Billy in Vermont after the crash. Despite having been told that "the true things were time-travel" (157), we recognize that this is a different type of time travel than had been previously presented. This time travel takes the form of memories that surface while Billy is unconscious. The structure of Billy's memories mirror what Vonnegut tells us about his own memories; they are disjointed, nonlinear, and incomplete. The events continue in Dresden as Vonnegut writes about Howard W. Campbell, Jr.'s visit to the prisoners, but Billy is still unconscious in a Vermont hospital as these past events are recalled.

The night before the firebombing, Billy falls asleep in the meat locker and "found himself" arguing with his daughter. Vonnegut does not identify this as anything other than a dreamed memory. Thus our journey into Billy's mind has become like nesting dolls; Billy is in a coma dreaming/time traveling of falling asleep in Dresden the night before the bombing and having a dream. The structure is:

> While in a coma in Vermont . . .
>> Billy dreams "true things" about Dresden . . .
>>> While dreaming about Dresden, Billy falls asleep and dreams . . .

The dream Billy has is inside a time-travel memory he is already having while in a coma. It is within this dream-within-a-dream while in a coma that Billy eventually *remembers* the firebombing of Dresden.

The structure of Billy's dream-within-a-dream while in a coma contains six parts, beginning where the first section ends (see leap 31) and ending with Billy telling Montana Wildhack a story about the destruction of Dresden. The dream-within-a-dream:

1. Recap of argument Billy has with his daughter, where she asks, "What are we going to *do* with *you*?" (165), and blames Kilgore Trout for Billy's condition.
2. Story of how Kilgore Trout and Billy met (166).
3. Trout at Billy's eighteenth wedding anniversary (170).
4. Billy goes upstairs during his anniversary, lies down, and remembers Dresden (177).
5. Montana Wildhack in the alien zoo asks Billy, "Tell me a story" (178).
6. Billy tells her about Dresden in the war. The story ends "very curiously in a suburb untouched by fire and explosions" (180), where Billy meets a blind innkeeper and his family.

At the start of chapter 9, the dream has ended and we are back at the hospital after the plane crash. Billy is presumably in the same state as before, as we are told, "Billy knew nothing about . . . [the death of his wife]. He dreamed on, and traveled in time and so forth" (183). While Billy is still unconscious, we learn about (1) his wife's auto accident and resulting death; and (2) Harvard history professor Bertram Copeland Rumfoord, who occupies the bed next to Billy and who is writing a history of World War II, including a section on the firebombing of Dresden.

Before Billy awakes, we are told about two other time-travel events, though the nature of these, like the other trips in time Billy has while unconscious, is in question. The first occurs when Billy's daughter visits him in the hospital and we are told that he is "ten years away, back in 1958," examining the vision of an "idiot" (188). This moment/memory follows in the wake of a long section illuminating Rumfoord's (and other military "experts") justification for the Dresden firebombing, inviting us to draw comparisons between Rumfoord and an idiot who cannot see clearly. This trip is followed by a moment/memory when Billy is sixteen and sitting in a waiting room with an old man "in agony because of gas" (189), inviting us to compare Rumfoord further to a gassy old man. Part 37 ends when Billy opens "his eyes in the hospital in Vermont" (189), regaining consciousness.

The Final Three Leaps (38-40)

Billy emerges from his coma to find his son, Robert, watching him. Robert, who had been a troubled child, is now a decorated soldier. The presence of Billy's son at the end of the long coma sequence signifies the inevitability of war. Robert represents the next generation, a generation that is just as involved with war as the last generation. As Vonnegut pointed out in chapter 1, antiwar books are as effective as an "anti-glacier book" (3). Vonnegut's point here, which is thematic to the novel, is ironic. The inhumanity of war seems to be inevitable, but to accept that belief is to adopt the Tralfamadorian view of time—to place your confidence in what you are told by green alien plungers who live in an atmosphere of cyanide. It is absurd.

With the final three leaps in time, Vonnegut returns to the filmic transitions he employed during the first thirty-one leaps.

Leap 38: From hospital in Vermont to World War II two days after the end of the war
(1968-1945)

> Rumfoord has no interest in listening to what Billy has to say about Dresden, though Billy was actually present during the firebombing. "Must we talk about it now?" Rumfoord says. Billy responds with a line that reflects Vonnegut's position in writing the novel: "We don't ever have to talk about it. . . . I just want you to know: I was there" (193). Then Billy closes his eyes and travels to what "he might have chosen as his happiest moment" during the war, when he is taking a "sun-drenched snooze" (195) in the back of a horse-drawn wagon after the end of the war.

TD: Closing eyes/snoozing

Leap 39: From end of the war to hospital in Vermont
(1945-1968)

> While Billy is in the wagon, he is approached by two obstetricians who scold "him . . . for the condition of the horses" (197), which were in "agony" and "insane with thirst" (196). Billy begins to weep because he had not noticed the suffering of the animals. We are told that "he hadn't cried about anything else in the war" (197). This scene articulates the absurdity of Tralfamadorian precepts, which mandate spending eternity only "looking at the pleasant moments" (117). To be human is to notice the suffering of others, a point that is stressed when Billy leaps in time back to Vermont where he tells Rumfoord about the horses, and we learn that Rumfoord is "reluctantly becoming interested in Billy as a human being" (197).

TD: Story of the horses

Leap 40: From New York City to alien zoo
(1968-unknown; see leap 30)

Billy is released from the hospital and eventually makes his way to New York City, where he finagles his way onto a radio talk show and tells everyone "about the flying saucers and Montana Wildhack" (206). He is expelled from the studio and returns to his hotel room, and then time travels "back to Tralfamadore" where Montana Wildhack is nursing their infant.

TD: Montana Wildhack

Chapter 10 closes the frame that began with chapter 1. We are again encountering Vonnegut talking about writing his famous Dresden novel. However, now Billy's story is intermingled with Vonnegut's as Vonnegut writes about the execution of Edgar Derby and the moment he (and Billy) discovered that "World War Two in Europe was over" (215).

Time and Memory

Vonnegut admits in the opening of *Slaughterhouse-Five* that "not many words about Dresden" came from his "mind" (2) when he first returned from the war, and that not many words came to him over two decades later when he was completing his novel. "The Dresden part of . . . [his] memory," he tells us, is "useless" (2). We might explain this gap in Vonnegut's memory in Freudian terms as the repression of something painful. S. A. Tannenbaum, working from Freud, points out that repression is related to an "individual's aversion to experiencing . . . emotional reactions, to his desire to deny the existence in him of tendencies conflicting with his ego-ideal" (419). Vonnegut, a freethinker and pacifist who descended from a long line of freethinkers and pacifists, would certainly find the corpse-mines and the inhumanity of war traumatic, which helps explain his repression of the specific events of the Dresden firebombing. And from a structural perspective, it helps us to understand Billy Pilgrim's narrative in the novel. As Vonnegut approaches the event he is most motivated to repress, the systematic control he exhibits over Billy's leaps in time crumbles and the structure of the narrative begins to reflect the nebulous structure of repressed memory. Billy, like Vonnegut, cannot easily confront the horrors of the firebombing. The details are too deeply buried within his unconscious. This burial is exposed in the structure of the second section, wherein the first specifics about the firebombing are *remembered* while Billy is *dreaming* inside another *dream* he has while *unconscious*. The horrors of the bombing are thus four removes from reality.

It is significant that when *Slaughterhouse-Five* moves past the Dresden bombing, the structure of the narrative regains control over Billy's time leaps, indicating that it is the key event, the bombing, which disrupts memory and disorients time, both of which are intimately linked and central to the structure of *Slaughterhouse-Five*. Time does not exist without memory—without the concepts of that which was, that which is, and that which will be—and time implies causality, as Paul Watzlawick points out when he writes, "When we say that one event is the cause of another, we obviously mean that the second event follows the first in time" (225). *Slaughterhouse-Five* raises questions about causality. What causes human atrocities? Is there anything people can do to prevent them? If we cannot identify the causes of atrocities, how can we ever hope to prevent them? The Tralfamadorian answer—the *absurd* answer—is that nothing can be done, so try not to pay attention to the bad times. Instead, pay attention to the pleasant moments. The Tralfamadorian view of the universe disempowers causality by detaching cause from effect. As a result, the linearity of time itself is disrupted. One event no longer leads to the next one. This is the condition of Billy Pilgrim in the novel, a man who has become "unstuck in time" and can do nothing to change the course of his life. But Vonnegut's position, which he stressed throughout his life and career, is that we need to try to effect change, even when we are unsure how to go about it, and that when we refuse to acknowledge atrocities and suffering, we become less human.

Notes

1. Billy Pilgrim wears "tri-focals" (62), implying that he can see three different distances from the same perspective—that he can see past, present, and future through one set of lenses. Though he can see them, he, like Vonnegut himself, cannot change them, as Vonnegut notes when he writes, "Among the things that Billy Pilgrim could not change were the past, the present, and the future" (60).

2. Vonnegut twice refers to himself in the novel as "an old fart with his memories" (2, 7).

Works Cited

Allen, William Rodney, ed. *Conversations with Kurt Vonnegut.* Jackson: UP of Mississippi, 1988.

Broer, Lawrence R. *Sanity Plea: Schizophrenia in the Novels of Kurt Vonnegut.* Rev. ed. Tuscaloosa: U of Alabama P, 1989.

Edelstein, Arnold. "*Slaughterhouse-Five*: Time Out of Joint." *College Literature* 1.2 (Spring 1974): 128-39.

Eisenstein, Sergei. *Film Form: Essays in Film Theory.* Trans. Jay Leyda. New York: Harcourt, 1969.

Gallagher, Brian. "Film Imagery, Literary Imagery: Some Distinctions." *College Literature* 5.3 (Fall 1978): 157-73.

Huss, Roy, and Norman Silverstein. *The Film Experience: Elements of Motion Picture Art.* New York: Dell, 1968.

Klinkowitz, Jerome, and Donald L. Lawler, eds. *Vonnegut in America: An Introduction to the Life and Work of Kurt Vonnegut.* New York: Delacorte Press, 1977.

Pinker, Steven. *How the Mind Works.* New York: W. W. Norton, 1997.

Tannenbaum, S. A. "Some Current Misconceptions of Psychoanalysis." *Journal of Abnormal Psychology* 12 (1918): 390-422.

Vonnegut, Kurt. Interview by David Standish. *Playboy* July 1973: 57-60, 62, 66, 68, 70, 72, 74, 214, 216.

_____. *Slaughterhouse-Five.* New York: Dell, 1969.

Watzlawick, Paul. *How Real Is Real?* New York: Vintage, 1977.

"The War Parts, Anyway, Are Pretty Much True":
Negotiating the Reality of World War II in
Slaughterhouse-Five and Catch-22_____

David Simmons

While a great deal of work has been done comparing Kurt Vonnegut's writing to that of other American authors, relatively little sustained analysis has been carried out discussing the links between Vonnegut's postwar oeuvre and that of some of his 1960s contemporaries.[1] It is clear that many of these writers share much in common, yet, as Christopher Gair points out in *The American Counterculture* (2007), "Oddly . . . recent studies of 1960s counterculture have largely erased literature from its history" (142). Such an inconsistency is all the more surprising when we consider Vonnegut's well-known and public friendship with the author of *Catch-22* (1961), Joseph Heller. In an oft-quoted 1992 *Playboy* magazine interview between the two authors, both display a warm and familiar rapport with one another, noting that their relationship goes back over twenty years to a literary festival that took place on the day that Martin Luther King, Jr., was shot. Heller recollects fondly of hearing Vonnegut talk on that day: "Kurt Vonnegut gave a speech that was probably the best speech I've ever heard. I think I haven't heard a better one since. He was so casual and so funny and it all seemed extemporaneous" (Mallory para. 16). Vonnegut is similarly complimentary toward Heller, commenting, "He's a comedian" and describing him as "screamingly funny" (paras. 216, 15). Among the wide range of topics that the two writers discuss is World War II and their firsthand knowledge of the conflict. Heller notes:

> It was fun in the beginning. We were kids, nineteen, twenty years old, and had real machine guns in our hands. Not those things at the penny arcades at Coney Island. You got the feeling that there was something glorious about it. Glorious excitement. (para. 80)

However, over the course of the interview, both writers suggest that this initial enthusiasm for the ennobling possibilities of war was soon quashed by the "reality" that they encountered, leading them to deem warfare "an atrocity." Indeed, the idea that the projected image of war differed from the "reality" the two authors experienced forms a central part of much of their writing. In his essay "The Great American Joke," author Louis D. Rubin, Jr., suggests that central to all humor is the juxtaposition of an ideal with the reality of life: "The essence of comedy is incongruity." In this essay I will argue that Rubin's proposal that a sense of incongruity "lies at the heart of American experience" (109) is of central importance to understanding the comparable satirical impulses behind both Vonnegut's and Heller's novels.

Slaughterhouse-Five (1969) and *Catch-22* are both frequently referred to as "war" or "antiwar" novels. Both texts engage, often on a personal level, with the effects and aftereffects of war on the individual. Rachel McCoppin concurs with such a sentiment, proposing in her chapter "'God Damn It, You've Got to Be Kind': War and Altruism in the Works of Kurt Vonnegut" that "World War II is a central component in many of Kurt Vonnegut's novels" (47). Such a claim can also clearly be applied to many of Heller's post-*Catch-22* works, including the play *We Bombed in New Haven* (1967), the *Catch-22* sequel *Closing Time* (1994), and Heller's autobiographical novel *Portrait of an Artist, as an Old Man* (2000). Indeed, in "Joseph Heller's Combat Experiences in *Catch-22*" Michael C. Scoggins lucidly argues for a reassessment of Heller's work in terms of its autobiographical elements: "Many of the characters and incidents in *Catch-22* were in fact drawn directly from Heller's tour of duty, and were simply modified or exaggerated for dramatic effect" (213).

McCoppin outlines the widely recognized semiautobiographical nature of Vonnegut's writing at the beginning of her chapter, highlighting the recurrent importance of the writer's experiences of the firebombing of Dresden:

Though it is not entirely certain that Vonnegut draws from his own life experiences for his novels, it seems likely. In 1944 Vonnegut was a prisoner of war in Dresden where he witnessed the slaughter of "135,000 civilian inhabitants—the largest massacre in European history. Vonnegut and his fellow prisoners were drafted as corpse miners, taking the dead Germans from their shelters and stacking them in funeral pyres across the ravaged city" ([Klinkowitz and Lawler] *Vonnegut in America* 13). Indeed, it is accepted critical knowledge that Vonnegut frequently mentions Dresden in his novels. (49)

Vonnegut's time in Dresden is one of the central themes in *Slaughterhouse-Five*. Right from the first chapter, the difficulty of recounting an orderly narrative of the events that took place in Dresden is presented as being of central importance to the construction of the novel.

I would hate to tell you what this lousy little book cost me in money and anxiety and time. When I got home from the Second World War twenty-three years ago, I thought it would be easy for me to write about the destruction of Dresden, since all I would have to do is report what I had seen . . . but not many words about Dresden came from my mind then—not enough of them to make a book, anyway. (2)

In "The Journey Home in Kurt Vonnegut's World War II Novels" Elizabeth Abele notes that "though Vonnegut had nothing to do with the bombing of Dresden, his obsessive return to the same narratives and themes reveals the responsibility he felt for his indirect acts of destruction" (73). Consequently, it is important to note that while the narrator of the novel (be this the "real" Vonnegut or a fictional stand-in) recognizes Dresden as an atrocity, he is simultaneously drawn back to it, stating, "I thought . . . it would be a masterpiece or at least make me a lot of money" (2). At this point of the novel, the narrator seems torn between a desire to capitalize on the heroic, romanticizing processes of the more conventional war narrative and his quite different, inherent feelings toward war, having experienced it firsthand: "One guy I knew *really* was shot in Dresden for taking a teapot that wasn't his" (1).

The narrator relates how his original draft of the novel would have had a much happier, more sentimental ending in which the soldiers "were flown to a rest camp in France, where we were fed chocolate malted milkshakes and other rich foods until we were all covered with baby fat. Then we were sent home, and I married a pretty girl" (5). However, this upbeat ending is rejected when the narrator goes to visit his old war buddy Bernard V. O'Hare. In a much-discussed passage of the novel, the narrator is confronted by O'Hare's wife, Mary, who protests angrily, "You'll pretend you were men instead of babies, and you'll be played in the movies by Frank Sinatra and John Wayne. . . . And war will look just wonderful, so we'll have a lot more of them. And they'll be fought by babies like the babies upstairs" (11). Upon realizing the truth of Mary's comments, the narrator vows not to follow this trend: the book is subtitled "The Children's Crusade" and dedicated to the woman who brought his attention to the dangerously glorifying tendencies of earlier war novels.

Central to the novel's rejection of such lionization is the character of Billy Pilgrim. Billy is presented as not befitting the heroic wartime model of the soldier; he is introduced to the reader "as a funny looking child, who became a funny looking youth—tall and weak" (17) and is described as not looking "like a soldier at all. He looked like a filthy Flamingo" (24). The fact that Billy becomes a chaplain's assistant rather than a soldier also makes him somewhat of a peripheral figure to the war. We are informed that Billy "was powerless to harm the enemy or to help his friends" (22). Indeed, in many ways Billy lacks the self-agency typically associated with the hero; instead, the novel emphasizes his lack of control, pointing out that he "has no control over where he is going next" (17). However, Billy does seem to exert some influence over what happens to him when he refuses to join in with the conflict taking place in Germany, even going so far as to refuse to carry a weapon throughout his time abroad. Instead, he suggests that what is needed is a more compassionate, pacifistic mindset; as I previously noted in *The Anti-Hero in the American Novel*: "[*Slaughterhouse-Five*] suggests that it is Billy's continued innocence, in a time of otherwise widespread madness, which enables him to retain his sanity." Billy does not embrace the militaristic desire to be the most effective soldier possible; rather, his "strong humanitarian stance causes him to respect life rather than to attempt to destroy it" (123).

McCoppin, writing about Vonnegut's self-professed belief in the importance of the social function of literature, suggests that *Slaughterhouse-Five* succeeds in "offering a message of pacifism in opposition to America's proclivity towards militarism" (61). In one particularly poignant episode in the future, Billy watches a documentary on World War II backward, reconfiguring an Allied attack on Germany into a healing rather than destructive sequence:

> The formation flew backwards over a German city that was in flames. The bombers opened their bomb bay doors, exerted a miraculous magnetism which shrunk the fires, gathered them into cylindrical steel containers, and lifted the containers into the bellies of the planes. (74)

Much like Billy Pilgrim, *Catch-22*'s John Joseph Yossarian also brings traditional wartime heroic models into question, and, like *Slaughterhouse-Five*, Heller's novel critiques the romanticized image of war as a noble cause. As the narrator of Heller's story states at the beginning of the book:

> It was a vile and muddy war, and Yossarian could have lived without it— lived forever, perhaps. Only a fraction of his countrymen would give up their lives to win it, and it was not his ambition to be amongst them. (77)

Yossarian's reluctance to "heroically" die for his country is partly a result of his superiors' complete lack of integrity. They set impossible and nonsensical rules, are more interested in appearances than the well-being of their squads, and are shown to be open to corruption. It is because of their duplicity that Yossarian finds himself effectively trapped in the Bombardier core, unable to escape because of a paradoxical rule that proposes that anyone that wants to leave combat is fit to stay and must stay: "Catch-22. Anyone who wants to get out of combat duty isn't really crazy" (52).

The question of Yossarian's sanity is a central theme of the book, and Heller uses the characters' dubious classification of Yossarian as "mad" to highlight the insanity of the actions of those around him. In particular the character of Clevinger, "a very serious, very earnest and very conscientious dope" (78), serves as a foil to Yossarian. Clevinger is an eternal optimist who believes that Yossarian is mad: "Clevinger enumerated Yossarian's symptoms: an unreasonable belief that everybody around him was crazy, a homicidal impulse to machine-gun strangers, retrospective falsification, an unfounded suspicion that people hated him and were conspiring to kill him" (23). Yet the irony is that many of the people Yossarian encounters are trying to kill him:

> But Yossarian knew he was right, because as he explained, to the best of his knowledge he had never been wrong. Everywhere he looked was a nut, and it was all a sensible young gentleman like himself could do to maintain his perspective amid so much madness. And it was urgent that he did, for he knew his life was in peril. (23)

Clevinger tries to explain Yossarian's paranoia away by suggesting that in a time of war people are trying to kill their enemies, but this circular logic proves to be ineffectual when Clevinger himself is brought up on contrived charges by Lieutenant Scheisskopf: "The case against Clevinger was open and shut. The only thing missing was something to charge him with" (81). Given the absurdity that the novel proposes becomes a part of everyday life during a time of war, it is clear that we are meant to see that Yossarian, though classified as mad by those around him, is the only truly rational character in the novel. As one of the doctors who treats Yossarian says of this incongruity: "That crazy bastard may be the only sane one left" (127).

Part of what keeps Yossarian sane is his refusal to believe that romanticizing war is a heroic act. Instead, Yossarian comes to believe that war only exacerbates humanity's worst characteristics: "When I look up, I see people cashing in. I don't see heavens or saints or angels. I see people cashing in on every decent impulse and every human tragedy" (510).

Like Billy Pilgrim, who refuses to carry arms in a time of conflict, Yossarian also chooses to reject military signifiers when- and wherever possible: he refuses to wear his uniform, preferring instead to parade in the nude; tries to be grounded from flying missions on the basis of insanity; and declines his superior officers' offer of a hero's discharge in exchange for his complicity. Ultimately, Yossarian will not partake of a system that seeks to restrict the freedom of the individual in such an illogical manner: "Yossarian was willing to be the victim of anything but circumstance. But that was war. Just about all he could find in its favor was that it paid well and liberated children from the pernicious influence of their parents" (77).

One of the few characters that choose to believe in the heroic wartime model in *Slaughterhouse-Five* is Ronald Weary. Weary, "a stupid and fat and mean" (25) antitank gunner, is enraptured with the notion that he and his fellow soldiers are fighting the heroic fight. Nicknaming the band of soldiers he finds himself lost with the Three Musketeers, Weary reconstructs the events he has witnessed in a decidedly romantic fashion: "Weary's version of the true war story went like this: There was a big German attack, and Weary and his antitank buddies fought like hell until everybody was killed but Weary" (30). In reality, Weary is a bully who considers it "absolutely necessary that cruelty be used" (25) whenever possible and ends up being ditched by his companions, captured by the Germans, and dying of gangrene while traveling in a boxcar to a prisoner of war camp.

Billy also encounters a group of British prisoners who have been captured and held by the Germans. Though they are imprisoned, a clerical error causes the Englishmen to be sent copious amounts of rations, to the point at which they are able to live in relative wealth and prosperity. Even their captors seem to be in awe of their enthusiasm and vigor:

> They were adored by the Germans, who thought they were exactly what Englishmen ought to be. They made war look stylish and reasonable, and fun. So the Germans let them have four sheds, though one shed would have held them all. And, in exchange for coffee or chocolate or tobacco, the Germans gave them paint and lumber and nails and cloth for fixing things up. (68)

The Englishmen take a great deal of pride in their personal appearance and seem overly enthusiastic: "I *envy* you lads" (106) one of them tells Billy when they find out that all of the American soldiers are to be shipped to Dresden to work as contract labor. Yet the novel suggests that the British soldiers are only able to maintain this zest by choosing to ignore the reality of the war that is going on around them. Emblematic of this disregard is the soldiers' staging of an amateur production of the fairy tale *Cinderella* amid the conflict.

While for much of the novel Billy is a passive, somewhat detached figure, embodying the novel's depiction of war as a state in which there flourishes "a sense of control by the trivial, the accidental, the degradingly unheroic" (Wright 103), it is during the period he spends in Dresden that Billy is, for the first time, provoked into a strong emotional response. On arriving in the city, Billy notes, "The skyline was intricate and voluptuous and enchanted and absurd. It looked like a Sunday school picture of heaven" (108). Following the horrendous bombing of the city, Billy and the remaining soldiers go looting in Dresden on horseback. In his happiness over the ending of the war, Billy does not realize that "the horses' mouths were bleeding, gashed by the bits, that the horses' hooves were broken, so that every step meant agony, that the horses were insane with thirst" (143). In what

McCoppin proposes "in many ways . . . is the thematic climax of the novel" (60), Billy breaks down crying when he discovers the horses' suffering: "When Billy saw the condition of his means of transportation, he burst into tears. He hadn't cried about anything else in the war" (144). Billy responds in this manner because he realizes his part in the pain inflicted on the horses. His ability to remain distanced from the horrors of the war is challenged by the implication that his impassivity has involuntarily led to the brutality inflicted on the innocent horses. As McCoppin explains, "Vonnegut uses the topic of war and his black humor to advocate the existential component of individual responsibility for one's actions in the modern and postmodern world" (47).

Following the ending of the war, and spurred on by his realization, Billy becomes an optometrist, devoting the rest of his life to helping others to see more clearly, both literally and metaphorically: "He was doing nothing less now, he thought, than prescribing corrective lenses for Earthling souls" (21). In the closing chapter of the book, the narrator tells us how he went back to Dresden yet again, this time with his fellow soldier Bernard V. O'Hare: "One of the nicest [moments] in recent times was on my trip back to Dresden" (154-55). It is here that the narrator seems to find some sort of conclusion, albeit ambivalent, to his relationship with what happened at Dresden. While on the plane O'Hare reads out from a notebook full of facts and figures:

> On an average, 324,000 new babies are born into the world every day. During that same day, 10,000 persons, on average, will have starved to death or died from malnutrition. So it goes. In addition 123,000 persons will die for other reasons. So it goes. This leaves a net gain of about 191,000 each day in the world. The population Reference Bureau predicts that the world's total population will double to 7,000,000,000 before the year 2000.
> 'I suppose they will all want dignity,' I said.
> 'I suppose so,' said O'Hare. (155)

We are then told that Billy is put to work as a corpse miner in the immediate aftermath of the bombing, searching out dead bodies for disposal: "They were cremated by soldiers with flamethrowers right where they were. The soldiers stood outside the shelters, simply sent the fire in" (157). The contrast between the narrator's suggestion that what is needed is an increased level of respect for human life and the undignified manner in which the burnt bodies are disposed of only serves to highlight how the narrator's knowledge of Dresden hinders him from believing in the possibility of a positive reformulation of society.

Abele suggests that the reasons for Vonnegut's desire to return to Dresden throughout his work are twofold. First, "His need to repeat the story of Dresden speaks to Vonnegut's obsession, whether due to the American public's continued lack of knowledge of Dresden (as compared to Hiroshima or Auschwitz) or possibly his own inability to come to terms with the event" (77). Yet Vonnegut's reasons for continually renegotiating his relationship with Dresden may be better explained by turning to the narrator's comment upon reading from his Gideon Bible at the start of the novel's first chapter: "Lot's wife, of course, was told not to look back where all those people and their homes had been. But she *did* look back, and I love her for that, because it was so human" (16).

Catch-22 also emphasizes the need to recognize the human cost of war; as Marguerite Alexander suggests, "[Heller's novel] was measurably subversive in effect: published in the early 1960s, it soon became a cult book among the young and helped fuel the protests against the Vietnam War" (106). Indeed, it is not hard to see why the novel chimed with the counterculture's resistance to Vietnam, presenting the reader, as it does, with a darkly comedic take on the absurdity and ineffectuality of the American military during wartime.

It is primarily through the character of Yossarian that we encounter the novel's humanism. Yossarian, like Billy Pilgrim, undergoes a change over the course of the novel from relative passivity toward a more active engagement with the world. At the beginning of the story, Yossarian is content to avoid his assigned flying missions by "hiding" in the field hospital, faking injuries to keep away from any potential danger. However, throughout the book Yossarian is haunted by his inability to save the life of a member of a previous flight crew when their plane was struck by antiaircraft fire: "'I'm cold,' Snowden whimpered. 'I'm cold.' 'There, there,' Yossarian said. 'There, there.'" (502). Yossarian continually experiences flashbacks to Snowden's death, recollecting snippets of the exchange between himself and the mortally wounded soldier in a manner that has clear parallels with the memories of Dresden that the narrator of *Slaughterhouse-Five* must try to cope with throughout that novel. The importance of dealing with repressed trauma brought on by a horrific wartime experience is a key component of *Catch-22*, and it is not until the novel is nearly over that we are allowed a further insight into the events of Snowden's death, as Yossarian eventually works through his memories of them. As Stanley Schatt notes in *Kurt Vonnegut, Jr.* (1976):

> Yossarian is compelled to think about Snowden's death yet finds it too painful and avoids the memory, so too is a reluctant Billy Pilgrim forced to return again and again to the firebombing of Dresden. Only when Yossarian and Billy Pilgrim learn to cope with mankind's inhumanity and the horrors of war are they able to describe the atrocities they have witnessed. (82)

Indeed, just as *Slaughterhouse-Five*'s narrator is able to arrive at a more conclusive relationship with Dresden once he has faced his remembered experience "head on," so Yossarian's full recollection of Snowden's death serves as a catalyst for the character to realize what he must do to find some sort of fulfillment. Comprehending through the dead soldier that "the spirit gone, man is garbage. That was Snowden's secret. Ripeness was all" (504), Yossarian vows to go on surviving: "That's just what I'm going to do from now on! I'm going to persevere. Yes, I'm going to persevere" (514). Spurred on by this humanist revelation, Yossarian chooses to reject his superior officers' offer that would enable him to leave the military at the cost of condoning their inhumane treatment because he is unable to place his own safety above that of the other men: "'Don't worry,' Yossarian said with a sorrowful laugh after several moments had passed. 'I'm not going to do it'" (498). As Richard Lehan and Jerry Patch propose in "*Catch-22*: The Making of a Novel" (2001), in making such a decision Yossarian displays a strong humanitarian concern for the welfare of others:

> Yossarian is indeed concerned about his own survival and with the forces that threaten it, but at the same time he is concerned for the survival of his friends, acquaintances, and mere colleagues. It is because of this that he is willing to pursue "through all the words in the world" the answer to his riddle, "where are the Snowdens of yesteryear?"; because of this that he mourns in his own unconventional way when Orr is lost over the Adriatic; because of this that he takes his life in his hands to break the news of Nately's death to the latter's girl friend. (82-83)

In addition to exploring the need to reconcile the incongruities caused by repressing the horrific experiences of wartime, the two novels share a comparable exploration of the disparity between an "official" heroic depiction of war and the "actual" experiences of the individuals involved in the conflict. Both *Slaughterhouse-Five* and *Catch-22* examine the sense of disparity that Rubin suggests is central to American humor. Gair notes that Vonnegut's writing is primarily concerned with representing "alternatives to the master narrative of American scientific, military and economic triumphalism" (144). The novel constantly reveals the mundane truth behind the heroic representation of World War II that history books have accustomed us to:

The photographer wanted something more lively, though, a picture of an actual capture. So the guards staged one for him. They threw Billy into shrubbery. When Billy came out of the shrubbery, his face wreathed in goofy good will, they menaced him with their machine pistols, as though they were capturing him. (42)

Similarly, Heller prefaces his novel with the following sardonic clarification, lest we mistake the novel's contents as being, in part, a true reflection of Heller's own war experiences: "The island of Pianosa lies in the Mediterranean Sea eight miles south of Elba. It is very small and obviously could not accommodate all of the actions described. Like the setting of this novel, the characters, too, are fictitious" (10).

Revealing the disparity between the ostensible truth and the actual reality of the situation is central to much of the satire found in *Catch-22*. This exposé is perhaps most apparent at the end of the novel when Yossarian confronts his commanding officer, Colonel Cathcart, with the news that he will not accept the commander's offer. Major Danby, one of the few officers sympathetic to Yossarian, refuses to believe the choice that he has made, informing him of the consequences: "Yossarian was taken back severely with surprise and disappointment. 'Another official report?' 'Yossarian they can prepare as many official reports as they want and choose whichever ones they need on any given occasion'" (506-507). The military's ability, and willingness, to create its own version of history causes Yossarian to realize the true nature of forces that can and will falsify history:

If you were court-martialed and found innocent, other men would refuse to fly missions, too. Colonel Cathcart would be in disgrace, and the military efficiency of the unit might be destroyed. So in that way it would be for the good of the country to have you found guilty and put in prison, even though you *are* innocent. (508)

By bringing the reader's attention to the "reality" of the experiences of those involved in World War II both Heller and Vonnegut seem to be suggesting a need for a change in how we think about the conflict. As I suggest in *The Anti-Hero in the American Novel: From Joseph Heller to Kurt Vonnegut* (2008), the two novels can be seen to possess a distinctly sociopolitical and humanist impetus that stands in contrast to much of the academic discussion that surrounds them. This is not to say that work carried out by critics including Tony Tanner, Helen Weinberg, and Marguerite Alexander is misplaced, rather that an inclination toward postmodernist readings has arguably elided the possibility of other, equally valid interpretations.

In *Flights from Realism: Themes and Strategies in Postmodernist British and American Fiction* (1990), Alexander examines the postmodernist depiction of war in three postwar American novels: Thomas Pynchon's *Gravity's Rainbow* (1973), Kurt Vonnegut's *Slaughterhouse 5*, and Joseph Heller's *Catch-22*. Alexander suggests that what distinguishes these novels as definably postmodern is their formal experimentation: "*Catch-22* in particular shows a keen awareness of the ways in which the devaluing of language assists the devaluing of the individual" (109); and their nihilistic outlook: "*Catch-22* makes the transition from comedy of the absurd to tragedy of the absurd" (110). While such a postmodernist reading of both novels contains much that is valid, I would suggest that it does not pay enough attention to the prominent humanist and idealist aspects of each text. For the formal experimentation of Heller's and Vonnegut's novels does not occur alongside a novelistic devaluing of characterization. Instead, and in contrast to Alexander's assertion that both novels possess "no stable centre" (166), we are presented with distinctive characters with which we are able to empathize. Similarly, Alexander's assertion that *Slaughterhouse-Five* and *Catch-22* should be read primarily as absurd tragedy seems at odds with both novels' themes of humanitarianism and compassion in the face of the absurd and nonsensical processes of war. While Alexander's reading of these novels is only one example, it

serves as a representative indication of the often overly nihilistic interpretations of the 1960s novel that exist within poststructuralist criticism. In their attempts to conceptualize 1960s fiction as belonging to a
deconstructionist mode, critics have displayed a tendency to imply that
all the significant novels of this period focus only upon depicting the
disorder or randomness experienced by the postwar individual, often
missing the fact that both Heller and Vonnegut attempt to suggest humanist alternatives for dealing with the dehumanizing experience of
war.

Note

1. See select parts of Stanley Schatt's *Kurt Vonnegut, Jr.,* and Scott MacFarlane's
The Hippie Narrative, in addition to Alberto Cacicedo's enlightening article "'You
Must Remember This': Trauma and Memory in *Catch-22* and *Slaughterhouse-Five.*"

Works Cited

Abele, Elizabeth. "The Journey Home in Kurt Vonnegut's World War II Novels."
    New Critical Essays on Kurt Vonnegut. Ed. David Simmons. New York:
    Palgrave, 2009. 67-88.
Alexander, Marguerite. *Flights from Realism: Themes and Strategies in Postmod-
    ernist British and American Fiction.* London: Edward Arnold, 1990.
Cacicedo, Alberto. "'You Must Remember This': Trauma and Memory in *Catch-
    22* and *Slaughterhouse-Five.*" *Studies in Contemporary Fiction* 46.4 (2005):
    357-68.
Gair, Christopher. *The American Counterculture.* Edinburgh: Edinburgh UP, 2007.
Heller, Joseph. *Catch-22.* London: Vintage, 1994.
_____. *Closing Time.* New York: Charles Scribner's Sons, 2003.
_____. *Portrait of an Artist, as an Old Man.* New York: Charles Scrib-
    ner's Sons, 2000.
_____. *We Bombed in New Haven.* Middlesex: Penguin, 1971.
Klinkowitz, Jerome, and Donald L. Lawler, eds. *Vonnegut in America: An Intro-
    duction to the Life and Work of Kurt Vonnegut.* New York: Delacorte Press,
    1977.
Lehan, Richard, and Jerry Patch. "*Catch-22*: The Making of a Novel." *Joseph
    Heller's "Catch-22."* Ed. Harold Bloom. Philadelphia: Chelsea House, 2001.
    81-90.
McCoppin, Rachel. "'God Damn It, You've Got to Be Kind': War and Altruism in

the Works of Kurt Vonnegut." *New Critical Essays on Kurt Vonnegut*. Ed. David Simmons. New York: Palgrave, 2009. 47-66.

MacFarlane, Scott. *The Hippie Narrative: A Literary Perspective on the Counterculture*. Jefferson, NC: McFarland, 2007.

Mallory, Carole. "The Joe and Kurt Show." *Playboy* May 1992. 18 Feb. 2010. http://www.Vonnegutweb.com/Vonnegutia/interviews/int_heller.html.

Pynchon, Thomas. *Gravity's Rainbow*. 1973. New York: Penguin, 2006.

Schatt, Stanley. *Kurt Vonnegut, Jr.* Boston: Twayne, 1976.

Scoggins, Michael C. "Joseph Heller's Combat Experiences in *Catch-22*." *War, Literature & the Arts* 15 (2003): 213-27.

Simmons, David. *The Anti-Hero in the American Novel: From Joseph Heller to Kurt Vonnegut*. New York: Palgrave, 2008.

Tanner, Tony. *City of Words*. London: Jonathan Cape, 1971.

Vonnegut, Kurt, Jr. *Slaughterhouse-Five*. London: Vintage, 2000.

Weinberg, Helen. *The New Novel in America: The Kafka Mode in Contemporary Fiction*. Ithaca, NY: Cornell UP, 1970.

Wright, Moorhead. "The Existential Adventurer and War: Three Case Studies from American Fiction." *American Thinking About Peace and War: New Essays on American Thought and Attitudes*. Ed. Ken Booth and Moorhead Wright. New York: Rowman, 1978. 101-10.

The Vietnamization of World War II in
Slaughterhouse-Five and *Gravity's Rainbow*_____
Christina Jarvis

> If World War II was the straightforward movie everyone could be in, Vietnam was the sequel that was so confused that it demanded a review of the original. Perhaps the seeds of a later confusion were present in the midst of seeming clarity.
>
> —George Roeder, *The Censored War*

On November 3, 1969 Richard Nixon announced to a politically divided nation that the war in South East Asia would be conducted according to a new plan of "Vietnamization."[1] Making good on Johnson's earlier promise that the United States was not going to send American boys "to do what Asian boys ought to be doing for themselves," Nixon's policy of Vietnamization meant that the United States would train the South Vietnamese army to wage the ground war on its own, allowing U.S. troops to withdraw in greater numbers.[2] Despite advocating a plan that placed more responsibility for fighting in the hands of the ARVN, Nixon adamantly declared that the U.S. was not lessening its commitments to the South Vietnamese people or to victory. In televised speeches on April 20 and 30, 1970, Nixon addressed the implications of Vietnamization along with his decision to invade Cambodia, justifying his policies in terms of America's power and prestige. During the April 20th speech on Vietnamization, Nixon avowed: "We are not a weak people. We are a strong people. America has never been defeated in the proud one-hundred-ninety-year history of this country, and we shall not be defeated in Vietnam" (qtd. in Carroll 11). Ten days later, employing more Cold War rhetoric, Nixon asserted that "the world's most powerful nation" could not afford to act "like a pitiful helpless giant"; freedom throughout the world was in jeopardy.[3] As historian Peter Carroll has noted, during the ten day period between speeches Nixon "ordered several screenings of the movie

Patton, a film which celebrated military toughness, high risk attacks, and the disregard of formal channels" (11). While screenings of *Patton* no doubt offered inspiration for his unauthorized attacks in Cambodia, they also remind us that Nixon, like his predecessors, was haunted by the specter of World War II—a war that offered Americans a clear-cut, decisive victory and positioned the U.S. as global superpower. In contrast to the "bad war" (Vietnam), the "good war" had become "the culminating myth of the American experience and national character" (Isaacs 7).

While Nixon was touting his new vision and plans for the war, another process of Vietnamization was taking place: the "Vietnamization" of World War II in American literature. Kurt Vonnegut's 1969 novel, *Slaughterhouse Five*, and Thomas Pynchon's 1973 masterpiece, *Gravity's Rainbow*, revealed that the war in Vietnam was shaping representations of World War II just as the legacies and cultural narratives of the Second World War were influencing policy in Vietnam. Following the lead of Joseph Heller's *Catch-22*, *Slaughterhouse-Five* and *Gravity's Rainbow* deconstructed the binary framing of America's "good war," offering a "Vietnamized" version, full of discontinuities, fragmented bodies, and multiple shades of gray.

Through readings of *Slaughterhouse-Five* and *Gravity's Rainbow*, this essay examines how the Cold War with its specific hot episodes in Vietnam created a prism for reimagining and reconfiguring cultural narratives about masculinity and the Second World War. Vonnegut and Pynchon's texts, I argue, simultaneously address World War II and Vietnam in an attempt to undermine the privileged space that "the good war" occupies in America's cultural imagination. While presenting revisionist accounts of World War II, these later postmodern novels also fragment and expand our notions of bodies in and at war, offering a shift away from an exclusive focus on the human body to other types of "bodies" (i.e., bodies of capital, bureaucracy, flows of excrement and technology, etc).

Slaughterhouse-Five: A New Kind of War Story

In the late 1940s, "the war film—with a full panoply of flags, insignia, martial music, and expressions of love for country—made a strong comeback" (Marling 127). After reaching a new height in popularity in 1943 when it accounted for approximately 30 percent of Hollywood's output, the combat film was no longer appealing to a war-weary nation in 1945, and it was virtually abandoned by the war's end. As the Cold War began to heat up in the Far East and the war against communism spread in the U.S., World War II narratives once again had appeal. Explaining this allure, Marling and Wetenhall write:

> World War II seemed clean, straightforward, refreshingly unambiguous in a Cold War world of espionage and ideology. In less than a decade, World War II and its symbols came to stand for the postwar ideal, for things as they should have turned out: American valor and know-how supreme; America always victorious. (127)

At the forefront of this wave of new World War II movies was Republic Pictures' 1949 film, *Sands of Iwo Jima*. With John Wayne playing Sergeant Stryker, the film introduced a somewhat troubled and unconventional protagonist, but still managed to celebrate the "hardboiled, blood-and-guts" heroism of American men. Cashing in on the patriotic fervor the movie created, Marine recruiters set up booths in the lobbies of theaters following the movie's March 1, 1950 general release. And in at least one theater, the R.K.O. Keith's in Richmond Hill, New York, where my father saw the film, young men were enlisting enthusiastically. Many of them would no doubt go on to serve in Korea.

Like his World War I predecessors—Ernest Hemingway, John Dos Passos, Siegfried Sassoon, Wilfred Owen—Kurt Vonnegut has long recognized the power war stories possess to engender additional armed conflicts. Re-viewing his war experiences through the prism of Vietnam, Vonnegut sets out in *Slaughterhouse-Five* not only to fracture American narratives about the "good war," but also to create a different kind of war story—one that will not produce other conflicts. While the novel clearly charts a larger pattern of violence in Western civilization, linking multiple conflicts from the Crusades to the fictional Tralfamadorian-initiated destruction of the universe, Vonnegut's primary goal is a specific revision of World War II narratives.

Vonnegut foregrounds this process of revision in his self-reflexive opening chapter, where the narrator describes the events leading up to creation of his "war book" (14). During a visit to an "old war buddy, Bernard V. O'Hare" (11), the narrator receives a chilly welcome from O'Hare's wife, Mary, who resents the idea of the veterans recalling old war memories. Fearing that the reminiscences will lead to another typical war story, Mary chastises the narrator:

> "You'll pretend that you were men instead of babies, and you'll be played in the movies by Frank Sinatra or John Wayne or some of those other glamorous, war-loving, dirty old men. And war will look just wonderful, so we'll have lots of more of them. And they'll be fought by babies like the babies upstairs." (14)

With her references to Frank Sinatra and John Wayne, Mary's remarks are intended as a specific critique of World War II films like *Sands of Iwo Jima* and *From Here to Eternity*, which present rugged, maverick, thoroughly masculine heroes. Reflecting on Mary's comments, the narrator further clarifies the connections between war fictions and actual conflicts: "she thought wars were partly encouraged by books and movies" (15).

Making good on his promise that there "won't be a part for Frank Sinatra or John Wayne" (15), the narrator offers a very different kind of war story—one which combines fact, fiction, and postmodern literary techniques to undermine the conventions of traditional narration itself. Not only does the narrator interrupt the already jumbled fragments of the story with asides about his presence at events or reflections on other characters, but he summarizes the entire story in the first chapter, quoting the opening and closing lines. In *Slaughterhouse-Five*, we are told, there will be no "climaxes and thrills and characterization and wonderful dialogue and suspense and confrontations" (5). In short, the novel will provide no fictional material for a glamorous war story.

To reinforce the importance of undermining traditional war narratives, Vonnegut mocks ideals of heroism and honor through his scenes describing the British POWs. In a rather Heller-esque passage, filled with dark humor, absurdity, and startling contrasts, the reader encounters a group of English officers in the middle of a concentration camp for Russian prisoners. Although it is late in the war and people all over Europe are starving, the Englishmen are "clean and enthusiastic and decent and strong" (94). (Because of clerical error, they are receiving five hundred Red Cross parcels of supplies each month instead of fifty.) For the Englishmen, the war is another game, to be mastered like "checkers and chess and cribbage and dominoes and anagrams and charades" (94).[4] It is also, like the play they put on, a scripted performance that involves "manly blather," "brotherly rodomontades," and other forms of male bonding (95). Although the Englishmen are themselves rendered absurd in their Cinderella costumes and half battle-half croquet dress, they clearly embody pre-World War I ideals. They even have *The Red Badge of Courage* in their library for authenticity. As the narrator explains, "They were adored by the Germans who thought they were exactly what Englishmen ought to be. They made war look stylish and reasonable, and fun" (94). Through this quote Vonnegut once again reveals the power of self-generating war fictions. The Englishmen perform gallant war roles from the past while simultaneously creating new ones for future wars.

While reconfiguring war narratives generally, *Slaughterhouse-Five* also revisions World War II specifically by linking it explicitly to events in Vietnam. By employing the vehicle of time travel and a fractured narrative that juxtaposes the firebombing of Dresden with reference to Vietnam, the narrator's story of World War II presents a narrative primarily about civilian deaths and concentration camps—not

heroic assaults and flag raisings. Vonnegut utilizes the morally ambiguous, fragmented lens of Vietnam to highlight the seedier, incomprehensible elements of the "good war."

At first glance, references to the Vietnam War in *Slaughterhouse-
Five* seem to serve as signposts for historicizing Billy Pilgrim's position in time/space travel or as vague specters of the then-current conflict. When examined more carefully, however, they reveal particular
parallels and continuities between the wars. In the narrator's description of Billy's trip to and luncheon at the Lions Club, for example,
World War II and Vietnam are linked in several important ways. Vonnegut first establishes the parallels between the wars by noting the odd
results of Billy's time travel: "Billy's smile as he came out of the shrubbery was at least as peculiar as Mona Lisa's, for he was simultaneously
on foot in Germany in 1944 and riding in his Cadillac in 1967" (58).
Not only are the two wars linked through Billy's presence in both time/
space dimensions, but the reassembled fragments of narration create a
new narrative in which World War II flows directly into Vietnam. On
his way to the Lions Club meeting, Billy drives through the burned-
out, wrecked neighborhood of "Ilium's black ghetto" (59). Invoking
race riots of the 1960s generally and the D.C. riots following King's assassination more specifically, the scene of destruction reminds Billy of
"Dresden after it was firebombed—[when it looked] like the surface of
the moon" (59).[5] Immediately following this depiction of a firebombed
Dresden, the narrator describes the speaker's keynote address at the
Lions Club, offering the following summary:

> He said that Americans had no choice but to keep fighting in Vietnam until
> they achieved victory or until the Communists realized that they could not
> force their way of life on weak countries. . . . He told of many terrible and
> wonderful things he had seen. He was in favor of increased bombings, of
> bombing North Vietnam back into the Stone Age, if it refused to see rea-
> son. (59-60)

Although supposedly a Marine major, the speaker is a thinly disguised Curtis LeMay, the general and commander of the Air Force who originally suggested that the U.S. should bomb the North Vietnamese "back to the Stone Age" (qtd. in Karnow 41, 400). With the allusion to LeMay, Vonnegut sets up multiple parallels and continuities between World War II and Vietnam. "A pioneer in strategic air warfare," LeMay played a key role in Allied bombing campaigns during the Second World War; he started the combined RAF and U.S. daylight bombing plan, "developed pattern bombing from lower altitudes . . . [and] the Norden bomb sight," and turned bombing raids on Japan "from nuisance to catastrophe" (Boatner 315-16). Credited with starting incendiary runs in the Pacific Theater, LeMay ordered the bombings of some 66 Japanese cities, including the firebombing of Tokyo.[6] Moreover, along with other top Air Force commanders, LeMay selected the targets for the atomic bombs dropped on Hiroshima and Nagasaki, and later advocated the use of nuclear weapons in Vietnam. Like Billy's earlier moment of straddling two time/space dimensions, the LeMay figure embodies continuities between World War II and Vietnam. Perhaps more than any other military figure, LeMay and his actions symbolize the trend of incorporating civilian targets in waging war. Through strategic "innovations" like LeMay's, civilian casualties comprised forty-four percent of war deaths in World War II (up from five percent in World War I) and ninety-one percent of war-related fatalities in Vietnam.[7]

The LeMay figure offers Vonnegut an ideal vehicle for graying America's black-and-white, clear-cut narratives about the Second World War. Once associated with his 1968 suggestion to "use anything that we could dream up, including nuclear weapons" to win a decisive victory in Vietnam, LeMay's earlier World War II actions seem morally suspect and cruel.[8] To reinforce parallels between the wars established in the Lions Club scene, Vonnegut scatters other references to Vietnam throughout *Slaughterhouse-Five*, allowing additional connections between Dresden and bombings in South East Asia to emerge in the cut-

and-paste narrative. We are told, for instance, that Billy treats a boy whose father had been killed in the "battle for Hill 875 near Dakto" (135) just before we hear of Billy's arrival in Dresden (136). Dakto, of course, was site of "the largest engagement of the war to date" in 1967 and the target of over "two thousand fighter-bomber assaults" (Karnow 539). Through artillery shells and chemical weapons, the area was turned into "a bleak landscape of crater and charred tree stumps" (Karnow 538-9). This reference to destroyed jungle terrain in Vietnam once again blurs the space/time boundaries between the craters of Dakto and lunar-like surface of Dresden.[9] Other allusions to Vietnam, like the napalm-dropping robot in Kilgore Trout's *The Gutless Wonder* reinforce these connections, further exposing the reprehensible burning of civilian bodies and buildings in both wars.

Perhaps one of the most important links between wars in the novels, though, is the familial connection between Billy and his son Robert, "a sergeant in the Green Berets—in Vietnam" (61). Realistic in the sense that many men who fought in Vietnam were sons of World War II veterans, the familial connection also symbolically represents the cycle of one war engendering another. Vonnegut emphasizes this cycle of war begetting war in the description of Robert's conception on Billy and Valencia's honeymoon. After consummating their marriage, Valencia asks Billy to tell her his war stories. As the narrator explains, "It was a simple-minded thing for a female Earthling to do, to associate sex and glamour with war" (121) because her expectations and associations are constructed by war films and books. While Billy tells her a few selected stories from the war, however, the figurative becomes literal. As Billy recounts his war experiences, simultaneously "in a tiny cavity of [Valencia's] great body she was assembling the materials for a Green Beret" (121). Vonnegut seems to suggest that Billy's war fictions contribute as much to Robert's creation as his and Valencia's genetic materials. It is interesting to note, then, that later in 1967—around the same time that Robert goes to Vietnam—Valencia is described as not having "ovaries or a uterus any more" (72). In addition to breaking the cycle of war begetting war, Valencia's sterility introduces other relationships between war and bodies.

Like most war fiction, *Slaughterhouse-Five* explores the impact of modern armed conflict on the body. Departing from conventions established in earlier World War II novels like Norman Mailer's *Naked and the Dead*, James Jones's *The Thin Red Line*, and Heller's *Catch-22*, *Slaughterhouse-Five* does not rely on "realistic" description as a means of presenting the corporeal horrors of the Second World War.[10] The novel offers no detailed accounts of rotting Japanese corpses, wounded American bodies, or the stewed tomatoes an airman had for lunch that are now visible through his wound. Although we do encounter "hundreds of corpse mines" (214) in the novel's final pages describing the destruction at Dresden, *Slaughterhouse-Five* depends primarily on other techniques to dramatize war's terrible effects on bodies. As literary critics Peter Freese, Cremilda Lee, and Peter Reed have observed, Vonnegut recognizes the failures of language to truly capture the horrors of war or to convey a shared "reality" in a postmodern age.[11] After all, "there is nothing intelligent to say about a massacre" (19). Moreover, in a world saturated with graphic violence in the media, any narrative accounts of war's impact on bodies either pale in comparison or get lost in a sea of other images.

Not wishing to contribute to this sea of violent images, Vonnegut refuses to detail the spectacle of battle. Instead of re-creating moments of corporeal destruction or recalling the primal space of the wound, which might glamorize war, Vonnegut explores World War II's bodily legacy through already damaged bodies. Naturally, Billy Pilgrim is the locus for this exploration. Through the fantastic vehicle of time travel, Billy is fragmented throughout space and time. Somewhat like a cubist painting, his body exists in multiple space/time dimensions simultaneously, allowing him to experience his birth, death, and World War II days over and over again. While Billy's body is never literally dismembered or scattered as many bodies at war are, his symbolic fragmentation is manifested in physical and mental ways. When we first encounter Billy behind German lines during World War II, for example, the narrator describes him as "bleakly ready for death" (32). His body is "preposterous—six feet and three inches tall, with a chest and shoulders like a box of kitchen matches" (32). As one of the Englishmen later remarks, it's not the body of "a man[;] It's a broken kite" (97). While the narrator's descriptions of Billy as a tall, lanky, ridiculously clothed figure emphasize his status as an anti-hero, they also provide a fitting state of embodiment for a war-damaged individual. Through references to Billy's stay as a mental patient at a VA hospital in 1948 (99) and the fact that "the war had ruined his stomach" (46), we see that the war has reterritorialized Billy's body, leaving lasting physical and mental legacies. To cope with these war legacies and to unify the fragments of his life, Billy is forced to turn to the numbing, passive philosophies of the Tralfamadorians.

As the novel unfolds, we see that Billy Pilgrim's body is not the only already damaged body in *Slaughterhouse-Five*'s accounts of the war in Europe. Roland Weary's overweight body is also unfit, and though supposedly a fresh replacement, it turns out to be "weary" on the long forced march. Moreover, Paul Lazzaro's gangly, sore-infested body is no better than those of the German soldiers and civilians who are "armed and clothed fragmentarily" (52), starving, and "crippled" (150). Offered as further commentary on the war's widespread impact on soldiers and civilians, this array of marred bodies provides a different cast of characters. With the exception of well-fed Englishmen and their "washboard" stomachs and muscles "like cannonballs" (94), the bodies in *Slaughterhouse-Five* are largely physically incapable of waging war. Thus their destruction seems even more senseless, heightening the cruelty of targeting non-combatants.

The novel's most incisive critique of war's impact on the body, however, is its examination of the dehumanizing lens through which bodies are viewed during war. This vision of bodies is perhaps captured most clearly in the narrator's comment about body counts in Vietnam: "And everyday my Government gives me a count of corpses created by military science in Vietnam" (210). Once again establishing continuities between World War II and Vietnam, *Slaughterhouse-Five* links this contemporary view of bodies with Nazi bureaucracy, racial hygiene theories, and other militaristic conceptualizations. By offering cool, detached analyses of bodies in terms of their use-value or social worth, the novel enacts the militaristic vision it hopes to critique. Many of the book's descriptions of women, for example, measure their potential reproductive value. Valencia's hysterectomy is noted because it prevents her from creating additional Green Berets; Montana Wildhack is brought to Tralfamadore to have a baby with Billy; and Maggie White is described as "a sensational invitation to make babies" (171). Other women like Billy's mother, meanwhile, are characterized in more militaristic terms: "She was a perfectly nice, standard-issue, brown-haired, white woman with a high school education" (102). We hear little about these women, in part because the novel resists offering any "real characters," but also because of the vision of bodies *Slaughterhouse-Five* enacts.

The most striking examples of militaristic, wartime views of bodies occur in the scenes depicting Billy's experiences as a POW. In these descriptions of German extermination camps, individual bodies blur into one another, becoming part of a larger, Nazi death-making machine. Describing American POWs on a train bound for the concentration camps, the narrator remarks:

> To the guards who walked up and down outside, each car became a single organism which ate and drank and excreted through its ventilators. It talked or yelled sometimes through ventilators, too. In went water and loaves of black-bread and sausage and cheese, and out came shit and language. (70)

This de-individualized, dehumanizing view of bodies is further reinforced by the Nazi guards at the extermination camp for Russian prisoners of war. These guards, we are told, "had never dealt with Americans before, but they surely understood this general sort of freight"

(80). By reducing the American POWs to a single "it" comprised of biological functions, a flow of human "freight," the narrator recreates the militaristic vision that led to the Holocaust and other mass death scenes of World War II. Like the bodies being counted in Vietnam, these people are reduced to numbers, who can be rendered "legally alive" (91) or "theoretically dead" (31) through military records or war games.[12]

As part of his process of Vietnamizing World War II, Vonnegut demonstrates that these dehumanizing views of bodies were not unique to the Nazis. Through excerpts from historical texts and speeches, Vonnegut reminds his readers of the mass civilian deaths caused by Allied bombings at Dresden, Tokyo, Hiroshima and Nagasaki, and their necessary role in "hasten[ing] the end of the war" (180). Bertram Rumfoord's opinions about war and the expendability of certain lives are perhaps the greatest example of American militaristic conceptions of bodies. Following his 1967 plane crash, Billy wakes up in a hospital room with Rumfoord, "a retired brigadier general in the Air Force [and] the official Air Force Historian" (184). As the narrator explains, Rumfoord not only views the bombing of Dresden as "a howling success" (191), but he thinks "in a military manner" (192), which allows him to see certain lives as disposable. Blurring the lines between the Nazi ideology and militaristic conceptions of bodies, Rumfoord often remarks to Billy and his companion Lily "that people who are weak deserve to die" (193). German or American, Second World War or Vietnam, militaristic conceptions of bodies are integral to the wholesale slaughter of civilians.

While Vonnegut's tools for telling his "war story"—his fragmented narrative, self-reflexivity, parody, pastiche, and black humor—are decidedly postmodern, his anti-war vision is distinctly humanist. Throughout *Slaughterhouse-Five* he contrasts militaristic views of bodies with frequent reminders that these bodies are indeed "human beings." And although he employs modernist and postmodern conceptions of bodies, in the end, he rejects metaphors that envision the body as a machine or as a cog in a larger social or military system. When human beings are envisioned in mechanistic ways, they become "targets" for napalm-dropping robots or fragmented, passive bodies like Billy's that take delight in "feel[ing] nothing and still get[ting] full credit for being alive" (105).

Redefining History/Rethinking the Body: *Gravity's Rainbow*

Published four years after *Slaughterhouse-Five*, Pynchon's *Gravity's Rainbow* offers a more extensive Vietnamization of the Second World War as well as a more in-depth exploration of relationships between war, bodies, and technology. Whereas Vonnegut's project of Vietnamization concerns itself primarily with breaking the cycle of armed conflict engendered by war narratives and reframing World War II as an event that killed millions of civilians, Pynchon's novel reconfigures multiple aspects of the "good war." Set primarily in Europe during the final months of the war and early postwar period, *Gravity's Rainbow* weaves together historical "fact," fiction, and the utterly fantastic to create a text that is at once encyclopedic and anarchistic. Often described as the postmodern novel par excellence, *Gravity's Rainbow* problematizes notions of history (along with other master narratives) while simultaneously offering a provisional revisionist account of World War II. The text not only explores the seeds of the Cold War sown in treaties, conferences, and the race for German technologies, but it also examines almost every facet of the war—from racial tensions and propaganda to the complex flows of capital, information, and technology that bridged national boarders. This reexamination of World War II, however, is not merely a product of temporal distance; it is a specific reexamination of the Second World War through the prism of Vietnam.

As literary critics Frederick Ashe and Eric Meyer have noted, despite its meticulously researched and historically accurate treatment of World War II, *Gravity's Rainbow* "is a novel of 'The '60s'—not only because it is *about* that now mythic period, but because it is demonstrably *of* it as well" (Meyer 81). Indeed, one can find echoes of the American youth, black power, and feminist movements as well as the "disparate discourses" of the 1960s "social text" (Meyer 81).[13] What has been largely glossed over in these examinations of *Gravity's Rainbow* as a novel of the 1960s, though, is the haunting presence of Vietnam. While many scholars have noted the novel's passing references to prisoners "back from Indo-China" (132) and the "eyes from Burma, from Tonkin" (132) in a description of London during the Blitz, few critics have seen these as anything but vague allusions to the war in South East Asia. Even Meyer, who offers the most extended treatment of references to Vietnam, still views the war in South East Asia as the "Absent War" in *Gravity's Rainbow*. Meyer argues that Vietnam's status as the "Absent War" in Pynchon's text speaks to "the difficulty activists had in making Vietnam a reality to a mediatized public" as well as to "the generalized derealization of cultural production in the postmodern period" (92). I would contend, however, that the Vietnam War is *quite* present in *Gravity's Rainbow*. Like a "second shadow" in Gerhardt's *Alpdrücken*, Vietnam serves as World War II's double or surrogate in the novel, complicating its narratives and reconfiguring its representations.[14]

Because evocations of Vietnam are often subtle and because, as Steven Weisenburger and Khachig Tölölyan have noted, *Gravity's Rainbow* fastidiously reconstructs details from events during the final stages of the war in Europe, it is worth examining the ways in which Vietnam is present in the novel.[15] I would suggest that we must examine the text's anachronistic elements closely because they offer such radical departures from the otherwise carefully woven fabric of late war and postwar periods. While the first overt reference to Vietnam does not occur until the mention of prisoners "back from Indo-China" and eyes "from Tonkin" (132), the novel's opening epigraph recalling Von Braun's remarks before the 1969 Apollo 11 launch helps establish a more contemporary lens through which to view the war. The epigraph coupled with the late war setting, which itself suggests a narrative about the Cold War rather than the "action" of World War II, prepare us for the more specific evocations of Vietnam in part one. During the seance scene in Snoxall, for example, the reader encounters a war in which ghosts are participants and the enemy is ambiguous. As the narrator remarks, many of the seance participants are from "the agency known as PISCES—Psychological Intelligence Schemes for Expediting Surrender. Whose surrender is not made clear" (34). Although the ghosts and unclear enemy and war aims speak to other motifs in the novel such as trafficking in the occult, conspiracies, and general paranoia, these characterizations of "the enemy" are more in keeping with Vietnam than World War II and its Frank Capra-esque framing. In Vietnam the Viet Cong were not only physically indistinguishable from their South Vietnamese counterparts, they were often invisible, "ghosts" that moved through the jungles and attacked unseen. Roger Mexico's reflection in the following episode that he should be "graphing Standardized Kill Rates Per Ton for the bomber groups" (40), is likewise more appropriate to Vietnam and its concepts of body counts and kill ratios.

The most compelling evidence for Vietnam's presence as a shadow or surrogate for World War II in *Gravity's Rainbow*, though, lies in Pynchon's October 8, 1969 letter to Thomas Hirsch, a graduate student interested in Sudwest material in *V.* Commenting on the role of the Herero in "the novel I'm writing now," Pynchon remarks:

> But I feel personally that the number done on the Herero head by the Germans is the same number done on the American Indian head by our own colonists and what is now being done on the Buddhist head in Vietnam by the Christianity minority in Saigon and their advisors . . . I don't like to use the word but I think what went on back in Sudwest is archetypical of every clash between the west and non-west, clashes that are still going on right now in South East Asia. (qtd. in Seed 241-2)

Given the parallels Pynchon draws between the situations in South West Africa and Vietnam here, it is hardly surprising that *Gravity's Rainbow* depicts the Zone Hereros as living "down in abandoned mine shafts" (315) and as the victims of "Search-and-destroy missions" (362) both in Sudwest and Europe. Invoking U.S. military raids on South Vietnamese villages and the elaborate networks of tunnels used by the VC and NVA, these references further reinforce Vietnam's shadowy presence in the book. In many ways the amorphous "Zone" of the novel is more like the "free fire zones" of Vietnam than the clearly demarcated occupation zones of World War II. As various episodes in the Zone make clear, the Herero are open targets for Americans, Germans, and Russians alike despite the fact that there are no clear political motivations for these assaults.

The novel's more obvious anachronisms—the rampant drug use among members of the military, the Counterforce spokesman's reference to "the years of grease and passage, 1966-1971" (739), allusions to Nixon's "Silent Majority" speech, and numerous other late 1960s and early 1970s details in the final episode—likewise provide connections to Vietnam. As Pynchon scholars have widely noted, the use of pot, hash, acid, cocaine, hallucinogenic mushrooms, opium, and numerous other drugs along with characters with names like "Geli Tripping" and "Acid Bummer" all highlight an element of "sixties radicalism" woven into the novel's "narrative fabric" (Ashe 69). Narcotics use in the novel, however, is especially reminiscent of the latter part of Vietnam, where drugs became an inoculation against the war. Faced with an increasingly unpopular and morally ambiguous war, in 1969 over half the soldiers serving in Vietnam admitted to using marijuana. By 1971, drugs like heroin, pot, and opium were claiming four times as many casualties as the war.[16] Given Vietnam's shadowy presence in the novel, then, it is not surprising that images of "human bodies" in "carefully tagged GI" body bags (368) and "big white bundles" that look "like Graves Registration back there" (643) are linked to drug use and that companies like Du Pont are working to dull the "real pain" produced by wars (348).

As *Gravity's Rainbow*'s final section highlights, Vietnam is also present through suggestions of the domestic conflicts and anti-war movements that occurred in the U.S. The most obvious embodiment of these conflicts is, of course, the textual opposition between The Counterforce and Richard M. Zhlubb, a thinly disguised Nixon described as "fiftyish and jowled, with a permanent five-o'clock shadow" (754). Depicted as activists trying to jam the corporate machinery of The Force, Counterforce members Pirate, Roger, and Bodine use their bodies, wit, and language (with all their abject imaginings) instead of violence as oppositional strategies. It is no wonder that Bodine has kept a fragment of Dillinger's bloody shirt as a "relic" to remind the Counterforce of the "blood of our friends" (739). While John Dillinger certainly signifies in his own right as an outlaw figure, one cannot help but hear echoes of David Dellinger, a leading anti-war activist and member of the Chicago Seven, who was also "ambushed" in Chicago for his involvement in the 1968 Democratic Convention anti-war demonstration. Like their Vietnam counterparts, the Counterforce is also characterized as "only a small but loud minority" (755). An allusion to Nixon's famous November 3, 1969 "Silent Majority" speech, this reference evokes the political rhetoric that clouded any clear understanding of the war in Vietnam.

But what do all these evocations of Vietnam in *Gravity's Rainbow* mean? One could argue that with its hard-to-determine plot, countless flashbacks and anachronisms, Pynchon's text speaks to the broader poststructuralist project of decentering master narratives. Certainly "history" becomes but one of many fragmented narratives, a set of discourses and practices better understood in terms of Foucault's notions of archeology and genealogy. *Gravity's Rainbow* is, after all, filled with comments about "the end of history" (56), history/war as a "set of points" (645), "human palimpsests" (50), and the disruption of history as a "the idea of cause and effect" (56). Within Pynchon's broader project of exploring the general constructedness and process of history, however, there is also a narrower task of re-visioning World War II, of creating a provisional "history" of that war to make sense of Vietnam's madness. While Pynchon does not seem to suggest as Vonnegut does that a reframing of the "good war" and its cultural narratives can prevent future Vietnams, he does recognize the importance of re-visioning World War II in order to come to terms with the present.

Pynchon registers the inadequacies of World War II's binary framing early in the novel through one of Roger's facetious reflections on "The War," "the great struggle of good and evil the wireless reports everyday" (54). Writing during the conflict in Vietnam, where not only were enemies and objectives unclear but the beginning and ending dates of the war were as well, Pynchon recognizes the problems of trying to frame any war in binary terms. To combat singular or monolithic framings, *Gravity's Rainbow* constantly shifts its characterizations of "the War." World War II is variously described as: "a *laboratory*" (49), "a celebration of markets" (105), "a long-time schiz . . . who believes that *he* is World War II" (131), a larger force "reconfiguring time and space into its own image" (257), "theater" (326), "fucking . . . done on paper" (616), a "set of points" (645), "Roger's mother" (39), etc. These shifting definitions highlight World War II's complex dimensions and establish a more fitting precursor to Vietnam—a conflict that still isn't universally recognized as a war or considered to be over by certain Americans.

Pynchon's reference to the Frank Capra-esque framing of the war likewise highlights the carefully controlled flows of information present during World War II. Although efforts were taken to curtail negative coverage of U.S. involvement in Vietnam, the sea of lies surrounding the war and its atrocities came to light through television coverage and a freer press in the 1960s. Re-viewing World War II though Vietnam's hazy and fractured lens, Pynchon exposes the fact that "the Home Front [was] something of a fiction and a lie" (41). In one stinging indictment of home front portrayals of World War II, for example, the narrator describes the bodily costs behind the propaganda:

Maybe [you] just left behind your heart at the Stage Door Canteen, where they're counting the night's take, the NAAFI girls, the girls named Eileen, carefully sorting into refrigerated compartments the rubbery maroon organs with their yellow garnishes of fat. . . . Everybody you don't suspect is in on this, everybody but you: the chaplain, the doctor, your mother hoping to hang that Gold Star . . . the lads in Hollywood telling us how grand it all is over there, how much fun Walt Disney had causing Dumbo the elephant to clutch to that feather like how many carcasses under the snow tonight among the white-painted tanks. (134-135; ellipses mine)

With its allusions to Disney's propaganda cartoons, USO events, the Gold Star program, and Hollywood interpretations of the war, the passage highlights the ways in which World War II was turned into a "children's story" (135) in the 1940s. What *Gravity's Rainbow* makes abundantly (and sometimes nauseatingly) clear is that the Second World War was anything but a "children's story." Like Vietnam, Pynchon's version of World War II is for "Adults Only"; his war is a series of pornographies—both literal and figurative.

In addition to exposing how World War II propaganda often hid the bodily costs of war, *Gravity's Rainbow* emphasizes the ways in which it concealed domestic racial tensions and contributed to racist perceptions of the Japanese enemy. One of the more overt examples of Vietnam's haunting presence in the narrative, the novel's reexamination of racial issues recasts the Holocaust as one part of a larger pattern of racial conflict during World War II. While the novel seems to establish the "archetypical" clash between white, westerners and racially marked non-westerners that Pynchon forecasts in his letter, *Gravity's Rainbow* also specifically examines the dynamics of American racial tensions. In a description of America's involvement in Operation Black Wing, a propaganda campaign designed to undermine Nazi racial theories by showing Germany's "dark, secret children" (75), for example, the narrator reminds readers that the program will have an added benefit: "Black Wing has even found an American, a Lieutenant

Slothrop, willing to go under light narcosis to help illuminate racial problems in his own country" (75). American involvement in Operation Black Wing highlights the complex and contradictory elements of U.S. homefront racial discourses. During the war, the U.S. government presented pluralistic, ethnically diverse images of itself—especially in contrast to the hateful, racist Nazi enemy—while it was simultaneously imprisoning Japanese Americans and maintaining a Jim Crow military. Re-viewing World War II from a late 1960s perspective, *Gravity's Rainbow* constantly reveals the shortcomings of the Office of War Information's "strategy of truth" (74) policy. Not only does Pynchon's text recall the Zoot Suit riots of 1943 and weave figures like Malcolm X and Ishmael Reed into its narrative, but it also calls attention to the intense racism surrounding the Pacific War. Sardonically recalling U.S. wartime popular culture, the narrator asks, "Who can ever forget the enormously popular juicy Jap, the doll that you fill with ketchup then bayonet through any of several access slots" (558). Shortly after this passage, the narrator reminds us that it was "100,000 little yellow folks" (588) who were killed at Hiroshima. Once again, the novel fractures cultural narratives of the "good war," creating a more fitting precursor to "American Death" and the "death-colonies" (722) in Vietnam.

Perhaps the most important rewriting of World War II that Pynchon's late 1960s perspective provides is *Gravity's Rainbow*'s examination of war's impact on the body. Like most World War II fiction, *Gravity's Rainbow* records the war's tremendous destruction of human bodies. As we have seen so far, the novel exposes the countless corpses left out of OWI presentations of the war as well as the human costs of genocide programs in Nazi Germany and colonial situations. *Gravity's Rainbow* moves beyond this focus on human corporeality and broadens the very concept of a "body" in war. In Pynchon's text the increasingly fragmented late modernist body becomes "scattered," assuming the form of what Gilles Deleuze and Felix Guattari have called the "body without organs" (BwO).

Drawing on their earlier notions of "desiring machines" and Antonin Artaud's writings, Deleuze and Guattari suggest in *A Thousand Plateaus* that we must move beyond notions of the body as an organic, unified entity. They offer instead a conception of the body, emptied of its interiorities (organs), in which it becomes a surface "populated only by intensities" (153). As Elizabeth Grosz explains, this "notion of the body as a discontinuous, nontotalizable series of processes, organs, flows, corporeal substances and incorporeal events" forces us to imagine body in terms of "its connections with other bodies, both human and nonhuman, animate and inanimate, linking organs and biological processes to material objects and social practices" (165). In short, the body becomes a site establishing links with other "bodies." Always in the process of "becoming"—forming assemblages with other entities—the BwO is understood in terms of what it can do rather than what it is. While Deleuze and Guattari posit the BwO as a locus of a "positive libidinal driving force," they nonetheless acknowledge that the body is "the surface of intersection between libidinal forces . . . and 'external' social forces" (Lash 277).[17]

More so than any World War II novel before it, *Gravity's Rainbow* undermines a relationship between war and bodies in which the forces of the former act on the latter. While earlier works suggest, often in passing, that war dissolves lines between soldiers and their weapons and machines, *Gravity's Rainbow* provides a web of complex assemblages and flows between organic and non-organic bodies.[18] "The White Visitation," for instance, creates in the name of war, an odd alliance that includes spirit mediums, Pavlovian scientists, a statistician, a senile masochistic World War I general, clairvoyants, a man who thinks he is World War II, a patient who can change the pigmentation of his skin, stolen dogs, an octopus, and countless other beings. Many of the members of this agency, we learn, are valued primarily for their ability to form linkages with other bodies. As we discover early in the novel, Pirate Prentice has a career in the agency as "a fantasist-surrogate" (12). He can get "inside the fantasies of others," experience their emotions, "get their erections for them" (12), dream their dreams. Like a BwO, Pirate's body becomes a surface of physical and psychological intensities and flows; he is no longer a separate entity but part of a larger systems of bodies connected through dreams and emotions. These connections, however, are not always full of freeing libidinal energies. The scene involving Pirate's decoding of a message written in "Kryptoplasm" (an invisible substance made discernible through seminal fluid) serves as a reminder that even "private" sexual desires are still shaped by the movies, pornography, and other cultural images.[19]

As the novel goes on to explore, many of the linkages between bodies are not restricted to human surfaces. The "schiz" who believes that he is the war, for example, becomes a site of intensities linked to the battles in Europe. "He gets no newspapers, refuses to listen to the wireless," the narrator informs us, "but still, the day of the Normandy invasion somehow his temperature shot up to 104°" (131). And whenever rockets fall, "he smiles, turns out to pace the ward, tears about to splash from the corners of his merry eyes" (131). Emptied out of a normal organizing system, his body becomes a surface on which the ebbs and flows of the war speed up and slow down. Other sites of "becoming" in the novel offer more concrete connections between organic and nonorganic bodies. In the "Byron the Bulb" story, for example, we see numerous flows and connections between assholes, light bulbs, flows of shit and power, revealing an array of strange assemblages.[20] Nevertheless, these assemblages are overshadowed by the novel's central connection between animate and inanimate bodies—the attempts to "become rocket."

From Enzian's wet dream about coupling with the rocket to fraternity boys' jokes to Rocket limericks, *Gravity's Rainbow* is littered with men's desires to fuse bodies and machinery. These collective desires culminate, of course, in the novel's final description of the launch of the 00000 rocket. Encased in Imipolex and attached to the rocket, Gottfried is the only character to achieve a true (though short-lived) merging with the rocket. The novel's treatment of this linkage is hardly celebratory, though. Gottfried does not ride to the moon, as Franz and others have hoped, but instead falls back to earth like "a bright angel of death" (760). Once again, *Gravity's Rainbow* provides a more fitting version of World War II to suit the present situation in Vietnam. As Susan Jeffords, Arnold Isaacs, and others have noted, one of World War II's chief legacies for the Vietnam generation was a blind confidence in and association with American technology. World War II was "such a triumph of American resources, technology, and industrial and military genius," Isaacs contends, that "Americans came to think the success of their society was guaranteed" (7). Indeed, "It was almost as if Americans were technology" (14) (Phillips qtd. in Jeffords 8).

Behind this "intense fascination with technology," Jeffords argues, is a desire to unify the fragments of the male body through weapons and technology (14). Jeffords writes, "In Vietnam representation, technology does not 'stand in for' the (male) body but is that body, because the body has ceased to have meaning as a whole and has instead become a fragmented collection of disconnected parts that achieve the illusion of coherence only through their display as spectacle" (14). Moreover, "because technology is the (male) body, that body achieves not only the illusion of coherence, but its power as well" (Jeffords 14). In keeping with its Vietnam-centered revisioning of World War II, *Gravity's Rainbow* captures this overwhelming male desire to unify the body through technology generally and the rocket specifically. Enzian speaks for most of the central male characters when he reflects, "He was led to believe that by understanding the Rocket, he would come to understand truly his manhood" (324). Indeed, throughout *Gravity's Rainbow* men from various nations literally and figuratively converge around the 00000 rocket, striving to "belong to the Rocket" (325).

Although *Gravity's Rainbow* generally resists assigning values or positing clear enemies, it is difficult to read the novel without viewing this particular coupling between masculinity and technology as harmful. Not only does the process of "becoming rocket" foreclose other possibilities of connection by unifying and sealing up the phallic male body, but it reifies binaries between male/female and technology/ nature. Whether discussing the Rocket's "victory" "over the feminine darkness" (324), the triumph of plastics because "chemists were no longer to be at the mercy of nature" (249), or Major Marvy's obsession with "thrust, impact, penetration, and such other military values" (606), the novel highlights the negative effects these relationships pro- duce. This is not to say, however, that Pynchon's text offers a broad in- dictment of technology. There are after all at least two Rockets, "a good Rocket to take us to the stars, and an evil Rocket for the World's suicide, the two perpetually in struggle" (727). Like Pynchon's provi- sional notion of history, the values of technology are never fixed.

Nonetheless, the question of the body's status in a technologized, postmodern world still remains. Whereas Vonnegut seemingly advo- cates rejecting late modernist notions of the body and adopting individ- ualized, humanist conceptions instead, Pynchon finds potential within postmodern discourses. Although subject to widespread surveillance and cultural conditioning, Slothrop finds a way to empty himself of the desire to become rocket and de/reterritorialize his body. In addition to changing his identity repeatedly, Slothrop becomes a BwO through his drug-enhanced encounter with Trudi. The narrator describes their en- counter:

> Trudi is kissing him into an amazing comfort, it's an open house here, no
> favored senses or organs, all equally at play . . . for possibly the first time in
> his life Slothrop does not feel obliged to have a hardon, which is just as
> well because it does not seem to be happening with his penis so much as
> with . . . oh mercy, this is embarrassing but . . . well his *nose* actually seems
> to be erecting, the mucus beginning to flow yes a nasal hardon. (439)

While perhaps a bit revolting to our own culturally conditioned de- sires, Slothrop's ability to reinscribe the site of his pleasures and de- sires from his penis to his nose offers an important instance of agency in the novel. Because Slothrop's body has been the culturally conditioned, heterosexually territorialized body par excellence, his ability to divest his body of these territorializations offers the hope of alternative libidinal economies and nondestructive becomings. Likewise, we can read Slothrop's later scattering as another site of possibility. As Jeffrey Nealon suggests, "Slothrop's scattering disrupts a kind of subjectivity that is part and parcel of the contemporary war state" (126). Instead of unifying his body through the rocket or other forms of destructive technology, Slothrop is "scattered all over the Zone" (712), assuming a form that is no longer recognizable "in the conventional sense" (712). In his new form of fragments, Slothrop survives well into the future, and we learn that he has appeared as "The Fool" on a Rolling Stones' album cover. The exact status of Slothrop's body is never pinned down. The text offers speculations ("Some believe that fragments of Slothrop have grown into consistent personae of their own" 742), but it resists offering a firm description of Slothrop's new embodied subjectivity. What *Gravity's Rainbow* seems to imply is that we need not determine what Slothrop is, what's more important is focusing on what his body can do. The potential for developing more positive relationships between bodies and technologies lies not in denying relationships or rejecting modernist and postmodern conceptions of the body but in thinking differently about them.

Many who fought in or experienced the war first-hand have long understood that World War II can not be neatly summed up in binary terms like good/evil, combatant/noncombatant, and truth/propaganda. Nevertheless, despite the unfathomable and terrifying elements of the war such as the Holocaust, the atomic bombs dropped on Hiroshima and Nagasaki, and the large-scale destruction of lives and property worldwide, a general binary framing of the war persisted as America moved into the postwar period. In fact, as the Cold War heated up in Korea and Vietnam, World War II seemed to become even more clear-cut and emblematic of American success. Soldiers, politicians, and civilians alike nostalgically looked to "the last good war" as the lack of moral purpose and clear goals in Vietnam tore the nation apart instead of unifying it. While Vietnam in many ways reified World War II's mythical status in the national imagination, it also opened the door for important revisions of the "good war"—revisions that showed there are no "good" wars, no matter what the spoils of victory are. Through their amalgam of fantasy, fiction, and history, *Slaughterhouse-Five* and *Gravity's Rainbow* offer two such important revisions. The novels not only address the idea of war as a way of seeing and the power of war narratives to engender other conflicts, but they open new doors for envisioning different relationships between bodies and technologies.

From *War, Literature & the Arts* 15, nos. 1-2 (2003): 95-117. Copyright © 2003 by the U.S. Air Force Academy. Reprinted with permission of the U.S. Air Force Academy.

Notes

1. As George Herring has pointed out, Nixon's "new" plan for the Vietnamization of the war was not so cutting edge; by November 3, 1969, "the program had been in effect for more than a year and a half" (230). The term itself was not Nixon's invention either; Secretary of Defense Melvin Laird coined the term in March 1969 as a euphemism for American troop withdrawals. For additional background on Nixon's policy of Vietnamization, see Peter Carroll's *It Seemed Like Nothing Happened*, George Herring's *America's Longest War*, Stanley Karnow's *Vietnam: A History*, and William O'Neill's *Coming Apart*.

2. Johnson's famous remark of 1964 turned out to be one of a web of lies that led to the famous "credibility gap" that haunted his and later administrations. See O'Neill's *Coming Apart*, pages 120-122, for the full text of Johnson's campaign quote.

3. Quoted in Herring's *America's Longest War*, page 236. See Herring and Nixon's public papers for additional background on these quotes and speeches.

4. Clearly, Vonnegut seems to be playing with the idea of the "war game" here as well.

5. Although the scene is supposedly set in 1967, the destruction from the riots and the intervention of "National Guard tanks" is far more characteristic of riots in 1968.

6. The damage caused by LeMay's incendiary runs on Japanese cities was immense. As Mark Boatner details, "some 100,000 tons of incendiaries on 66 cities killed about 260,000 people, injured more than 412,000, left 9,200,000 homeless, and destroyed an estimated 2,210,000 dwellings" (316).

7. This figure comes from page 1 of David Craig and Michael Egan's *Extreme Situations* (1).

8. LeMay made this remark during a televised press conference on October 3, 1968,

while explaining his goals as George Wallace's running mate on the American Independent Party ticket.

9. Throughout *Slaughterhouse-Five* the key simile for illustrating the destruction at Dresden is that it "looked like the moon" (179).

10. I am not suggesting, of course, that *Catch-22* relies on conventionally realistic narration.

11. See Peter Freese's "Kurt Vonnegut's *Slaughterhouse-Five* or, How to Storify an Atrocity," Cremilda Lee's "Fantasy and Reality in Kurt Vonnegut's *Slaughterhouse-Five*," and Peter Reed's "Authenticity and Relevance: Kurt Vonnegut's *Slaughterhouse-Five*."

12. The novel also highlights the "use value" of bodies in German concentration camps. Describing the candles and soap in the British compound, the narrator remarks, "The British had no way of knowing it, but the candles and soap were made from the fat of rendered Jews and Gypsies and fairies and communists, and other enemies of the State" (96).

13. See Eric Meyer's "Oppositional Discourses, Unnatural Practices: Gravity's History and 'The '60s'" and Frederick Ashe's "Anachronism Intended: *Gravity's Rainbow* in the Sociopolitical Sixties" for further study of 1960s cultural elements in Pynchon's text.

14. While the "lighting scheme of the two shadows" in *Alpdrücken* is designed to give each character specific shadows—Cain and Abel—the pattern of doubling it presents reoccurs throughout the novel. The multiple pairings of the Franz/Schlepzig/Slothrop, Greta/Leni/Katje, and Bianca/Ilse/Gottfried relationships, for example, demonstrate a broader scheme of shadowing—one in which the "shadows of shadows" begin to double back on themselves (429). In terms of The War, I would argue that World War II likewise has two shadows in *Gravity's Rainbow*, Vietnam and World War I. Because of the scope of this essay, however, I will only examine the former of these shadows. Please see Paul Fussell's conclusion to *The Great War and Modern Memory* for a discussion of World War I's legacy in the novel.

15. Both Khachig Tölölyan and Steven Weisenburger provide excellent, thorough examinations of the complex web of texts used to recreate details from the late war period. See Tölölyan's "War as Background in *Gravity's Rainbow*," Weisenburger's *A Gravity's Rainbow Companion*, and McLaughlin's "IG Farben's Synthetic War Crimes and Thomas Pynchon's *Gravity's Rainbow*" for further study.

16. In 1971, for example, only 5,000 U.S. servicemen were treated for wounds while approximately 20,000 were hospitalized for drug addiction. This figure is cited in Peter Arnett's *Vietnam: The Ten Thousand Day War.*

17. Elizabeth Grosz's chapter "Intensities and Flows" in *Volatile Bodies* and Scott Lash's "Genealogy and the Body: Foucault/Deleuze/Nietzsche" provide excellent analyses of Deleuze's writings on bodies.

18. Mailer's *Naked and the Dead*, for example, contains several comments about the extension of men's bodily surfaces to incorporate their weapons or gear into notions of "self." The narrator comments that Croft "could not have said at that moment where his hands ended and the machine gun began" (122) and, describing a march, remarks "the weight of their packs was crushing, but they considered them as part of

their bodies, a boulder lodged in their backs" (393).

19. The cultural programming of desire and sexuality is a recurring motif in the novel. While Slothrop's conditioned erections provide the most notable example, the text calls attention to other instances of culturally managed desire and sexual response. Katje's careful applications of cosmetics to make her look like "the reigning beauties of thirty or forty years ago" (233) for her encounters with Brigadier Pudding and remarks like "How the penises of Western men have leapt, for a century, to the sight of this singular point at the top of a lady's stocking, this transition from silk to bare skin and suspender!" (396) are just two of many examples. For further discussion of Pirate's sexual conditioning see Timothy Melley's "Bodies Incorporated: Scenes of Agency Panic in *Gravity's Rainbow.*"

20. Because so much scholarship on *Gravity's Rainbow* describes the flows of technology and capital between nations before and during the war, I will not discuss them here. See Weisenburger, McLaughlin, Tölölyan.

Works Cited

Ashe, Frederick. "Anachronism Intended: *Gravity's Rainbow* in the Sociopolitical Sixties." *Pynchon Notes* 28-29. Spring-Fall (1991): 59-75.

Boatner, Mark. *Dictionary of World War II.* San Francisco: Presidio, 1996.

Carroll, Peter. *It Seemed Like Nothing Happened: The Tragedy and Promise of America in the 1970s.* New York: Holt, Rinehart and Winston, 1982.

Craig, David, and Michael Egan. *Extreme Situations: Literature and Crisis from the Great War to the Atom Bomb.* Totowa, NJ: Barnes & Noble, 1979.

Deleuze, Gilles, and Felix Guattari. *A Thousand Plateaus: Capitalism and Schizophrenia.* Minneapolis: University of Minnesota Press, 1987.

Freese, Peter. "Kurt Vonnegut's *Slaughterhouse-Five* or, How to Storify an Atrocity." *Historiographic Metafiction in Modern American and Canadian Literature.* Ed. Bernd Engler and Kurt Muller. Munich: Ferdinand Schöningh, 1994. 209-22.

Fussell, Paul. *The Great War and Modern Memory.* New York: Oxford University Press, 1975.

Grosz, Elizabeth. *Volatile Bodies: Toward a Corporeal Feminism.* Indianapolis: Indiana University Press, 1994.

Heller, Joseph. *Catch-22.* 1961. New York: Dell, 1985.

Herring, George. *America's Longest War: The United States and Vietnam, 1950-1975.* 2nd ed. New York: Alfred Knopf, 1986.

Isaacs, Arnold. *Vietnam Shadows: The War, Its Ghosts, and Its Legacy.* Baltimore: Johns Hopkins University Press, 1997.

Jeffords, Susan. *The Remasculinizaton of America: Gender and the Vietnam War.* Bloomington: Indiana University Press, 1989.

Jones, James. *The Thin Red Line.* 1962. New York: Bantam Doubleday Dell, 1998.

Karnow, Stanley. *Vietnam: A History.* New York: Viking Press, 1983.

Lash, Scott. "Genealogy and the Body: Foucault/Deleuze/Nietzsche." *The Body: Social Process and Cultural Theory.* Ed. Mike Featherstone, Mike Hepworth, and Bryan S. Turner. London: Sage, 1991. 256-280.

Lee, Cremilda Toledo. "Fantasy and Reality in *Slaughterhouse-Five.*" *Journal of English Language and Literature* 37.4 (1991): 983-91.

Limon, John. *Writing After War: American War Fiction from Realism to Postmodernism.* New York: Oxford University Press, 1994.

Mailer, Norman. *The Naked and the Dead.* New York: Signet, 1948.

Marling, Karal Ann, and John Wetenhall. *Iwo Jima: Monuments, Memories, and the American Hero.* Cambridge, MA: Harvard University Press, 1991.

McLaughlin, Robert. "IG Farben's Synthetic War Crimes and Thomas Pynchon's *Gravity's Rainbow.*" *Visions of War: World War II in Popular Literature and Culture.* Bowling Green, OH: Popular Press, 1992. 85-95.

Melley, Timothy. "Bodies Incorporated: Scenes of Agency Panic in *Gravity's Rainbow.*" *Contemporary Literature* 35.4 (1994): 709-738.

Meyer, Eric. "Oppositional Discourses, Unnatural Practices: Gravity's History and 'The '60s.'" *Pynchon Notes* 24-25 (1989): 81-104.

Nadel, Alan. *Containment Culture: American Narratives, Postmodernism, and the Atomic Age.* Durham: Duke University Press, 1995.

Nealon, Jeffrey T. "*Gravity's Rainbow* and the Postmodern Other." *Double Reading: Postmodernism after Deconstruction.* Ithaca: Cornell University Press, 1993. 107-131.

O'Neill, William. *Coming Apart: An Informal History of America in the 1960s.* New York: Quadrangle Books, 1971.

Phillips, Jayne Anne. *Machine Dreams.* 1984. New York: Simon & Schuster, 1991.

Pynchon, Thomas. *Gravity's Rainbow.* 1973. New York: Penguin, 1995.

Reed, Peter J. "Authenticity and Relevance: Kurt Vonnegut's *Slaughterhouse-Five.*" *Censored Books: Critical Viewpoints.* Metuchen, NJ: Scarecrow Press, 1993. 464-470.

Roeder, George, Jr. *The Censored War: American Visual Experience During World War II.* New Haven: Yale University Press, 1993.

Seed, David. *The Fictional Labyrinths of Thomas Pynchon.* London: Macmillan Press, 1988.

Tölölyan, Khachig. "War as Background in *Gravity's Rainbow.*" *Approaches to Gravity's Rainbow.* Ed. Charles Clerc. Columbus: Ohio State University Press, 1983. 31-67.

Vonnegut, Kurt. *Slaughterhouse-Five, or the Children's Crusade.* 1969. New York: Bantam, Doubleday Dell, 1991.

Weisenburger, Steven. *A Gravity's Rainbow Companion: Sources and Contexts for Pynchon's Novel.* Athens: University of Georgia Press, 1988.

CRITICAL READINGS

Vonnegut's *Slaughterhouse-Five* and the Fiction of Atrocity_____

Donald J. Greiner

With the publication of *Slaughterhouse-Five* in 1969, Kurt Vonnegut, Jr., stepped to the front rank of contemporary American novelists. Acclaim for the novel, coming after nearly two decades of obscurity for Vonnegut, was something of a surprise. A National Book Award nomination and best-seller sales testify to *Slaughterhouse-Five*'s acceptance by both professional critics and casual readers. Why did the novel finally gain for Vonnegut the kind of stature he deserves? *Slaughterhouse-Five* is not, after all, so different from his earlier fiction. Short and episodic, it is also, like *Mother Night* (1961) and *Cat's Cradle* (1963), an irreverent novel which mixes horror and humor while bordering on science fiction.

Several secondary factors contributed to its success. Certainly the support of university students, who find his untraditional war fiction relevant, and the novel's publication during the Viet Nam war were two significant, although unmeasurable, contributions. The appearance of some scholarly material on Vonnegut's work, particularly Robert Scholes' analysis,[1] initiated necessary critical interest. Vonnegut's recent contract with Delacorte Press, a publisher willing to get his earlier fiction back into print, aided the effort to introduce him to increased numbers of readers. But the reason for the book's success goes deeper. Vonnegut's latest novel summarizes his thoughts on war which until now have been scattered throughout his previous fiction—the other novels seem a build-up to the climax of *Slaughterhouse-Five*. War has always been a significant subject for him, but until *Slaughterhouse-Five* he has never revealed his personal anguish. *Mother Night* and *Cat's Cradle*, of course, focus on war. Even his novels which do not treat war as the primary subject nevertheless comment on its effects. In *The Sirens of Titan* (1959), for example, Vonnegut satirizes the Martians and their military regimentation as they plan their unsuccessful attack on earth. And in *God Bless You, Mr. Rosewater* (1965), Eliot Rosewater suffers from the memory of a World War II episode during which he mistakenly kills a German boy. But in all of these novels the humorous antics and the sheer delight of the science fiction fantasies ease the shock which the descriptions of war produce.

Most of the major characters from the earlier fiction turn up in *Slaughterhouse-Five* as if to take a final bow: Kilgore Trout, Eliot Rosewater, Howard Campbell. With its publication, Vonnegut wraps up a series of novels about war, a topic he has brooded on since that night in February, 1945, when Allied bombers leveled Dresden. Because the novel crowns twenty-three years' work, we can understand why he has since tried other mediums, film scripts, for example, and the play *Happy Birthday, Wanda June*. His producer Lester Goldsmith goes so far as to say that Vonnegut has finished writing fiction[2] (although a new novel, *Breakfast of Champions*, has been mentioned). His latest book, then, may climax his novelistic efforts to treat war from the perspective of his comic imagination.

Significantly, *Slaughterhouse-Five*, although funny, is not as wildly humorous as his previous fiction. The lack of outrageous comedy is not a flaw but rather a comment upon how deeply Vonnegut feels about the bombing of Dresden. Although *Mother Night* and *Cat's Cradle* are surely serious novels, something is boisterously funny about Howard Campbell's trials or about ice-nine destroying the world and all of the Bokononist faithful. The seriousness of *Slaughterhouse-Five* is always before us so that the Vonnegut brand of comedy takes second place to the subject's gravity. The novel seems to convey a somber tone because its subject, the Dresden bombing, is a historical fact, and unlike the purely imaginative subjects of *Mother Night* and *Cat's Cradle*, a holocaust which Vonnegut suffered through and lived to write about.

Laughing at war is a protective measure in *Mother Night*, possible because the war is kept abstract, peopled with imaginary characters who are as irrational as war. Although Vonnegut's Dresden experiences are mentioned in an introduction he wrote for the 1966 re-issue of *Mother Night*, the historical facts are not developed in the book it-self. He reduces *Mother Night*'s one historical figure, Adolf Eichmann, to a minor character and a crazed clown whose chief worry is whether he needs a literary agent to handle his memoirs. Laughter shields us from the specter of Eichmann's six-million murders because in *Mother Night* it seems to be the only sane response to the insanity of war. In *Slaughterhouse-Five* Vonnegut negates the possibility of abstracting war when he focuses on one particular historically verifiable atrocity and lets us know that he literally experienced the event. His close rela-tionship to the subject contributes to the noticeable seriousness of his novel. Brooding on the Dresden nightmare for twenty-three years, he cannot help but treat the subject somberly. *Slaughterhouse-Five*'s suc-cess seems to come primarily from Vonnegut's personal involvement in the atrocity, and the result is a novel of definitely darker tone which is not totally a product of his comic imagination. An examination of the way Vonnegut fictionalizes the Dresden raid will help us better to un-derstand his personal reaction to an atrocity of unbelievable magni-tude.

The My Lai massacre and the resulting national debate have made atrocity and its effects on victims and victimizers a popular topic. Rob-ert Jay Lifton comments on "the increasing gap we face between our technological capacity for perpetrating atrocities and our imaginative ability to confront their full actuality."[3] He wonders if individuals— and nations—require a psychic numbing as a necessary defense against full realization of what they suspect has happened, and he warns that such emotional paralysis can be malignant. Lifton admits that his experience with Hiroshima victims changed his feelings about his own death as well as about collective deaths. For the first time he realized that suspicions of apocalypse could no longer be laughed away as a delusion of the world coming to an end. Survivors of the Hi-roshima atrocity experienced a sense of dislocation and absurdity which destroyed their previous assumptions of a rational universe.

Lifton's analysis of atrocity is particularly relevant to Vonnegut's novel. By writing *Slaughterhouse-Five*, Vonnegut narrows the gap between his realization of the technological capacity for total destruction and his ability to confront barbarity because the book is a fictionalized account of an atrocity personally experienced. Surviving the annihilation of 135,000 civilians not only sharpened awareness of his own death but also brought home his relationship to collective death on a nearly unimaginable scale. One of Lifton's conclusions is especially pertinent here: "Survivors felt guilty about remaining alive while others died, and also experienced an amorphous sense of having been part of, having imbibed, the overall evil of the atrocity." No one can speak for Vonnegut's private reactions, of course, but his novel suggests that Billy Pilgrim suffers the same sense of guilt by virtue of his unusual status during the Dresden raid. He is, as was Vonnegut, an American who survived the destruction of a German city by British and Americans. As an American Billy shares the guilt of both the Allied victimizers who slaughtered and the German victims who survived. Vonnegut must have experienced the same sort of double guilt, and the guilt of survival may have inhibited for years his efforts to write, as he ironically calls *Slaughterhouse-Five*, "my famous book about Dresden."[4] Certainly Billy Pilgrim suffers from immersion in the collective deaths of 135,000 civilians and from the guilt of survival. His trips to Tralfamadore suggest the kind of psychic numbing which Lifton discusses. If we take Billy as a partial mask for Vonnegut, then the seriousness of the novel probably results from Vonnegut's own experience with atrocity. The writing of *Slaughterhouse-Five* has likely been a liberating process, for expression of the experience eases the pressures caused by identification with both victim and victimizer.

That expression has not come easily, as the novel's first chapter testifies. Written in Vonnegut's own voice rather than from Billy Pilgrim's point of view, the chapter serves as a prologue in which Vonnegut admits the difficulty of trying to write about Dresden. Note the serious tone and the evident frustration:

I would hate to tell you what this lousy little book cost me in money and anxiety and time. When I got home from the Second World War twenty-three years ago, I thought it would be easy for me to write about the destruction of Dresden, since all I would have to do would be to report what I had seen. And I thought, too, that it would be a masterpiece or at least make me a lot of money, since the subject was so big. But not many words about Dresden came from my mind then—not enough of them to make a book, anyway. And not many words come now, either. (2)

The comment illustrates the difference between *Slaughterhouse-Five* and *Mother Night* or *Cat's Cradle*. As Vonnegut says on the first page, "All this happened, more or less. The war parts, anyway, are pretty much true." His personal involvement with the novel's subject has cost him a great deal, but his imaginative reconstruction of the experience has produced a truer, a more deeply felt, and a more somber-toned fiction.

The result of immersion in so many deaths is a novel in which Vonnegut reveals his awareness and fear of mankind's possible collective death. Surviving an apocalyptic experience diminishes the need to affix blame or to divide the victims into allies and enemies. As the novel suggests, the next atrocity might kill us all. Thus, Vonnegut refuses to point his finger or to accuse anyone. Designation of guilt is not his concern. He comments in the first chapter that he never wrote a novel with a villain in it, although he is fully aware that the Germans were slaughtering Jews while the Allies were bombing Dresden's defenseless civilians. When both sides indulge in atrocities, little value can come from attempts to single out good guys and bad. All he can do is promise not to glamorize war, to avoid creating a hero's "part for Frank Sinatra or John Wayne." Yet, as Vonnegut admits at the end of Chapter One, the novel may be a failure because nothing intelligent can be said about a massacre. When he celebrates the humanity of Lot's wife for glancing back at the destruction of Sodom and Gomorrah, he hints that the primary accomplishment of *Slaughterhouse-Five* may indeed be personal. By finally completing his "famous book about Dresden," he suggests that he may have regained his sympathy with humanity which was threatened by the numbing experience of a double-edged guilt. The successful expression of such deeply felt personal emotion without sentimentality is one of the reasons for *Slaughterhouse-Five*'s success.

With Chapter Two Vonnegut shifts from his own direct statements to the adventures of Billy Pilgrim, but significantly he never lets us forget that the novel is based on a historically verifiable event even though it borders on science fiction. He keeps in touch with the facts of Dresden by citing passages from David Irving's *The Destruction of Dresden*, particularly quotations from the introduction by Ira C. Eaker, USAF, retired, and from the foreword by British Air Marshal Sir Robert Saundby. A reading of Irving's book reveals why Vonnegut chooses parts of the Eaker and Saundby prefaces for quotations. General Eaker, for example, passes the buck for the Dresden raid from the senior military commanders to the Allied heads of state, describes civilians as enemies, and ignores the question of whether Dresden was "a proper military target."[5] The paragraph which Vonnegut quotes argues that those who weep for Dresden should recall the German bombings of England. Marshal Saundby's foreword is a little more humane, for he at least suggests that those responsible for the decision to crush Dresden were "too remote from the harsh realities of war" to realize the destructive power they were unleashing. With minimal indirect commentary, Vonnegut scorns General Eaker's reasoning, not because he tries to excuse Dresden, but because he assumes that to balance an Allied atrocity with a German one is to neutralize both and, thus, to expiate guilt. For Eaker guilt belongs nowhere since both sides did the same thing, but for Vonnegut the guilt is universal. General Eaker's "war is hell" attitude makes Vonnegut's suffering more intense.

Irving's book is a valuable complement to *Slaughterhouse-Five*, corroborating many of the novel's events and statements. Of particular significance is Irving's discussion of Dresden's obvious vulnerability, since Vonnegut stresses the same point. Although the city was never declared "open," it was not worthy of the industrial and military importance which the Allies tried to give it. According to Irving its strategic significance was "scarcely marginal." By 1944 it was an administrative center, never with important industrial or military sites. What railroad yards existed were located far from the city's center. When Dresden's anti-aircraft guns were dismantled in October of 1944, the civilian population had every right to believe that the city would not be bombed. Irving writes that "only papier-mâché dummies remained on the hills outside to defend the city." Thus, by 13 February 1945, the date of the raid, Dresden was virtually undefended, bursting with hundreds of thousands of refugees plus 26,000 prisoners (including 2,207 Americans of which Vonnegut was one).

Irving cites two key reasons for the attack. The British Air Chief Marshal Sir Arthur Harris advocated, with the support of Prime Minister Churchill, indiscriminate area bombing of population centers, as opposed to precision bombing of military targets, as a means to shatter German morale. Harris hoped to destroy all sixty of Germany's major cities, although the Dresden raid was the first time that a fire-storm, created by bombing civilians with incendiaries, was planned as part of the attack. The second reason which Irving cites is that Churchill wanted to impress the Russians with Allied air power. The Red Army was advancing so quickly from the east that Churchill feared being forced into an inferior position at the Yalta talks. Ironically, the Yalta meetings ended before the Dresden raid. The extraordinary devastation (American pilots even strafed the city in their Mustang fighters) caused Churchill to question the concept of area bombing by trying to shift the blame from the British Government to the bomber commanders. Although he contributed much of the incentive for the terror raid, the Prime Minister was looking beyond the war to the time when blame would be placed. Irving shows that Churchill later rephrased his criticism of the bombing to erase the implication that he had been misled by his military advisers. Irving also quotes the Prime Minister's only comment in his memoirs about the massacre: "We made a heavy raid in the latter month on Dresden then a centre of communications of Germany's Eastern front."

These frantic efforts to avoid blame and the subsequent attempts to hush up the raid mystify and infuriate Vonnegut. In a telling understatement, he writes, "There hadn't been much publicity." Vonnegut informs us in Chapter One that he once wrote the United States Air Force asking for details about Dresden, who ordered the raid, why it was carried out, what the desirable results were. The Air Force officer's reply calls forth Vonnegut's despair: "He said that he was sorry, but that the information was top secret still. I read the letter out loud to my wife, and I said, 'Secret? My God—from *whom*?'" Mention of the effort to cover up the attack is just one example of the way Vonnegut keeps the historical validity of his subject before us even while he creates the science fiction of space travel and little green men.

Like Irving, for example, he calls attention to the fact that Dresden was not only defenseless but that it had retained its pastoral beauty in spite of the war. A fellow prisoner of Billy Pilgrim, Edgar Derby, writes his wife and urges her not to worry because the prisoners are being taken to Dresden, a city that "will never be bombed." To Billy, Dresden looks "intricate and voluptuous and enchanted and absurd" like a picture of Heaven (129). Similarly, Billy Pilgrim's report of the fire-storm squares with Irving's historical account: "There was a fire-storm out there. Dresden was one big flame. The one flame ate everything organic, everything that would burn. . . . Dresden was like the moon, now, nothing but minerals. The stones were hot. Everybody else in the neighborhood was dead" (153). Even Billy's descriptions of the charred bodies resembling little logs because arms, legs, and heads had been burned off, or of "the bodies of schoolgirls who were boiled alive in a water tower by my own countrymen, who were proud of the fighting pure evil at the time" (100) are verified by Irving's book. The suggestion that most of the casualties died, unmarked, from suffocation and the description of the way the bodies were stacked before the mass cremations—first layer with heads pointed left, second layer with feet pointed left—find support in Irving's historical account of the raid's aftermath. Perhaps the novel's two most shocking events with historical validity are the American strafing and the execution of Edgar Derby for taking a teapot. The strafing incident, although minor when compared to the tons of firebombs dropped, illustrates the Allied policy of total destruction and underscores the senselessness of the atrocity. Vonnegut writes ironically: "Absolutely everybody in the city was supposed to be dead, regardless of what they were, and that anybody that moved in it represented a flaw in the design. There were to be no moon men at all." The idea of strafing the surviving civilians, he tells us, was "to hasten the end of the war" (155). The irony of Derby's execution after the raid is supported by Irving's account of American and French-Canadian prisoners being shot for taking food from wrecked shops. Both Vonnegut and Irving note the warped sense of justice in a world which can gloss over the Dresden horror and yet meticulously observe the letter of the law as it applies to petty looting. To make sure we get the point, Vonnegut tells us in his own voice that Derby's execution is the novel's climax: "I think the climax of the book will be the execution of poor old Edgar Derby. . . . The irony is so great. A whole city gets burned down, and thousands and thousands of people are killed. And then this one American foot soldier is arrested in the ruins for taking a teapot. And he's given a regular trial, and then he's shot by a firing squad" (4).

Vonnegut makes a considerable effort to fictionalize isolated incidents which can be certified as factual and to establish his painful, personal involvement in an atrocity of such magnitude that it numbed his ability to write about it for twenty-three years. Because he is writing a novel, rather than a documented history, which underscores his pain and fear, he deliberately omits discussion of the complex motives and details leading to the Dresden raid. To his credit, he controls his outrage and refuses to use the novel to specify blame. He is interested not in realistic detail but in effect, yet the historicalness of the novel's subject poses problems for readers who are unaware of the raid's complexity. Some knowledge of the facts is necessary to understand how Vonnegut gains an effect from the application of fiction to this historical event.

Irving's study is useful, for it analyzes the Dresden attack in depth. Equally important is Noble Frankland's *Bomber Offensive*, which places Dresden in the context of all major raids on Europe.[6] Frankland tells us, for example, that the decision to bomb German civilian centers in an effort to destroy morale was the result of a directive issued as early in the war as 14 February 1942. More significantly, he discusses the terrible pressures on the Allied Bomber Command late in the war which led to the Dresden attack. By 1945 the Allies sensed victory, only to be frustrated by a dramatic German counterattack in the Battle of the Bulge. Although the attack was repulsed in January 1945, it testified to the strength of German resistance. The Allies feared an outbreak of guerilla warfare following formal defeat, and they hoped that a devastating blow from the air would shock Berlin into total surrender. Something spectacular had to be tried to hasten the end of the war. When frustration at the inability to force surrender and fear of prolonged guerilla action are joined to the pressure applied by the Russian Army's rapid advance, the complicated background to Dresden becomes clear. Never once does Frankland use these facts to excuse the raid, calling it "too much and too late" with "gross" over-bombing. But he clarifies for Vonnegut's readers that the atrocity was a good deal more complex than we are allowed to see in *Slaughterhouse-Five*.

To be aware of these complexities is to understand better the importance of Dresden not only to Vonnegut's personal experience but to his feelings about the problem of war in general. As he says, most of us do not know much about the raid because it was hushed-up. Both the historical validity of the novel's subject and Vonnegut's closeness to it contribute in great measure to *Slaughterhouse-Five*'s success. In spite of Vonnegut's own comments in Chapter One and the novel's various verifiable events, he reverses his narrative method following the first chapter and uses most of the novel to create distance between himself and his protagonist, even though he pointedly gives Billy Pilgrim his own birth date. He interrupts the third-person narrative several times to speak in the first person and to tell us, "I was there," but for the most part he uses indirection, understatement, and dispassionate description to create distance.

Beginning with the second chapter, the novel becomes more "unreal" when he develops fictional distance by creating an obviously imaginary character who indulges in space travel. In general, verisimilitude is avoided. At least two reasons justify his choosing this method to recreate imaginatively a true experience which obviously means so much to him. First is the pressure imposed by the guilt of survival and by the resulting consciousness of the scope of potential collective death. He is so close to his material that his guilt could stifle his expression. He is forced to stand back from his subject in spite of the personal comments in Chapter One and to insist upon the distance between himself and Billy Pilgrim in the remainder of the novel. Second, Vonnegut needs to convey his sense of outrage at the raid, but that he never describes in detail his experience during the bombing or its aftermath suggests that he knew he was too close to his subject. In a century saturated with wars and threatened by the specter of nuclear annihilation, one more account of the horrors of war with realistic details and stacks of statistics would not express a personal sense of shock to a reading public inundated with daily reports of violent death. Vonnegut makes the problem quite clear when he mentions without comment other atrocities—the assassinations of Robert Kennedy and Martin Luther King and the United States Government's invention of the body count in Viet Nam. Taking the other approach, he understates the Dresden horrors dispassionately so that the apparently unconcerned manner communicates his grief.

The phrase "so it goes" which is repeated at every reference to death, be it champagne or civilians, is his most effective means to create distance. The refrain of apparent indifference is also a clue to the reason Vonnegut partially separates himself from the narrative. Not only does "so it goes" communicate his awareness of the equality of all deaths, whether 135,000 at one time or just one, it also expresses the futility he suffers when he tries to convey his feelings about any death. The Dresden experience forced home to Vonnegut the truth that appropriate responses to death do not exist. His use of the silly phrase "so it goes" makes us realize not only that death is everywhere and final but also that we can do nothing about it. If one could have an appropriate reaction to death or an adequate response to Dresden, then both death and Dresden could be effectively dealt with, and the pain eased. Vonnegut does not want to negate the shock and undercut the magnitude of the atrocity. In the novel's last chapter, he again speaks in his own voice, reinforcing his distance from Billy Pilgrim while simultaneously revealing how close he remains to the Dresden experience. Billy has learned from the Tralfamadorians a casual approach to death which accepts it as no more than one moment in a string of moments. According to the little green men, a dead person may be dead in one moment but alive in another. Thus, death's pain and finality are neutralized. But while Billy can come to terms with death and Dresden, Vonnegut cannot. Haunted by the memory of the fire-storm and fearful of man's capacity for future atrocity, he pointedly divorces himself from Billy's lesson and hints that eternal life in a world which tolerates death and war is no blessing: "If what Billy Pilgrim learned from the Tralfamadorians is true, that we will all live forever, no matter how dead we may sometimes seem to be, I am not overjoyed. . . . East Germany was down below, and the lights were on. I imagined dropping bombs on those lights, those villages and cities and towns" (182-3).

The use of Tralfamadore and of the various trappings of science fiction also establishes and maintains narrative distance. Lifton's interviews with those who perpetrated atrocities at Hiroshima and My Lai suggest that the experience can be "a dreamlike affair" committed by men who seem to be outside of normal human society. Similarly, the survivors of atrocity feel trapped by an unreal sense of doom to the point of being immobilized. These two descriptions certainly fit Billy Pilgrim's dismissal of everyday reality following his rescue from Dresden and his dreamlike, immobile trances which result in trips to the imaginary planet. Rather than undercut the seriousness of *Slaughterhouse-Five*, the use of science fiction reveals how keenly Vonnegut understands atrocity. Billy Pilgrim suffers the psychological aftereffects of both victimizer and victim which Lifton describes. Permitting Vonnegut to be detached and dispassionate, the science fiction fantasies convey the outrageousness of the truth about Dresden. The firestorm had to occur as if in another world—we remember Billy describing the destroyed city as looking like the moon. Vonnegut implies that science fiction can help us cope with an irrational experience like Dresden when he comments on Billy, who had seen the "greatest massacre in European history," and on Eliot Rosewater, who had killed a fourteen-year-old German: "So they were trying to re-invent themselves and their universe. Science fiction was a big help" (87). That statement goes a long way toward explaining Vonnegut's method and tone in *Slaughterhouse-Five*.

Vonnegut took twenty-three years to ponder his survival of Dresden, writing pure science fiction, like *The Sirens of Titan*, before he could liberate himself from the guilt of survival by expressing the experience in *Slaughterhouse-Five*. In one sense the novel is the result of his effort to re-invent himself and his universe. His extraordinary closeness to the subject matter and the theme accounts for the restrained and serious tone, in turn revealing how the experience damaged his spirit. His attempt to establish the historical validity of the subject matter poses the problem of narrative distance, but it also gives the novel a foundation in fact which his earlier war fiction lacks. The apocalyptic imagination, so funny as to seem unreal in *Mother Night* and *Cat's Cradle*, reinforces the reality of Dresden in *Slaughterhouse-Five*. Vonnegut's juggling of Billy Pilgrim's imaginary adventures with a dispassionate account of his personal experiences at Dresden is a way of balancing his efforts to maintain an objective view of the atrocity and his need to convey his closeness to it. Successfully handling a complex technique, Vonnegut creates in *Slaughterhouse-Five* a novel that clearly surpasses his earlier work.

From *Critique* 14, no. 3 (1973): 38-51. Copyright © 1973 by Heldref Publications. Reprinted with permission of Heldref Publications.

Notes

1. Robert Scholes, "Mithridates, He Died Old: Black Humor and Kurt Vonnegut, Jr.," *The Hollins Critic*, 3 (Oct. 1966), 1-12; and "Fabulation and Satire," *The Fabulators* (New York: Oxford Univ. Press, 1967), pp. 35-55.

2. Lester Goldsmith, *Show Magazine* (April 1971).

3. Robert Jay Lifton, "Beyond Atrocity," *Saturday Review* (27 March 1971), p. 23.

4. Kurt Vonnegut, Jr., *Slaughterhouse-Five, or The Children's Crusade* (New York: Delacorte, 1969), p. 16. All subsequent references are to this edition.

5. David Irving, *The Destruction of Dresden* (New York: Ballantine, 1968), p. 7.

6. Noble Frankland, *Bomber Offensive: The Devastation of Europe* (New York: Ballantine, 1971).

Slaughterhouse-Five:
Novel and Film

Joyce Nelson

The recent film, *Slaughterhouse-Five*,[1] based on the best-selling novel by Kurt Vonnegut, Jr., is a remarkable achievement in its own right. Director George Roy Hill has managed to capture and convey the essential spirit of a novelist who has, at times, baffled and dismayed his critics in their attempts to deal with his work. Since Vonnegut himself receives top billing on many marquees advertising the George Roy Hill-Paul Monash production, it is interesting to compare the film with the novel.

One of the most striking stylistic elements of the novel is its nineteen-page first chapter, which is more an author's preface giving personal background and attitudes. "All of this happened, more or less. The war parts, anyway, are pretty much true . . . ,"[2] Vonnegut begins his novel. He gives us the prototypes for certain characters (Roland Weary, Edgar Derby, Paul Lazzaro): "One guy I knew really was shot in Dresden for taking a teapot that wasn't his. Another guy I knew really did threaten to have his personal enemies killed by hired gunmen after the war" (p. 1). Throughout this first chapter there is a kind of pleading insistence, a desire to impress upon the reader the fact that the author has experienced the horrors and sincerely felt the grief: "People aren't supposed to look back. I'm certainly not going to do it anymore. I've finished my war book now. The next one I write is going to be fun. This one is a failure, and had to be, since it was written by a pillar of salt" (p. 19). The moral, intimate tone of the chapter serves, in a sense, to justify the ironic detachment which characterizes the rest of the novel. Perhaps fearing that his ennui, this detachment will be misunderstood, Vonnegut sometimes overemphasizes his intent. Relating an incident during the writing of the novel, he gives us this conversation between himself and a friend's wife: Mary O'Hare says, "You'll pretend you were men instead of babies, and you'll be played in the movies by Frank Sinatra and John Wayne or some of those other glamorous, war-loving, dirty old men. And war will look just wonderful, we'll have a lot more of them. And they'll be fought by babies like the babies upstairs." In answer, Vonnegut says, "I don't think this book of mine is ever going to be finished. I must have written five thousand pages by now, and thrown them all away. If I ever do finish it, though, I give you my word of honor: there won't be a part for Frank Sinatra or John Wayne" (p. 13).

George Roy Hill's casting is faithful to this promise. The part of Billy Pilgrim is played by Michael Sacks, whose versatility is extraordinary. Not only has Sacks convincingly created many phases of Billy's life, from a youth in the war to an old man, but he has managed to subtly convey the range of emotions which make Billy seem so fragile. Like the novel's Billy Pilgrim, who tries to transcend experience, Michael Sacks's Pilgrim seems poised between emotional numbness and crushing despair.

There is a sense in which Vonnegut's characters (Valencia, Robert, Montana Wildhack, Edgar Derby) are created, in the novel, more by suggestion than by fullness of description. Verging on the cartoon-like, they are sketched through ironic placement, key bits of dialogue, and events. The result is a delicacy of characterization, a certain fragility as in Pilgrim, which easily could have been shattered through overexaggeration in the film, but was not.

While protecting the fragility of character, the film achieves a sense of poignancy by bridging the emotional distance created in the novel. For example, the scenes involving Edgar Derby (Eugene Roche) are dealt with more thoroughly and directly, though faithful to the novel in detail. Derby watches over Pilgrim in the prison camp, is elected leader of his fellow prisoners, is shot for plundering; but in the film the father-son relationship between Derby and Pilgrim is heightened to make more painful the death of Derby. Exemplary of Vonnegut's style, Derby's death in the novel is completely understated, starkly ironic through brevity: "Somewhere in there the poor old high school teacher,

Edgar Derby, was caught with a teapot he had taken from the cata-combs. He was arrested for plundering. He was tried and shot. So it goes" (p. 186). In the film, the plundering (here, a figurine exactly like one his son had broken long ago) is not mere thievery, but has a de-lighted innocence surrounding it. Derby even shows it to his German guards, attempting to share his joy at finding it. As we then see him car-ried off, in long-shot, to the wall and executed, our own horror is ines-capable. The emotional detachment created in the novel by the reoc-currence of the phrase, "So it goes," is lacking in the film. Time and again we are confronted with characters and events which call forth a greater emotional response than the novel will allow. When Pil-grim's son Robert (Perry King), wearing the uniform of the Green Be-rets, comes to his father's bedside to apologize and assure him that he's "straightened out," Pilgrim, without a word, slowly turns his head slightly away and toward the window. The gesture perfectly cap-tures the combination of frustration, forgiveness and growing detach-ment.

Fortunately, the film includes most of the minor figures from the novel: Wild Bob ("If you're ever in Cody, Wyoming, just ask for Wild Bob"); the hobo in the prisoner-of-war train ("I've been in worse places than this, this ain't so bad"); Howard W. Campbell, Jr. (the Nazi recruiting men for the Free American Corps); Rumfoord, the war his-torian hospitalized next to Pilgrim ("I could carve a better man out of a banana").

However, one character that the film does not include is Kilgore Trout, the science fiction writer who appears in three Vonnegut novels and who functions importantly in the novel of *Slaughterhouse-Five*. It is through reading Trout's fiction that Pilgrim first achieves transcen-dence over his grief, first reads of the Tralfamadorians. It is important to any literary analysis of Vonnegut's works that Trout seems a kind of self-parody: "Trout's unpopularity was deserved. His prose was fright-ful. Only his ideas were good" (p. 95).

The novel gives us summaries of several Trout stories and two brief glimpses of his character, but the tone of these sections and their function are more appropriate to the novel than to the film. For the latter. Trout is perhaps wisely eliminated, which also facilitates Hill's decision to leave the Tralfamadorians invisible, although they are described in the novel. Because of these changes, there is another key difference between novel and film.

Because of the detail given to Trout and to the Tralfamadorians, including more of their philosophy and Billy's trip to their planet, the novel seems to create a greater distinction between Pilgrim's life on earth and his life on Tralfamadore. As a result, there is a greater feeling of schizophrenia and exaggeration in the novel. Coupled with this element is the author's tendency to always alert us to Billy's time-travel: "The terrific acceleration of the saucer as it left Earth twisted Billy's slumbering body, distorted his face, dislodged him in time, sent him back to the war. When he regained consciousness, he wasn't on the flying saucer. He was in a boxcar crossing Germany again" (pp. 66-67). In the novel this technique often works brilliantly to heighten the irony of certain juxtapositions and to unify certain pervasive images and recurring symbols. But in the film the time-travel is more easily accomplished within the flow of the editing. And by eliminating the more bizarre elements of the Tralfamadorian world (flying saucer, their appearance, etc.), Hill makes Pilgrim's transitions between realms seem less jarring (both to Pilgrim and to us). The result seems to be a greater sense of continuity in Pilgrim's life, as well as a greater credibility surrounding his extra-terrestrial experiences. For example, the cut from Pilgrim seated on his bed watching an approaching light, to Pilgrim appearing in the space dome, seems quite "natural" when compared to a more startling, "real" scene: the appearance of the skiers wearing face masks in the airport crowd, and their finding Pilgrim after the plane crash, staring down in startling close-up.

This seeming naturalness of the film's Tralfamadorian dimension is in keeping with yet another major difference between novel and film: Montana Wildhack and the element of sex. Vonnegut's novel is asexual, almost anti-sexual. During the war scenes of the novel, the sexual imagery is either disgusting and lewd (Roland Weary's picture of a woman attempting intercourse with a Shetland pony) or pathetically impotent: "The naked Americans took their places under many shower-heads along a white-tiled wall. There were no faucets they could control. They could only wait for whatever was coming. Their penises were shriveled and their balls were retracted. Reproduction was not the main business of the evening" (p. 73). In the postwar scenes, sex is equally non-beautiful: "Billy was on top of Valencia, making love to her. One result of this act would be the birth of Robert Pilgrim, who would become a problem in high school, but who would then straighten out as a member of the famous Green Beret. . . . Billy made a noise like a small, rusty hinge. He had just emptied his seminal vesicles into Valencia, had contributed his share of the Green Berets" (p. 102). In another scene. Pilgrim browses through a pornographic bookshop and Vonnegut writes of the store and its owners: "They were making money running a paper-and-celluloid whorehouse. They didn't have hard-ons. Neither did Billy Pilgrim. Everybody else did. It was a ridiculous store, all about love and babies" (p. 175).

Thus, it is appropriate that the novel's Montana Wildhack seems silly and irrelevant, especially in her pregnancy:

> Montana was six months pregnant now, big and rosy, lazily demanding small favors from Billy from time to time. She couldn't send Billy out for ice cream or strawberries, since the atmosphere outside the dome was cyanide, and the nearest strawberries and ice cream were millions of light years away. She could send him to the refrigerator . . . or, as now, she could wheedle, "Tell me a story, Billy boy." "Dresden was destroyed on the night of February 13, 1945," Billy Pilgrim began. (pp. 153-54)

In contrast, the film's sexual overtones are more poignant than pathetic, more optimistic and potent. The war scenes include the adolescent love of a German couple, and a Pilgrim who stares in fascination at the women in the windows of Dresden. But it is in the character of Montana Wildhack that the main difference remains. Charmingly portrayed by Valerie Perrine, the film's Montana, a starlet snatched away from earth to be Pilgrim's mate, is just on the borderline between parody and sensitive portrayal. But, like Pilgrim, she has an aura of innocence about her, which prevents her sensuality from appearing immoral or ridiculed. Perhaps as a consequence, the film ends with a family portrait: Billy, Montana and their baby being applauded by their Tralfamadorian hosts. In contrast, the novel closes upon an almost deserted Dresden street of ruins at the end of World War II.

Although George Roy Hill (with Stephen Geller's screenplay) has effectively bridged the ironic detachment of the novel, thereby losing something of the Vonnegut humor and satire, he has retained the "quietness after a massacre" which is such a part of the Vonnegut style. The prisoners of war emerge slowly and silently from their bomb shelter to the ruins of a once beautiful Dresden. Only once do we see a pile of bodies, ignited to facilitate burial. In keeping with the tone of the novel, what is not said or shown is as overwhelming as what is.

By selecting and expanding the more visual aspects of Vonnegut's work (Valencia's wild ride to the hospital), and by leaving out the more verbal sections (such as Rumfoord reading Truman's war speeches), Hill has perhaps lessened the anti-war didacticism of the novel, but to the film's advantage. For George Roy Hill's film convinces us of the grief behind the transcendence, the emotion which Vonnegut, "the pillar of salt," felt he could not convey.

From *Literature/Film Quarterly* 1, no. 2 (April 1973): 149-153. Copyright © 1973 by Salisbury University. Reprinted with permission of Salisbury University.

Notes

1. Produced by Paul Monash. Directed by George Roy Hill. Screenplay by Stephen Geller; based on the novel *Slaughterhouse-Five, Or the Children's Crusade* by Kurt Vonnegut, Jr. Director of Photography: Miroslav Ondricek. Film Editor: Dede Allen. Sound: Milan Novotny, James Alexander. Makeup: Mark Reedall, John Chambers. Music: Glenn Gould. With: Michael Sacks, Ron Leibman, Eugene Roche, Sharon Gans, Valerie Perrine, Holly Near, Perry King, Kevin Conway, Friedrich Ledebur, Nick Belle. A Universal-Vanadas Productions, Inc. Picture.

2. New York: Dell, 1969. All references to the novel are to this edition.

Slaughterhouse-Five:
Time Out of Joint_____

Arnold Edelstein

I

Kurt Vonnegut's *Slaughterhouse-Five* is a strange little book. It jux-taposes satiric glances at suburban life in America during the Fifties and Sixties, the horrors of death and war—especially the fire-bombing of Dresden during the last days of World War II—and Billy Pilgrim's problematic adventures in space and time. Its obvious contempora-neity—it contains references to Vietnam, John Wayne, and the deaths of Martin Luther King and Robert Kennedy—and its great popularity with the counter-culture seem to invite the application of political and sociological criteria rather than literary ones. In a way, the book is what Vonnegut calls it on the title-page: schizophrenic. Its subject is very se-rious—war and death—but the treatment can be totally whimsical at times, as the title-page itself indicates. Most readers leave the book happy that they have read it, delighted by a few new Vonnegut gems, but confused if they try to explain either their delight or their happi-ness.

The basic question for every reader of *Slaughterhouse-Five* is sim-ple: how seriously are we to take Billy Pilgrim's Tralfamadorian the-ory of time? Is it happy fantasy, like the harmoniums in *The Sirens of Titan*? Is it fictionalized but serious speculation about the nature of time? Is it a large, philosophical metaphor of man's existential condi-tion? One reviewer takes the theory very seriously indeed and sees that one of the novel's possible themes is that

> it could be best simply to hold onto some second-rate resignation, sigh, af-fect the attitude of one who has seen too much history, who knows too much of the future, and who counts tragedy an odd notion of the inhabit-ants of the water planet. And so it goes.

132 Critical Insights

Another reviewer calls it a "sci-fi fantasy that flies up from the local disaster to a fanciful, cosmological redefinition of death."[1]

On first reading, at least, the theory of the simultaneity of all time and its implication of a thorough-going determinism in which man is totally incapable of changing his condition do seem to constitute either an avoidance of moral responsibility or a metaphysical horror story. The world is both real and totally determined from its beginning to its end. We are bugs trapped in the amber of an unalterable spacial display of simultaneous moments that only seem to succeed each other. Instead of vainly trying to free ourselves from the amber, we should take the Tralfamadorians' advice and "ignore the awful times, and concentrate on the good ones" (p. 102).[2] This kind of first reading, which takes the time theory at face value, is encouraged by the similarities between Vonnegut's own experience and Billy Pilgrim's and by the presence in the novel of both Vonnegut in his own voice and characters from his earlier novels. Nevertheless, there is overwhelming evidence throughout *Slaughterhouse-Five* that every element of Billy's "sci-fi fantasy" can be explained in realistic, psychological terms.

Perhaps aware of the reader's temptation to identify the author with his central character after hearing the author speaking in his own voice in the first chapter, Vonnegut begins the second chapter with a clear assertion of narrative distance. Billy "has seen his birth and death many times, *he says*, and pays random visits to all the events in between. *He says. . . .* He is in a constant state of stage fright, *he says . . .*" (p. 20).[3] Two pages later, Vonnegut repeats this emphasis.

He said, too, that he had been kidnapped by a flying saucer in 1967. The saucer was from the planet Tralfamadore, *he said*. He was taken to Tralfamadore, where he was displayed naked in a zoo, *he said*. (p. 22)[4]

Vonnegut maintains the narrative distance that is established here throughout the novel by a rather complex formal structure which distinguishes, sometimes not too clearly, between four levels of narration:

Vonnegut's present tense (chapters one and ten); *Billy's present tense* (his trip to New York and its aftermath); *a novelistic past tense of historical fact* (the war experiences, Billy's eighteenth wedding anniversary and the plane crash); *and Billy's travels in time and space*, which contain both historical events and the Tralfamadorian episodes (generally woven throughout the war experiences). Only the last level, the flash-forwards, raise any problems. Most of these problems vanish, however, when we reconstructed a chronological time-sequence from the bits and pieces that Vonnegut gives us. For then we discover that the flash-forwards are actually reinterpretations of Billy's past experience in the light of a time fantasy that takes twenty years to develop, but that achieves full form only a short while before he communicates it during his visit to New York City.

Such a chronological reconstruction would begin with the events that disturb the pattern of Billy's life in 1944: basic training and the death of his father. In quick succession after that, Billy is sent to Europe, is cut off from his unit, is taken prisoner by the Germans, and becomes a survivor of the fire-bombing of Dresden. Three years later, after the war and during his last year in optometry school, Billy breaks down and commits himself to a veterans' hospital. While in the hospital, he reads Kilgore Trout's science fiction novel *The Big Board*, "about an Earthling man and woman who were kidnaped by extraterrestrials" and "put on display in a zoo on a planet called Zircon-212" (p. 174). The seeds for the space-travel elements of Billy's fantasy, then, were planted as early as 1948, twenty years before Billy communicates the fantasy to anyone else (in the actual telling, Vonnegut withholds the information until the end of the novel).

Billy is released from the hospital, marries the daughter of the school founder and president, and, for eighteen years, lives an exemplary suburban life. He makes lots of money, invests his money wisely, owns a Cadillac that exhibits ultra-conservative bumper-stickers, attends Little League banquets, becomes an important member of the Lions Club, is unfaithful to his wife (but only once), and raises two children he really does not know or understand. On the night of his eighteenth wedding anniversary, however, the war returns to Billy's consciousness. In the middle of the hilarity of the celebration, he associates the optometrists' barbershop quartet with the four German guards who survived the fire-bombing of Dresden along with the American prisoners. Billy reacts to the memory called up by this association by having what seems to be a cardiac seizure. Kilgore Trout, whom Billy had accidentally met a few days earlier and had invited to the party, speculates that Billy has seen the past or the future through a time window. Billy denies it, but since he has seen the past, the time-travel element of his fantasy has been added to the idea of being kidnapped by extraterrestrials. The entire incident is given authorial support by being described in novelistic past tense, not as one of Billy's travels in time.[5]

After the anniversary party, Billy's world begins to crumble. He falls asleep in his office while taking care of his patients; he cannot care about the future of European optometry; the scene of a riot in Ilium's black ghetto frightens him and the scene of Ilium's attempt at urban renewal seems more desolate than Dresden; a pro-Vietnam war speaker at the Lions Club leaves him unmoved, although his own son is a Green Beret; seeing two cripples working a racket depresses him; and the loneliness of his house causes him to weep. Indeed, as only his doctor knows, "every so often, for no apparent reason, Billy Pilgrim would find himself weeping" (p. 53). This first stage of his breakdown climaxes in the absolute emptiness he feels on the night after his daughter's wedding—the night on which he chooses to be abducted by the Tralfamadorians.

Three earlier scenes help explain this emptiness; each relates to old age, and two are clearly associated with war. In 1965 his mother, recuperating from pneumonia in a nursing home, had asked him, "How did I get so *old*" (p. 38)—associated with the war because Billy thumbs through *The Execution of Private Slovik* a few minutes later in the waiting room. When he was sixteen, a man suffering horribly from gas had told him, "I knew it was going to be bad getting old. . . . I didn't know it was going to be *this* bad" (p. 163)—associated with the war because it is recalled while Billy is in bed next to Bertram Copeland Rumfoord, the official historian of the Air Force, and is discussing the bombing of Dresden. Finally, on one of the days that Billy falls asleep at the office, he notices the license plate of his Cadillac, dated 1967, and wonders: "Where have all the years gone?" (p. 49). His son a sergeant in Vietnam, his daughter married, his house empty, Billy has nothing to look forward to but old age and death—and nothing to look back to but Dresden.

Billy's collapse is completed by two accidents—when the plane taking him to a convention of optometrists crashes, killing everyone but Billy; and when his wife dies of carbon monoxide poisoning after rushing to see him in the hospital. The plane crash is associated with Dresden in a number of ways. The barbershop quartet from the anniversary party is singing just before the plane goes down—although Vonnegut obscures the connection by having the crash precede the party in the telling. Rumfoord, the military historian, is in the bed next to Billy. When the Austrian ski instructors from Sugarbush are bending over Billy, he whispers "Schlachthoffünf"—slaughterhouse-five—his address in Dresden. Finally, he is again a survivor.

Soon after his release from the hospital, Billy, possibly suffering the aftereffects of a broken skull, sneaks off to New York City to communicate his time theory and its source to the world. Before he can get on a talk show, however, he wanders into a bookstore that specializes in pornography and thumbs through two books by Kilgore Trout—including the one about being kidnapped by extraterrestrials that he had read years earlier in the veterans' hospital. He also sees a girly magazine with the headline, "What really became of Montana Wildhack" (p. 176) and part of a blue movie that Montana had made as a teenager. The fantasy is now complete. The clearest indication that Vonnegut means us to see it as fantasy is his use of the same phrases, with the pronouns made singular in the second instance, to describe the photographs of

Montana in the girly magazine and the photograph of Montana's mother on her locket, which Billy says he sees in the zoo on Tralfamadore: "They were grainy things, soot and chalk. They could have been anybody" (pp. 177, 180). Significantly, the message on the other side of the locket is the same as the prayer on the wall of Billy's office: "God grant me the serenity to accept the things I cannot change, courage to change the things I can, and wisdom always to tell the difference" (pp. 181, 52). It is clear at this point that all the significant details of Billy's life on Tralfamadore have sources in Billy's life here on Earth.

That night, Billy tells about Tralfamadore on a radio talk show. A month later, he writes a letter about Tralfamadore to the Ilium *News Leader* and is working on a second when his daughter interrupts him. A few days after that, he tries to comfort a boy whose father has been killed in Vietnam by telling him the Tralfamadorian's theory about death. The chronology ends with Billy's daughter taking him home and saying: "Father, Father, Father—what *are* we going to *do* with you?" (p. 117). The chronology ends, that is, if we do not include Billy's time-travel version of his death in 1976.

Billy is happy at the end of the novel, no matter what his daughter thinks. Significantly, however, the time-travel elements of his fantasy—those flash-forwards based on historical fact—bring Billy no peace at all. They cause that stage fright he feels at never knowing "what part of his life he is going to have to act in next" (p. 20). They are, then, an excellent metaphor for a man's inability to keep the horrible experiences of his past from invading the relative serenity of his present. They are more frightening in Vonnegut's version because the earlier experiences are not just remembered; they are *relived*. The space-travel to Tralfamadore and what Billy learns there about time provide him with a framework in which he can make peace with both the horrors of his past and the horrors of his impending old age, and in which his entire life has meaning—a framework that neither reality nor the time-travel elements alone could provide. Instead of a lost, little man whose life is empty and filled with horror, Billy becomes a saviour, "prescribing corrective lenses for Earthling souls" (p. 25). As a prophet of the Tralfamadorian "way," Billy can now foresee a life that has direction and significant meaning—and he can foresee a martyr's death that is completely antithetical to the painful meaninglessness of his mother in the nursing home and the old man afflicted with gas. These saviour elements of Billy's fantasy also have their source in his actual experience: the "ghastly crucifix" on his wall (p. 33) and Kilgore Trout's novel about a time-traveler who wants to see Jesus (pp. 174-176).

If Billy were an actual person, not a literary character, we could say that his resigned "so it goes," the leit-motif of the novel, is earned at a price terrible enough to be psychologically consistent with the horror of Billy's experiences. The only way he can live with his memories of the past and his fear of the future and find meaning in both is to withdraw from reality into a pleasant but neurotic fantasy. Vonnegut's restructuring of the chronological sequence prolongs our confusion about what is going on until the end of the novel and allows us to see in a single moment of insight—the scene in the bookstore—exactly what Dresden has done to Billy. This ending has a potentially enormous emotional impact.

The restructuring also gives Vonnegut an opportunity for some biting ironic juxtapositions that bring the war scenes and the suburban scenes into the same complex of influences on Billy's life and help explain the total emptiness that drives him away from reality. Billy packed into an orange and black cattle car in 1944, for example, flashes forward to his daughter's wedding in 1967, which takes place under an orange and black tent. How different are the two events and yet how similar—dehumanized flesh markets in Halloween colors. Or totally powerless Billy, about to be thrashed by Roland Weary, flashes forward to Billy the self-assured optometrist, about to speak as president of the Lions Club. Which is the real Billy? How self-assured can Billy the president be when he is built upon Billy the soldier?

Other juxtapositions relate causes and effects or problems and possible solutions. In the middle of the cattle-car episodes, we flash forward to Billy's malaise in 1967. The intensity of the experience is different in each incident, but Billy is equally unwanted and powerless in both. In the middle of the prison camp episode, which describes the further dehumanization of the American prisoners in ironic contrast to the fraternity heroics of the British officers, Billy flashes forward to the veterans' hospital and his honeymoon, episodes in which we see his first withdrawal from reality in ironic contrast to both his mother's and his wife's inability to understand what he has been through in Dresden.

In short, Billy's fantasy provides him with a hard-won escape from the horrors of death—both the violent death of Dresden and the natural death that he faces in the future—and from the moral responsibility of having to do something about war, his meaningless existence, the generation gap, ghetto riots, cripples who work magazine rackets, and so on. In the next section, we shall see exactly how pervasive the escape theme is in *Slaughterhouse-Five* and in the last section we shall examine Vonnegut's relation to Billy's fantasy.

II

Billy Pilgrim's withdrawal from reality is not a random one. Its pattern is obscured by Vonnegut's restructuring of the chronological sequence but becomes obvious when we take the Tralfamadorians' advice and look at only the pleasant moments in Billy's life. Oddly, Billy's most pleasant moments include the potentially terrifying incidents in which he is dropped into a pool by his father, is crammed into a cattle car with other prisoners of war, is stripped and scalded in a delousing station, is carried through Dresden after the bombing, and then is kidnapped by creatures that resemble green machines and displayed in a zoo. As we shall see, the pattern is almost the same in all of these incidents: completely passive Billy is placed in a situation that is pleasant because it provides all the necessities of life and precludes anxiety but then is jolted back into reality.

Two of the incidents are very simple and indicate the direction of the entire group. At first, Billy's plunge into the pool is "like an execution," but then it changes:

> When he opened his eyes, he was on the bottom of the pool, and there was beautiful music everywhere. He lost consciousness, but the music went on. He dimly sensed that somebody was rescuing him. Billy resented that. (p. 38)

The scalding water of the delousing station brings on a flashback of Billy being bathed by his mother, but his gurgling and cooing is then interrupted by a flash-forward of Billy playing golf and Billy being told that he is "trapped in another blob of amber" and has no free will (p. 74). In both incidents, Billy accepts the lure of infancy but is propelled back into adulthood.

The cattle car and the horse-cart take Billy back from infancy into the womb itself. Each cattle car

> became a single organism which ate and drank and excreted through its ventilators. It talked or sometimes yelled through its ventilators too. In went water and loaves of blackbread and sausage and cheese, and out came shit and piss and language. (p. 61)

But the womb of the cattle car is pleasant: "When food came in, the human beings were quiet and trusting and beautiful. They shared" (p. 61). Later, Billy is delivered from the car and must face the horrors that await him.

The destruction of Dresden and its aftermath constitute the most complex example of this pattern. The American soldiers, who have been herded about like children and who have survived by eating syrup, are saved from the fire-bombing because they are being kept deep in the basement of a concrete slaughterhouse. A few days later, Billy is sleeping in the back of a "coffin-shaped green wagon. . . . He was happy. He was warm. There was food in the wagon, and wine . . ." (p. 167). We are told that this ride was Billy's "happiest moment" (p. 168). Complete with Billy's own tears and blood dripping from the horse's mouth, Billy is delivered from the wagon-coffin-womb by two obstetricians (p. 170). Once again, Billy is reborn from a womb-like, pleasant death (the obstetricians look at the suffering of the horse as they would have looked at Christ being taken down from the cross) not into paradise but into a life that is filled with the horrors of actual death.

If Billy's escape from the horrors of reality is ultimately unsuccessful in each of these actual incidents, the final escape—into the fantasy of the zoo on Tralfamadore—is completely successful. The zoo is a geodesic dome that contains a simulated Earth environment, including a lounge chair which had been Billy's "cradle during his trip through space" (p. 96). Billy is appropriately naked within his geodesic womb; the necessities of life are provided by the Tralfamadorians; and Billy can not escape even if he wants to: "the atmosphere outside the dome was cyanide, and Earth was 446,120,000,000,000,000 miles away" (p. 97). While in the zoo, Billy is indoctrinated with the Tralfamadorians' theories, which seem designed to free him from his anxieties:

> On other days we have wars as horrible as you've ever seen or read about. There isn't anything we can do about them, so we simply don't look at them. We ignore them. We spend eternity looking at pleasant moments— like today at the zoo. (p. 101)

But Billy is not alone on Tralfamadore. He is mated with Montana Wildhack, a pleasant, buxom, movie starlet with a jaded past. Why is Montana in the fantasy at all? The easiest answer is simply that Montana has apparently always lived her life in accordance with the prayer on Billy's wall. She accepts what she cannot change and adapts to her condition whether she is making pornographic movies, living high in Hollywood as a starlet, or being held prisoner in a zoo on Tralfamadore. She can be seen, then, as something of a contrast to Billy and we may take the contrast on its own terms or see it as a terrible irony: only mindless movie starlets can be happy in this world.

Montana as part of the general environment on Tralfamadore, however, is a contrast of another kind as well. She is a twenty-year-old movie star whose naked body reminds Billy of the "fantastic architecture in Dresden, before it was bombed" (p. 115). In spite of the disparity in their ages and in physical attractiveness—Billy is "shaped like a bottle of Coca Cola" (p. 20)—Montana "came to love and trust Billy Pilgrim" (p. 115). Their first lovemaking was "heavenly." Further, she is a great contrast to Valencia, Billy's wife—who had been pleasant, but fat and ugly—and to Barbara, Billy's daughter—who is not much older than Montana but who is described as a "bitchy flibbertigibbet" (p. 25) who takes Billy's "dignity away in the name of love" (p. 114). Montana—the big-breasted, yielding, ideal woman of adolescent masturbation fantasies—supplements the Tralfamadorians' theories as a defense against Billy's feelings of impotence and his fear of death.

The frequent references to Eden indicate that, on one level, we are meant to take Billy and Montana as another Adam and Eve. Eden myths, however, frequently mask and attempt to dignify escapist, regressive fantasies of the kind we have been discussing here. Significantly, just before he is kidnapped, Billy is watching a war movie on television that moves backwards from the landing of a decimated squadron in England after a bombing raid. Billy sees bullets being sucked out of planes and bombs returning from the ground into the bellies of the planes. Finally, in Billy's imagination, "everybody turned into a baby, and all humanity, without exception, conspired biologically, to produce two perfect people named Adam and Eve" (pp. 64-65). This backwards movie may be one of Vonnegut's gems in the novel but it also indicates the function of the Eden imagery and its relation to the womb imagery. In the long run, Eden and the womb seem identical—places of retreat beyond which Billy cannot regress.

Billy Pilgrim, Vonnegut's everyman-schlemiel-hero, reacts to the horrors of the world around him by withdrawing totally from reality. Billy is not merely an ostrich who hides his head in the pleasant moments of his past rather than facing the difficulties of the present and the future; but one who crawls back into the egg itself. It remains to be seen how Kurt Vonnegut—at least the Kurt Vonnegut of the first and last chapters—views this defensive behavior.

III

In one sense, the first chapter of *Slaughterhouse-Five* is an overture that introduces themes, characters, and certain verbal snatches that will reappear in Billy's part of the novel. The most significant parallel between the two parts, of course, is between Vonnegut's and Billy's war experiences in Dresden; but there are many others. Roland Weary, for example, the trench-knife-carrying sadist who tries to kill Billy when they are captured by the Germans, is previewed by the newspaperwoman who tells Vonnegut to "get a statement" from the wife of a veteran who has just been crushed to death by an elevator. Vonnegut underscores the parallel by showing us the newspaperwoman eating a "Three Musketeers Candy Bar" (p. 8)—a clear reference to Weary's idealized relationship to the two scouts with whom he and Billy are caught behind the lines. Another parallel is between Rumfoord, the historian and apologist for the Air Force who has no combat experience, and Vonnegut's boss at G.E., who "had been a lieutenant colonel in public relations in Baltimore" (p. 9).

The first chapter of *Slaughterhouse-Five* also creates a clear image of the implied author of the novel—the image of himself that Kurt Vonnegut wants the reader to have before he describes the experiences of Billy Pilgrim. This implied Kurt Vonnegut reappears in his own voice at the beginning of the last chapter and makes at least two authorial intrusions into the war experiences of Billy to assert that he, Kurt Vonnegut, had been there too (pp. 58, 129). The presentation of Vonnegut in his own voice and the parallels between Vonnegut's and Billy's experiences, although risking further muddying of narrative distance, serve two important functions. First, since Vonnegut is not Billy Pilgrim but has experienced what Billy has, the Vonnegut of the first and last chapters offers the reader an alternative way of reacting to common experiences. Second, and more important, the Vonnegut of the first chapter creates attitudinal norms by which we are to judge Billy's experience.

The central incident of the first chapter is Vonnegut's meeting with Bernard V. O'Hare, his old war buddy, and with O'Hare's wife, Mary. Although Mary is neither a bitch, like Billy's daughter, nor a vegetable, like Billy's wife, she effectively destroys—not Vonnegut's dignity, but Vonnegut's male image of "two leather chairs near a fire in a paneled room where two old soldiers could drink and talk." Instead of the paneled room, "Mary had prepared an operating room" (p. 11). Mary's indignation against war is powerful and sincere:

You'll pretend you were men instead of babies, and you'll be played in the movies by Frank Sinatra and John Wayne or some of those other glamorous war-loving, dirty old men. And war will look just wonderful, so we'll have a lot more of them. And they'll be fought by babies like the babies upstairs. (p. 13)

Vonnegut promises that his book will not have a part in it for John Wayne and says that he will call it "The Children's Crusade"—which becomes the subtitle of *Slaughterhouse-Five*. A discussion of the actual Children's Crusade of the Thirteenth Century follows, in which a clear distinction between history and romance is made that parallels Mary's distinction between babies and men, and that parallels the split in Billy's experience between reality and fantasy. Nevertheless, knowledge of these distinctions does not lead to the kind of action that Vonnegut's anti-war critics demand. Rather, it leads to the resignation of "so it goes."

Mary O'Hare's indignation is bracketed by two passages that emphasize this reading. The first describes Harrison Starr's reaction to an anti-novel:

"I say, 'Why don't you write an anti-glacier book instead?'"
What he meant, of course, was that there would always be wars, that they were as easy to stop as glaciers.

More significant than Vonnegut's agreement with Starr is the comment that follows—placed in a paragraph by itself. "And, even if wars didn't keep coming like glaciers, there would still be plain old death" (p. 3).

The second passage, quoted from Erika Ostrovsky's *Céline and His Vision*, elevates plain old death into truth. For Céline, "No art is possible without a dance with death" (p. 18)—and "A Duty-Dance with Death" becomes the second subtitle of *Slaughterhouse-Five*. Vonnegut's implication, in spite of his own indignation at war, seems to be that there is no life, as well as no art, without a dance with death—an implication that is emphasized by Billy's fear of his own old age and death as well as by the leit-motif of "so it goes," which is a response, specifically, to death.

The final chapter of the novel begins with the following paragraphs:

Robert Kennedy, whose summer home is eight miles from the home I live in all year round, was shot two nights ago. He died last night. So it goes.
Martin Luther King was shot a month ago. He died too. So it goes. My father died many years ago now—of natural causes. So it goes. He was a sweet man. He was a gun nut, too. He left me his guns. They rust. (p. 182)

Vonnegut knows the horrors as well as Mary O'Hare, but he answers the moral indignation of his critics with the paradox of his father: "He was a sweet man. He was a gun nut, too." Billy Pilgrim retreats into wish-fulfilling fantasy—the romance of the crusades; Vonnegut, at least, lets the guns rust. There may not be a part in *Slaughterhouse-Five* for John Wayne; Vonnegut may train his sons to avoid taking part in massacres (p. 17); Mary O'Hare's indignation may move us—but the paradox of human nature remains. "*Eheu, fugaces labuntur anni*. My name is Yon Yonson. There was a young man from Stamboul" (p. 10).

Slaughterhouse-Five ends with a demonstration of Billy Pilgrim following the Tralfamadorians' advice. Instead of showing us the Maori's physical disgust at the dead bodies in the ruins of Dresden or the senseless execution of Edgar Derby, the novel's final scene begins a retelling of Billy's paradisiacal ride through the streets of Dresden— the happiest moment of his life. More rational than Billy and more aware of the horrors of life and death, Kurt Vonnegut—at least the implied Kurt Vonnegut of *Slaughterhouse-Five*—might nevertheless agree with the Tralfamadorians. After seeing the New York World's Fair's version of the future, Vonnegut asks himself "about the present: how wide it was, how deep it was, how much was mine to keep" (p. 16). Billy and Vonnegut, finally, in spite of narrative distance, are one.

As human beings, we may—perhaps must—ask ourselves whether or not Vonnegut's response to World War II and to the chaotic Nineteen-Sixties is adequate, but the standards with which our judgment will be made are extra-literary. Politically, Vonnegut's solution may not get us anywhere, perhaps because it is based on a resigned and pessimistic, although loving, view of human nature; psychologically, like the solution implied in so many other American novels, it attempts to deny the responsibilities of adulthood by escaping into a pre-sexual, pre-fall past. Nevertheless, as readers, we must recognize that *Slaughterhouse-Five* makes eloquent sense within its own aesthetic limits. Our objections, if any, are to the limits, not to Vonnegut's achievement within them.

From *College Literature* 1, no. 2 (Spring 1974): 128-139. Copyright © 1974 by *College Literature*. Reprinted with permission of *College Literature*.

Notes

1. Jack Richardson, "Easy Writer," *The New York Review of Books* (2 July 1970) p. 8; Benjamin DeMott, "Vonnegut's Otherworldly Laughter," *Saturday Review* (1 May 1971) p. 29.

2. All parenthetical references are to Kurt Vonnegut, Jr., *Slaughterhouse-Five* (New York; Delta, 1969).

3. Italics mine.

4. Italics mine.

5. I am indebted to Philip Damon for pointing out that Vonnegut's command of his chronology breaks down here. He tells us that Billy meets Trout "for the first time in 1964" (p. 142) and that "Billy invited Trout to his eighteenth wedding anniversary which was only two days hence" (p. 146). But if Billy marries Valencia after his time in the veterans' hospital (1948), then the eighteenth wedding anniversary should take place in 1966, not 1964. A similar two-year confusion occurs in Vonnegut's statements about Billy's age.

The Arbitrary Cycle of *Slaughterhouse-Five*:
A Relation of Form to Theme_____

Wayne D. McGinnis

Surely the biggest question asked in Kurt Vonnegut, Jr.'s fiction—
and asked almost consistently in his novels—is one patently unanswerable from without: "What is the purpose of life?" Like any good existentialist, Vonnegut, putting himself in league with writers like Barth
and Borges, finally answers the question by affirming that man must
arbitrarily make his own purpose. The real interest for the writer of fiction in *how* the purpose is made has resulted in an emphasis on the skill
and intricacy involved in the process in both Vonnegut's *fiction* and
that of his contemporaries who take the view of the arbitrary nature of
fiction itself. Today, many of the best writers are indeed writing about
art, primarily. *Slaughterhouse-Five*, Vonnegut's major achievement, is
essentially different from Nabokov's *Pale Fire* or Borges's *ficciones*,
however, because it insists on both the world of fiction or fantasy
(Tralfamadore) and the world of brutal fact (Dresden). Vonnegut's
novel urges the primacy of the imagination in the very act of facing one
of history's most infamous "massacres," the fire-bombing of Dresden
in World War II, the source of its great originality.

The poignancy and force of *Slaughterhouse-Five* derive largely from
an attitude about art and life that Vonnegut apparently shares with Louis-
Ferdinand Céline, whom he quotes in the first chapter as saying two
things: "No art is possible without a dance with death" and "the truth is
death."[1] Taking his cue from Céline, Vonnegut calls his novel A DUTY-
DANCE WITH DEATH on the title page. Ultimately, however, *Slaughterhouse-Five* goes beyond the fatalism implied in Céline's statements
by stressing survival through the use of the imagination. Vonnegut has
said that the novel "was a therapeutic thing. I'm a different person now.
I got rid of a lot of crap."[2] Although strikingly similar to Lawrence's notion that "one sheds one's sicknesses in books," the important thing is to
go on, to escape the paralyzing emotional rigidity that can turn one into

a pillar of salt. The ability to go on, to escape fixity by motion in time is precisely what *Slaughterhouse-Five* is about, and its success comes from being able to effect a regeneration in reader as well as writer.

In keeping with the theme of regeneration, the form of the novel avoids the climax and denouement typical of linear narration, as indicated by Vonnegut's rejection of the grid-like outline of the story he proposes in the first chapter, with its climax at Edgar Derby's execution for taking a teapot and its ending in a POW trade made after the destruction of Dresden. Essentially, Vonnegut avoids *framing* his story in linear narration, choosing a circular structure. Such a view of the art of the novel has much to do with the protagonist of *Slaughterhouse-Five*, the author's alter ego, Billy Pilgrim, an optometrist who provides corrective lenses for Earthlings. For Pilgrim, who learns of a new view of life as he becomes "unstuck in time," the lenses are corrective metaphorically as well as physically. Quite early in the exploration of Billy's life the reader learns that "frames are where the money is" (21), a statement which has its metaphorical equivalent, too, and helps to explain why Vonnegut chose a non-linear structure for his novel. Historical events like the bombing of Dresden are usually "read" in the framework of moral and historical interpretation. Such is the viewpoint of the several documentary works mentioned in the novel, most significantly including Harry Truman's announcement that an atomic bomb had been dropped on Hiroshima and David Irving's *The Destruction of Dresden*, with forewords by Lt. General Ira C. Eaker and Air Marshal Sir Robert Saundby. The Truman speech and Eaker's foreword attempt to explain historical events within the framework of war priorities, and both are rather frightening within the context of *Slaughterhouse-Five*.

Vonnegut's decision to cast his Dresden experience in a "nonexplainable" work of the imagination ("I don't know how people explain the imagination, anyway. My books are protests against explanations."[3]) is a movement away from framing and toward a more unresolved circular structure. Vonnegut supplies strong hints of the circular nature of *Slaughterhouse-Five* in Chapter One. He is reminded, he says, of a particular song when he thinks of "how useless the Dresden part of my memory has been, and yet how tempting Dresden has been to write about":

> My name is Yon Yonson,
> I work in Wisconsin,
> I work in a lumbermill there.
> The people I meet when I walk down the street,
> They say, What's your name?
> And I say,
> "My name is Yon Yonson,
> I work in Wisconsin . . ."

And so on to infinity. (2-3)

Vonnegut's own life (and memory) is a model of the Yon Yonson cycle: "And [our babies] are all grown up now, and I'm an old fart with his memories and his Pall Malls. My name is Yon Yonson. I work in Wisconsin, I work in a lumbermill there" (6). The message of the song is that life is cyclical, self-renewable—at least part of the implication of Roethke's "The Waking," the first stanza of which Vonnegut quotes in Chapter One. The paradox of the villanelle (a form which, through complexity and artificiality, should give an impression of simplicity and spontaneity, like *Slaughterhouse-Five* itself) is its circularity, both in form and content. Vonnegut invokes the same sort of circularity when he begins the fictional part of his novel by writing at the end of the first chapter,

> This book is a failure, and had to be, since it was written by a pillar of salt. It begins like this:
> > *Listen*:
> > Billy Pilgrim has come unstuck in time.
> > It ends like this:
> > Poo-tee-weet? (19)

The rather strange preamble, then, helps to create the essentially cyclical nature of the novel, for here we have beginning and end in one place, the cycle completed in a small space.

The cyclical nature is inextricably bound up with the large themes of *Slaughterhouse-Five*, time, death, and renewal. Once again, the first chapter, the autobiographical one, prepares the reader for the full exploration of these themes in the novel itself. Vonnegut uses Céline to start two of the themes when he writes,

> Time obsessed him. Miss Ostrovsky [author of *Céline and His Vision*] reminded me of the amazing scene in *Death on the Installment Plan* where Céline wants to stop the bustling of a street crowd [end of Chapter 123]. He screams on paper, *Make them stop. . . . don't let them move anymore at all. . . . There, make them freeze. . . . once and for all! . . . So that they won't disappear anymore!* (19)

In Céline's novel—and persistently in his other works—time means change and is, obviously, equivalent to death: hence, the title, *Death on the Installment Plan*. What Céline would have as an antidote in the passage Vonnegut quotes is fixity, which would prevent the flow of time and the constant encroachment of death. The agonizing paradox here, of course, is that fixity or rigidity is also associated with death. Lot's wife is punished for looking back on the burning cities of Sodom and Gomorrah with death, the rigidity of a pillar of salt. While Vonnegut loves Lot's wife for looking back "because it was so human," obviously he, like anyone desiring life, wants not to be rigid. Stopping the flow of time is at once a solution and no solution.

The Tralfamadorian answer to the problem is hinted at from the very first page. After telling of the German taxicab driver, Gerhard Mueller, whose mother "was incinerated in the Dresden fire-storm," Vonnegut begins what will be a persistent refrain throughout the novel, the phrase "so it goes." The reader does not know until the second chapter, however, that this is what the Tralfamadorians, those mythical creatures who live on a distant planet in Billy Pilgrim's mind, say about dead people. The philosophy of Tralfamadore on time and death, as Billy explains it, is an escape from the concept of linear time, just as their novels are an escape from linear narration:

> The most important thing I learned on Tralfamadore was that when a person dies he only *appears* to die. He is still very much alive in the past, so it is very silly for people to cry at his funeral. All moments, past, present, and future, always have existed, always will exist. The Tralfamadorians can look at all the different moments just the way we can look at a stretch of the Rocky Mountains, for instance. They can see how permanent all the moments are, and they can look at any moment that interests them. It is just an illusion we have here on Earth that one moment follows another one, like beads on a string, and that once a moment is gone it is gone forever. (23)

The Tralfamadorians, then, avoid the "duty-dance with death" by ignoring death as a finality. Their little formula "so it goes," said ritualistically throughout the novel whenever any death, no matter how trivial, is mentioned, is, from the human point of view, the height of fatalism. The most important function of "so it goes," however, is its imparting a cyclical quality to the novel, both in form and content. Paradoxically, the expression of fatalism serves as a source of renewal, a situation typical of Vonnegut's works, for it enables the novel to *go on* despite—even because of—the proliferation of deaths. Once again we come upon a paradox: death keeps life in motion, even the life of the novel, but the movement is essentially unaided in Vonnegut's silent universe. As he emphasizes in *The Sirens of Titan*, beyond man's interior universe is only the emptiness of space eternal. In a world where life must renew itself arbitrarily, the mental construct becomes tremendously important. The phrase "so it goes" is a sign of the human will to survive, and it recurs throughout the novel as an important aid to *going on*.

Vonnegut's fiction deals heavily with survival by the arbitrary imposition of meaning on meaningless reality, as demonstrated most force-fully in *Cat's Cradle*. Tralfamadore is another mental construct, like Bokononism, that goes beyond the question of true or false. As Eliot Rosewater says in *Slaughterhouse-Five* to the psychiatrists: "I think you guys are going to have to come up with a lot of wonderful *new* lies, or people just aren't going to want to go on living" (87-8). The statement is certainly a clue to the meaning of Tralfamadore, since it comes right af-ter the statement that Rosewater and Billy had found life meaningless, partly because of what they had seen in the war: "So they were trying to re-invent themselves and their universe. Science fiction was a big help." Vonnegut lets us know that an act of re-invention is going on within the novel, just as the novel is Vonnegut's own re-creation of his past and even of his other novels. Mental constructs like Bokononism and Tralfamadore, both re-inventive fictions, are models of Vonnegut's own fiction, throughout which one can see the pattern of meaninglessness/re-invention.[4]

That Tralfamadore is ultimately a "supreme fiction," a product of the imagination, and that Vonnegut emphasizes using the imagination as a method of survival are obvious from his preoccupation with the value of works of art, especially in the novels from *Cat's Cradle* on. (A work of art even plays a pivotal role in *Breakfast of Champions*.) Espe-cially interesting is Vonnegut's source for his idea of Tralfamadore; ev-idence shows that, characteristically, Vonnegut was inspired by modern science in creating his fiction. Shortly after *Slaughterhouse-Five* was published, Vonnegut wrote an article in which he quotes from another book arranged along the lines of a trip into space, Guy Murchie's popu-larization of the great body of science, *Music of the Spheres*. In his arti-cle Vonnegut writes, "I had lifted a comment Murchie made about time for a book of my own."[5] (The book must surely be *Slaughterhouse-Five*.) The quotation from Murchie that Vonnegut cites occurs at the end of "Of Space, Of Time," a chapter on relativity—the part deleted by Vonnegut is placed in brackets:

I sometimes wonder whether humanity has missed the real point in raising the issue of mortality and immortality [—whether perhaps the seemingly limited time span of an earthly life is actually unlimited and eternal—] in other words, whether mortality itself may be a finite illusion, being actually immortality and, even though constructed of just a few "years," that those few years are all the time there really is, so that, in fact, they can never cease.[6]

Although Vonnegut does not quote further, Murchie goes on to ask, "Indeed, if time is the relation between things and themselves, how can time end while things exist? Or how can time have ever begun, since either a beginning or an end would logically and almost inevitably frame time in more of itself?"

Vonnegut, then, is apparently trying to get away from "framing" in *Slaughterhouse-Five* by means of circularity. Both the Tralfamadorian concept of time and the Murchie passage from which it is probably lifted imply a kind of cyclical "return,"[7] though, of course, Billy Pilgrim's *movement* in time embodies this return, rather than the Tralfamadorian idea of fixity expressed by the mountain range image. The Murchie comment seems to echo the idea of eternal recurrence that Nietzsche propounded in *Thus Spake Zarathustra*, without, of course, the Nietzschean will to improvement. A colloquy in the Third Part between Zarathustra and his "dwarf" concerns the nature of time:

"Behold this gateway, dwarf!" I continued. "It has two faces. Two paths meet here; no one has yet followed either to its end. This long lane stretches back for an eternity. And the long lane out there, that is another eternity. They contradict each other, these paths, they offend each other face to face; and it is here at this gateway that they come together. The name of the gateway is inscribed above: 'Moment.' But whoever would follow one of them, on and on, farther and farther—do you believe, dwarf, that these paths contradict each other eternally?"

"All that is straight lies," the dwarf murmured contemptuously. "All truth is crooked; time itself is a circle."[8]

Time as a circle is eternal, timeless. The location of the circle is in the human mind, which is where Zarathustra's eternal return to the self-same life ultimately occurs. As Frederick Hoffman has written, "Perhaps the most remarkable of all speculative adventures in the history of man's adjustment to death is his struggle to understand the paradoxical relationship of time to eternity."[9] Nietzsche's great imaginative "solution" was the myth of eternal recurrence, a myth which sought to answer what Hoffman calls "the last paradox of self-assertion: the effort to make aspects of mortality seem or even validly be guarantors of 'immortality.' Death is either annihilation or it is the 'mother of beauty,' the ultimate challenge to the imagination, that it make as much as it can of the threat of impermanence" (320-1).

What Nietzsche proposed as part of his world view is the nature of the cycle. Billy Pilgrim, too, is engaged in a quest to make mortality (which he knows so well from Dresden) a guarantor of immortality; at least he has an affinity with the philosopher in believing that death is the ultimate challenge to the imagination. He essentially experiences circularity when he goes from life to death to life and then back to pre-birth in the novel; we are told that when he first became unstuck in time,

His attention began to swing grandly through the full arc of his life, passing into death, which was violet light. There wasn't anybody else there, or anything. There was just violet light—and a hum.

And then Billy swung into life again, going backwards until he was in pre-birth, which was red light and bubbling sounds. (37)

Circularity is what Billy also affirms when, having "memories of the future," he talks of his own death while preaching his Tralfamadorian gospel: "'If you protest, if you think that death is a terrible thing, then you have not understood a word I've said.' Now he closes his speech as he closes every speech—with these words: 'Farewell, hello, farewell, hello'" (123). His little ritual manifests the ever present possibility of renewal through the imagination.

The Tralfamadorian concept of time, with the suggestion of cyclical return embodied in Billy's time travels, reflects the fact that timelessness is a product of the irrational, the unconscious, the imagination itself. Although we might be tempted to see *Slaughterhouse-Five* as a "plotless" novel allied to the stream of consciousness novel, Billy's psyche is not as fully explored as, say, Mrs. Dalloway's or Benjy Compson's, for he is too effaced and manipulated by the author to have the kind of independent being required for the stream of consciousness novel. While *Slaughterhouse-Five* cannot fully employ the stream of consciousness technique because it simply does not deal with the internal psychic processes of a fully developed character, it does make a secondary use of the technique by providing certain signals to help predict time and space shifts in the "durational" world of the novel. Among these images or attitudes are feet of blue and ivory, the black and orange color of a POW train, nestling like spoons, sleeping and waking, and having tears in the eyes. With the use of these signals the reader gets a strong feeling that Billy's time travels are manipulated from outside—by Vonnegut. As the narrator rather mockingly says of Billy's becoming unstuck in time, "He has seen his birth and death many times, he says, and pays random visits to all the events in between. He says. Billy is spastic in time, has no control over where he is going next, and the trips aren't necessarily fun" (20). The idea of being "spastic" captures the immediate quality of Billy's travels in the regenerative cycle.

The novel seems, indeed, allied not so much to stream of consciousness or any novelistic tradition as it is to the Tralfamadorian novel which is invented by Vonnegut-Pilgrim. Part of the description on the title page of *Slaughterhouse-Five* states that THIS IS A NOVEL SOMEWHAT IN THE TELEGRAPHIC SCHIZOPHRENIC MANNER OF TALES OF THE PLANET TRALFAMADORE. Billy has the Tralfamadorian novel explained to him when he observes that its arrangement of "brief clumps of symbols separated by stars" suggests a telegram:

There are no telegrams on Tralfamadore. But you're right: each clump of symbols is a brief, urgent message—describing a situation, a scene. We Tralfamadorians read them all at once, not one after the other. There isn't any particular relationship between all the messages, except that the author has chosen them carefully, so that, when seen all at once, they produce an image of life that is beautiful and surprising and deep. There is no beginning, no middle, no end, no suspense, no moral, no causes, no effects. What we love in our books are the depths of many marvelous moments seen all at one time. (76)

The Tralfamadorian novel is arranged by space, then, and not by time, a quality that could loosely be called "cinematic." Here again we see that *Slaughterhouse-Five* has at least an affinity with the stream of consciousness novel, which, as Robert Humphrey has noted, often employs cinematic devices, such as montage:

Among the secondary devices are such controls as "multiple-view," "slow-ups," "fade-outs," "cutting," "close-ups," "panorama," and "flash-backs." "Montage" in the film sense refers to a class of devices which are used to show interrelation or association of ideas, such as a rapid succession of images or the superimposition of image on image or the surrounding of a focal image by related ones. . . . The secondary techniques are methods for achieving the effect of montage; devices for overcoming the two-dimensional limitation of the screen.[10]

Humphrey goes on to explain that the analogy for fictional technique rests in the fact that "montage and the secondary devices have to do with transcending or modifying arbitrary and conventional time and space barriers," and he notes David Daiches' distinction between time-montage (subject remains fixed in space and his consciousness moves in time) and space-montage (time is fixed and the spatial element changes). Montage, then, is one of the things that take the place of plot in the stream of consciousness novel; when viewed from such perspective, *Slaughterhouse-Five* is seen to combine space- and time-montage techniques.

Actually, *Slaughterhouse-Five* is cinematic to a degree, especially in the sense described by Humphrey; it has also been made into a motion picture directed by George Roy Hill and much praised by Vonnegut himself. The montage technique, however, does not fully explain the form of the novel:

> Vonnegut books are noted for their great patches of color—blue, azure, silver, for example—which serve to sharpen the images and make the tale more vivid. A series of impressions and images are given with swift and clean cuts in and out both in *Cat's Cradle* and *Slaughterhouse-Five*. The result is a quality critic Richard Schickel called speaking specifically of *Mother Night*, "an artful, zestful cartoon." Young writers call it cinematic.
>
> Whatever it is called, Vonnegut believes a kaleidoscopic technique has limitations.
>
> "What limits you is that the reader would have to conjure up images in his head. Going too far with kaleidoscopic images would be like making hi-fi records for a very poor stereophonic set. Except for a very few people who could be quite skillful, the reader could not do what the writer would hope he could do."[11]

What is also limiting for the technique—cinematic, kaleidoscopic, or spatial-form—is the fact that at least in reading literature one can never completely experience "the depths of many marvelous moments seen all at one time." Form in literature appears, finally, to be linked with temporality, although attempts have been made to read much modern literature as atemporal. Although Joseph Frank appears to have begun something of a revolution with his ideas of "spatial form," his claim that spatialization in the major works of modern literature "eliminates any feeling of sequence by the very act of juxtaposition"[12] has not gone wholly uncontested. John Lynen, for instance, acknowledges that many critical terms like *form, structure, focus,* and *point of view* recognize spatial effects, but he offers a major reservation:

> It is true that literature *seems* to break free of chronological arrangement, and that writers can use language to conceal the movement of time, suggesting simultaneity and thus, often, an effect of spatialization. But this does not mean that a writer can in fact efface the sequential nature of literature. Words, paragraphs, events, facts do follow in sequence, and whatever fiction leads us to imagine, we encounter them in sequence as we read. . . . Because language is the medium of literature, the sequence in which the elements are presented is a necessary means of creating form.[13]

The rather simple point is that Vonnegut himself cannot really write fully in the Tralfamadorian mode, but Lynen's stress on the sequential nature of literature is relevant to *Slaughterhouse-Five.* The form created in the novel is essentially circular, not spatial or linear; because its "sequence" is that of the circle, *Slaughterhouse-Five* is a novel without climaxes, since its real subject matter and formal arrangement is renewal. In this sense it is like the Tralfamadorian novel, a novel without beginning, middle, and end, without suspense and without a moral. Like the Roethke villanelle, it learns by going where it has to go. While the Tralfamadorian style implies an indirect statement of the novel's aesthetic, the real impression one is left with is based on its form, that of continual self-renewal. That the renewal is arbitrary is the thematic point of the novel, and even the novel's circular form shares the arbitrary quality. Aside from the specific question of how Tralfamadorian *Slaughterhouse-Five* is, its echo of cinematic technique is quite loose and appears especially loose when one considers how closely other novels have reflected their formal references—the echo of the fugue in the Sirens section of *Ulysses* or the echo of musical counterpoint in *Point Counter Point*, for example. The debt of *Slaughterhouse-Five* to cinema is enough to establish a general basis for considering its cinematic technique, but not enough to say that it does more than loosely borrow from the formal pattern that film has to offer the novel. Neither does the form of *Slaughterhouse-Five* share more than a certain affinity with the technique of the stream of consciousness novel. Humphrey states that two of the ways in which stream of consciousness novels supply necessary form or pattern without the help of plot are by the formal patterns of "natural cyclical schemes (seasons, tides, etc.)" and of "theoretical cyclical schemes (musical structures, cycles of history, etc.)" (86). The cyclical scheme of *Slaughterhouse-Five*, however, is "arbitrary" in that its continual self-renewal is essentially unaided by an echo of some general outside form.

What makes self-renewal possible in *Slaughterhouse-Five* is the human imagination, which is what the novel finally celebrates. Many critics have failed to perceive how strongly the novel affirms the value of the mental construct and have attacked it either for urging passivity or being hopelessly ambiguous about the Tralfamadorian ethic—which does, of course, deny free will and support Billy's passivity. Willed action is simply not stressed in Vonnegut's fictional world. In *Breakfast of Champions*, Vonnegut finally stresses that "our awareness is all that is alive and maybe sacred in any of us. Everything else about us is dead machinery."[14] The imagination, then, beholds the immaterial core of every living thing, the "unwavering band of light" that the minimalist artist in that novel paints. Billy Pilgrim is a kind of artist, too, as Howard W. Campbell, Jr., Bokonon, and Eliot Rosewater have been before him. Like Vonnegut's other protagonists-artists, Billy must use an artistic stance to survive in a basically absurd world. As a doer Billy is ineffectual—thus, he simply drives through a burned-out ghetto, for example. Despite his lack of enthusiasm about living, Billy does go on, largely through the aid of his Tralfamadorian fiction. Neither he nor Vonnegut can change the fact of Dresden, but they both can survive it by the use of the imagination. Vonnegut's television special, "Between Time and Timbuktu," ended with a scene in heaven in which death (in the form of Hitler) fights the imagination and loses.[15] The duel represents in stark outline the great theme of Vonnegut's work.

Finally, the fixity of death at Dresden, which reduces people to "seeming little logs lying around" (154), is overcome in *Slaughterhouse-Five* by the novel's arbitrary cycle. Appropriately, the novel "ends" with a re-cycling back to the Dresden experience. Billy's liberation from his German captors is described:

> Billy and the rest wandered out onto the shady street. The trees were leafing out. There was nothing going on out there, no traffic of any kind. There was only one vehicle, an abandoned wagon drawn by two horses. The wagon was green and coffin-shaped.
>
> Birds were talking.
>
> One bird said to Billy Pilgrim, "*Poo-tee-weet?*"

Vonnegut's "famous Dresden book," then, comes to its open end with the symbol of renewal that had saved the narrator Jonah from suicide in *Cat's Cradle* and had awakened Eliot Rosewater in *God Bless You, Mr. Rosewater* to the potential of living a life of the absurd, the bird that asks, "*Poo-tee-weet?*" With the faint echo of the cycle of nature, the green and coffin-shaped wagon, we realize that the cycle itself reflects man's own nature as he experiences the regeneration of immortality in his mind. In using the idea of regeneration to integrate both theme and form, Vonnegut has written in *Slaughterhouse-Five* his best and even most hopeful novel to date.

From *Critique* 17, no. 1 (1975): 55-68. Copyright © 1975 by Heldref Publications. Reprinted with permission of Heldref Publications.

Notes

1. Kurt Vonnegut, Jr., *Slaughterhouse-Five or The Children's Crusade: A Duty-Dance with Death* (New York: Dell-Delta, 1969), p. 18. All subsequent references are to this edition.

2. Richard Todd, "The Masks of Kurt Vonnegut, Jr.," *New York Times Magazine*, 24 January 1971 , p. 17.

3. Todd, p. 26.

4. Wayne D. McGinnis, "Kurt Vonnegut, Jr.'s Confrontation with Meaninglessness," Diss. Arkansas, 1974.

5. Kurt Vonnegut, Jr., "Excelsior! We're Going to the Moon! Excelsior!" *New York Times Magazine*, 13 July 1969 , p. 11.

6. Guy Murchie, *Music of the Spheres* (Boston: Houghton Mifflin, 1961), p. 589.

7. John L. Somer, "Quick-Stasis: The Rite of Initiation in the Novels of Kurt Vonnegut, Jr.," Diss. Northern Illinois, 1971 , pp. 237, 254-7 et passim, uses the implications of the Murchie passage in a different way and mentions the idea of eternal return, although he does not make the connection with Nietzsche; indeed, he believes that "Vonnegut is not espousing a cyclical view of time." His thesis is that *Slaughterhouse-Five* argues for the creation of an "artificial" or "schizophrenic" time as part of a modern rite of initiation. Somer's argument is reprinted in substance in "Geodesic Vonnegut; or, If Buckminster Fuller Wrote Novels," in *The Vonnegut Statement*, ed. Jerome Klinkowitz and John Somer (New York: Delacorte Press/Seymour Lawrence, 1973), pp. 221-54. Vonnegut's personal philosophy on finality, expressed in speaking of the ending of his play, *Happy Birthday, Wanda June*, is interesting since it reflects both the idea of eternal recurrence and the particular form of Billy Pilgrim's time travels: "I hate endings— they are strictly technical. Nothing in this world is ever final—no one ever ends—we keep bouncing back and forth in time, we go on and on ad infinitum." (Quoted in Patricia Bosworth, "To Vonnegut, the Hero Is the Man Who Refuses to Kill," *New York Times*, 25 October 1970, sec. 2, p. 5.)

8. *The Portable Nietzsche*, trans. Walter Kaufmann (New York: Viking, 1968), pp. 269-70.

9. Frederick J. Hoffman, *The Mortal No: Death and the Modern Imagination* (Princeton: Princeton Univ. Press, 1964), p. 341.

10. Robert Humphrey, *Stream of Consciousness in the Modern Novel*, Perspectives in Criticism, 3 (Berkeley: Univ. of California Press, 1954), p. 49. Sergei Eisenstein, the inventor of montage, describes it in "The Image in Process," *The Modern Tradition: Backgrounds of Modern Literature*, ed. Richard Ellmann and Charles Feidebon, Jr. (New York: Oxford Univ. Press, 1965), pp. 167-8: "Montage has a realistic significance when the separate pieces [or shots] produce, in juxtaposition, the generality, the synthesis of one's theme. This is the image incorporating the theme." According to Eisenstein, the image is first envisioned by the creator and then is "concretized" into "a few basic partial representations which, in their combination and juxtaposition, shall evoke in the consciousness and feelings of the spectator, reader, or auditor, that same initial general image which originally hovered before the creative artist." "This," Eisenstein believes, "is actually the final aim of every artist's creative endeavor."

11. Loretta McCabe, "An Exclusive Interview with Kurt Vonnegut," *Writer's Yearbook '70*, p. 101.

12. Joseph Frank, "Spatial Forum in Modern Literature," *The Widening Gyre: Crisis and Mastery in Modern Literature* (New Brunswick: Rutgers Univ. Press, 1963), p. 59. Several critics have applied Frank's analysis of spatial form to *Slaughterhouse-Five* (see the articles by Glenn Meeter and John Somer in *The Vonnegut Statement*).

13. John F. Lynen, *The Design of the Present: Essays on Time and Form in American Literature* (New Haven: Yale Univ. Press, 1969), pp. 20-1.

14. Kurt Vonnegut, Jr., *Breakfast of Champions or Goodbye Blue Monday* (New York: Delacorte Press/Seymour Lawrence, 1973), p. 221.

15. Kurt Vonnegut, Jr., *Between Time and Timbuktu or Prometheus-5: A Space Fantasy* (New York: Dell-Delta, 1972), pp. 256-68.

The Ironic Christ Figure in *Slaughterhouse-Five*_____
Dolores K. Gros Louis

"Why are English teachers always asking us to look for the Christ figures in fiction?" is a question I've received from students more than once. The query frequently implies that teachers are reading between the lines, projecting meanings that are not in the fiction at all. The answer, usually supported if not offered by other students (the perceptive ones!), is that teachers ask students to look for the Christ figure because it is there and it is important to the author's meaning. Why is it there? First, the redeemer theme and the death-and-resurrection theme are archetypal, appearing around the world in various forms. Second, in Western culture the story of Jesus is "still the greatest story ever told, or at least, the most familiar one."[1] If the story of Jesus is still the greatest or the most familiar story, then writers may draw on it freely with the assumption that most of their readers will recognize the major parallels to the gospel story.

Novelists use the gospel story in many ways and for many different purposes. Some use it to structure their work of fiction. Some use it as an aid in characterization, either to elevate a protagonist or to deflate him by his contrast to Jesus. Others adapt the story to show how Jesus himself might exist and act in a particular modern situation. Some writers use only casual allusions and metaphors to broaden the meaning of certain incidents and events. Some create a Christ figure, either ironic or serious, to convey a contemporary religious, political, or social theme. Still others use the Christ story as a rhetorical device for indirect authorial comment.

In *Slaughterhouse-Five*, Kurt Vonnegut is using the Christ story in the last two ways. Through Billy Pilgrim's similarities to Jesus, Vonnegut creates a Christ figure who is a resurrected survivor with a philosophical message for the world. Vonnegut's own, contrasting message is conveyed indirectly, through his deflation of Billy Pilgrim as an ineffectual and immoral messiah. Vonnegut's implied moral is the antithesis of the gospel preached by his ironic Christ figure.

In his excellent study *Fictional Transfigurations of Jesus*, Theodore Ziolkowski describes fictional transfigurations as adaptations with essentially formal parallels, not ideological ones. In a fictional transfiguration, a modern Christ figure's qualities and actions are described in terms paralleling those of Jesus as he is portrayed in the Gospels; but the *meaning* of the Christ figure may have little or nothing to do with Christianity. Ziolkowski's five categories of fictional transfiguration are Christian socialist, psychiatric, mythic, Marxist, and Fifth Gospels. He doesn't discuss *Slaughterhouse-Five*; but it clearly belongs in the category of Fifth Gospels, which Ziolkowski defines as ironic adaptations by writers who are detached and neutral toward the New Testament, who view the story of Jesus primarily as a myth and feel free to adapt it in any way they wish.

Slaughterhouse-Five is a complex novel. A *Christian Science Monitor* reviewer states, "To quote that rarity, a truthful book jacket blurb, Mr. Vonnegut's book is 'a miracle of compression.' One could write a Talmudic commentary on every other paragraph."[2] In this compressed, complex novel, the Christ motif is not immediately apparent to a casual reader, nor even to some serious readers. My commentary concentrates on the descriptions, situations, and actions of Billy Pilgrim which parallel those of Jesus in the Gospels. When seen all at once—"many marvelous moments seen all at one time"—these parallels form a pattern which is, clearly, consciously intended by Vonnegut. I have not rearranged these parallels to follow the gospel story chronologically, because Vonnegut, as is well known, has not used the story of Jesus to order his time scheme. Thinking about this, one realizes a major ironic contrast between Billy Pilgrim and Jesus: when Billy Pilgrim lives again after having been shot, there is no change in his life nor in anyone else's; through time-travel, he simply repeats again and again various moments of his life.

There are, however, many similarities between Billy and Jesus. The epigraph, a quatrain from the carol "Away in the Manger," hints that in some way "the little Lord Jesus" is related to the meaning of the novel. Early in the novel, in two oblique references to the carol, "Billy Pilgrim would find himself weeping. . . . It was an extremely quiet thing Billy did, and not very moist." "But sleep would not come. Tears came instead. They seeped."[3] The emphasis upon the moderateness of Billy's crying suggests that it is motivated by a profound and sincere grief. As Vonnegut quoted Shakespeare in his 1970 Bennington College address, "To weep is to make less the depth of grief." Much later in the novel, after stating again that Billy "would weep quietly and privately sometimes, but never make loud *boohooing* noises," Vonnegut repeats the epigraph and explicates it explicitly:

> Which is why the epigraph of this book is the quatrain from the famous Christmas carol. Billy cried very little, though he often saw things worth crying about, and in *that* respect, at least, he resembled the Christ of the carol. (p. 197)

This authorial comment—"in *that* respect, at least, he resembled the Christ of the carol"—indicates that Vonnegut is certainly conscious of other possible resemblances between Billy and Jesus. We may note that here, as throughout the novel, it is only Vonnegut who is aware that Billy Pilgrim is a Christ figure. Billy himself is never conscious of any similarity between himself and Jesus.

A second major resemblance is Billy's compassionate desire to comfort people, "Billy's belief that he was going to comfort so many people with the truth about time" (p. 28). The solace he offers is in his extraterrestrial message, the essence of which is the negligibility of death—or, in Christian terms, the eternity of life. "Isn't that comforting?" he asks the fatherless boy after informing him "that his father was very much alive still in moments the boy would see again and again" (p. 135). The first part of Billy's Tralfamadorian message has to do with the true nature of time; that is, the fourth-dimension, omniscient, Godlike view of time: "All moments, past, present, and future, always have existed, always will exist. . . . How permanent all the moments are" (p. 27). The second part of the message follows from that: if all the moments always were, always are, and ever will be, then "we will all live forever, no matter how dead we may sometimes seem to be" (p. 211; see also pp. 26-27).

After learning this comforting truth on Tralfamadore, Billy develops a somewhat messianic sense of having a special mission to the poor souls on Earth:

> . . . he was devoting himself to a calling much higher than mere business.
>
> He was doing nothing less now, he thought, than prescribing corrective lenses for Earthling souls. So many of those souls were lost and wretched, Billy believed, because they could not see as well as his little green friends on Tralfamadore. (p. 29)

"He was going to tell the world about the lessons of Tralfamadore" (p. 199) on the New York City radio talk show, in his letters to the Ilium newspaper, and later, in public lectures.

At the beginning of his teaching, Billy encounters the same reaction as Jesus did early in his ministry: "When his family heard it, they went out to seize him, for people were saying, 'He is beside himself'" (Mark 3:21). Billy's family, especially his daughter Barbara, and other people in Ilium think "that Billy [is] evidently going crazy" (p. 135) when he teaches the lessons of Tralfamadore. On several occasions Barbara attempts to take charge of him (pp. 25-26, 29-30, 135). After the publication of his first letter in the Ilium *News Leader,*

> She said he was making a laughing stock of himself and everybody associated with him.
>
> "Father, Father, Father—" said Barbara, "what are we going to *do* with you? Are you going to force us to put you where your mother is? . . .
>
> "It's all just crazy. None of it's true!" (p. 29)

Billy, like Jesus, persists nevertheless, with serenity and confidence. He maintains his sense of mission, his compassion for people, and his belief in his otherworldly message about the eternal nature of time and the insignificance of death. And like Jesus, Billy will eventually gain a large following. At the time of his death, which he has foreseen happening on February 13, 1976, "Billy is speaking before a capacity audience in a baseball park. . . . There are police around him as he leaves the stage. They are there to protect him from the crush of popularity" (p. 142).

Billy's foreseeing his own death is one example of his belief that whatever happens to him had to be so; that since all time is all time, all the moments in his life have already been structured. This reminds us that Jesus frequently does certain things "so that the prophecies might be fulfilled," though Jesus, of course, freely chooses to fulfill the prophecies. Billy's foreknowledge of his own death is mentioned several times in the novel:

He has seen his birth and death many times. . . . (p. 23)

His attention began to swing grandly through the full arc of his life, passing into death, which was violet light. (p. 43)

Billy Pilgrim says now that this really *is* the way he is going to die, too. (p. 141)

Billy predicts his own death within an hour. (p. 142)

The conscious modern difference is that, instead of telling his disciples, Billy describes his death to a tape recorder:

As a time-traveler, he has seen his own death many times, has described it to a tape recorder. . . . *I, Billy Pilgrim,* the tape begins, *will die, have died, and always will die on February thirteenth, 1976.* (p. 141)

The description of Billy's death includes several gospel parallels. When the crowd protests his announcement of his imminent death, "Billy Pilgrim rebukes them. 'If you protest, if you think that death is a terrible thing, then you have not understood a word I've said'" (p. 142). Not only the verb "rebukes" but also the rebuking statement recall Jesus' words: "Do you not yet perceive or understand? Are your hearts hardened? Having eyes do you not see, and having ears do you not hear? And do you not remember? . . . Do you not yet understand?" (Mark 8:17-18, 21). Then there are the offers to help save his life—"The police offer to stay with him. They are floridly willing to stand in a circle around him all night, with their zap guns drawn" (p. 142)—offers which Billy rejects. "'No, no,' says Billy serenely. 'It is time for you to go home to your wives and children, and it is time for me to be dead for a little while— and then live again.' . . . So Billy experiences death for a while" (pp. 142-43). This passage echoes John 16:16-19, "A little while, and you will see me no more; again a little while, and you will see me. . . . A little while, and you will not see me, and again a little while, and you will see me."

Some thirty years before his death, Billy is compared several times to Jesus on the cross. First is the near-identification of Billy (a non-Catholic) with the "ghastly crucifix" which he had contemplated twice daily as a child:

Billy, after all, had contemplated torture and hideous wounds at the beginning and the end of nearly every day of his childhood. Billy had an extremely gruesome crucifix hanging on the wall of his little bedroom in Ilium. A military surgeon would have admired the clinical fidelity of the artist's rendition of all Christ's wounds—the spear wound, the thorn wounds, the holes that were made by the iron spikes. Billy's Christ died horribly. He was pitiful. (p. 38)

Just four pages later, "He was pitiful" is Roland Weary's evaluation of Billy as a footsoldier. As a war prisoner on a crowded boxcar, Billy is repeatedly described in terms of the crucifixion:

Billy stood by one of these [ventilators], and, as the crowd pressed against
him, he climbed part way up a diagonal corner brace to make more room.
(p. 67)

And Billy let himself down oh so gradually now, hanging onto the diagonal
cross-brace in the corner in order to make himself seem nearly weightless
to those he was joining on the floor. He knew it was important that he make
himself nearly ghostlike when lying down. He had forgotten why, but a reminder soon came. . . . So Billy stood up again, clung to the cross-brace.
(p. 78)

Billy Pilgrim was lying at an angle on the corner-brace, self-crucified,
holding himself there with a blue and ivory claw hooked over the sill of the
ventilator. (p. 80)

Besides reinforcing the Christ parallel fairly early in the novel, these
apparently conscious references to the crucifixion suggest that being a
war prisoner is a crucifying experience.

After he is shot in 1976 and "experiences death for a while," Billy
experiences a Tralfamadorian resurrection as "he swings back into life
again" (p. 143). The first place he returns to is the stage setting of the
prisoners' production of *Cinderella*, a story which is an analogue of the
theme of rebirth. Vonnegut himself suggests a particular analogy when
he describes *Cinderella* as the gospel story is usually described—"the
most popular story ever told" (p. 96). In Cinderella's silver boots, Vonnegut tells us, "Billy Pilgrim was Cinderella, and Cinderella was Billy
Pilgrim" (p. 145). Cinderella is reborn in her transformation from an
abused, humble servant into a princess; Billy is reborn when he swings
back into life again, to relive the moment when he discovered that
Cinderella's boots "fit perfectly"; and man's servant, Jesus, arises from
death to eternal life.

Later in the novel (though much earlier in his life), Billy experiences
a miraculous survival which is almost a resurrection: after the fire-

bombing of Dresden, he emerges from "an echoing meat locker which was hollowed in living rock under the slaughterhouse" (p. 165). Jesus rose, we recall, from a tomb "hewn in the rock" (Matt. 27:60). After climbing the staircase out of the tomblike meat locker, Billy Pilgrim sees a new kind of world he never could have imagined. Dresden after the firebombing is an apocalyptic scene of total destruction; everything organic has been killed, including 135,000 human beings. Under the city, Billy Pilgrim was very close to death; when he emerges, he sees nothing but death. Yet he goes on living.

The psychohistorian Robert J. Lifton calls *Slaughterhouse-Five* "Vonnegut's great survivor novel."[4] In his book *Death in Life*, Lifton defines the survivor in terms of rebirth applicable to Billy Pilgrim: "We may define the survivor as one who has come into contact with death in some bodily or psychic fashion and has himself remained alive."[5] In his later essay "Survivor as Creator," Lifton describes the survivor as "dying and 'being reborn,'" as "rejoining the living" after his "death immersion" (p. 40). In Lifton's terms, then, we may view Billy's survival of the Dresden firebombing as a psychic resurrection.

In addition to the major parallels between Billy and Jesus, further occasional biblical allusions reinforce the identification. First, before his capture by the Germans, Billy is "a dazed wanderer" in the wilderness "without food or maps" (p. 32). Second, in the German boxcar moving slowly toward the war prison, Billy is scorned and reviled by his fellow prisoners (pp. 78-79) just as Jesus is "mocked," "derided," and "reviled" by soldiers, passersby, chief priests, scribes, and even by the two robbers who were crucified with him (Mark 15:17-32). Billy is falsely accused, as Jesus is, and is made a scapegoat by Roland Weary; in 1976, he will be unjustly killed by Paul Lazzaro's hired murderer.

Fourth, as Billy leads the parade of prisoners to the Dresden-bound train, he had some resemblance to Jesus: "He had silver boots now, and a muff, and a piece of azure curtain which he wore like a toga. Billy still had a beard" (p. 147). His arrival in Dresden is an ironic parallel to the triumphal entry into Jerusalem:

And then they saw bearded Billy Pilgrim in his blue toga and silver shoes, with his hands in a muff. . . . Billy Pilgrim was the star. He led the parade. Thousands of people were on the sidewalks, going home from work. (pp. 149-50)

Then, after the destruction of Dresden, Billy and one hundred other prisoners of war "came at nightfall to an inn" where they are allowed to sleep in the stable, to bed down in the straw (pp. 180-81). Finally, if Jesus is the new Adam, the New Testament Son of God who will atone for Adam's fall, Billy Pilgrim is the old Adam before his fall. Immediately after he sees Adam and Eve in the highly polished boots of a German corporal, he looks up into the face of "a blond angel . . . as beautiful as Eve" (p. 53)—a juxtaposition suggesting that Billy is Adam. More important, Billy resembles Adam in the zoo on Tralfamadore where he lives naked and innocently ("guilt-free") with his mate in the Tralfamadorian ideal of human paradise.

With these minor allusions and the major parallels to the gospel story, Vonnegut endows his time-traveling optometrist with many similarities to Jesus. In descriptions, he compares Billy to the infant Jesus, to Jesus in his triumphal entry into Jerusalem, and to the mocked and crucified Christ. Even more parallels exist in Billy's actions: he wanders in the wilderness, he acts out of a sense of mission to the world, he preaches a message about eternal life, he is thought by many people to be out of his mind, he preaches to crowds, he foresees his own death, he is mocked and scorned, he is falsely accused and unjustly killed, and he returns to life after death. This extensive pattern of parallels makes Billy Pilgrim a modern Christ figure.

The elaborate and conscious identification is undercut, however, by the important ways in which Billy Pilgrim differs from Jesus. By important differences I don't mean omitted gospel details such as the Last Supper but, rather, morally significant contrasts. First, Billy's death is not a sacrifice. Second, his death has no redemptive value for other people. And third, unless we believe the Tralfamadorian values taught by Billy, his teaching is unlike Jesus' in that it doesn't change our lives or suggest new values worth living by. Vonnegut clearly rejects—and wants us to reject—the Tralfamadorian view of time and its implications for human life.

Why, then, does Vonnegut make Billy Pilgrim a Christ figure of this sort? Isn't Billy Pilgrim a Vonnegut hero? What is the point of a savior who saves no one?

There are several answers to these questions. Since he is so ineffectual, Billy Pilgrim is an ironic Christ figure, that is, one resembling Jesus in many ways but ultimately lacking the all-important redemptive, sacrificial death. This irony is appropriate in a novel, and in a world, where there is such irony as Edgar Derby's being executed for stealing a teapot while no one is punished for the destruction of Dresden.

Then, too, an ironic Christ figure fits in with Vonnegut's pessimistic and satiric view of humanity in today's world. A poor imitation of Jesus may be all we can expect in a society which covers up and then justifies the needless firebombing of Dresden. Maybe an ironic Christ figure is appropriate in a society whose values are reflected in the American dream that is Billy's miserable life in Ilium.

At the same time, Vonnegut's use of the gospel story, his allusions ranging from the first Christmas Eve to the resurrection, suggest a nostalgia, a kind of yearning that the Christ story might be true. This yearning is part of Vonnegut's search for meaning in an absurd world (he alludes to the Creator, Jesus, or God in his other novels). His use of the gospel story is nearly blasphemous; yet the fact that he does use it, doesn't ignore it, suggests that it has some appeal for him. As one critic has stated, "The question [of God] haunts Vonnegut at every turn."[6]

The most important reason for Billy's being an ineffectual, ironic Christ figure, however, is that this allows Vonnegut indirectly to counter Billy's Tralfamadorian message with his own very different, very worldly message. Vonnegut is qualified to oppose Billy's teachings because, as he tells us several times, his experiences in the prison camp and in Dresden were the same as Billy's. Vonnegut is very conscious of this; Billy is a semiautobiographical character, at least in the war parts of *Slaughterhouse-Five*. There are many similarities between Vonnegut and his protagonist: both were born in 1922; both have the same souvenir of war (a Luftwaffe ceremonial saber [pp. 6 and 195]); both are interested in science fiction as a help in "trying to re-invent themselves and their universe" (p. 101); both have messages to help mankind. Most important, both rise from near-death "in an echoing meat locker which was hollowed in living rock" and cannot understand why they were among the 105 survivors of the massacre of 135,000 people. Vonnegut comes close to identifying himself with Billy when he intrudes into the narrative four times to say, "I was there." Yet, though he was there, and though he had many of the same war experiences as Billy, Vonnegut's ultimate reaction to those experiences differs greatly from Billy's ultimate reaction.

Vonnegut's survival of the Dresden raid, like Billy's, ironically occurred in a slaughterhouse. It is well known from his other writing and from interviews that, to Vonnegut, his survival of Dresden was more than an irony—it seemed like a miracle. The sight of Dresden was an unforgettable nightmare. The absurd massacre, the total destruction of everything living, was an experience it took him twenty-three years to write about. He did, of course, allude to it in other novels, most specifically in his preface to *Mother Night*; and fires and firemen appear often in his fiction. He had seen an apocalyptic vision of the end of the world ("Dresden was like the moon now, nothing but minerals" [p. 178]), and he had "survived to tell the tale"—not to escape to a science fiction paradise. In an interview in 1966, Vonnegut talked about Dresden and the writing of *Slaughterhouse-Five*:

> Yes, I'm working on it now. It's what I've been working on for a long time, and it's extremely hard to think about. You know, you have these enormous concentration camps full of corpses, and then you have a city full of corpses, and, you know, is the city full of corpses right or wrong? . . . Well,

I think the only thing I have been able to think of doing as a result of seeing the destruction of that city there and knowing at the same time about the great crimes of Germany, is to become the impossible thing, which is a pacifist, and I figure I'm under an obligation, having seen all this, you know, that that's the only possible conclusion I can come to, is that we must not fight under any conditions.[7]

This statement of pacifism, "that we must not fight under any conditions," combined with his compulsion to *look back* at Dresden and other appalling massacres in history, marks the most important distinction between Kurt Vonnegut and Billy Pilgrim. In 1967, Vonnegut goes *back* to Dresden (p. 1), while in the same year Billy goes *away*, to Tralfamadore (p. 25). True, this first time Billy goes as a captive, but he is nevertheless an enthusiastic learner of the Tralfamadorian views; in 1968 he writes to the newspaper, "They had many wonderful things to teach Earthlings, especially about time" (p. 26).

Through his Tralfamadorian lessons, Billy Pilgrim learns a resigned tolerance of war ("So—I suppose that the idea of preventing war on Earth is stupid, too" [p. 117]) and an acceptance of whatever will be, will be (and always was, and always will be). Vonnegut, most obviously in his autobiographical first chapter but also throughout the novel, challenges Billy's postwar philosophy of serene acceptance. Billy's office sign and Montana Wildhack's locket say, "God grant me the serenity to accept the things I cannot change. . . ." According to Billy's view of time, he can change *nothing*; but Vonnegut, on the other hand, is only ironic when he says, "So it goes."

The Tralfamadorian lesson taught by Billy is "All moments, past, present, and future, always have existed, always will exist" (p. 27). Therefore, "we will all live forever, no matter how dead we may sometimes appear to be" (p. 211). Therefore, also, there is nothing we can do to prevent war, nothing we can do to prevent the end of the world ("A Tralfamadorian test pilot presses a starter button, and the whole Universe disappears. . . . He has *always* pressed it, and he always *will*" [p.

117]). So the thing to do as we visit various moments during eternity is to select the happy moments, the pretty moments. The Tralfamadorian guide tells Billy, "On other days we have wars as horrible as any you've ever seen or read about. There isn't anything we can do about them, so we simply don't look at them. We ignore them. We spend eternity looking at pleasant moments . . ." (p. 117). This is the gospel from outer space, the view of history that leads Billy Pilgrim to say about the destruction of Dresden, "It was all right. *Everything* is all right . . ." (p. 198).

This complacent gospel, preached by the ironic Christ figure, is rejected by Vonnegut himself. The author's extensive research on Dresden, and his writing of this novel with its overt pacifism, show that for him everything is *not* all right. Unlike the Tralfamadorians, Vonnegut the narrator looks back at many *horrible* moments: the destruction of Sodom and Gomorrah, the drowning or enslavement of the thousands of children in the Children's Crusade, the 1760 devastation of Dresden by the Prussians, the extermination of millions of Jews by the Nazis, the firebombing of Dresden, the atomic bombing of Hiroshima, the bombing of North Vietnam, the napalm burning of the Vietnamese, the assassination of Robert Kennedy, the assassination of Martin Luther King, the daily body count from Vietnam.

Like Billy Pilgrim, Kurt Vonnegut also has a message for the world. If we are to avoid another Dresden, if we are to break out of the Tralfamadorian inevitability of war and the end of the world, "we must not fight under any conditions." "I have told my sons," he writes,

> that they are not under any circumstances to take part in massacres, and that the news of massacres of enemies is not to fill them with satisfaction or glee.
>
> I have also told them not to work for companies which make massacre machinery, and to express contempt for people who think we need machinery like that. (p. 19)

Comparing himself to Lot's wife, Vonnegut says it is human to look back on a massacre; he implies that it is *inhuman* to forget or ignore it. Looking back in *Slaughterhouse-Five*, he reminds us that war is awful, that it is absurd, that it creates many grotesque ironies.

Slaughterhouse-Five is not a Christian book, but it is a compassionate and moral one in its concern for man and his fate. Through an ironic Christ figure, Vonnegut presents and rejects an extraterrestrial gospel which leads away from moral responsibility, away from guilt, away from active protest against war. As reborn survivor, Billy preaches a view of life which negates guilt, negates responsibility, negates active concern for the past or for the future. "*Everything* is all right." As reborn survivor, Vonnegut transcends Billy's Tralfamadorian vision of life. He transcends it by offering us his own earthly vision, a vision which has nothing to do with science fiction. Although he is skeptical about the success of his message, Vonnegut teaches the "impossible" pacifism to which he converted after his experience of Dresden: Do not kill. Do not burn. Do not fight in war. Do not condone war. Everything is *not* all right.

Although Billy Pilgrim ends up as a resurrected time-traveler whose gospel helps no one, there is a positive aspect to some of his other similarities to Jesus. Billy's genuine suffering, and his deeply sincere desire to help humanity, suggest that there may be something of Jesus even in a nobody. In *these* respects, at least, Billy seriously resembles the Christ of the Gospels. This identification extends the significance of Billy's role in the novel. He is, however, also a pilgrim traveling away from the city of destruction. The inverted parallels to Jesus, such as the negative quality of Billy's message and the inefficacy of his death, add an ironic dimension of meaning to his role. As an ironic Christ figure whose gospel is both untrue and ultimately immoral, Billy Pilgrim is opposed by the moral, real narrator, who travels *back* to the city of destruction and arrives at an active pacifism.

To understand Billy's ambivalent role as a modern version of Jesus, we and our students must be familiar with the gospel story. Knowledge of that story is necessary for the aesthetic pleasure of recognizing the biblical allusions in *Slaughterhouse-Five* and for the intellectual pleasure of recognizing both the serious and the ironic parallels between Billy Pilgrim and Jesus. Most important, however, we and our students need the gospel background in order to recognize Billy's *failure* as a *savior*, to recognize the immorality and the ineffectiveness of his serene vision of time and death. If we perceive Billy as a Christ figure, then we will perceive the important ways in which he is *unlike* Jesus: his death redeems no one; and his particular vision of eternal life leads to a passive acceptance of war, which if not unchristian is certainly immoral, inhuman, and uncompassionate. Only unfeeling and unthoughtful readers could find anything of positive value in the guilt-free, passive Tralfamadorian gospel. Vonnegut's pacifism and active moral concern are much closer to the teachings of Jesus as recorded in the Gospels.

From *Biblical Images in Literature*, edited by Roland Bartel, with James S. Ackerman and Thayer S. Warshaw (1975), pp. 161-175. Copyright © 1975 by Abingdon Press. Reprinted with permission of Abingdon Press and Donald C. Farber. Quotations from *Slaughterhouse-Five* taken from *Slaughterhouse-Five* by Kurt Vonnegut, Jr. Copyright © 1968, 1969 by Kurt Vonnegut, Jr. Used by permission of Dell Publishing, a division of Random House, Inc.

Notes

1. Theodore Ziolkowski, *Fictional Transfigurations of Jesus* (Princeton: Princeton University Press, 1972), p. 232.

2. John Reed, "Billy Pilgrim's Progress: A Fable About Sanity," *Christian Science Monitor*, April 17, 1969, p. 15.

3. Kurt Vonnegut, Jr., *Slaughterhouse-Five* (New York: Dell Publishing Co., 1971), pp. 61 and 62. Subsequent quotations, cited parenthetically in the text, are to this edition. The novel was first published in 1969 by Delacorte Press.

4. Robert J. Lifton, "Survivor as Creator," *American Poetry Review*, January/February, 1973, p. 41.

5. Robert J. Lifton, *Death in Life: Survivors of Hiroshima* (New York: Random House, 1967), p. 479.

6. Ernest W. Ranly, "What Are People For?" *Commonweal*, May 7, 1971, p. 209.

7. Robert Scholes, "A Talk with Kurt Vonnegut, Jr.," *The Vonnegut Statement*, ed. Jerome Klinkowitz and John Somer (New York: Delacorte Press, 1973), pp. 117-18.

Slaughterhouse-Five:
Kurt Vonnegut's Anti-Memoirs_____
Maurice J. O'Sullivan, Jr.

"People should be changed by world wars," I said, "else what are world wars for?"

—Mother Night

The appearance of Kurt Vonnegut's *Slaughterhouse-Five* in 1969 was hailed by many as, if not the cultural or literary capstone of that tumultuous decade, at least the most accessible countercultural event of a confusing year. Much of the work's success arose from its ability to offer a little something to everyone. Apologists for science fiction argued, intensely but prematurely, that Vonnegut had finally achieved for their genre a respectability similar to the one Ross Macdonald had won for the detective novel; anti-war activists saw the book as a denunciation of the mindlessness of war in general and of the Vietnam debacle in particular; neo-transcendentalists found in it a justification for ignoring precisely what their more politically oriented peers were protesting; and critics busy forecasting the death of the traditional novel—a more popular pastime in the sixties than the seventies—greeted it as new evidence for their theories. For many of the same reasons that it was welcomed, however, it was also condemned: as a subliterary, or at least subgeneric, excrescence, a polemical tract, an escapist fantasy, or a pop fiction. The comforting ambiguity in the book's form, with its introductory *apologia pro libra sua*, its apparently fractured time sequence, and its lack of concern with the psychology of its protagonist,[1] aided both defenders and opponents by creating difficulties in determining the criteria with which to judge it. The work could be praised or damned as apologue, satire, novel, or autobiography depending on the needs of the reviewer or critic.

Perhaps the finest recent discussion of the typology of prose fictions is that of Sheldon Sacks in his *Fiction and the Shape of Belief*,[2] and Sacks's categories suggest the difficulties involved in defining the form of Vonnegut's book. For many of its readers, *Slaughterhouse-Five* seems, in Sacks's terms, either an apologue, "a work organized as a fictional example of the truth of a formulable statement or a series of such statements," or a satire, "a work organized so that it ridicules objects external to the fictional world created in it." Both of these views tend to focus on the character of Billy Pilgrim. If *Slaughterhouse-Five*'s primary purpose is to promulgate a new philosophy, to convert its readers into Tralfamadorians, it supplies a nicely simplified, two-dimensional model, a twentieth-century version of Bunyan's Christian, who becomes the prophet for a new religion that teaches man to avoid unpleasantness by manipulating time. Such a technique has a serious value for it can provide us, as it does Billy, with an easy escape from the potentially threatening realities of homely wives, reactionary in-laws, aggressive children, and empty lives. On the other hand, if the book's purpose is to ridicule contemporary analogues of the philosophy Billy adopts, his prophetic role is merely a variation of the classic naif of satire, the Simplicius Simplicissimus or Gulliver, praising folly and embracing chaos. It is, however, difficult to believe that Sacks's third category, the novel, "a work organized so that it introduces characters, about whose fates we are made to care, in unstable relationships which are then further complicated until the complication is finally resolved by the removal of the represented instability,"[3] applies to Billy and his story. We might find Billy's uncomplicated innocence appealing (like the little Lord Jesus in the headnote he never grows up, even to the point of retaining, on the advice of his father-in-law, the childish diminutive Billy for his name) but there is not enough texture in his character to arouse more than momentary affection. He resembles both the holy fool and the miles gloriosus, with all the folly of the former but none of the cunning the latter occasionally acquired, and like these two stock characters he lacks the qualities necessary to attract sustained interest. Yet there is a character in *Slaughterhouse-Five* about whose fate we are made to care: the authorial persona who dominates the first chapter and appears periodically thereafter.

Slaughterhouse-Five, however, is not autobiography. The "I" of the first chapter is no more a perfect parallel of Vonnegut than the personae of many other works are of their authors; he functions, in fact, like the "I" of Pope's *Epistle to Arbuthnot*, a consciously crafted figure who can be identified with the author's public personality but who exists primarily to serve the ends of the work of art. This authorial persona, the key if not central character in the book, is Vonnegut's venture in *Slaughterhouse-Five* into fictional autobiography. But the work as a whole is less autobiography than inverted or anti-autobiography, an attempt by the persona, and ultimately by Vonnegut, to define himself and his values negatively through a fable he constructs around Billy Pilgrim. Unlike the classic framed narrative, however, in this case the storyteller appears in his tale *in propria persona* to underline the primary reason for his parable: Billy Pilgrim represents a standard—an essentially negative although often sympathetic standard—against which the persona measures himself. The point at which the two characters intersect, converging like the lines crayoned by the author on his daughter's wall, is Dresden, or, more precisely, before boarding a train to a POW camp that both pass through. Before this they were apparently very similar, two of the innocents embarked on what the author later comes to realize was a Children's Crusade. What is important about them is the direction each takes after they cross in the story. Billy wanders thoughtlessly in life, eventually adopting a philosophy which justifies his purposelessness. The author, on the other hand, is driven like Coleridge's mariner to relive his story by retelling it. It is the oblique manner of his retelling that has confused readers into identifying the authorial persona with Vonnegut and both of them with Billy. Ignoring the sophistication of Vonnegut's technique invariably leads to the kind of critical obtuseness suffered by Dr. Johnson in one of his rare critical lapses when he dismissed *Gulliver's Travels* with the comment, "When once you have thought of big men and little men, it is very easy to do all the rest."[4]

The opening chapter of the book is crucial to an understanding of both the novel's form and the persona's character. What appears to be a

By reappearing occasionally in the fable, the persona shows a fundamental similarity of experience with Billy to balance his fundamentally dissimilar response to those experiences.

The key to Billy's philosophy is expressed in the apparent form of the novel and in the beliefs he discovers among the Tralfamadorians. The assertion on the title page of *Slaughterhouse-Five* that "this is a novel somewhat in the telegraphic schizophrenic manner of the tales on the planet Tralfamadore" has misled many readers into identifying the entire book as a Tralfamadorian novel. The author, however, is very careful to describe such a work:

> Billy couldn't read Tralfamadorian, of course, but he could at least see how the books were laid out—in brief clumps of symbols separated by stars. Billy commented that the clumps might be telegrams.
>
> "Exactly," said the voice.
>
> "They *are* telegrams?"
>
> "There are no telegrams on Tralfamadore. But you're right: each clump of symbols is a brief, urgent message—describing a situation, a scene. We Tralfamadorians read them all at once, not one after the other. There isn't any particular relationship between all the messages, except that the author has chosen them carefully, so that, when seen all at once, they produce an image of life that is beautiful and surprising and deep. There is no beginning, no middle, no end, no suspense, no moral, no causes, no effects. What we love in our books are the depths of many marvelous moments seen all at one time." (p. 76)

But *Slaughterhouse-Five* is, of course, only "somewhat" in this manner. In fact the author is able to allow his hero to become "unstuck in time" (p. 20) only by setting up a fairly firm chronological narrative of Billy's pilgrimage through World War II to the firebombing of Dresden. Around this narrative the author weaves the story of Billy's life and the voyage to Tralfamadore, with the juxtaposed sequences invariably revealing overt and covert relationships. Chapter Four, for example, begins with Billy in bed on his daughter's wedding night waiting to be kidnapped by a flying saucer. He arises, wanders about thinking of his daughter's childhood, and finally settles in front of his television to watch a World War II movie which recalls the reader to the primary story. Billy then becomes unstuck in time and sees the film backward, extrapolating in fact all the way back to Adam and Eve, and forward. After this he goes out to meet the saucer which captures and anesthetizes him. When he wakes up, he is not in the saucer but in a boxcar, a prisoner of the Germans rather than the Tralfamadorians. The chapter then follows his trip on the boxcar to a POW camp. In the showers at the camp he briefly swings back to infancy, then to a golf game in middle age, and finally he awakens to hear a Tralfamadorian deny free will, a denial which will form the basis for his new religion. Thus states of innocence and the hope of rebirth exist, ironically, only within a context of war and the limitation of freedom.

The Tralfamadorians' aesthetic develops directly from their metaphysics and ethics, and central to all is a belief in fatalism. When Billy accuses one of his Tralfamadorian cantors of not believing in free will, the creature answers: "'If I hadn't spent so much time studying Earthlings . . . I wouldn't have any idea what was meant by "free will." I've visited thirty-one inhabited planets in the universe, and I have studied reports on one hundred more. Only on Earth is there any talk of free will.'" This denial of man's capacity to control his life leads inevitably to the twin principles, "There is no why" (p. 66) and "The moment is *structured* that way" (p. 101). Tralfamadorians escape the potential despair of such principles by a theory of the universality of time—all time is eternally present—which allows them to slip away from present difficulties into past or future happiness. Billy himself summarizes the Tralfamadorian view in a letter to his hometown newspaper:

"All moments, past, present, and future, always have existed, always will exist. The Tralfamadorians can look at all the different moments just the way we can look at a stretch of the Rocky Mountains, for instance. They can see how permanent all the moments are, and they can look at any moment that interests them. It is just an illusion we have here on Earth that one moment follows another one, like beads on a string, and that once a moment is gone it is gone forever.

"When a Tralfamadorian sees a corpse, all he thinks is that the dead person is in bad condition in that particular moment, but that the same person is just fine in plenty of other moments. Now, when I myself hear that somebody is dead, I simply shrug and say what the Tralfamadorians say about dead people, which is 'So it goes.'" (p. 23)

But such a fatalistic acceptance as Billy's and the Tralfamadorians' is a position that the persona will not adopt. His rejection of it is, however, paradoxical. Although he feels that the Tralfamadorian doctrine may be true, he believes that, even if it is, adopting such a system would be a denial of his humanity. For the author, man creates his freedom by postulating it and acting according to that postulate. An incident in Billy's POW camp illustrates the author's recognition of the difficulties involved in dealing with the problem of freedom and responsibility:

As the Americans were waiting to move on, an altercation broke out in their rear-most rank. An American had muttered something which a guard did not like. The guard knew English, and he hauled the American out of ranks, knocked him down.

The American was astonished. He stood up shakily, spitting blood. He'd had two teeth knocked out. He had meant no harm by what he'd said, evidently, had no idea that the guard would hear and understand.

"Why me?" he asked the guard.

The guard shoved him back into ranks. "Vy you? Vy anybody?" he said. (pp. 78-79)

Despite the American's question and the German's answer, there was a reason, if not a very good one, for the guard to single out the prisoner. It was an act of cruelty, but not of random cruelty. What for Billy is simply another instance of the ultimate purposelessness behind man's actions, is for the author rather an example of man's unwillingness to search for, examine, or evaluate the reasons behind those actions. This aversion to a careful scrutiny of motives leads to the adoption of easy rationalizations and facile, self-justifying philosophies, escapes which form the essential object of the author's protest. His protest, however, despite its vivid, affective presentation, is tinged with a scepticism about the possibility of improvement. In his opening chapter the persona mentions telling Harrison Starr, "the moviemaker," that he is writing an anti-war book. To which Starr responds, "'Why don't you write an anti-*glacier* book instead?'" And the persona finds himself in some agreement with this objection: "What he meant, of course, was that there would always be wars, that they were as easy to stop as glaciers. I believe that, too" (p. 3). Nevertheless he writes an anti-war book. Although the author recognizes the possibility that the world is ruled by chance, he refuses to accept such a possibility. Unlike Billy and the Tralfamadorians, who deny responsibility for their actions by denying freedom of the will, the author, in a rather more complex position, understands the probable futility of such an action as writing an anti-war novel but at the same time realizes the need to make such a gesture, even if it is merely a gesture. His morality is in fact a twentieth-century version of classical scepticism, qualified by a hope for, if not confidence in, man.

Questions of moral responsibility and free will set against a background of destruction and war have dominated much of Vonnegut's longer fiction. Like the persona of *Slaughterhouse-Five*, Vonnegut has never escaped his sense of involvement in the devastation of Dresden: *Player Piano, The Sirens of Titan, Mother Night, Cat's Cradle, God Bless You, Mr. Rosewater,* and *Breakfast of Champions* all reflect their author's attempts to deal with his memories of the war. In a review of *Mother Night,* Vonnegut's finest novel, Doris Lessing has pointed out the fundamental concern underlying all his work: "What Vonnegut deals with, always, is responsibility: Whose fault was it all—the gas chambers, the camps, the degradations and the debasements of all our standards? Whose? Well, *ours* as much as *theirs*."[6] Vonnegut phrased the same idea somewhat differently in a typically oblique epigram prefacing *Mother Night* when he warned, "We are what we pretend to be, so we must be careful about what we pretend to be."[7] Even a comment on a minor character in *Breakfast of Champions*, his most recent novel,[8] mirrors this concern with the interrelationship of identity, war, and will. In describing Harold Newcomb Wilbur, the second most decorated veteran of Midland City and currently bartender in the cocktail lounge at the piano bar of the Holiday Inn, Vonnegut notes, "He won all those medals in the Second World War, which was staged by robots so that Dwayne Hoover could give a free-willed reaction to such a holocaust" (p. 202). Hoover, the book's protagonist, reacts by going mad. Near the end of *Breakfast of Champions* Vonnegut suggests that he has finally exorcised himself of the demons of Dresden when he has his persona in that book offer Kilgore Trout, the phenomenally unsuccessful science fiction writer and proxy for Vonnegut in many of the novels, an apple, a symbol of the possibility of new knowledge and the promise of a new fall proffered by one Vonnegutian surrogate to another.

In *Slaughterhouse-Five* Vonnegut offers art as the only potential form of transcendence. A pornographic snapshot of a pony and a girl appears to have the capacity for timelessness, reappearing at different times and in different places throughout the novel, but the very fact of its survival simply mocks man's inability to escape time. Men who, like Billy, fail to see or attempt to flee responsibility become negative models from whom we can learn to refashion our own lives more carefully. It is a characteristic folly of the age that Billy has become for so many a hero. Vonnegut appears to have anticipated this, and some would say encouraged it in these anti-memoirs, for his ironies, reflections of the schizophrenia noted on the title page, act as a defense from a world going mad; they function as a Laingian placenta, nourishing and protecting ideas from a world which is generally too distracted to care. But despite its madness, Vonnegut is telling us, this world is our world and its traumas our burden: escape is impossible and resignation immoral. When Kilgore Trout in *Breakfast of Champions* finds the question, "What is the purpose of life?" scribbled in the men's room of a pornographic movie theater, he answers as a man, an artist, and a Vonnegut deputy:

> To be
> the eyes
> and ears
> and conscience
> of the Creator of the Universe,
> you fool. (p. 67)

But, a true product of Vonnegut's sceptical idealism, he cannot actually write the words because he has nothing to write with.

From *Essays in Literature* 3, no. 2 (Fall 1976): 244-250. Copyright © 1976 by Western Illinois University. Reprinted with permission of Western Illinois University.

Notes
1. Unlike the baseball world of J. Henry Waugh in Robert Coover's *The Universal Baseball Association, Inc.*, the Tralfamadorian episodes in *Slaughterhouse-Five* reveal neither states of awareness nor dynamic creative activity on Billy's part; his mind, in fact, functions like a pinball, jolted without conscious control from memory to memory.
2. *Fiction and the Shape of Belief: A Study of Henry Fielding with Glances at Swift, Johnson and Richardson* (Berkeley: Univ. of California Press, 1964). The definitions cited in this paragraph are on p. 26.
3. Sacks's subtitle suggests some of the limitations of his work. While his definitions are most valuable in dealing with the early English novel (with the obvious exception of *Tristram Shandy*), they also offer a useful frame for discussing even contemporary works of fiction. The specific application of all the details in his definitions (e.g., "the removal of the represented instability") is, of course, impossible for many modern works.

4. *Boswell's Life of Johnson*, ed. George Birkbeck Hill and L. F. Powell (Oxford: Clarendon, 1934), II, 319.

5. *Slaughterhouse-Five* (New York: Delacorte, 1969), p. 17. Citations from *Slaughterhouse-Five* are from this edition.

6. "Vonnegut's Responsibility," *New York Times Book Review*, 4 Feb. 1973, p. 35.

7. "Introduction," *Mother Night* (New York: Delacorte, 1966), p. v.

8. *Slaughterhouse-Five* and *Breakfast of Champions* (New York: Delacorte, 1973) originally formed a single book, and Vonnegut's decision to separate the two was a wise one, for the latter book merely makes explicit what was implicit in the former. Citations from *Breakfast of Champions* are to the Delacorte Press edition.

The "New Reality" of *Slaughterhouse-Five*_____

James Lundquist

"*It is my duty* to describe something beyond the imagination of mankind," the correspondent for the London *Times* began his dispatch in April 1945, after British troops marched into Belsen—the first Nazi prison camp to be exposed to world scrutiny—and discovered over forty thousand malnourished and dying prisoners and more than ten thousand corpses.[1] The problem that Vonnegut faces in all of his novels is essentially the same as the one the correspondent had to face at Belsen—the increasing gap between the horrors of life in the twentieth century and our imaginative ability to comprehend their full actuality.

For Vonnegut, the subject matter is not simply Nazi atrocity; it is many other things—runaway technology, inflated views of human destiny, amoral science, the distribution of wealth in America, the senselessness of war as continued experience, and insanity in Midland City—but the aesthetic problem remains the same, whether the scene is the crystallization of the oceans or the firebombing of Dresden: How to conceptualize and define the night terrors of an era so unreal, so unbelievable, that the very term *fiction* seems no longer to have any currency.

Given the difficulty of the problem that dogs Vonnegut (and most contemporary novelists, for that matter), there is bound to be considerable debate concerning his success in solving it. The technique he employs in *Player Piano* offers little in the way of innovation, and Vonnegut falls considerably short of making a computerized future seem all that frightening. There are troublesome deficiencies in some of his other novels as well—the science-fiction motifs in *The Sirens of Titan*, as humorously as they are used, occasionally seem hackneyed; the flat characterization in *God Bless You, Mr. Rosewater* makes it difficult to see Eliot Rosewater as much more than a "tinhorn saint"; and Vonnegut's own appearance at the Holiday Inn cocktail lounge near the end of *Breakfast of Champions* is, just about any way one looks at it, a little contrived.

These are, of course, not major objections to any of the novels cited, and good arguments could be made for their artistic merit on other grounds. But there have been sustained attacks on Vonnegut's writing ever since the start of his career, doubts that were pretty well summed up in P. S. Prescott's strident review of *Breakfast of Champions*. "From time to time, it's nice to have a book you can hate—it clears the pipes—and I hate this book for its preciousness, its condescension to its characters, its self-indulgence, and its facile fatalism: all the lonely people, their fates sealed in epoxy," Prescott writes. "Mostly I hate it for its reductiveness, its labored denial of man's complexity and resilience. Life cannot, as Vonnegut insists, be summed up with 'and so on' and 'ETC.'—or at least not without more wit and insight than Vonnegut can master."[2]

Such attacks are not a symptom of vindictiveness alone. To many critics, Vonnegut's novels do read as if they are haphazard in structure and simplistic in thought. Robert Scholes has tried to reply to all this by pointing out that "Serious critics have shown some reluctance to acknowledge that Vonnegut is among the great writers of his generation. He is . . . both too funny and too intelligent for many, who confuse muddled earnestness with profundity."[3] But the only effective reply is to take a close look at what is probably Vonnegut's most widely read novel and perhaps his best, *Slaughterhouse-Five*.

"I felt after I finished *Slaughterhouse-Five* that I didn't have to write at all anymore if I didn't want to," Vonnegut has said. "It was the end of some sort of career."[4] *Slaughterhouse-Five*, with its non-linear time scheme and its complex interweaving of science-fiction fantasy and the realities of World War II, makes his earlier novels, as innovative as some of them are, appear to be ordinary and uncomplicated by comparison, even if they are far from being that. The reason for this is that Vonnegut reveals himself in *Slaughterhouse-Five*, as do Alexander Trocchi in *Cain's Book* and Thomas Pynchon in *V*, to be "highly self-conscious of the novel as an abstract concept that examines a condition that never yields itself up completely as itself."[5] In other words, the novel functions to reveal new viewpoints in somewhat the same way that the theory of relativity broke through the concepts of absolute space and time. *Slaughterhouse-Five* thus gains its structure from Vonnegut's essential aesthetic problem—how to describe a reality that is beyond human imagination.

The method he chooses is outlined in the explanation given Billy Pilgrim of the Tralfamadorian novel as he is being transported toward that whimsical planet. His captors offer him the only book in English they have, Jacqueline Susann's *Valley of the Dolls*, which is to be placed in a museum. "Billy read it, thought it was pretty good in spots," Vonnegut writes. "The people in it certainly had their ups and downs. But Billy didn't want to read about the same ups and downs over and over again."

The Tralfamadorians allow him to look at some of their novels, but warn that he cannot begin to understand them. The books are small; it would take a dozen of them to even approach *Valley of the Dolls* in bulk, and the language is impossible for Billy. But he can see that the novels consist of clumps of symbols with stars in between. Billy is told that the clumps function something like telegrams, with each clump a message about a situation or scene. But the clumps are not read sequentially as the chapters are in an earthling novel of the ordinary sort. They are read simultaneously. "There isn't any particular relationship between all the messages," the speaker says to Billy, "except that the author has chosen them carefully, so that, when seen all at once, they produce an image of life that is beautiful and surprising and deep. There is no beginning, no middle, no end, no suspense, no moral, no causes, no effects. What we love in our books are the depths of many marvelous moments seen all at one time."

Slaughterhouse-Five is an approximation of this type of novel. Its chapters are divided into short sections (clumps if you will), seldom more than a few paragraphs long. The time-tripping, both by Billy and the narrator, produces an effect somewhat like that achieved in the Tralfamadorian novel—to see many moments at once. The time-tripping also serves to eliminate suspense. (We know not only of Billy's assassination long before the novel ends, but also how the universe will end—the Tralfamadorians blow it up experimenting with a new fuel for their flying saucers.) And the conclusion Vonnegut comes to after examining the causes and effects of Dresden is that there indeed is no moral, only the *Poo-tee-weet* of the bird call that Billy hears when he discovers that the war in Europe is over and he wanders out onto the shady streets of springtime Dresden.

What the Tralfamadorian structure does for Vonnegut is to enable him to embody a new reality in his novel—at least new in contrast to the sequential ups-and-downs reality of the traditional novel. Vonnegut's method accords well with the major changes in the conception of physical reality that have come out of contemporary science. "Change, ambiguity, and subjectivity (in a sense these are synonyms) thus become ways of defining human reality," Jerry H. Bryant writes in commenting on the relationship between twentieth-century physics and recent fiction. "Novelist after novelist examines these features, and expresses almost universal frustration at being deprived of the old stability of metaphysical reality."[6] But not Vonnegut. His Tralfamadorian scheme enables him to overcome the problems of change, ambiguity, and subjectivity involved in objectifying the events surrounding the fire-bombing of Dresden and the involvement of Billy Pilgrim and the author in them.

This is a difficult idea, but one way to understand it is to consider the distinction Bertrand Russell makes in *The ABC of Relativity* between the old view of matter (that it has a definite identity in space and time) and the new view (that it is an event). "An event does not persist and move, like the traditional piece of matter," Russell writes; "it merely exists for a little moment then ceases. A piece of matter will thus be resolved into a series of events. . . . The whole series of these events makes up the whole history of the particle, and the particle is regarded as *being* its history, not some metaphysical entity to which things happen."[7]

This is just the paradoxical conception of Billy that Vonnegut develops. Billy at first seems to be merely an entity to which things happen—he is lost behind the lines during the Battle of the Bulge, he and Roland Weary are captured by the Germans, he survives the fire-bombing of Dresden, he marries, he is the sole survivor of a plane crash, he hallucinates that he is kidnapped by the Tralfamadorians, he appears on crackpot talk-shows, and he is finally gunned down in Chicago. But through the constant movement back and forth in time that constitutes Vonnegut's narrative, we see Billy becoming his history, existing all at once, as if he is an electron. And this gives the novel a structure that is, to directly state the analogy, atomic. Billy whirls around the central fact of Dresden, the planes of his orbits constantly intersecting, and where he has been, he will be.

Of course, all of Vonnegut's earlier central characters are somewhat like Billy in that they are seen as aspects of a protean reality. (Again, the name of Paul Proteus suggests how persistent this representation of personality is.) But it is not until *Slaughterhouse-Five* that Vonnegut develops a way of fully representing the context of that reality. The sudden changes that come over Malachi Constant, Eliot Rosewater, and others make them seem as illusive and problematic as the absurd universe they occupy. By oversimplifying his characters, Vonnegut does manage to suggest something of the complexity of human nature by indirection. But they still tend to linger in the mind as cartoon figures (the Dell paperback covers of *The Sirens of Titan* and *Mother Night* certainly suggest so).

This is not the case with Billy Pilgrim. The Tralfamadorian structure through which his story is told (*sent* might be a better word) gives Billy dimension and substance and brings him eerily to life despite his pale ineffectuality. "Vonnegut's reluctance to depict well-developed characters and to supply them with conventional motives for their actions serves as a conscious burlesque of the whole concept of realism in the novel," Charles B. Harris in his study of the contemporary novel of the absurd has pointed out.[8] But with *Slaughterhouse-Five*, the conscious burlesque is diminished because Vonnegut has come up with a representation of Billy Pilgrim's universe that is in itself a new concept of realism—or reality.

Slaughterhouse-Five is thus as much a novel about writing novels as it is an account of Billy Pilgrim and Dresden. In relating the difficulty he had in dealing with Dresden, Vonnegut prefaces *Slaughterhouse-Five* with an account of his own pilgrimages through time as he tried to write about his Dresden experience. The opening section consists of jumps back and forth in the author's life—from his return to Dresden on a Guggenheim grant to his return home from the war two decades earlier, from a conversation on the telephone with his old war buddy to the end of the war in a beet field on the Elbe outside of Halle, and then on to the Chicago City News Bureau, Schenectady and General Electric, visiting O'Hare in Pennsylvania, teaching writing at the University of Iowa, and then Dresden and the Guggenheim trip once more.

The concern is always with the problem of writing the book—how to represent imaginatively things that are unimaginable—but in detailing his frustrations, Vonnegut conceptualizes his own life the way he later does Billy's, in terms of Tralfamadorian time theory. The structure of the chapter about writing the novel consequently prefigures the structure of the novel itself.

In that opening section, Vonnegut outlines his essential difficulty by elaborating on the misconception with which he began work on the novel. He states that he thought the book would be easy to write—all he would have to do is to simply report what he had seen. But this does not work. Too many other things get in the way. Why was Dresden, a supposedly safe city, bombed? Why did the American and British governments cover up the facts about the raid? What does the Dresden attack imply about American and British civilization? And, more important, why must Vonnegut's life always lead up to and go back to what he saw when he emerged from the slaughterhouse meat locker and looked at the moonscape that was once perhaps the most beautiful city in Europe?

The conflict Vonnegut is indicating is that of the old Henry James-H. G. Wells debate on what the novel as a literary form should be. James felt that it should be mimetic, realistic, that it should relate human experience as accurately as possible through detailed characterization and careful construction. Wells, on the other hand, believed that social pronouncements and ideas are more important, and that art should be subordinate to both. Wells was not even certain that the novel should be taken seriously as an art form. For him, characterization was just something to be got through so that an idea or a "ventilation" of the novel's social, political, or philosophical point can be got across as clearly as possible.[9]

Wells's influence is certainly a factor in the development of the science-fiction novel, and James must be taken into account in any discussion of the so-called mainstream or art novel. Vonnegut, as he indicates in his preface to *Slaughterhouse-Five*, is caught somewhere in the middle of the debate. His earlier books are mainly novels of character written to a thesis, an approach that leads to the direct statement of a moral in *Mother Night*.

But *Slaughterhouse-Five* is different; Vonnegut's impulse is to begin with his own experience, not with characters or ideas, but the ideas soon get in the way.

Two structural possibilities come to mind. The first is suggested in the song Vonnegut remembers as he thinks about how useless, yet how obsessive, the Dresden part of his memory has been:

> My name is Yon Yonson,
> I work in Wisconsin,
> I work in a lumbermill there,
> The people I meet when I walk down the street,
> They say, "What's your name?"
> And I say,
> "My name is Yon Yonson,
> I work in Wisconsin . . ."

When people ask him what *he* is working on, Vonnegut says that for years he has been telling them the same thing—a book about Dresden. Like Yon Yonson, he seems doomed to repeat the answer endlessly. But the maddening song suggests something else—the tendency many people (perhaps all) have to return to a central point in their lives in reply to the question of identity ("What's your name?").

The song also crudely suggests the time theory that is later developed in the novel with its emphasis on infinite repetition. But repetition leads nowhere, especially in a novel, so Vonnegut considers another possibility. He takes a roll of wallpaper, and on the back of it tries to make an outline of the story using his daughter's crayons (a different color for each of the characters). "And the blue line met the red line and then the yellow line," Vonnegut writes, "and the yellow line stopped because the character represented by the yellow line was dead. And so on. The destruction of Dresden was represented by a vertical band of orange cross-hatching, and all the lines that were still alive passed through it, came out the other side." This is an outline for a Jamesian novel with an essentially linear time scheme. But it does not work as a representation of the experience Vonnegut is anxious to write about.

For one thing, characters do not actually come out the other side and inevitably go on from there. Like Vonnegut himself, like Yon Yonson, they compulsively return, moving back and forth on their lines. And as for the lines that stop, the beginning and middle of those lines are still there. What does Vonnegut do? He comes up with a structure that includes both the Yon Yonson story and the wallpaper outline. It is as if he rolls the wallpaper into a tube so all of the characters and incidents are closely layered, so they are in effect one unit, and the reader must look at them from the side. The tube then becomes a telescope through which the reader looks into the fourth dimension, or at least into another dimension of the novel. The story goes around and around, yet it still leads somewhere, and yet the end is very close to the beginning.

It may well be that, as Karen and Charles Wood suggest, *Slaughter-*

house-Five is a new form of novel representing the mature fusion of science fiction and Jamesian literature of experience.[10]

The search for an approach also takes Vonnegut through an investigation of other works of literature that deal with catastrophe and the attitudes that surround it. He mentions an account of the Children's Crusade in a nineteenth-century book, *Extraordinary Popular Delusions and the Madness of Crowds*. This account is used to underscore the contrast he draws between the serious business of war and the naiveté of Billy Pilgrim, Roland Weary, and most of the other soldiers he depicts. He mentions *Dresden, History, Stage and Gallery*, by Mary Endell (published 1908), and its account of how Dresden, with all of its beauty, has been attacked repeatedly.

He quotes some lines from Theodore Roethke's *Words for the Wind* to suggest both his own confusion and the sense he has that, simply by moving ahead and back in time, the meaning of Dresden was being sorted out:

> I wake to sleep, and take my waking slow.
> I feel my fate in what I cannot fear.
> I learn by going where I have to go.

He mentions Erica Ostrovsky's *Céline and His Vision* and recounts how death and time also obsessed the insomniac French writer after he was wounded in World War I. And then he mentions the story of the destruction of Sodom and Gomorrah in the Bible and how Lot's wife, because of her compulsive looking back at the burning cities when she was told not to, was turned into a pillar of salt.

All of these references either give Vonnegut ideas and material or else they relate to his own reaction to Dresden, but they do not quite offer him the approach he is after. This, as we have seen, he had to discover for himself.

The structure Vonnegut chooses is indicated right at the start of Billy Pilgrim's story. It is a structure that, for all of the later explanation and illustration of its basis in Tralfamadorian time theory, actually develops out of Vonnegut's central character. Vonnegut, in the guise of an oral storyteller, asks us to "Listen." Then, in two paragraphs he introduces Billy and sets up the pattern that will be followed throughout the rest of the novel: "Billy Pilgrim has come unstuck in time. . . . He has seen his birth and death many times, he says, and pays random visits to all the events in between."

Vonnegut proceeds to outline Billy's life in the next few pages—what happens to him during the war, his marriage, the airplane crash, the flying saucer, and his appearances on talk shows—to build irony and to bring out the sudden and often absurdly sad changes in Billy's life that make his time-tripping largely a survival reaction.

Billy's survival seems at first to depend simply on his thinness as a character, his ineffectuality, and his utter insignificance. But the imagery associated with Billy, as it expands and cuts back and forth through the novel, suggests otherwise. He is said at times to look like a Coke bottle in shape and like a filthy flamingo in dress, and he is said to have a "chest and shoulders like a box of kitchen matches." But before his capture by the Germans he is portrayed "like a poet in the Parthenon." When he is elected president of the Ilium Lions Club in 1957, he gets up to give his acceptance speech in a voice that is a "gorgeous instrument." He becomes as "rich as Croesus." At another point in his travels through time, he is clearly identified with Christ, "self-crucified, holding himself there with a blue and ivory claw hooked over the sill of the ventilator." Billy is anything but a thin character; he is another illustration of Vonnegut's concept of Protean man. Billy *needs* to travel back and forth in time not only to understand himself but also to endure himself, to become his history. He is many personalities, many selves existing together at once. He is a living Tralfamadorian "clump."

One of the surprises in the novel is that the personality that seems the most ridiculous—Billy as an optometrist—turns out to be the most important symbolically. Throughout the novel there is considerable emphasis on seeing things, and there is a near continuous contrast between the way the world looks to Billy and the way others see him. At times Billy appears to be a poet and at other times, such as when he appears in Dresden wrapped in an azure curtain and wearing silver-painted combat boots, he looks the fool. For Billy himself, there is considerable development in the way he views what has happened to him.

The change that comes over Billy is mainly a result of the way he is forced to look at many things—Weary's triangular-bladed knife with its brass-knuckle grip, the picture of a woman attempting sexual intercourse with a Shetland pony, the German corporal's boots (in which Billy sees a vision of Adam and Eve), his Cadillac El Dorado Coupe de Ville in the suburban shopping center parking lot outside his office, the spastic salesman who comes to the door trying to peddle phony magazine subscriptions, St. Elmo's fire around the heads of the guards and his fellow prisoners, the cozy interior of the guards' railroad car, the clock on his gas stove an hour before the flying saucer comes to pick him up, the backward movie he watches on television while he is waiting for the Tralfamadorians, and so on. Through recapitulating imagery, Vonnegut suggests how the simultaneous relationship of everything Billy sees and experiences is slowly revealed and how Tralfamadorian time theory, instead of merely being a comic example of Vonnegut's fondness for science-fiction motifs, develops naturally and logically out of Billy's unconscious awareness of his own life.

Vonnegut's use of recapitulating imagery can be seen on almost every page of the novel, but the backward movie will serve as one of the best examples of this technique. Billy suddenly sees a movie of World War II running backward in his head. The bombers suck the fire and the bombs back into their bellies, the bombs are shipped back to the factories and dismantled, and the dangerous contents are reduced to mineral form and returned to the ground. The fliers turn in their uniforms and become high school kids. Hitler and everyone else turns into a baby and, as Vonnegut writes, "all humanity, without exception, conspired biologically to produce two perfect people named Adam and Eve. . . ." The reference to Adam and Eve recapitulates the vision Billy saw in the German corporal's boot years before; and the barking of the dog he hears outside his house recapitulates the barking Billy heard just before the corporal captured him.

A further use of this type of imagery occurs when Billy hears what he thinks is the cry of a melodious owl, but the sound turns out to be the whine of the flying saucer. All his professional life he has been working with an "owl" of another sort. During one of his time trips, Billy opens his eyes and finds himself "staring into the glass eyes of a jade green mechanical owl. The owl was hanging upside down from a rod of stainless steel. The owl was Billy's optometer in his office in Ilium. An optometer is an instrument for measuring refractive errors in eyes—in order that corrective lenses may be prescribed." With this recapitulation of imagery, a major theme in the novel is brought into focus.

Of all that Billy is forced to look at, the most significant is what is revealed to him by the Tralfamadorians. The flying saucer becomes an optometer that measures the refractive errors in Billy's outlook and the Tralfamadorians are able to suggest a prescription. But it is Billy's job as an optometrist to help others see, and this is what he tries to do. At first, he is not very effective. He is able to attend the Ilium School of Optometry for only one semester before he is drafted (and he is enrolled only in *night* sessions at that). And after the war, despite all his success, Billy is dealing less in vision than in fashion: "Frames are where the money is." But through his flying-saucer journey, he gains a new conception of what his job should be—prescribing "corrective lenses for Earthling souls" so that they can see into the fourth dimension as the Tralfamadorians do.

This development of Billy's vision is handled in a deceptively ambiguous way, of course. The repetition of imagery together with the juxtaposition of disparate events in Billy's life suggests that his trip to Tralfamadore is an hallucination and that the prescription he winds up advocating is essentially the result of the associative powers of his mind. The substance of his trip to Tralfamadore may well be the consequence of reading a Kilgore Trout novel, and the whole business of time travel and the simultaneous existence of events may well be simply another of the human illusions Vonnegut attacks so frequently in his earlier novels.

But the point for Billy is that the Tralfamadorians *are* real, that the years of his life are the only time there is, and he is going to live every moment over and over again. In addition, there is the pragmatic value of his vision—it enables him to deal with the horror of Dresden and to get around the question of "Why me?" that echoes through the novel. Are his lenses rose-colored or not? It perhaps depends on the reader's own willingness to look into the fourth dimension with him. *Slaughterhouse-Five*, at any rate, gives us a glimpse of what that dimension might be like, and shows us at the very least how it is possible to gain a sense of purpose in life by doing what Billy Pilgrim does—he re-invents himself and his universe.

The process of re-invention is made vivid by Vonnegut's style with its hesitant short sentences and his tendency to return again and again to the same images. His abruptness works well in describing the time shifts Billy suddenly goes through, and it contributes a sense of Billy's new vision, his re-invented universe, being formulated piece by piece. But the overall effect of the direct, often choppy, sentences and the brief paragraphs (several times consisting of only a few words) is to suggest the whirring of basic particles, of electrons that really cannot be seen. What we think of when we think of the structure of the atom is not actually there at all—it is only a model, an illusion. And the same thing can be said of *Slaughterhouse-Five* and Billy Pilgrim's erratic revolutions in time around Dresden. But as a model, it is, through its recapitulating imagery, its optometric symbolism, its positively charged sentences, and its telegraphic-Tralfamadorian-atomic structure, one of the best solutions we have to the problem of describing the unimaginable.

Unfortunately, one cannot say the same of the movie version of the novel released in 1972. Although Michael Sacks as Billy Pilgrim and

Valerie Perrine as Montana Wildhack are effective and director George Roy Hill (who also directed *Butch Cassidy and the Sundance Kid*) and writer Stephen Geller treat the story with reverence, the film does not match the sophistication of statement to be found in the book. One problem is that while Billy's time-tripping is handled in an artistically justifying way by Vonnegut, it is merely cinematically familiar on the screen where flashbacks and flash-forwards only serve to diminish its intellectual force.

There are many nice touches in the film, however. One is Billy's changing into Nazi-looking steel-rimmed glasses in middle age (a device that hints at the recapitulating imagery in the novel). And there are some brilliantly conceived scenes, such as one of American soldiers marching through Dresden, past the spires and statues of the city, while the Fourth Brandenburg Concerto comes over the soundtrack. Much of the film was shot in Prague by Miroslav Ondricek, the Czech photographer who did Forman's *Loves of a Blonde* and Ivan Passer's *Intimate Lightning*, and Ondricek deserves much of the credit for the visually pleasing aspects of the production. But, as one reviewer wrote, "In its elaborate structure and editing, its leaping bounds between fact and fancy, the film is like a version of *Last Year in Marienbad* revised for showing on *Sesame Street*."[11]

Of course, no film could document the way Vonnegut confronted his own ambiguous nature in working out the story of Billy Pilgrim. The character who is developed the most fully in the novel is Vonnegut himself.[12] This is why Vonnegut can get away with repeating the phrase "So it goes" after every tragic or pathetic incident. He has established himself, through his preface, as one of the characters in the book. His is a human voice, not just that of an omniscient narrator, and this in itself adds poignancy to the inhuman acts his subject matter forces him to describe.

Vonnegut's way of dealing with that subject matter results in a novel that is, by any standard, highly complex. It is a novel that works toward the resolution of Vonnegut's own obsessions at the same time it works toward the resolution of several nervous questions concerning the viability of the genre itself. Like many of his contemporaries, Vonnegut accepts the idea of an absurd universe that is chaotic and without meaning. But unlike Beckett and Robbe-Grillet, he does not develop an antistyle, even though he seems to share their fear of the loss of distinctions between fact and fiction. Instead, he chooses to rely upon many traditional devices (among them burlesque and parody) in conjunction with the new reality of twentieth-century physics and the motifs of science fiction to come up with a radical use of fictional form that reveals a regained joy in storytelling and is also true to his cosmically ironic vision.

Notes

1. Cited by Alfred Kazin, *Bright Book of Life: American Novelists and Storytellers from Hemingway to Mailer* (Boston: Atlantic/Little, Brown, 1973), p. 81.
2. P. S. Prescott, *Newsweek*, 14 May 1973, p. 114.
3. Robert Scholes, *New York Times Book Review*, 6 April 1969, p. 1.
4. Kurt Vonnegut, Jr., *Wampeters, Foma & Granfalloons* (New York: Delta, 1975), p. 280.
5. Jerry H. Bryant. *The Open Decision* (New York: Free Press, 1970), p. 36.
6. Bryant, p. 22.
7. Bertrand Russell, *The ABC of Relativity* (London: Kegan Paul, 1925), p. 209.
8. Charles B. Harris, *Contemporary American Novelists of the Absurd* (New Haven: College and University Press, 1971), p. 74.
9. For a detailed study of the Wells-James debate, see Leon Edel and Gordon N. Ray, *Henry James and H. G. Wells* (Urbana: University of Illinois Press, 1958).
10. Karen and Charles Wood, "The Vonnegut Effect: Science Fiction and Beyond," in *The Vonnegut Statement*, p. 154.
11. *Time*, 10 April 1972, p. 77.
12. Tim Hildebrand, "Two or Three Things I Know about Kurt Vonnegut's Imagination," in *The Vonnegut Statement*, p. 132.

Slaughterhouse-Five and the Comforts of Indifference_____

C. Barry Chabot

There is a scene near the end of *Slaughterhouse-Five* which nicely captures Vonnegut's posture toward the world he would address. Having recently survived an airplane crash fatal to many acquaintances, including his father-in-law, and immediately thereafter suffering the accidental death of his wife, Billy Pilgrim journeys to New York City for the purpose of spreading the good news he has learned from the Tralfamadorians. While he has known this news for a considerable period, he had previously confined his missionary efforts to stray patients in need of comfort, such as a boy whose father had been killed in Vietnam. Now, however, the time is "ripe," and he comes to New York to address the populace at large. He checks into the Royalton Hotel and is assigned a room with a terrace overlooking Forty-fourth Street. As he prepares for his mission of mercy, he chances to look "down at all the people moving hither and yon. They were jerky little scissors. They were a lot of fun."[1] The derision this passage directs against those whom Billy Pilgrim would succor compromises the comfort he would give, and this tangle of motives—concern and contempt— typifies not only Pilgrim's attitude toward his fellows, but Vonnegut's as well.

If the Tralfamadorian vision of things holds out for Pilgrim some relief from the harsh terms of his life, it must be recognized that to some extent Vonnegut himself concocted that vision in an attempt to come to terms with his experience of the bombing of Dresden and all that experience had come to represent. The facts that they were both at Dresden, that both at least give mouth service to the Tralfamadorian vision, that both seek some comfort from it, and that both broadcast it to their fellows bespeak the extent to which Pilgrim stands in for his author. We need not question either the genuineness of their distress at the lot and the conduct of man or their sincerity in addressing their audiences in suggesting that that vision is cruelly inadequate, that its comforts are the comforts of indifference, that it is the opiate of the terminally weary, the defeated. Its solace is purchased only at the cost of accommodating oneself to the things one would otherwise regret, thereby insuring that they will multiply. If *Slaughterhouse-Five* urges such attitudes on us, it nonetheless provides us with an opportunity to understand the impasse they represent and to locate the slippage which transforms indignation into indifference, concern into taunt apathy.[2]

I

Slaughterhouse-Five begins in pain and indignation. It is, we are told, Vonnegut's attempt to recount and come to terms with the trauma of witnessing the destruction of Dresden while a prisoner of war. He had initially assumed that it would be a comparatively simple undertaking, a recital of facts and observations. Of course he was mistaken; words came slowly, seemed inadequate to the task, and he did not finish the novel for twenty-three years. The book completed, he remains dissatisfied, as he tells his editor in the first chapter: "It is so short and jumbled and jangled, Sam, because there is nothing intelligent to say about a massacre. Everybody is supposed to be dead, to never say anything or want anything ever again" (p. 19). What can one say about wanton destruction on this scale? Is it sufficient simply to tot up the losses, so many buildings, so many casualties, men, women and children?

As if the bombing of Dresden were not enough, during the course of the novel Vonnegut makes it emblematic of the destruction wrought by war generally. Thus he makes references to the concentration camps, the destruction of European Jewry, the bombing of Hiroshima, and behind them, as if to insist that such murderousness is no historical anomaly, to the children's crusades of another era. Beside these instances of mass slaughter, he sets references to smaller events, such as the executions of Private Slovik and Edgar Derby, which would seem comically disproportionate were their consequences not so dire. Corpses litter his pages. Since these deaths are all the fruits of man's own murderousness, they suggest that we are all secretly Roland Weary's and Paul Lazzaro's who derive some immense compensatory pleasure in the torture and destruction of our fellows. Of course this sense of man as casually destructive fully warrants Vonnegut's rage at such acts, and partially accounts for the particular acerbity of his depiction of the species as a whole.

However, deaths of another order are also recounted in *Slaughterhouse-Five*. The final chapter begins with these brief paragraphs:

> Robert Kennedy, whose summer home is eight miles from the home I live in all year round, was shot two nights ago. He died last night. So it goes.
>
> Martin Luther King was shot a month ago. He died, too. So it goes.
>
> And every day my Government gives me a count of corpses created by military science in Vietnam. So it goes.
>
> My father died many years ago now of natural causes. So it goes. He was a sweet man. He was a gun nut, too. He left me his guns. They rust. (p. 210)

While they extend the reign of murderousness both into the present and outside warfare, the first three paragraphs are nonetheless of a piece with the other incidents we have recounted: they offer further evidence of the murderousness of man. The final paragraph introduces another dimension; Vonnegut's father died of natural causes, not at the hands of others. However, the fact that it can be included as merely another item in this series, the fact that it too is punctuated by "So it goes," suggests that Vonnegut takes it to be loosely equivalent to the previous items in the series. This conflation of natural death with murders of various sorts is a consistent feature of *Slaughterhouse-Five*. Thus we are told early on in the novel that even were wars somehow eliminated (an unlikely eventuality, it is made clear), thus no longer being occasions for human misery and subsequent outrage, we would still be left with "plain old death" (p. 4). Twice Billy Pilgrim hears people agonizing about aging, once his mother (p. 44), and once an old man waiting to see a doctor: "'Oh God—' he said, 'I knew it was going to be bad getting old.' He shook his head. 'I didn't know it was going to be *this* bad'" (p. 189). Finally, I take it that the fact that the odor released as decomposing bodies are excavated from the ruins of Dresden—"the stink was like roses and mustard gas" (p. 214)—is identical to that of Vonnegut's own breath (p. 4) suggests his concern for his own mortality, for the workings of "plain old death."

The extent to which death as such comes to replace human murderousness as the especial regret of *Slaughterhouse-Five* must qualify Vonnegut's rage at the latter. Even if men did not visit violence upon their fellows, they would still, one and all, be subject to the reign of "plain old death." If death itself is the outrage, then humans cannot be held accountable for it, since it is built into the very structure of things. While their actions might hurry it in any particular instance, human violence brings nothing to pass that would not occur in any event. Thus when Vonnegut broadens the scope of his complaint to include the mere fact of death—that is, when he equates gratuitous murder with passing away in one's sleep—he deprives himself of any reason for holding any special animus toward those who perpetrate the mass slaughters which so exercise him.

The novel actually carries this deflation one step further. Not only people die, but so do champagne (p. 73), water (p. 101), and the novel (p. 205). The death of each is punctuated by "So it goes," thereby suggesting that they are all of a piece, roughly equivalent. Thus it is not just murder, not even the fact of human mortality, which outrages Vonnegut; it is rather the fact that all things in this universe apparently have some tropism toward death. Thus what began as an anguished outcry against particular atrocities becomes a lament at the manner in which the world happens to be put together. At this point one must ask if this does not trivialize the destruction of Dresden. Is there no difference among the items in this series: the bombing of Dresden, the assassinations of Kennedy and King, the executions of Slovik and Derby, the accidental death of Pilgrim's wife, and the deaths of champagne and water in a still glass? Are we to take each of them in the same way?

II

Vonnegut never lets us forget about death in *Slaughterhouse-Five*. The punctuation is insistent, relentless. By the time they have read any considerable portion of the novel, many readers find the reiterated phrase annoying, and I suspect that to some extent Vonnegut wants us to be annoyed. If the phrase "So it goes" insists that we attend to each and every death recounted in the novel, however, it also suggests a way to minimize its impact. We are told that the phrase, used by both Vonnegut and Pilgrim, originates with the Tralfamadorians, and if their version of things is accurate, death is not the terminal event we three-dimensional beings take it to be.

"The most important thing I learned on Tralfamadore," says Billy Pilgrim, "was that when a person dies he only *appears* to die." He continues:

> He is still very much alive in the past, so it is very silly for people to cry at his funeral. All moments, past, present, and future, always have existed, always will exist. . . . When a Tralfamadorian sees a corpse, all he thinks is that the dead person is in bad condition in that particular moment, but that the same person is just fine in plenty of other moments. Now, when I myself hear that somebody is dead, I simply shrug and say what the Tralfamadorians say about dead people, which is "So it goes." (pp. 26-27)

This obviously spatializes time, transforms moments into points on an eternal landscape. The future has already happened; it is just that those of us in three dimensions are ignorant of what is there. And if the future has already happened, if the next moment has already occurred someplace else, there can be no question of free will (p. 86): our actions are thoroughly determined, our lives laid down like railroad tracks we simply travel along. Let us consider several consequences of this view.

First, if everything has already happened, from some perspective there can be no suspense. In other words, suspense is a function of our ignorance of an already existent future, not the result of the structure of a world whose figure remains to be made. This accounts for the structure of Tralfamadorian novels:

> . . . the books were laid out . . . in brief clumps of symbols separated by stars. . . . [Each] clump of symbols is a brief, urgent message—describing a situation, a scene. We Tralfamadorians read them all at once, not one after the other. There isn't any particular relationship between all the messages, except that the author has chosen them carefully, so that, when seen all at once, they produce an image of life that is beautiful and surprising and deep. There is no beginning, no middle, no end, no suspense, no moral, no causes, no effects. What we love in our books are the depths of many marvelous moments seen all at one time. (p. 88)

The subtitle announces that *Slaughterhouse-Five* is something of a Tralfamadorian novel, and it surely meets many of the specifications. While we cannot read them at once, the novel is built up out of a series of brief fragments or episodes, which are in turn organized in such a manner that terms such as beginning, middle, and end do not capture its sequence. More substantially, Vonnegut deliberately undercuts the development of any suspense: the first chapter ends by providing the reader with the final words of the novel, and Edgar Derby is never mentioned without reference to the fact that he is to be executed for stealing a teapot, an event which is not finally narrated until the final pages of the novel. Each mention of Derby's fate serves as a reminder that his fate is already an accomplished fact.

Secondly, if there can be no question of human volition—if, as it were, determinism goes all the way down—people are relieved of all responsibility for their actions, for in such circumstances it cannot make sense to hold human agents accountable for their various doings. If Paul Lazzaro is craven and vicious, if he is to kill Billy Pilgrim, so be it. In this view he cannot be blamed; he is, like his victim, merely another bug caught in a particular piece of amber. He suffers his actions in the same manner that Billy Pilgrim does: he is, so to speak, simply a conduit for behavior that passes through him. Thus, in the Tralfamadorian view of things, guilt is a meaningless and empty notion; it can play no formative role in the conduct of human life (p. 207). Moreover, not only are men absolved from the consequences of their actions, but they are relieved as well from the responsibility for acting at all; that is, this view thrusts an individual into a passive relationship to his own actions. A life is something to be suffered or endured, not something one makes. Thus, although he cannot know it until much later, the utter passivity of Billy Pilgrim throughout his life comes to seem prescient once he has been schooled on Tralfamadore.

Finally, since all moments, happy and painful alike, already exist, and since the Tralfamadorians have access to a fourth dimension, on the principle of making the best of what is allotted them the Tralfamadorians attend only to the happy moments. While telling Pilgrim about the wars which mark their history, a Tralfamadorian guide tells him that "There isn't anything we can do about them, so we simply don't look at them. We ignore them. We spend eternity looking at pleasant moments—like today at the zoo. Isn't this a nice moment" (p. 117). The guide goes on to urge that earthlings too conduct their lives on such a policy, and a passing remark in the first chapter suggests that Vonnegut has taken the advice—at least he will try to forget the pain he has lived through (p. 22). Such a policy obviously removes the sting from disappointment and suffering; events which occasion them now take place behind one's back, without one ever submitting to their duration. With this move we are effectively immunized against death in any form.

III

Actually, this final piece of Tralfamadorian view of things introduces a telling inconsistency into the putative fabric of the novel. If all one's actions are as thoroughly determined as claimed, how is it that one can choose to "ignore the awful times, and concentrate on the good ones" (p. 117)? One could not. The only way this contradiction could be redeemed would be to grant the existence of psychic freedom in the midst of a physically determined universe. One can think what one will, but of course one's thought cannot alter the course of events, which will be what it must be. Thus psychic freedom has been purchased only at the cost of rendering thought impotent, of severing it completely from the events which otherwise compose one's life. This impotence in turn suggests another: for all that he would avail himself of this psychic freedom, Vonnegut seems unable to talk himself into complete accommodation to the ways of the world.

He surely tries. His accumulated distress and anger at all that he has witnessed of human perversity seem to have initially soured him on his fellows, and subsequently compelled him to search out some means to accommodate himself to the human scene. The means he hits upon are extreme: it seems that nothing less will do than to will his own indifference to the very things that cause him anguish. Remembering the destruction of Dresden during a time which suggested that it was anything but an aberration, that is, during the midst of the Vietnam War, Vonnegut seeks to anesthetize himself to his own grief. His allusion to Lot's wife is instructive, for *Slaughterhouse-Five* is a novel written by a man who would be stone (p. 22).

Were he successful, Vonnegut would be impervious to the stresses of events and the claims of those about him. However, he would achieve this peace only at the cost of trivializing the very events that make it necessary. If the destruction of Dresden (or of Vietnam) is on a par with natural deaths, much less with that of water in a still glass, there is no reason to single it out for special lament or comment. On this view, in fact, there is not even any viable reason to prefer peace (nor any means to achieve it) over distress; one should be indifferent even as regards such temporary mental states. The truth is, of course, that Vonnegut cannot sustain such indifference: his mask of indifference is repeatedly broached by his irrepressible rage at the events he documents.

Vonnegut is angry despite himself, and that anger keeps him from altogether assuming the angelic transcendence of the things of this world that he would otherwise affect. The problem, however, is that his rage consistently misses its mark. By making death itself rather than particular atrocities his object, he can only rail at presumed injustices that reach us all. By making all human action seem contemptible rather than certain human acts, his scorn must fall on all alike, the foolish and innocent as well as the wicked. We see this most clearly in the first and last chapters, those in which Vonnegut speaks in the first person. After reading that the world's total population is likely to double prior to the year 2000, Vonnegut sarcastically adds that he supposes that all will lay claim to being treated with "dignity" (p. 212). When in the first chapter he reports that Mary O'Hare, to whom the book is in part dedicated, is a trained nurse, he must add that that "is a lovely thing for a woman to be" (p. 12), a comment I can only read as gratuitous irony. Such diffuse anger constantly belies Vonnegut's claim that "Everything was Beautiful, and Nothing Hurt" (p. 122) could aptly serve for his, as well as Billy Pilgrim's epitaph.

The residual anger testifies to the futility of Vonnegut's cultivation of indifference. It is futile on several scores. To the extent that social life provides the impetus, such quietism can only insure the triumph of all that one regrets, for it leaves the issue uncontested. Further, even were human events as impervious to concerted intervention as Vonnegut seems to think, it is not at all clear that the mere shrug of one's shoulders is thereby the sole or most appropriate response. Might one not still comfort the hapless in ways more substantial than simply suggesting that they ignore their distress and think instead of happier times? that they are, in a way, wrong to feel pained at all? The cultivation of indifference is also futile in the sense of being finally impossible. Despite the human capacity for self-deception, its project can never reach completion, if only because of the vigilance with which one must guard against the encroachment of what one would forget. In *Slaughterhouse-Five* Vonnegut's rage—however now wide of its mark, however displaced—constitutes the last remnant of his concern; if its presence marks a failure, it is a failure that saves the novel from being an inhuman exercise.

Notes

1. Kurt Vonnegut, Jr., *Slaughterhouse-Five* (1969; rpt. New York: Dell, 1971), p. 199. All subsequent references will be to this readily available edition and will be incorporated into the text.

2. As should already be clear, my reading of the novel differs widely from the many which praise it as either a revelation of "the human condition" or a breakthrough toward something called "post-modernism." On the one hand I remain skeptical of ahistorical accounts of the human condition or the absurd; on the other I judge that the break with modernism is neither so complete nor triumphant as is usually claimed. On both scores, see Gerald Graff, *Literature Against Itself: Literary Ideas in Modern Society* (Chicago: Univ. of Chicago Press, 1979).

"This Lousy Little Book":
The Genesis and Development of *Slaughterhouse-Five* as Revealed in Chapter One_____

T. J. Matheson

Critics cannot agree on the meaning of Kurt Vonnegut's *Slaughterhouse-Five*. To Robert Merrill and Peter Scholl, the novel is best appreciated as a satire where "The object of satiric attack turns out to be a complacent response to the horrors of the age,"[1] in particular the Second World War. Though Dolores Gros Louis agrees, seeing the novel as a plea for "active pacifism,"[2] Maurice O'Sullivan believes the solution offered is more personal and argues that "Vonnegut offers art as the only potential form of transcendence"[3] from such horrors. In contrast, Robert Uphaus claims that Vonnegut, dealing "with the all-encompassing problem of human imagination pitted against the forces of historical extinction,"[4] offers no clear solution to the problem, and Patrick Shaw, of all the critics the most pessimistic, concludes that "Vonnegut's theme [is] that history, sex, religion, and life in general are all waste products of a world which is itself universally inconsequential."[5]

Most critics are agreed that *Slaughterhouse-Five* is a carefully structured work, while at the same time recognizing how difficult it is to determine the reasons behind the novel's structural pattern. For both the structure of the work and the author's treatment of his subject present many problems that do not admit to easy resolution. The first of these problems is encountered in the unusual opening chapter where Vonnegut, apparently speaking as himself, gives an account of the novel's genesis that cannot help but strike us initially as being carelessly written and filled with irrelevant, peripheral observations that seem to lead nowhere. Attempts to account for the purpose of Chapter One and its importance to the rest of the novel have been limited. Charles Harris, in one of the best essays on *Slaughterhouse-Five*,[6] is alone in investigating the matter in any detail. He shows that many of the images in the first chapter reappear later and is able to establish its importance accordingly. All the same, one is still left wondering why Vonnegut chose to introduce the novel in this way and is at something of a loss to explain how many of the seemingly random comments and observations relate to the rest of the book.

Upon inspection, it will be seen that the first chapter of *Slaughterhouse-Five* is of great importance in providing us with a means of tracing the author's evolving attitude both to the horrors of war and to the composition of his book as well. In this capacity, it outlines an artist's developing moral and aesthetic responses to a major aspect of the age in which he lived. Just as importantly, it also contains suggestions as to how *we* should respond intellectually and morally to war in particular and evil generally. For Vonnegut's theme is not as obscure as the structure of the work might imply. Indeed, there is every indication that his most fundamental concern is more traditional than has hitherto been assumed and is not so much with achieving "Henri Bergson's world of pure inner duration"[7] or even with the "psychological impact of time, death, and uncertainty"[8]—though these elements are undoubtedly present but simply with the problem of living in the midst of, and responding in a responsible manner to, evil as it is encountered in the modern world.

It should be noted that there is little agreement concerning the relationship of the narrator—who purports to be Vonnegut himself—to the novel as a whole. Donald Greiner believes the book was "written in Vonnegut's own voice,"[9] but to O'Sullivan "The 'I' of the first chapter is no more a perfect parallel of Vonnegut than the personae of many other works are to their authors. . . ." Rather, he is "a consciously crafted figure."[10] This latter view seems more likely to be the case; it is a view shared by Harris, who is without question correct to argue "that the Vonnegut of Chapter One is, indeed, a character in *Slaughterhouse-Five*."[11] But if he is a distinct character, it is also important to realize he is one to whom we are meant to respond ironically. There are several hints of this in the opening paragraphs. Even the first sentences of Chapter One are designed to give the reader pause, for we are informed that "All this happened, *more or less*," and that "The war parts, any-way, are *pretty much* true."[12] Since writers do not as a rule remind us of the extent to which their work is a fictional construct and not literally "true," Vonnegut may be trying to alert the reader to the fact that the naturalistic details of the book are not of primary importance, as they tend to be in many war novels. Furthermore, in that the comment distances the narrator from the subject of his narration, it enables us to see him as an entity distinct from the story he will subsequently tell and having an importance all his own.

If they missed this clue, even obtuse readers could not fail to be alerted when the narrator remarks that "I would hate to tell you what this lousy little book cost me in money and anxiety and time" (p. 2). Since such a contemptuous reference to a novel by the novelist himself is not something we normally encounter, the reader can safely conclude that Vonnegut is speaking ironically and is not making a straight-forward statement about the novel's literary worth, for if he genuinely did regard it as inferior—the usual meaning of the slang term "lousy"—he would surely not publish it in a form he found unsatisfactory. Obviously then, since the very appearance of the book is proof that Vonnegut regards it seriously, it is plain that he is not using the word "lousy" in the usual way. Since he does not appear to be speaking sarcastically, we are led to ask how the book might be "lousy" while not also being inferior. It is this question the remainder of Chapter One is concerned with answering.

Paradoxically, though here the narrator has just stated an apparent reluctance to outline the history of the novel's composition and his relationship to it, he proceeds to do just that and describes this history in considerable detail, in the process of which it becomes evident that we are also reading a history of the development of his character, as revealed through his evolving intellectual and artistic relationship not only to the book, but also to the central experience on which the book was based, the bombing of Dresden. As far as his actual character is concerned, Vonnegut wishes us to see the narrator (as a young man) as having been shallow, materialistic, and immature, and more than a little insensitive, for it is plain he initially regarded his war experiences as important primarily in terms of how they could advance his writing career. As a young man fresh from the Front, he naively "thought it would be easy for me to write about the destruction of Dresden, since all I would have to do would be to report what I had seen" (p. 2). With equal naiveté, he conceived his novel originally in epic terms suggestive of *Gone With the Wind*, "since the subject was so big," and thought it would virtually write itself and of its own accord emerge a "masterpiece" or at least make him "a lot of money." Epic war novels that make their authors rich likely have a mass appeal. To achieve this appeal, one suspects some sort of romantic sugarcoating of events— many of which are intrinsically grisly, horrid, and far from glamorous—must often take place, whereby they are rendered palatable to a mass audience. Evidently, the young author originally conceived his novel in such terms, probably as a romantic work that, if no true masterpiece, would nevertheless enjoy wide sales, in a word, a potboiler. However, "not many words" came from his mind, suggesting both that he soon learned it is not easy to write—about Dresden or anything else, for that matter—and also that on a deeper level, there was for all his immaturity a sense somewhere of moral and artistic responsibility to the events concerned.

The narrator then returns us to his present, reminding us that he has aged, having "become an old fart with his memories and his Pall Malls, with his sons full grown" (p. 2), presumably of an age to fight in yet another war. The real Vonnegut, incidentally, can scarcely be considered all that old (in 1968 he was forty-six), a discrepancy alerting us again to the distinction between the real novelist and his fictional narrator-persona. But what of his memories? Musing on the uselessness of his Dresden experiences, he is led inexplicably to recall a mildly vulgar limerick together with the well-known nonsense song "Yon Yonson":

There was a young man from Stamboul,
Who soliloquized thus to his tool:
"You took all my wealth
And you ruined my health,
And now you won't *pee*, you old fool."

    * * * * * * * * * * * *

My name is Yon Yonson,
I work in Wisconsin,
I work in a lumbermill there,
The people I meet when I walk down the street,
They say, "What's your name?"
And I say,
"My name is Yon Yonson,
I work in Wisconsin . . ."

And so on to infinity. (pp. 2-3)

Critics have experienced an understandable difficulty accounting for the relevance of the limerick; surely Rubens's dismissal of it as merely "scatological"[13] is insufficient, given the prominence obviously attached to it. It will be noted that the poem deals explicitly with penile dysfunction, presumably as a consequence of excessive sexual activity, expressed comically and employing the child's common euphemism for urination. Obviously a now-older man, for whom the possibility of sexual dysfunction is not so remote and as such not so easily laughed at, is revealing himself as perhaps a bit self-conscious about his advancing age and the possible loss of potency therein. But there is also a hint that in the very irrelevance of the memory recalled, Vonnegut is making a subtle point about the fallibility of the human memory and its inability to retain a sense of perspective or stay on subjects of great importance for any length of time. It is also interesting to note that in Legman's definitive collection of limericks, the example in question does not appear, suggesting, however obliquely, that the narrator is wrong to regard it as "famous" and that his sense of perspective is perhaps askew.[14]

With the "Yon Yonson" poem much the same points can be made, but in this latter example the preoccupation with irrelevance could be perpetuated to infinity, given the endlessly repetitive nature of the song. Surely the entire section is highly ironic, for what we have been presented with is a discussion of memory by a narrator who, though thinking of himself as laden with significant memories, is able only to recall nonsense rhymes and quite likely imperfectly at that.[15] The human mind has an inevitable tendency, it seems, to lose sight of the past, try as we might to keep it in view.

The narrator's inability to recall where his old girlfriends live also attests to this imperfection of memory. But the most compelling evidence of this deficiency is seen in his attempt to stimulate his memory of the war by having a reunion with Bernard O'Hare, his old war buddy. Although ostensibly a sincere effort to face the past, it is plain that his approach to the proposed book is not yet well thought out. That he is taking neither the events of the war themselves nor the writing of the novel very seriously is suggested by the fact that he is drunk when he first contacts O'Hare. Childishness is also evident in the narrator's very diction, as seen when he explains to O'Hare that he would "'like some help remembering stuff'" (p. 4).

It should come as no surprise, then, to learn that the novel as he originally conceived it was to have had a form, tone, and structure far different from that which *Slaughterhouse-Five* eventually assumed. By the narrator's own account, it appears to have been conceived along the lines of a conventional, popular war novel, full of action and suspense, easily understood by an unsophisticated reader and culminating in a conclusion wherein all issues appear to be resolved. It is plain, however, that the narrator will receive no help in this direction from the more mature O'Hare, a man too sensitive to the horrors of war ever to collaborate with a writer who would trivialize such experiences in fiction. Virtually alone among the prisoners of war, "O'Hare didn't have any souvenirs," possibly because war was so hideous to him that he refused to acquire any kind of booty or trophy that might become glamorous with the passage of time. Lest we miss this point, souvenir-hunting itself is portrayed as being either revoltingly ghoulish, in the case of the deranged Paul Lazzaro who "had about a quart of diamonds and emeralds and rubies" taken "from dead people in the cellars of Dresden" (p. 5), or simply vulgar and garish, like the Englishman so impressed over his worthless and tawdry "plaster model of the Eiffel Tower." Notably, the young narrator also possessed a souvenir.

Understandably, O'Hare is "unenthusiastic" about the reunion and claims "he couldn't remember much" (p. 4), possibly because the memories are so painful, but more likely because he senses that the book the narrator is planning to write, as described, will fail to do justice to the truth. O'Hare has every reason to suspect the narrator of intending to exploit the war for his own purposes. There is something unmistakably unfeeling in the way the narrator alludes so enthusiastically to the death of "'poor old Edgar Derby'" (p. 4), seeing it as an event important solely in terms of its irony and its resulting suitability as a possible climax for his novel, having more literary than human significance to him. This callous and cynical attitude to death suggests the narrator is not taking the war all that seriously; little genuine feeling is evident as he speaks. His very enthusiasm over the subject indicates he does not feel very deeply about it; one feels the sheer magnitude of the carnage ought to have a more sobering effect on a truly mature man. For that matter, the very importance he attaches to the novel's climax is significant when we recall that the word as a literary term usually heralds the appearance of the denouement, wherein all is resolved or unravelled. Clearly, the narrator himself intends to give the appearance in his novel of resolving issues that a more sensitive individual would see were beyond any such simplistic resolution, if they were resolvable at all. When asked "'where the climax should come'" O'Hare replies drily, "'That's your trade, not mine'" (p. 4), his use of the word "trade" revealing his awareness of the extent to which the narrator's methods are, after all, more those of a mechanic or laborer than of a truly creative artist.

At this point, the narration shifts again to the novelist's present, from which vantage point the older narrator, seeing his initial approach to the novel's composition from a better perspective, recognizes himself as having been nothing more than a would-be "trafficker in climaxes and thrills and characterization and wonderful dialogue and suspense and confrontations . . ." (p. 4). Vonnegut's use of the word "trafficker" is particularly apposite, for in addition to the immediate suggestion of a dealer in illicit drugs, one of the meanings of the word "traffic" is "unlawful or improper trade." Since a trafficker, then, is one who engages in improper trade—precisely as the astute O'Hare recognized, one notes—a "trafficker" in literature must be a writer who presents for consumption something artistically improper, a kind of literary contraband or drug. It follows that any war novel designed as the narrator originally conceived his, to be merely thrilling and suspenseful, providing a merely pleasurable experience for the reader, is also a drug of sorts in that the reader's responses are being dulled as effectively as the body is by a chemical opiate.

The drugging process alluded to is not the product simply of an author having romanticized war and its participants. Even the normal method of structuring a historical novel—especially a war novel— with a strict reliance on chronology, of necessity will present the reader with an illusion of logic and meaning by virtue of the apparent causal pattern therein. This positioning of the events of war in relation to their chronological sequence appears to give a coherence to the totality of the experiences themselves and makes sense of a series of occurrences that have no rational basis, as far as Vonnegut is concerned. Significantly, the "best outline" the young narrator ever made—presumably by "best" he means the most complete and symmetrical ordering of the events—he also describes as the "prettiest one," that is, the one most superficially attractive to the mind. This particular outline is drawn on a roll of wallpaper with his daughter's crayons, hinting that the very attempt to find such order is a puerile activity. Although Vonnegut's description of the outline seems to belabor the obvious—"One end of the wallpaper was the beginning of the story, and the other end was the end, and then there was all that middle part, which was the middle" (p. 5)—it is inserted to draw our attention to how the war as depicted would visually appear as the wallpaper scroll was unrolled. Each event would pass quickly before our eyes, first in and then out of sight: "The destruction of Dresden was represented by a vertical band of orange cross-hatching, and all the lines that were still alive passed through it, came out the other side" (p. 5). The vertical band itself, of course, along with the many thousands of implied lines that were not still alive, all disappear conveniently as the scroll is turned, located as the event is on only one point on the wallpaper.

In thus reducing the destruction of Dresden to one of many events specific in space and time, the outline also reduces it in importance, allowing it to be seen and then dismissed as something that was merely part of a causal process that otherwise ends happily with the release of the still-living prisoners of war. The horror of the firebombing, the countless deaths, the magnitude of the carnage and the evil behind it: all have been safely rolled away and consigned to oblivion. Interestingly enough, as the narrator recalls this original plan for the book, he does not stop neatly at the point where the novel as originally conceived was to close, but continues, returning us again to the immediate present, seeing himself as before as an "old fart" and recalling the "Yon Yonson" poem once more, a recollection that indicates he has since learned that he lives *not* in a world where events can disappear conveniently from his consciousness once they have been experienced, but one where even trivial events through memory keep returning to consciousness, in the sense suggested both by the endless circularity of the song and by his repeated recollection of it. Moreover, particularly unpleasant or unsettling memories cannot be dismissed by honest individuals and must form part of the baggage all sensitive men and women carry with them as a consequence of their sensitivity. Such people recognize that there are certain occurrences which, through their sheer magnitude, contain a kind of eternal relevance and must be acknowledged as forever important; what they tell us about the human condition is simply too valuable to be allowed to forget.

At the same time, there are many forces in society working to encourage such forgetfulness. As a civilian attempting to learn why Dresden was bombed, the narrator encounters resistance everywhere from military public relations men. Public relations itself is presented in *Slaughterhouse-Five* as a profession almost exclusively concerned with suppressing truth; importantly, the narrator after the war was in public relations. His boss in PR, we are told, joins the Dutch Reformed Church. This seemingly irrelevant bit of information, upon reflection, can be seen as ironically appropriate in light of that institution's Calvinistic emphasis on the total depravity of man. For that matter, the boss, through his profession and his attitude to war—an officer (in PR!) during the war, he sneers at the narrator for not having been an officer too—becomes himself convincing proof that the church's assumptions about human evil are correct.

With his conventionally attired little girls, the narrator appears at the O'Hare house, expecting a comfortable evening of drink, good fellowship, and pleasant reminiscences. To his surprise Mary O'Hare, refusing to cater to his expectations, seats them on "two straight-backed chairs at a kitchen table with a white porcelain top. That table top was screaming with reflected light from a two-hundred watt bulb overhead" (p. 11), a far cry from the snug and cozy scene the narrator had sentimentally imagined, of "two leather chairs near a fire in a paneled room, where two soldiers could drink and talk" (p. 11). Unwilling to provide the narrator with an atmosphere conducive to nostalgia, Mary O'Hare presents them with "an operating room," the better to examine (and perhaps dissect) their memories honestly. O'Hare himself is unable to drink and as such cannot enter into the world of alcoholic sentimentality the narrator had anticipated. Not surprisingly, under such conditions neither man "could remember anything good" (p. 12), because in truth nothing good can ever be said of war. At this point Mary, angrily aware of the tendency in popular novels to find something of positive value in war, accuses the narrator of intending to do likewise and ignore the fact that wars are not fought by "'glamorous, war-loving, dirty old men'" but by babies, "foolish virgins . . . at the end of childhood" (p. 13). Mary recognizes that the very attempt to romanticize such horrors makes them palatable to a subsequent generation of "babies" who, ignorant of the hideous realities, rush headlong into new wars in a pathetic and misguided attempt to gain experience they mistakenly conclude their forefathers found meaningful.

At this point, the narrator attains a new level of understanding. To his credit, he both recognizes and sympathizes with what angered Mary and vows that he will write a book for which no parts could be played by Frank Sinatra or John Wayne, two actors we easily associate with typically unsophisticated and glamorous war movies. Furthermore, he promises to subtitle his book "The Children's Crusade" in acknowledgment of what Mary has taught him.

Once having seen this, the narrator's approach to his subject begins to change dramatically. In curiosity, he and O'Hare turn to an account of the original Children's Crusade, Charles Mackay's *Extraordinary Popular Delusions and the Madness of Crowds* (London, 1841), wherein much is made of the vast difference between the dispassionate historical record which reveals the Crusades as a particularly distasteful chapter in human history—the Children's Crusade was nothing more than the result of an attempt by two cynical monks to sell homeless children into slavery in Africa—and the romantic account, which *"dilates upon their piety and heroism, and portrays, in her most glowing and impassioned hues, their virtue and magnanimity, the imperishable honor they acquired for themselves, and the great service they* [supposedly] *rendered to Christianity"* (p. 14). Later that night he reads a history of Dresden left at his bedside by O'Hare which further sensitizes him to the fact that man's inhumanity to man is a recurring, if not also permanent, aspect of the human condition, be it manifested in the Children's Crusade, the destruction of Dresden by Frederick the Great, or even the American Revolutionary War. Through this reading, the narrator comes to see that there are, broadly speaking, two approaches he can take to historical manifestations of evil, one straightforward, the other disingenuous: he can face all the facts squarely, letting them speak for themselves, or he can edit history by romanticizing or flatly ignoring events that are intrinsically sordid, unpleasant, or ugly, as he had originally intended to do.

At the World's Fair, the narrator encounters displays portraying "what the past had been like, according to the Ford Motor Car Company and Walt Disney" (p. 16). These allusions are particularly appropriate when we recall Henry Ford's contemptuous dismissal of history as "bunk" and are reminded of the Disney Studio's sentimental—but very profitable!—interpretations of American history; both are essentially exploiting the past in a manner that reminds us of how far the narrator has progressed beyond his initial approach to his subject. His ensuing question about time—"how wide it was, how deep it was, how much was mine to keep" (p. 16)—also serves to reveal his new awareness that the past is not his personal property which he has a right to manipulate or dispose of irresponsibly.

Following his meeting with O'Hare, the narrator spends time at the Writers' Workshop at the University of Iowa, initially still at work on his "famous book about Dresden" (p. 16). But the O'Hares have had a lasting effect on his original plan for the novel; upon completion, he refers simply to it as—"'the book,'" "short and jumbled and jangled . . . because there is nothing intelligent to say about a massacre" (p. 17). Of course, by speaking of his novel as jumbled, Vonnegut is not implying that the structure is unplanned and truly meaningless, that the novel is poorly thought-out or unintelligible, or that *Slaughterhouse-Five* is the work of a moral cynic and aesthetic nihilist. For the narrator adds in strong and unequivocal language a statement indicating that his abhorrence of war is absolute and unqualified, having told his "sons that they are not *under any circumstances* to take part in massacres, and that the news of massacres of enemies is not to fill them with satisfaction or glee" (p. 17, my italics). Chaotic though the book may appear, it was neither conceived nor put together indifferently, at least in its final form. On the contrary, the apparently haphazard movement of the novel, the purposeful violation of normal chronological sequence, and the absence of conventional attitudes regarding the subject matter, are all purposefully inserted to prevent the reader from emerging from the work with a comfortable sense that moral order has been restored with the ending of the war, or that the factors that precipitated the carnage have been resolved or eradicated.

The narrator-author has also come to see that almost all historical war novels distort the truth in conveying the impression that objective order and rationality prevail, just because various occurrences such as the events of World War II can be arranged on the basis of their chronological sequence. Even acknowledging the premise that a war has a beginning, a middle, and an end in a novel could detract from our ability to comprehend fully the actual madness behind it. To prevent all of this from happening in his own war novel, Vonnegut tampers throughout with temporal structure, presents us with a non-hero so weak and passive it is impossible not to regard him with ambivalence, and denies this figure even the ability to remain rooted in causal time. But Billy's inability to put the events of time forever behind him is a trait shared by the reader of *Slaughterhouse-Five*, who is also at the mercy of the "Tralfamadorian" structure of the novel as engineered by the author, where all key events—the bombing of Dresden, the death of Edgar Derby, etc.—are repeated again and again. That the reader is never allowed to lose sight of these events reinforces what is surely one of Vonnegut's main themes in the novel: that since man's destructive nature is always with us, events should never be forgotten, if we are ever to stand a chance of preventing them from recurring.

As a means of keeping the memory of Dresden fresh in his mind, Vonnegut and O'Hare make plans to return to that city. Waiting for his delayed plane in a hotel, the narrator remarks that "The time would not pass. Somebody was playing with the clocks, and not only with the electric clocks, but the wind-up kind, too. The second hand on my watch would twitch once, and a year would pass, and then it would twitch again" (p. 18). Here, Vonnegut is reminding us that there are many ways of viewing time. Our common perception of it as a linear procession of discrete but causally linked events, where the past is generally regarded accordingly as less relevant to us than the present, is arbitrary and only a convention we adopt for convenience's sake. Although we must submit to the convention for practical purposes—the narrator sees that "As an Earthling, [he] had to believe whatever clocks said—and calendars" (p. 18)—this does not mean that past and present are not of equal importance. Doubtless for this reason he is often ignorant of the time, seeing as he does that "knowing what time it is" and being able to place oneself securely in time provide us with a potentially deceptive security and a not very valuable kind of knowledge.

Two books the narrator takes with him to Dresden also influence his final conception of the novel. From the first, a volume of Theodore Roethke's poetry, the narrator quotes the following lines from "The Waking":

> *I wake to sleep, and take my waking slow.*
> *I feel my fate in what I cannot fear.*
> *I learn by going where I have to go.* (p. 18)

Here, what impresses the narrator is Roethke's recognition that the sensitization of consciousness is related directly to facing what one *must* face, that integrity consists in part in choosing or deciding to embark on a path one has come to see as essential both to one's growth and one's being.

The second passage, taken from Céline (another author scarred by an earlier war), is also relevant; the narrator recalls "the amazing scene in *Death on the Installment Plan* where Céline wants to stop the bustling of a street crowd. He screams on paper, *Make them stop . . . don't let them move anymore at all . . . There, make them freeze . . . once and for all! . . . So that they won't disappear anymore!"* (pp. 18-19). What bothers Céline and now the narrator as well is the notion of time's events as consisting of movement first in and then out of consciousness. Céline's desire to stop the crowd on the street—in itself a most appropriate metaphor for time as perpetual flux—is the expression of a wish to extricate himself from the movement of present events into the irretrievable past, to "freeze" or suspend time in one's consciousness to keep it from being lost forever. In a sense, the final structure of *Slaughterhouse-Five* is an attempt to do just that, by moving beyond the wallpaper outline and satisfying Céline's demand that the crowd be "stopped." By continually reminding us throughout the novel of the slaughter that occurred in Dresden, by telling us of his originally intended climax—the absurd death of Edgar Derby—in the opening paragraph and reminding us of it repeatedly, and by never allowing readers the luxury of putting the novel's atrocities into our own intellectual "pasts," he keeps the eternal importance of the horror together with his own message constantly before our eyes.

The narrator then turns to the Bible for one of the first recorded "firebombings" in history, the destruction of Sodom and Gomorrah. In this final recollection, past and present meet.[16] Like Lot's wife, also permanently devastated by what she saw—he describes himself as a "pillar of salt" (p. 19)—he too is one who dared to look back whatever the consequences and write his "lousy little book," a failure in popular, conventional terms,[17] containing no suspense, no climax as such, and no surprises in plot. Even Billy's unusual relationship to time is discussed at the outset of Chapter Two, and the first few pages go on to delineate with scrupulous fidelity to chronology the major events in Billy's life, thus getting the mere sequence of events out of the way, as it were, and virtually forcing the reader to concentrate on the more important aspects of the book. The final sentences of Chapter One, containing the cryptic first and last sentences of the novel that follows, remind us that terms like "beginning" and "end" have no meaning or

---

importance as far as this novel is concerned. But, in preventing us from enjoying his war novel in the usual way, the very unsettling nature of the ensuing work does far greater justice to the subject matter and enables us to see the permanent, lasting evil of war with a greater degree of clarity and to respond with more sensitivity to it than we would otherwise have been able to do.

From *Studies in the Novel* 16, no. 2 (1984): 228-240. Copyright © 1984 by the University of North Texas. Reprinted with permission of the University of North Texas.

Notes

1. "Vonnegut's *Slaughterhouse-Five*: The Requirements of Chaos," *Studies in American Fiction*, 6 (1978), 65-76.

2. "*Slaughterhouse-Five*: Pacifism vs. Passiveness," *Ball State University Forum*, 18, No. 2 (1977), 3-8.

3. "*Slaughterhouse-Five*: Kurt Vonnegut's Anti-Memoirs," *Essays in Literature* (Western Illinois University), 3 (1976), 244-50.

4. "Expected Meaning in Vonnegut's Dead-End Fiction: *Breakfast of Champions* and Others," *Novel*, 8 (1975), 164-74.

5. "The Excrement Festival: Vonnegut's *Slaughterhouse-Five*," *Scholia Satyrica*, 2, No. 3 (1976), 3-11.

6. "Time, Uncertainty, and Kurt Vonnegut Jr.: A Reading of *Slaughterhouse-Five*," *Centennial Review*, 20 (1976), 228-43.

7. Philip M. Rubens, "Nothing's Ever Final: Vonnegut's Concept of Time," *College Literature*, 6 (1979), 64-72.

8. Harris, p. 228.

9. "Vonnegut's *Slaughterhouse-Five* and the Fiction of Atrocity," *Critique*, 14, No. 3 (1973), 38-51.

10. O'Sullivan, p. 245.

11. Harris, p. 230.

12. Kurt Vonnegut, Jr. *Slaughterhouse-Five* (New York: Delacorte Press, 1969), p. 1, my italics. All subsequent references are to this edition and appear in the text.

13. Rubens, p. 68.

14. The one similar reference to penile dysfunction that does appear in Legman is expressed in explicit, sexually coarse language: to wit, "But now you've quit fucking, you fool!" See G. Legman, ed., *The Limerick: 1700 Examples, with Notes, Variants, and Index* (New York: Bell, 1969), note to limerick #1098, p. 435.

15. Is it possible that Vonnegut has purposely left out half of the sixth line of "Yon Yonson"? Although there is no authoritative source for this nonsense song, the version

I (and others) recall runs as follows: "They say 'What's your name?'/ And I say *just the same,/* 'My name is Yon Yonson . . .'" etc. Obviously, the addition to the line completes the metric regularity of the song; the version the narrator recalls is more jarring, and, if consciously left out by Vonnegut, might be designed to alert us to the fact that the narrator has forgotten part of a line.

16. Edward A. Kopper, Jr. ("Operation Gomorrah in *Slaughterhouse-Five*," *Notes on Contemporary Literature*, 8, No. 4 [1978], 6) has made the interesting suggestion that the cities of Hamburg and Dresden, both firebombed during the war, are a modern equivalent of the biblical Sodom and Gomorrah, and offers as proof the fact that the "name of the Allied operation against the city of Hamburg was 'Gomorrah,'" thus justifying Vonnegut's allusion to the Old Testament cities further and adding to our sense of history as endlessly repetitive and of evil as perpetually present.

17. Vonnegut, at the time he wrote these words, could not have predicted the tremendous commercial success his novel would enjoy.

Adam and Eve in the Golden Depths:
Edenic Madness in *Slaughterhouse-Five*_____

Leonard Mustazza

Critics of *Slaughterhouse-Five* have long recognized Billy Pilgrim's need to "create," albeit involuntarily, his Tralfamadorian experience. Wayne McGinnis writes that "what makes self-renewal possible in *Slaughterhouse-Five* is the human imagination, . . . the value of the mental construct."[1] "Tralfamadore is a fantasy," argue Robert Merrill and Peter Scholl, "a desperate attempt to rationalize chaos, but one must sympathize with Billy's need to create Tralfamadore. After all, the need for supreme fictions is a very human trait."[2] More specifically, a few commentators have noticed (mostly in passing) that Billy's space fantasy reflects Edenic yearnings. Frederick Karl, for instance, calls Billy's fantasy "sentimentalized, a golden age, the Edenic place, all to give Billy an alternative experience."[3] Along somewhat different lines, Glenn Meeter argues that Billy's backward movie, which ends with Adam and Eve in Eden, reflects a vision of history as sin and shows that "the fall of man for Vonnegut is a fall from timelessness into history, as it is in heretical readings of *Paradise Lost*."[4] Others have made similar points.[5]

In this chapter, I would like to look closely at the linkage that Vonnegut draws in this, his most successful novel, between Eden and Tralfamadore. From the moment he comes "unstuck in time," Billy Pilgrim tries to construct for himself an Edenic experience out of materials he garners over the course of some twenty years. Although Billy's Eden differs very much from Paul Proteus's, Malachi Constant's, and Howard Campbell's, Vonnegut subtly manipulates here the same familiar myth; and ironically, the pathetic protagonist of *Slaughterhouse-Five* is the most successful of his central figures in realizing his pursuit of Genesis. In order to throw the contours of this myth into sharper relief, I will use here not the Genesis account, for, in itself, it is far too underdeveloped. Instead, Milton's *Paradise Lost* provides a useful framework within which to consider Billy's myth, which, like Milton's Edenic sequences, reflects universal preoccupations with such matters as life and death, free will, the acquisition of knowledge, the fall into history, and the narrative recapturing of the perfect place where all answers are available, where everything is neatly ordered. Milton's epic provides a convenient and remarkably revealing exostructure[6] against which we might compare Billy's Edenic yearnings.

It soon becomes quite clear in *Slaughterhouse-Five* that Billy Pilgrim's madness is one with a method in it: his "trip" to Tralfamadore and the "knowledge" he brings back reflecting his own desperate yearnings after peace, love, immutability, stability, and an ordered existence. To come to terms with the horrors he has witnessed in the war, Billy, taking his cue from the well-known Eliot Rosewater, his fellow patient at a veterans' hospital, tries to "re-invent [himself] and [his] universe," in which reinvention "science fiction was a big help" (101). It comes as no surprise, of course, that the writer Rosewater recommends to Billy is none other than Kilgore Trout, whose fanciful plots, supplemented by some other outside details, help Billy to forge his illusory trip into outer space. That trip proves to be mythic in that, like traditional mythic narratives, it provides answers, decidedly idiosyncratic ones, to the existential problems confronting humanity. Joseph Campbell's distinction between myth and dream can well apply in Billy's case. Campbell defines *dream* as "personalized myth" and *myth* as "depersonalized dream," the former "quirked by the peculiar troubles of the dreamer," the latter making problems and solutions valid for all of humanity.[7] One might fairly easily substitute *madness* for Campbell's *dream*. Like the dreamer's involuntary nightly visions, the schizophrenic's involuntary hallucinations obliquely reflect his or her own peculiar troubles. Unlike the dreamer, however, the schizophrenic cannot readily awaken and allow reality to take control, and so it is with Billy. His hallucinations must, therefore, become his reality, making him a permanent dreamer. Unlike the dreamer, too, Billy will not leave his "personalized myth" on the personal level. Rather, he depersonalizes it and tries to make it valid for everyone by sharing it on a New York radio program. In a very limited sense, what also depersonalizes his story is the fact that we can discern in it some familiar contours of other mythic narratives, and the fact that he uses the science fiction form, which Northrop Frye, among others, has associated with earlier mythic narratives, calling it "a mode of romance with a strong inherent tendency to myth."[8] Thus, Vonnegut brilliantly turns Billy's self-generated truths into both a schizophrenic delusion and an age-old universal means of coming to terms with life's hidden meanings. As such, he also adapts this very human need for supreme fictions to the sad circumstances of Billy's life while making a wry comment on the persistence of such fictions.

The specific connection between the Tralfamadorian experience and the myth of Eden occurs subtly but unmistakably. Shortly after Billy comes "unstuck in time" during the war, he and his unwilling companion (and now would-be murderer), Roland Weary, are taken prisoner by a group of misfit German soldiers, one of whom, a middle-aged corporal, is wearing golden cavalry boots taken from a dead Hungarian soldier on the Russian front:

> Those boots were almost all he owned in this world. They were his home. An anecdote: One time a recruit was watching him bone and wax those golden boots, and he held one up to the recruit and said, "If you look in there deeply enough, you'll see Adam and Eve."
>
> Billy Pilgrim had not heard this anecdote. But, lying on the black ice there, Billy stared into the patina of the corporal's boots, saw Adam and Eve in the golden depths. They were naked. They were so innocent, so vulnerable, so eager to behave decently. Billy Pilgrim loved them. (53)

By contrast, the pair of feet next to the corporal's are swaddled in rags, and yet the imagery surrounding the owner of those feet is comparable to the mythic references used to describe the corporal's boots.

Those feet belong to a fifteen-year-old boy whose face was that of a "blond angel," a "heavenly androgyne." "The boy," the narrator tells us, in a most significant analogy, "was as beautiful as Eve" (53). What all of these images reveal is that Billy's preoccupations are rapidly moving away from the personal level toward the cosmic, from his own real and perceived experiences there on the black ice to those of the race. Shortly before Billy's capture, at the point where he becomes unstuck in time, the narrator says that "Billy's attention began to swing grandly through the full arc of his life." Specifically, he considers three pleasantly passive moments: pre-birth ("red light and bubbling sounds"), being thrown into a swimming pool by his father ("there was beautiful music everywhere"), and his own death ("violet light—and a hum") (43-44). The common thread running through these "experiences" is Billy's desire for inaction, passivity, semi-loss of consciousness, a sort of *regressus ad uterum*.[9] When he sees Adam and Eve in the golden boots, however, his concerns are suddenly enlarged to include not only his own vulnerability to forces beyond his control but all of humanity's, a condition that represents, mythically, a fall from Adam's and Eve's primal innocence. In other words, he begins by considering his own passive innocence and moves backwards to the innocence of the species, although, conveniently, he does not acknowledge the fact that those mythic figures in the golden depths were themselves far from passive, and that their "activity" is what is said to have caused the dire condition in which he finds himself.

Likewise, on his daughter's wedding day later in his life, Billy comes "slightly unstuck in time" and "watches" a war movie backwards, beginning with German planes sucking bullets out of American planes and ending with specialists whose job it is to bury the minerals with which bombs are made so that those minerals can never hurt anyone again. Significantly, however, Billy's wish-fulfilling movie, his imaginative effort, in Jerome Klinkowitz's words, "to turn things around"[10] does not end there:

The American fliers turned in their uniforms, became high school kids. And Hitler turned into a baby, Billy Pilgrim supposed. That wasn't in the movie. Billy was extrapolating. Everybody turned into a baby, and all humanity, without exception, conspired biologically to produce two perfect people named Adam and Eve, he supposed. (75)

Vonnegut gives us unmistakable clues here as to the direction Billy's creative fantasies are taking. Billy's extrapolations and suppositions enable him to go well beyond the limits of the movie, and his additions to the film suggest his preoccupations not merely with the state of individual "babyhood,"[11] but with the innocent perfection of the race.

By the same token, however, Billy's delusions and extrapolations and his subsequent creation of a "solution" also suggest his awareness of the race's inability to go backwards. Knowing that the biblical past itself is unrecoverable, therefore, he uses various materials—his longings, his readings, his experiences—to forge a world, Tralfamadore, which is futuristic to all appearances but which, in effect, carries out all of the functions of the mythic world he yearns after. Billy finds what prove to be his most important source materials in a tawdry Times Square bookstore that he visits in 1968, over twenty years after the war. First he notices a Kilgore Trout novel entitled *The Big Board*, which concerns an Earthling couple who have been kidnapped by extraterrestrials and put on display in a zoo. The visitors to this zoo are entertained by the Earthlings' reactions to the rising and falling prices of their supposed investments on Earth. In reality, however, the telephone, the big board, and the ticker with which they monitor their "fortunes" are fakes, designed only as "stimulants to make the Earthlings perform vividly for the crowds at the zoo . . ." (201). In the same bookstore, Billy also sees a pornographic magazine with a question on its cover, "What really happened to Montana Wildhack?" (204), and he subsequently watches a film on a movie machine of an erotic performance by Wildhack (205). All of these details, modified to suit his needs, will become quite significant in Billy's space fantasy; and Vonnegut takes pains to show whence those details derive. In this regard, the novel proves to be realistic, providing us with a portrait of a pathetic man. Yet, there is also a larger context for Billy's myth-making. His alterations to his source materials to create his personal myth again reflect his longings—as do his view of Adam and Eve in the corporal's boots in 1945 and, much later in his life, his extrapolations and suppositions about Adam and Eve while watching the backward movie. It is with these alterations that Billy is finally able to bridge the gap between his longing for Eden and the dire facts of his life. Before considering those alterations and what they imply, however, I would like to look briefly at the actions and concerns of Milton's Adam and then compare Billy's to those of the race's mythic progenitor.

Barbara Lewalski correctly observes that "in *Paradise Lost* the Edenic life is radical growth and process, a mode of life steadily increasing in complexity and challenge and difficulty but, at the same time and by that very fact, in perfection."[12] We may best discern this increasing complexity if we consider their earliest experiences. Upon awakening to life, Adam soon realizes that he can speak; and he immediately asks "Ye Hills and Dales, ye Rivers, Woods, and Plains/ And ye that live and move, fair creatures" (8.275-76) who made him. The very act of inferring the existence of "some great Maker" from the beauty and rational order he beholds demonstrates the start of the "radical growth" that Lewalski comments upon. (It might be noted here that, in contrast to Adam's extrapolations, which lend complexity to his initial experiences, Billy's are intended to take him in the opposite direction, from horrifying complexity to simple innocence.) Before long, Adam's Maker does appear to him in "shape Divine," and gives him the "Garden of Bliss," his "Mansion," his "seat prepar'd." There Adam does two significant things: he names the creatures over which he has been given dominion, and he debates with his Maker for a mate, one in whom he can find "rational delight" and "By conversation with his like to help,/ Or solace his defects" (8.418-19). We soon learn that this debate was not so much persuasive as instructional, for God used it to observe Adam's ratiocinative powers ("for trial only brought,/ To see how thou couldst judge of fit and meet" [447-48]) and to instruct him in disputation and reasoning. Adam, who has passed this trial admirably, is then put to sleep, and his request for a mate is granted. The result, as Adam exclaims, is magnificent:

> On she came,
> Led by her Heav'nly Maker, though unseen,
> And guided by his voice, nor uninform'd
> Of nuptial Sanctity and marriage Rites:
> Grace was in all her steps, Heav'n in her Eye,
> In every gesture dignity and love.
>
> (8.484-89)

As always, the context in which we derive all of this information is important. Adam reveals these details in a conversation with the angel Raphael, whom Adam refers to variously as "glorious shape" (5.309; 362), "Divine instructor" (5.546), "Divine Interpreter" (7.72), and "Divine Historian" (8.6-7). For his part, Raphael's function is to inform Adam about things that "surmount the reach/ Of human sense" (5.571-72), that "human sense cannot reach" (7.75); and Adam's deferential epithets reveal his awareness of the privilege conferred upon him by his angelic visitor.

Interestingly, virtually all of these elements—a prepared habitat, instruction by a higher power, a mate whom he regards as perfect—can be discerned in Billy's mythic space fantasy. Frederick Karl has noted that, "even though Billy is exhibited in a zoo, as an animal to their human, Tralfamadore represents paradise . . ."[13] and, viewed against the background of Milton's Edenic milieu, this "paradise" comes into sharper focus.

The initial linkage of space fantasy and Eden is accomplished by Vonnegut's juxtaposing of scenes. Immediately after Billy watches his backward movie, extrapolating that the film begins/ends with Adam and Eve, he goes into the backyard to meet his Tralfamadorian kidnappers. They take him aboard their craft and introduce an anesthetic into the atmosphere so that he will sleep. When he awakens, like Adam, he finds himself in his new "Mansion," on display under a geodesic dome, the symbolic counterpart of "the uttermost convex/ Of this great Round" in *Paradise Lost* (7.266-67). Within this domed enclosure, he breathes air. He cannot exist outside of it for the element of his transcendent masters is cyanide.

The environment in which Billy finds himself, though very different from Adam's on the surface, is also ironically comparable. The beauty of Milton's Eden is such that it fills the angels who behold it with awe, a place of stunning natural loveliness and utility, where "Out of the fertile ground [God] caus'd to grow/ All Trees of noblest kind for sight, smell, taste" (4.216-17). Billy's paradise is, likewise, a perfect place for him as a middle-class, middle-minded, twentieth-century Earthling. The natural habitat may be fine for Adam, but only the best in ornamental conveniences will do for Billy; and these come not from the hand of God but from a Sears Roebuck warehouse in Iowa City:

> There was a color television set and a couch that could be converted into a bed. There were end tables with lamps and ashtrays on them by the couch. There was a home bar and two stools. There was a little pool table. There was wall-to-wall carpeting in federal gold, except in the kitchen and bathroom areas and over the iron manhole cover in the center of the floor. There were magazines arranged in a fan on the coffee table in front of the couch.
>
> There was a stereophonic phonograph. The phonograph worked. The television didn't. There was a picture of one cowboy killing another one pasted to the television tube. (112)

In this familiar place, Billy goes about the routines of life—eating "a good breakfast from cans," washing his plate and eating utensils, exercising, taking showers, using deodorant—and the visitors to the zoo are fascinated by his appearance and his actions. Milton's Adam and Eve are also on display to the angels, as is made clear when a disguised Satan tells Uriel that he wishes "with secret gaze,/ Or open admiration" (3.671-72) to behold the newly created beings in Eden, and when Adam tells Eve that "Millions of spiritual Creatures walk the Earth" and admire God's works (4.677-80), which works include the human creatures themselves. Although Milton is, of course, serious in his portrayal of the prime creatures of the new creation and the admiration they inspire in the superior spiritual beings who behold them, Vonnegut's comic portrayal nevertheless evokes a similar sense of Billy's special place in his new environment. This special status conferred (or self-conferred) on the otherwise pathetic Billy Pilgrim is further evidenced by another parallel with Adam. Like Adam in his "naked Majesty" (4.290), Billy is naked in his contrived new home (111), and wryly evoking Adam's shameless nakedness and proud majesty, Vonnegut indicates that, since the Tralfamadorians could not know that Billy's body and face were not beautiful, "they supposed that he was a splendid specimen," and "this had a pleasant effect on Billy, who began to enjoy his body for the first time" (113). In short, Billy has found a way to make himself like the prime of men.

By the same token, he also finds a way to make his overlords different from, and yet superior to, the weaker human species, a relationship that is also obtained in *Paradise Lost*. Although Milton's angels are invisible spirits, Raphael takes on a form when he goes to meet Adam, and here is how the narrator describes the angel's "proper shape":

> A Seraph wing'd: six wings he wore, to shade
> His lineaments Divine; the pair that clad
> Each shoulder broad, came mantling o'er his breast
> With regal Ornament; the middle pair
> Girt like a Starry Zone his waist, and round
> Skirted his loins and thighs with downy Gold

And colors dipt in Heav'n; the third his feet
Shadow'd from either heel with feathered mail
Sky-tinctur'd grain. Like *Maia's* son he stood,
And shook his Plumes, that Heav'nly fragrance fill'd
The circuit wide.

(5.277-87)

The divine shape (taken from Isaiah 6:2), the heavenly colors, the likening of the angel to Mercury (Maia's son) all serve to ennoble Raphael and to underscore his superior otherworldliness. Moreover, just as angels are superior to human beings in appearance, so are they above humans intellectually. Raphael soon makes clear to Adam that, while both angels and human beings have been endowed with the ability to reason, human reasoning is often carried out discursively while angels reason intuitively, the two modes "differing but in degree, of kind the same" (5.486-90). In other words, Raphael must make certain accommodations in order to adapt the information he conveys to Adam, whose powers of comprehension are more limited than those of the angels.

Likewise, various corporeal and ratiocinative differences between human beings and Tralfamadorians are evident in *Slaughterhouse-Five*. The aliens' shape is the most humorous and provocative:

. . . they were two feet high, and green, and shaped like plumber's friends. Their suction cups were on the ground, and their shafts, which were extremely flexible, usually pointed to the sky. At the top of each shaft was a little hand with a green eye in its palm. (26)

Whereas Milton ennobles his "divine shapes" by making them grander than humans, Vonnegut presents the otherworldliness of the Tralfamadorians comically, simultaneously letting us share in Billy's wonder and undercutting their superiority by means of absurdity. Yet, like Milton's angels, the Tralfamadorians are far superior intellectually to their human guests. They are able to see in four dimensions, and they pity Earthlings for being able to see only in three (26). Moreover, like the intuitively reasoning angels, the Tralfamadorians communicate telepathically; and so, lacking voice boxes, they must make accommodations so that Billy can understand them. The accommodation here is "a computer and a sort of electric organ" to simulate human sounds (76). Again, Vonnegut's portrayal of these beings relies upon machinery, in this case, twentieth-century gadgets, and again, unlike Milton, he uses these familiar instruments to compel us to look from dual perspectives. From the mythic perspective, which is Billy's viewpoint, the Tralfamadorians are no more or less bizarre than the mythic shapes that people the works of Homer or Dante or Spenser, whereas, from the literal perspective, they are ridiculous. Though we might find it natural to look from this latter viewpoint, we must also acknowledge Billy's real belief in these beings. Virtually nothing is considered absurd to the true believer, and, conversely, any belief that is radically different from one's own must strike the viewer as ludicrous to some extent or other. Hence, if we judge Billy's belief from the mythic perspective, however idiosyncratic and inadequate it may be, we can sympathize with the impulse he yields to.

One final correspondence must be observed before we proceed to the more significant matter of the revelations Billy receives. As we saw, Milton's Adam, aware of his own limitations, "persuades" his creator to make a mate for him. That mate proves to be not merely a woman, but the perfect woman for Adam. Eve, on the other hand, does not see things in quite the same way initially, and so she must be brought to Adam by the creator's leading voice and, in effect, taught to love him. Similarly, Billy's fantasy involves an Eve-figure with whom he may share his Eden; and, as usual, Vonnegut both evokes the familiar myth and looks ironically at the situation by making Billy's ideal mate an erotic film star, Montana Wildhack. Like Milton's Eve, Montana is brought to Billy by their masters; like Eve, too, she initially fears her mate, but eventually learns to trust him, and they become friends and then lovers. Significantly, the narrator describes their love making as "heavenly" (133), an adjective that is quite telling and, I think, not used casually. Finally, Billy's relationship with his mate is, like that of Milton's Adam, based not primarily on sex but on their mutual delight in conversation as evidenced by her request at one point that he tell her a story, which, not surprisingly, turns out to be one about the bombing of Dresden (178-79). In short, despite Vonnegut's joke about the kind of woman Billy sees as perfect, there is something serious, something touching, and something that partakes not at all in the stuff of erotic fantasies that one might expect from Billy's choice of women. Rather, for Billy, as for Adam, the perfection of Eden depends to a large extent upon having a partner with whom to converse and to share in the blissful state. Paradise, in other words, would be sorely lacking without a peer who is much more than a mere sex object.

These evocative surface correspondences are, however, ultimately less important than the information that Billy acquires from his sage captors, just as the information that Raphael conveys to Adam is far more important in the great scheme of things than the Edenic life itself. Indeed, in both cases, continued bliss depends upon the information conveyed, for both characters are being given a unique opportunity, in Milton's words, "to know/ Of things above his World" (5.454-55), things "which human knowledge could not reach" (7.75). The things essentially concern four principal topics: free will, time, death, and the destiny of the universe. In both works, moreover, these issues are intimately linked, but the "answers" provided by the superior beings differ radically in each case.

Raphael's main charge is to inform Adam and Eve of the dangers that Satan poses to their happy state and of the fact that everything depends upon their exercising the right reason to bring their wills into conformity with God's singular commandment. God's charge to Raphael is explicit:

> such discourse bring on
> As may advise him of his happy state,
> Happiness in his power left free to will,
> Left to his own free will, his will though free,
> Yet mutable; whence warn him to beware
> He swerve not too secure. . . .
>
> (5.233-38)

The emphasis upon free will and upon the direct relationship between willed action and consequence is unmistakable here, and Raphael accordingly underscores this point at every turn, even in his sociable chatter. For instance, his account of angelic modes of reasoning serves as a basis for his point that human beings can aspire to higher intellectual gifts "If ye be found obedient" (5.501). He thus makes it clear that the responsibility resting upon their shoulders, though easy enough in the observance, is immense because death, the fall of the universe into corrosive time,[14] and the fate of their descendants all hinge upon a single act of theirs.

Moving in the opposite direction from Adam, Billy Pilgrim begins from the fallen state and expresses an overwhelming desire to move symbolically backwards, going from horrid experience into a dimension where will and action are inconsequential, where time's ravenous activity is rendered unimportant, and where human destiny is in itself insignificant. Further, in forging answers to (or simply evading) the questions "where had he come from, and where should he go now?" (124), Billy effectively "corrects" the Edenic account so that human responsibility plays no role in the present state of affairs and the inherent nature of things obviates any concern one might have for consequences. What Tony Tanner calls Billy's "quietism" derives from the determinism with which he replaces willed and, therefore, consequential actions. In so doing, Tanner writes, Billy "abandons the worried ethical, tragical point of view of Western man and adopts a serene conscienceless passivity."[15] To use Milton's vision again as a point of comparison, whereas the epic poet's God asserts "What I will is Fate" (7.173), Billy, upon instruction from his Tralfamadorian overlords, asserts "If the accident will" (2).

Specifically, Billy's godlike instructors tell him what he desperately wishes were true: (1) that there is no such thing as linear time, but "all moments, past, present, and future, always have existed, and always will exist" (27); thus, the sting of time is removed, its ability to corrode is undermined, and the tragic view that the aging process makes for is eliminated; (2) that, as a result of time's non-linear nature, no one really dies except in brief moments (27); (3) that, since non-linear time contains both good and bad times, one would do well to concentrate on only the good ones (117); (4) that there is no such thing as free will, and so human action is really irrelevant; all things happen as they must, and individuals are thus like "bugs trapped in amber" (77, 86); (5) that the end of the universe is as ludicrous as its existence, the end caused not by human design or natural catastrophe, but by Tralfamadorians' testing of a new fuel (116-17). This last item is particularly suggestive, for it subtly parodies, in a Swiftian manner, the arrogance that human beings often display in our technologically dangerous time. Supposing that humankind will cause the end of life as we know it, such people reflect a kind of Lilliputian belief that we are the terrors of the universe rather than small cogs in a vast machine.

Billy himself has no such arrogant illusions except insofar as his diseased mind involuntarily makes him a form maker. "Among the things Billy Pilgrim could not change," we are told, "were the past, the present, and the future" (60); but, to a large extent, Billy's myth-making belies this statement. By making the alterations in the only place where they ultimately count—in his own mind—he eases the anxiety he hitherto felt. However limited, his personal myth carries out the same function that all myths do. It gives meaning to the apparently meaningless; it provides cause for hope; it affords relief from the otherwise horrible awareness of aging, death, decay, and meaningless sacrifice.

Near the end of Milton's *Paradise Lost*, the warrior angel, Michael, is sent by God both to expel Adam from paradise and to provide a preview of life in the fallen world. This preview includes many of the horrors of biblical history (for example, the murder of Abel by Cain) and the fallen natural world (for example, disease and hardship); but it also includes hopeful visions, specifically, Christ's messianic role and the possibility of salvation through willing obedience to God. Thus, Adam's view of time, though linear, is rendered complete by knowledge of the outcome—Christ's Second Coming, the resurrection of the just, and the final defeat of the evil Satanic powers. Although Billy is a Christian, he cannot bring himself to take comfort in such eschatalogical "solutions." Instead, he transforms himself into what Mircea Eliade has called "traditional man," who periodically abolishes or devalues or gives time a metahistorical meaning and who accords the historical moment no value in itself.[16] Both Billy and Milton's Adam leave their "hills of foresight" armed with the knowledge that time is not as deadly as it might seem and that death's sting is not all that sharp, but the kinds of comfort they take from their knowledge are vastly different. They have to be. Adam needs the knowledge he has acquired to arm himself against the world of suffering he is about to enter. Billy, on the other hand, is leaving the Adamic world of suffering to discover timelessness.

The cosmic and mundane questions that Vonnegut and Milton seek to address in their works, then, are comparable even if their views of life and beyond differ radically, being, as they are, products of their times and belief. The motions of Milton's Adam reflect the poet's own belief in God as the ground of all goodness. By contrast, Vonnegut's Billy Pilgrim reveals a lack of faith in God and, to a large extent, a lack of confidence in humanity. The only paradise that Billy can hope to inhabit is a self-generated one where there are "no conflicts or tensions,"[17] where he can be "absolved from the guilts of war without the cost of compassion,"[18] where humankind, though "no longer the image of God, the center of the universe,"[19] is, for that very reason, no longer responsible for the horrors of history. Giannone has pointed out that the

Tralfamadorians "play God, but without his merciful concern for creation"[20]—a concern that is abundantly evidenced throughout Milton's theodicean epic. But this concern is, of course, deliberately missing from Billy's reinvented world view, replaced by a deterministic existence in which nothing needs to be explained or rectified since free will can do nothing to change conditions.

To be sure, Billy's solution does not answer the needs of all of humanity. It is too contrived, idiosyncratic, and self-serving for that; and it would be a mistake to believe that Vonnegut himself is advancing any such notion. In fact, some critics have interpreted the novel's meaning in just this way, arguing that Vonnegut reveals in *Slaughterhouse-Five* his own indifference to questions of ethical conduct and his preference for facile and fantastic moral code.[21] Nothing can be further from the truth, however. If anything, Vonnegut's novels are a plea for ethical action, for the exercise of reason, for human will to be placed at the service of peace. Billy Pilgrim is not Kurt Vonnegut, nor is Billy the sort of person that Vonnegut is inviting his readers to emulate, though, to a limited extent, we cannot but sympathize and therefore identify with him. As I have noted elsewhere, one of Vonnegut's great strengths as a writer is his ability to force us to look at the world from dual perspectives—as, so to speak, outsiders and insiders. Like all ironic fictions, *Slaughterhouse-Five* invites the reader to look down upon the characters and events of the fiction. From a safe and superior intellectual distance, we regard Billy Pilgrim as a pathetic figure, at once weak-willed, passive, and victimized by both his own diseased mind and the brutal forces of politics. By the same token, however, Vonnegut also allows us glimpses into Billy's internal reality—his desire for peace and love, for innocence, for stability and escape from the world's madness. These glimpses are meant to appeal to our own common yearnings. Seen from that perspective, Billy Pilgrim, the Pilgrim-Everyman, is indeed all of us.

This duality of vision is what allows *Slaughterhouse-Five* to be more than the lurid and ludicrous tale of a lone madman and his obsessive behaviors. Rather, its subtext, like that of all of Vonnegut's novels, is a plea for responsible action, for change, for the pursuit of Genesis not as a lost mythic ideal but as an attainable state of innocence. And, as we will see, that plea will grow more and more pronounced in Vonnegut's more recent novels.

Notes

1. Wayne D. McGinnis, "The Arbitrary Cycle of *Slaughterhouse-Five*: A Relation of Form to Theme," *Critique* 17 (1975): 66.

2. Robert Merrill and Peter A. Scholl, "Vonnegut's *Slaughterhouse-Five*: The Requirements of Chaos," *Studies in American Fiction* 6 (1978): 69. Merrill and Scholl add, "But finally Billy Pilgrim is not Everyman. One may sympathize with his attempt to make sense of things, but the fact remains that some men have greater resources than others" (70). I agree that, as a mythology, Billy's specific "solution" proves to be adequate for himself alone. Yet it is also true that his elaborate fiction reflects recognizable and universal longings that have traditionally become the stuff of myths.

3. Karl, *American Fictions: 1940-1980*, 347.

4. Glenn Meeter, "Vonnegut's Formal and Moral Otherworldliness: *Cat's Cradle* and *Slaughterhouse-Five*, in *The Vonnegut Statement*, ed. Jerome Klinkowitz and John Somer (New York: Delacorte Press/Seymour Lawrence, 1973), 216.

5. Others have noticed Billy's desire to forge what Stanley Schatt calls "a Heaven of sorts" (*Kurt Vonnegut, Jr.*, 93). In his review of the novel at the time of its publication, Wilfred Sheed suggests that Billy's "solution is to invent a heaven out of 20th Century materials" ("Requiem to Billy Pilgrim's Progress," *Life*, 21 March 1969, p. 9). Likewise, Willis McNelly writes that Billy "will spend eternity contemplating only the happy, pleasurable moments when the universe is not destroyed, when no one dies, when Dresden does not burn, when peace endures, and Pilgrim mankind has eternal hope. In short, heaven—the eternal present" ("Science Fiction the Modern Mythology," in *SF: The Other Side of Realism*; ed. Thomas Clareson [Bowling Green, OH: Bowling Green University Popular Press, 1971], 196-97). While what these writers call "heaven" is not exactly synonymous with "Eden," the terms certainly have affinities.

6. I have borrowed this term from Kathryn Hume's "Kurt Vonnegut and the Myths and Symbols of Meaning," where Hume describes the ways in which Vonnegut employs and distorts the traditional modes of embodying meaning in fictional texts—the

conventional self-defining quest motif, as described by Joseph Campbell; and the use of *exostructures*, preexisting stories used to provide a context for a fiction.

7. Joseph Campbell, *The Hero with a Thousand Faces* (1949; rpt., Princeton: Princeton University Press, 1972), 19.

8. Frye, *Anatomy of Criticism*, 49.

9. In *Myth and Reality* (trans. Willard R. Trask [New York: Harper and Row, 1963]), Mircea Eliade uses the term *regressus ad uterum* to describe a symbolic stage in initiation rites. The return to origins, he writes, "prepares a new birth, but the new birth is not a repetition of the first physical birth. There is properly speaking a mystical rebirth, spiritual in nature—in other words, access to a new mode of existence (involving sexual maturity, participation in the sacred and in culture; in short, becoming 'open' to Spirit). The basic idea is that, to attain a higher mode of existence, gestation and birth must be repeated; but they are repeated ritually, symbolically" (81). Something akin to this pattern is evident in Billy's mental movement from the triple wombs to his mystical "experience," which he subsequently tries to share with the world.

10. Klinkowitz, *Literary Disruptions*, 52.

11. Mary Sue Schriber has argued that Billy does not develop in the course of his experiences. "He is surrounded with baby imagery," she writes, "and is very purposefully called 'Billy.' 'Billy' he remains throughout" ("Bringing Chaos to Order," 291). From a rational perspective, Schriber is right, of course. However, on the symbolic level, Billy develops a great deal, moving from a passive and childlike viewer of life to an aggressive preacher of special "knowledge." His solution may not be realistic, but he does change.

12. Barbara Kiefer Lewalski, "Innocence and Experience in Milton's Eden," in *New Essays on "Paradise Lost,"* ed. Thomas Kranidas (Berkeley: University of California Press, 1971), 88.

13. Karl, *American Fictions: 1940-1980*, 347.

14. Time of sorts does exist in Milton's Eden, as Raphael notes parenthetically: "For time, though in Eternity, appli'd/ To motion, measures all things durable/ By present, past, and future" (5.580-82). Moreover, there are in the poem clearly marked days and nights, times of work and times of rest. It is noncorrosive time; time that measures motion but not the process of decay and death. The latter—what Frye in *Anatomy of Criticism* calls the movement of time commencing with the fall from liberty into the natural cycle (213)—begins with Adam and Eve's transgression. By contrast, this "natural cycle" is all too apparent in *Slaughterhouse-Five*, and Billy finds it unendurable. For instance, in a touching recollection, Billy's mother, who is in a nursing home, asks him during one of his visits, "How did I get so *old?*" (44). Later, Billy recalls an old man he once met who said to him, "I knew it was going to be bad getting old. . . . I didn't know it was going to be *this* bad" (189). Thus, his wish-fulfilling fantasy serves to eliminate the tragic view of life implied by the aging process.

15. Tanner, *City of Words*, 198.

16. Mircea Eliade, *The Myth of the Eternal Return, or Cosmos and History*, trans. Willard R. Trask (Princeton: Princeton University Press, 1954), 141.

17. Karl, *American Fictions: 1940-1980*, 347.

18. Olderman, *Beyond the Waste Land*, 212.

19. Mayo, *Kurt Vonnegut*, 4.

20. Giannone, *Vonnegut*, 92.

21. See, for instance, C. Barry Chabot's *"Slaughterhouse-Five* and the Comforts of Indifference," *Essays in Literature* 8 (1981): 45-51.

Works Cited

Campbell, Joseph. *The Hero with a Thousand Faces*. 1949. Reprint. Princeton: Princeton University Press, 1972.

Chabot, C. Barry. *"Slaughterhouse-Five* and the Comforts of Indifference." *Essays in Literature* 8 (1981): 45-51.

Eliade, Mircea. *Myth and Reality*. Translated by Willard R. Trask. New York: Harper and Row, 1963.

_____. *The Myth of the Eternal Return, or Cosmos and History*. Translated by Willard R. Trask. Princeton: Princeton University Press, 1954.

Frye, Northrop. *Anatomy of Criticism: Four Essays*. 1957. Reprint. Princeton: Princeton University Press, 1971.

Giannone, Richard. *Vonnegut: A Preface to His Novels*. Port Washington, NY: Kennikat, 1977.

Hume, Kathryn. "Kurt Vonnegut and the Myths and Symbols of Meaning." *Texas Studies in Literature and Language* 24 (1982): 429-47.

Karl, Frederick. *American Fictions: 1940-1980*. New York: Harper and Row, 1983.

Klinkowitz, Jerome. *Literary Disruptions: The Making of a Post-Contemporary American Fiction*. Urbana: University of Illinois Press, 1975.

_____, and John Somer, eds. *The Vonnegut Statement*. New York: Delacorte Press, 1973.

Lewalski, Barbara Kiefer. "Innocence and Experience in Milton's Eden." In *New Essays on "Paradise Lost,"* edited by Thomas Kranidas, 86-117. Berkeley: University of California Press 1971.

Mayo, Clark. *Kurt Vonnegut: The Gospel from Outer Space*. San Bernardino, CA: Borgo Press, 1977.

McGinnis, Wayne D. "The Arbitrary Cycle of *Slaughterhouse-Five.*" *Critique* 17 (1975): 55-68.

McNelly, Willis E. "Science Fiction the Modern Mythology." In *SF: The Other Side of Realism*, edited by Thomas D. Clareson, 193-98. Bowling Green, OH: Bowling Green University Popular Press, 1971.

Meeter, Glenn. "Vonnegut's Formal and Moral Otherworldliness: *Cat's Cradle* and *Slaughterhouse-Five.*" In *The Vonnegut Statement*, edited by Jerome Klinkowitz and John Somer, 204-20. New York: Delacorte Press/Seymour Lawrence, 1973.

Merrill, Robert, and Peter A. Scholl. "Vonnegut's *Slaughterhouse-Five*: The Requirements of Chaos." *Studies in American Fiction* 6 (1978): 65-76.

Milton, John. "*Paradise Lost.*" In *John Milton: Complete Poems and Major Prose.* Ed. Merritt Y. Hughes. Indianapolis: Odyssey, 1957.

Olderman, Raymond. *Beyond the Waste Land: A Study of the American Novel in the Nineteen-Sixties.* New Haven: Yale University Press, 1972.

Schatt, Stanley. *Kurt Vonnegut, Jr.* Boston: Twayne, 1976.

Schriber, Mary Sue. "Bringing Chaos to Order: The Novel Tradition and Kurt Vonnegut, Jr." *Genre* 10 (1977): 283-97.

Sheed, Wilfred. "Requiem to Billy Pilgrim's Progress." Rev. of *Slaughterhouse-Five. Life*, 21 March 1969: 9.

Tanner, Tony. *City of Words: American Fiction 1950-1970.* New York: Harper and Row, 1971.

Vonnegut, Kurt. *Slaughterhouse-Five.* 1969. Reprint. New York: Dell, 1971.

Slaughterhouse-Five _____

William Rodney Allen

Nearly a quarter of a century passed between the night Kurt Vonnegut survived the firebombing of Dresden in World War II and the publication of his fictionalized account of that event, *Slaughterhouse-Five*. As Vonnegut says, "It seemed a categorical imperative that I write about Dresden, the firebombing of Dresden, since it was the largest massacre in the history of Europe and I am a person of European extraction and I, a writer, had been present. I *had* to say something about it."[1] But the problem was, as Vonnegut remarks in the novel itself, "There is nothing intelligent to say about a massacre."[2] Consequently he was frustrated in his early attempts to tell the single story he felt he had to tell: "I came home in 1945, started writing about it, and wrote about it, and *wrote about it*, and WROTE ABOUT IT. . . . The book is a process of twenty years of this sort of living with Dresden and the aftermath."[3] Precisely because the story was so hard to tell, and because Vonnegut was willing to take the two decades necessary to tell it—to speak the unspeakable—*Slaughterhouse-Five* is a great novel, a masterpiece sure to remain a permanent part of American literature.

The story of Dresden was a hard one for an American to tell for a simple reason: it was designed by the Allies to kill as many German civilians as possible, and it was staggeringly successful in achieving that aim. Because the government rebuffed his attempts shortly after the war to obtain information about the Dresden bombing, saying only that it was classified, it took Vonnegut years to realize the scale of the destruction of life on the night of February 13, 1945. What he eventually learned was that, by the most conservative estimates, 135,000 people died in the raid—far more than were killed by either of the atomic bombs the United States dropped later that year on Hiroshima and Nagasaki. Vonnegut was not killed himself in the attack by purest chance: he and a few other American POWs and their guards had available to them perhaps the only effective bomb shelter in the city, a meat locker two stories underground. They and only a handful of others survived the attack. This massive destruction of life was achieved by a technological breakthrough of sorts—the combination of two kinds of bombs that produced far greater devastation than either could have alone. As Vonnegut explained in an interview:

> They went over with high explosives first to loosen things up, and then scattered incendiaries. When the war started, incendiaries were fairly sizeable, about as long as a shoebox. By the time Dresden got it, they were tiny little things. They burnt the whole damn town down. . . . A fire storm is an amazing thing. It doesn't occur in nature. It's fed by the tornadoes that occur in the midst of it and there isn't a damned thing to breathe. . . . It was a fancy thing to see, a startling thing. It was a moment of truth, too, because American civilians and ground troops didn't know American bombers were engaged in saturation bombing.[4]

In another interview he said, "When we went into the war, we felt our Government was a respecter of life, careful about not injuring civilians and that sort of thing. Well, Dresden had no tactical value; it was a city of civilians. Yet the Allies bombed it until it burned and melted. And then they lied about it. All that was startling to us."[5]

Yet as crucial as Vonnegut's experience at Dresden was to his life and his fictional career, he has resisted the temptation to overdramatize it, to raise it to an apotheosis of the sort Hemingway did of his wounding in World War I at the Italian front. When asked if the events at Dresden changed him, Vonnegut replied, "No. I suppose you'd think so, because that's the cliché. The importance of Dresden in my life has been considerably exaggerated because my book about it became a best seller. If the book hadn't been a best seller, it would seem like a very minor experience in my life."[6] Dresden, then, was no road-to-Damascus-like conversion to a totally new way of thinking for Vonnegut; he was, after all, a young man convinced like most Americans of the necessity of destroying Nazism by whatever means necessary. The change came gradually, as a long process of thinking about the nature of war and writing about it, at first unsuccessfully. Finally, Vonnegut was less affected by the actual experience of Dresden than he would be by the fame that came with the enormous popularity of his book on the subject.

As James Lundquist puts it, Vonnegut's task in writing the novel was somehow to bridge "the increasing gap between the horrors of life in the twentieth century and our imaginative ability to comprehend their full actuality."[7] Indeed, what *can* one say about the madness in our time of human beings slaughtering their fellow human beings—coldly, methodically, scientifically, in numbers heretofore inconceivable? In his book *The Great War and Modern Memory*, Paul Fussell says that World War I was such a shock to those who experienced it that the only response they found adequate to describe it in literature was a searing irony. One thinks of such literary products of the war as Wilfred Owen's "Dulce et Decorum Est," a poem contrasting the martial phrase from Cicero that it is "sweet and proper" to die for one's country with the grotesque, panic-stricken death of soldiers in a mustard gas attack. But if World War I was a shock with its machine guns, its heavy artillery, and its trench-warfare charges into no-man's land, what of the next war with its saturation bombings, its death camps, its atomic bombs? Like the post-World War I writers Vonnegut had to find a new way to convey the horror, a new form to reflect a new kind of consciousness. He used irony, to be sure, but he went further, by altering the fundamental processes of narration itself. More than a conventional reminiscence of war, *Slaughterhouse-Five* is an attempt to describe a new mode of perception that radically alters traditional conceptions of time and morality.

Put most simply, what Vonnegut says about time in the novel is that it does not necessarily "point" only in one direction, from past to future. As Lundquist observes, "The novel functions to reveal new viewpoints in somewhat the same way that the theory of relativity broke through the concepts of absolute space and time."[8] Twenty years after the publication of *Slaughterhouse-Five*, theoretical physicists like Stephen F. Hawking are becoming more convinced that there is no reason why under some circumstances the "arrow of time" might point from future to past rather than from past to future.[9] If such a reversal is possible, then the famous description in *Slaughterhouse-Five* of a backwards movie (in which air force planes suck up bombs into themselves from the ground and fly backwards to their bases, where soldiers unload the bombs and ship them back to the factories to be disassembled) might be more than a wistful fantasy of a peaceful world. Of course, Vonnegut is less interested in new theories in physics than he is in his characters' confrontations with a world that makes no sense in terms of their old ways of seeing it. Hence, rather than beginning his story by quoting Einstein, Vonnegut puts a particular person in a very particular situation: "Listen: Billy Pilgrim has come unstuck in time" (19).

But that striking opening sentence comes not in chapter 1 but in chapter 2. Chapter 1 consists of Vonnegut speaking in his own voice about the difficulties of writing *Slaughterhouse-Five*. Beginning with his 1966 introduction to the reissued *Mother Night*, Vonnegut had begun to speak more openly about himself and about the autobiographical connections underlying his writing. In the opening and closing chapters of *Slaughterhouse-Five*, however, he takes that process much further. By making the autobiographical "frame" of the novel part of the novel itself (rather than setting those sections apart as a preface and an afterword) Vonnegut, as Lundquist puts it, "conceptualizes his own life the way he later does Billy's, in terms of Tralfamadorian time theory. The structure of the chapter about writing the novel consequently prefigures the structure of the novel itself."[10] Vonnegut jumps from how he returned to Dresden in 1967 on a Guggenheim fellowship with his "old war buddy," Bernard V. O'Hare, to what it had been like to try to write about Dresden just after the war, to his first meeting after the war with O'Hare in Philadelphia, to his time teaching in the Writers' Workshop at the University of Iowa. Yet as Reed observes, "There is surprisingly little difficulty in following this seemingly disjointed nar-

phorically into a pillar of salt, into an emblem of the death that comes to those who cannot let go of the past. To get to the heart of the matter of Dresden, moreover, Vonnegut felt he had to let go of the writer's usual bag of chronological tricks—suspense and confrontations and climaxes—and proceed by a different logic toward the future of the novel form.

Thus Vonnegut gives away what would be the traditional climax of his book—the execution of Billy's friend Edgar Derby "for taking a teapot that wasn't his"—in the novel's first paragraph. Throughout the novel he intentionally deflates suspense by mentioning in advance the outcome of any conflict he creates. The readers learn early, for example, that Billy will be kidnapped and taken to the planet Tralfamadore in 1967, where he will learn of the very different ways the Tralfamadorians view the universe. He learns as well that Billy will be shot to death on February 13, 1976, by Paul Lazzaro, a paranoid sadist Billy had been captured with in the war. He even learns with Billy the ultimate fate of the universe: the Tralfamadorians will accidentally blow it up while experimenting with a new type of rocket fuel. Thus, rather than being like a straight line, the narrative chronology of *Slaughterhouse-Five* is more like an ascending, widening spiral that circles over the same territory yet does so from an ever higher and wider perspective. Finally, like most science fiction writers, Vonnegut hopes to push the reader's perceptual horizon as far as he can toward infinity—toward the union of all time and all space. There mystery remains, even though suspense disappears, since suspense is a function of a lack of knowledge at a single point in time and space.

Paradoxically, in creating this cosmic, nonlinear narrative Vonnegut uses fragments of all sorts of traditional narrative forms, much as a bird might use twigs, bits of string, and its own feathers to construct a nest, something very different than the sum of its parts. As Richard Giannone observes, "Graffiti, war memos, anecdotes, jokes, song—light operatic and liturgical—raw statistics, assorted tableaux, flash before the readers eye."[12] The most important linear narrative underlying all of these is the Judeo-Christian Bible, which is itself a central motif in *Slaughterhouse-Five*. There time proceeds from the creation to man's fall to the birth, crucifixion, and resurrection of Christ to the end of time with the Second Coming. Giannone suggests that the Gospels were "an amalgamation of language forms that were available to early Christians to spread their good tidings, rather than a fixed ideal shape sent down out of the blue. . . . [Yet] the old forms were inadequate to convey the momentous news, so primitive Christians made their own."[13] Thus Vonnegut tries in *Slaughterhouse-Five* to do what the Gospel writers attempted to do in their time: construct a new form out of the fragments of old forms.

That Vonnegut was conscious of doing so—that he found the Christian, linear vision of time no longer adequate—is apparent by his remarks in the novel on a book by Kilgore Trout called *The Gospel from Outer Space*. According to Trout, the traditional Gospels are flawed because they seem to suggest that the moral lesson one should learn from Jesus' crucifixion is: "*Before you kill somebody, make absolutely sure he isn't well connected.*" In Trout's revised version of the story, rather than being the Son of God, "Jesus really *was* a nobody, and a pain in the neck to a lot of people with better connections than he had. He still got to say all the lovely and puzzling things he said in the other Gospels" (94). Yet when this nobody is crucified, the heavens open up with thunder and lightning, and God announces that he "will *punish horribly anybody who torments a bum who has no connections*" (95). In the course of the novel it becomes clear that the weak, hapless, clownishly dressed Billy Pilgrim is precisely this "bum who has no connections"—that he is in effect a sort of new Christ. Such observations as the fact that Billy lay "self-crucified" (69) on a brace in his German POW boxcar, or that Billy "resembled the Christ of the carol" (170) that Vonnegut takes as the novel's epigraph ("The cattle are lowing,/ The baby awakes./ But the little Lord Jesus/ No crying he makes.") make clear that this identification of Billy as a Christ-figure is Vonnegut's conscious intention.

Like Christ, Billy brings a new message to the world, although it is a very different one from his predecessor's. And like Jesus he is an innocent who accepts his death, at the hands of an enemy who reviles and misunderstands him, as an opportunity to teach mankind the proper response to mortality. Both Billy and Jesus teach that one should face death calmly, because death is not the end. In the Christian vision the self after death proceeds forward in time eternally, either in heaven or hell; for Billy, however, "after" death the soul proceeds backward in time, back into life. As Billy learns from the Tralfamadorians,

> When a person dies he only *appears* to die. He is still very much alive in the past, so it is very silly for people to cry at this funeral. All moments, past, present, and future, always have existed, always will exist. The Tralfamadorians can look at all the different moments just the way we can look at a stretch of the Rocky Mountains, for instance. They can see how permanent all the moments are, and they can look at any moment that interests them. It is just an illusion we have here on Earth that one moment follows another one, like beads on a string, and that once a moment is gone it is gone forever. (23)

Thus Billy, the new Christ, preaches that human beings *do* have eternal life—even if there is no life after death.

The literary consequence of the Tralfamadorian conception of time is the Tralfamadorian novel, which consists of "brief clumps of symbols read simultaneously." As the Tralfamadorians tell Billy, these symbols, or messages, when seen all at once "produce an image of life that is beautiful and surprising and deep. There is no beginning, no middle, no end, no suspense, no moral, no causes, no effects" (76). *Slaughterhouse-Five* is of course itself an attempt to write this sort of book, as Vonnegut announces in his subtitle: "This is a novel somewhat in the telegraphic schizophrenic manner of tales of the planet Tralfamadore." While human beings cannot read all the passages of the book simultaneously, its short length, its scrambled chronology, its deft juxtapositionings of different times to make thematic points, and its intricate patterns of imagery all combine to give the reader something of that effect. Once he finishes the novel—after a few hours, perhaps in one sitting—the reader can visualize all of Billy's moments stretched out before him like the Rocky Mountains; further, he can see the author's life in the same way, all the way from World War II to the assassination of Robert Kennedy in 1968, when Vonnegut was composing the last pages of *Slaughterhouse-Five*.

Yet while the novel boldly attempts to do away with traditional chronological narration on one level, it still gives the reader a story that builds toward the bombing of Dresden, which is recounted in greatest detail late in the book. Rather than being a traditional novel or a purely experimental, "Tralfamadorian" novel, *Slaughterhouse-Five* is more like one superimposed on the other. One can easily follow the traditional *Bildungsroman* of Billy's life. Born in 1922, like his creator, he endured a childhood marked by intense fears—of drowning when his father subjected him to the "sink or swim method," of falling into the Grand Canyon on a family trip, of the total darkness when the guides extinguished the lights in Carlsbad Caverns. These early images have great relevance for Billy's fear and ineptitude in the war and afterward. His refusal to try to swim and consequent passive sinking to the bottom of the pool is a symbolic wish to return to the safety of the womb. Billy falls constantly in the novel—into ditches, from boxcars, from the sky in a plane crash—despite his intense fear of falling epitomized by his Grand Canyon experience. Finally, the darkness in Carlsbad Caverns prefigures that in the meat locker two stories underground in Dresden—the most important symbolic womb into which Billy retreats for safety. One of the many ironies of the book is that such a passive person should be one of the few to survive the destruction of the city. As Vonnegut says simply of his hero, "He was unenthusiastic about living" (52).

After this shaky childhood Billy attends college for only a few weeks before going off to war as an unarmed chaplain's assistant. In no time he is captured, along with a hapless tank gunner named Roland Weary, in the Battle of the Bulge, the last great German counteroffensive of the war. Freezing in inadequate clothing, hungry, frightened out of his wits, Billy becomes "unstuck in time" for the first time, finding himself living moments out of his past or his future. Weary dies in transit to the POW camp of gangrene of the feet, which he had claimed was caused when the time-tripping Billy abstractedly stepped on him. Before he dies, Weary tells his story to Paul Lazzaro, who vows to avenge Weary's death by tracking Billy down after the war and killing him. Lazzaro is an emblem of the fact that a soldier can never really escape his war experiences—that they will always "track him down" even years later. In the POW camp the dispirited group of Americans is greeted by some hale and hearty Englishmen who have been there most of the war, growing healthy on good Red Cross food (sent by mistake in excessive amounts), exercise, and English optimism. They are the opposite of Billy, the fatalistic, disheveled weakling who simply drifts from one disaster to the next in helpless resignation. After a falling out with the Englishmen over personal hygiene and philosophical attitudes, the Americans are sent to Dresden, a supposedly "open" city, where they soon have their rendezvous with the most significant day in the city's history, February 13, 1945.

After the war Billy does far better than one would expect, since he becomes an optometrist, marries the boss's daughter, and is soon driving a Cadillac, living in an all-electric home, and pulling in over $60,000 a year. But the thematic reason Vonnegut makes Billy so successful is perhaps more important than the slight problem of verisimilitude: Vonnegut wants to show that all Billy's material comforts—his magic fingers bed, the expensive jewelry he gives Valencia, his wife, his fancy car (which will be the cause of his wife's death)—can do nothing to smooth over the pain of what he has experienced. Shortly after the war Billy had checked himself into a mental hospital, where he received shock treatments for depression. Today his problem would be called posttraumatic stress syndrome. Late in the novel, as he feels agony while listening to a barbershop quartet sing "That Old Gang of Mine" at a party celebrating his wedding anniversary, Billy realizes that "he had a great big secret somewhere inside," even though "he could not imagine what it was" (149). His secret is of course the awareness of the horrors of war and the certainty of death—an awareness the frantic materialism of postwar America was desperately trying to cover up.

The cracks in the American dream show through Billy's apparently successful postwar life. Valencia is a parody of consumerism, since she constantly consumes candy bars while making empty promises to lose weight in order to please Billy sexually. Billy's son appears to be headed for jail as a teenager before he joins the Green Berets and goes off to fight in Vietnam. On his way to the office Billy stops at a traffic light in a burned-out ghetto area and drives away when a black man tries to talk with him. Vonnegut was obviously responding to the incredible social tensions of the late 1960s, which saw the burning of major portions of several American cities in race riots, the assassinations of John F. Kennedy, Martin Luther King, Jr., and Robert Kennedy, and the seemingly endless acceleration of the war in Vietnam. A major reason *Slaughterhouse-Five* had the enormous impact it did was because it was published at the height of the conflict in Vietnam, and so delivered its antiwar message to a most receptive audience. In a book of powerful passages, there is no more powerful one than this at the end of the novel, in Vonnegut's autobiographical chapter 10: "Robert Kennedy, whose summer home is eight miles from the home I live in all year round, was shot two nights ago. He died last night" (182). One of Robert Kennedy's promises in his presidential campaign was to stop the war, and when he died that hope seemed to die with him. For Vonnegut, and for Billy, it must have seemed that Dresden was happening all over again in Vietnam.

In 1967, on the night of his daughter's wedding, Billy is picked up by a flying saucer and taken in a time warp to Tralfamadore, where he is displayed in a sort of Tralfamadorian zoo by his abductors. Since Billy had not been very happy on earth, he finds that during his stay of several years (in terms of Tralfamadorian time, not Earth time) he is "about as happy as I was on Earth" (98). His happiness is increased when the Tralfamadorians kidnap a sexy movie actress, Montana Wildhack, and bring her to the zoo as Billy's "mate." So while Billy enjoys sexual bliss for the first time with the willing Ms. Wildhack, he gets instruction from the Tralfamadorians on the true nature of the universe. Billy and Montana appear as a sort of new Adam and Eve, who live in the confines of a perfect world, until Billy eats of the tree of knowledge, in effect, by learning the true nature of time and the place of conscious beings in the universe. He is expelled from his symbolic garden when the Tralfamadorians (for unexplained reasons) send him back to Earth. An enlightened Billy then begins his mission of preaching his new gospel to his fellowmen—who are understandably skeptical about his claims.

Vonnegut leaves room for the idea that Billy's trip to Tralfamadore is all in Billy's mind. This sort of "escape hatch" from fantasy into realism is characteristic of the sci-fi genre: in *A Connecticut Yankee in King Arthur's Court* Twain has his hero receive a blow on the head and probably dream the novel's events. In *Slaughterhouse-Five* Billy had been in a mental hospital and received shock treatments. During his stay there he had met Eliot Rosewater, who makes a cameo appearance from Vonnegut's previous novel in order to introduce Billy to the sci-fi works of Kilgore Trout. One of the novels Billy reads, *The Big Board*, concerns an Earth couple kidnapped by aliens and displayed on their planet in a zoo. An event in 1968, moreover, suggests a physical explanation for the Tralfamadorian episodes: Billy survives a plane crash on the way to an optometrists' convention that kills everyone else and leaves him with a serious head injury. In chapter 1 of the novel Vonnegut mentions the French writer Céline, who had received a head wound fighting in World War I, and who had thereafter heard voices and had written his death-obsessed novels during his sleepless nights. Like Billy, Céline too was obsessed with time: Billy's Tralfamadore experience may be seen as the equivalent of Céline's—and Vonnegut's—

attempts to deal with the problem of mortality through writing fiction. As Vonnegut observes of Rosewater and Billy, "They had both found life meaningless, partly because of what they had seen in war. . . . So they were trying to re-invent themselves and their universe. Science fiction was a big help" (87).

Billy's trip to Tralfamadore, then, finally begins to look more like a metaphor than a literal description of events. His space travel is simply a way for Vonnegut to describe the growth of his own imagination out of the Christian, linear vision of time to the cosmic perspective of time as the fourth dimension. This is not to say, however, that Vonnegut offers the Tralfamadorian *attitudes* toward that vision as final truth. Tralfamadorians—"real" or imagined—are not human beings, so that their attitude of absolute indifference toward the terrors of the universe—even to the ultimate terror of its annihilation—could never work for humans. If *Slaughterhouse-Five* is a combination of the traditional narrative and the Tralfamadorian novel, it is also a synthesis of Christian and Tralfamadorian morals: the reader is not so much urged to choose the latter over the former as to superimpose the two. When Billy passionately implores the Tralfamadorians to tell him how they live in peace, so that he can return to give that knowledge to Earth, his hosts reply that war and peace come and go at random on Tralfamadore as they do everywhere else. Their response to any frustration on Billy's part—to his profoundly human need—to know why—is simply that "there is no *why*" (66). When Billy wonders why the universe must blow up, they respond that "the moment is structured that way." The Tralfamadorians claim that "only on Earth is there any talk of free will" (74). Such profound indifference could never suffice for human beings, nor does Vonnegut imply that it should.

Slaughterhouse-Five is built on the paradox that it appears to offer acceptance and even indifference as responses to the horrors of the twentieth century, when in fact it is a moving lament over those horrors—a piercing wail of grief over the millions of dead in World War II. Emblematic of this paradox is a short phrase from the novel that has become probably the best-known and most often repeated by his readers of any in Vonnegut's work: "So it goes." In *Palm Sunday* Vonnegut explains that the phrase was his response to his reading of Céline's *Journey to the End of Night*: "It was a clumsy way of saying what Céline managed to imply . . . in everything he wrote, in effect: 'Death and suffering can't matter nearly as much as I think they do. Since they are so common, my taking them so seriously must mean that I am insane.'"[14] Every time someone dies in the novel—from Wild Bob to Valencia to Billy Pilgrim himself to Robert Kennedy—Vonnegut repeats "So it goes." Once this pattern is established, Vonnegut has fun with it, as when he has Billy pick up a bottle of flat champagne after his daughter's wedding: "The champagne was dead. So it goes" (63). Thus the phrase finally embodies all the essential attitudes toward death in the novel—acceptance, sorrow, humor, outrage. If at times "So it goes" reads like a resigned "Let it be," it more often comes through as the reverse: "Let it be *different*—let all these dead live!" So Vonnegut does let them live, in effect, by positing the Tralfamadorian idea that they are always alive in their pasts.

Despite its mask of Tralfamadorian indifference *Slaughterhouse-Five* conveys at times an almost childlike sense of shock that the world is such a violent place. Children form an important motif in the book, which is subtitled "The Children's Crusade." Vonnegut had chosen that ironic phrase as a way to reassure Mary O'Hare, Bernard's wife, that he was not going to portray war as a glamorous affair fought by "Frank Sinatra and John Wayne or some of those other glamorous war-loving, dirty old men" (13). When the British POWs, after several years in captivity, see Billy and the other recently captured Americans, they confess that "we had forgotten that wars were fought by babies" (91). Before recounting the bombing of Dresden, Billy and his young German guard see a group of adolescent girls taking a shower. They are "utterly beautiful" (137). Yet when the bombs begin to fall, Vonnegut records that "the girls that Billy had seen naked were all being killed. . . . So it goes" (152).

But *Slaughterhouse-Five* does not stop with the pathos of innocent children being killed. It refuses to be a self-satisfied antiwar book like, say, *Johnny Got His Gun*. While conveying a sense of outrage, horror, regret, and even despair over the insanity of war, Vonnegut does not think that stopping war is a realistic possibility or that, if it were, this would end the pain of the human condition. In chapter 1, when talking about his Dresden project to a movie producer, Vonnegut had gotten the response, "'Why don't you write an anti-*glacier* book instead?' What he meant, of course, was that there would always be wars, that they were as easy to stop as glaciers. I believe that, too" (3). Even more significant is Vonnegut's admission that "if wars didn't keep coming like glaciers, there would still be plain old death" (3). Finally, while Vonnegut accepts war and death as inevitable, he refuses to endorse the sentimentalized, childlike attitude of acceptance of the inevitable epitomized in the prayer hanging on Billy's office wall and inside a locket on a chain hanging around Montana Wildhack's neck: "God grant me the serenity to accept the things I cannot change, courage to change the things I can, and wisdom always to tell the difference" (52, 181). As Vonnegut observes, "Among the things Billy Pilgrim could not change were the past, the present, and the future" (52). Dresden has happened, is happening, and will always happen.

Yet if the war is always going on, it is always ending, too. Life comes out of death, as surely as Billy survives the bombing of Dresden in a slaughterhouse. In chapter 1 Vonnegut describes the end of the war, when thousands of POWs of all nationalities were gathered in a beetfield by the Elbe River. This moment of liberation of the soldiers of all countries would grow for twenty years in Vonnegut's mind until it became the central image in *Bluebeard*, his most recent novel. The last sound in *Slaughterhouse-Five* is not that of bombs falling, but of a bird chirping just after the war: "*Poo-tee-weet?*" By making the chirp a question Vonnegut seems to ask all the survivors of the war, "Despite everything, would you like to try again?"

Reed speaks for most critics of Vonnegut's writing when he says that "*Slaughterhouse-Five* remains a remarkably successful novel . . .

[that] neither falters from, nor sensationalizes the horrors it depicts, and tenaciously avoids pedantic or moralistic commentary; no small achievement given the subject matter and the author's personal closeness to it."[15] Vonnegut was indeed close to the events of *Slaughter-house-Five*, but it took him nearly a quarter of a century to get far enough away from them in time to have the proper perspective. The authority of that perspective perhaps most forcefully rings through the simple phrase Billy utters about Dresden near the novel's end: lying in his hospital bed after his plane crash, listening to Bertrand Rumfoord belittle the "bleeding hearts" who would mourn the loss of innocent life in the Allied firebombings, Billy responds: "I was there" (165). Finally, *Slaughterhouse-Five* gains its power not as an act of moralizing, but of witness.

Notes

1. *Conversations with Kurt Vonnegut*, ed. William Rodney Allen (Jackson: University Press of Mississippi, 1988) 230. Hereafter *CKV.*

2. *Slaughterhouse-Five* (New York: Delacorte/Lawrence, 1969) 17. Subsequent references are noted parenthetically.

3. *CKV* 163.

4. *CKV* 173-74.

5. *CKV* 95.

6. *CKV* 94.

7. James Lundquist, *Kurt Vonnegut* (New York: Ungar, 1976) 69.

8. Lundquist 71.

9. Stephen F. Hawking, *A Brief History of Time* (New York: Bantam, 1988).

10. Lundquist 75.

11. Peter J. Reed, *Kurt Vonnegut, Jr.* (New York: Warner, 1972) 179.

12. Richard Giannone, *Vonnegut: A Preface to His Novels* (Port Washington, NY: Kennikat Press, 1977) 84.

13. Giannone 85-86.

14. *Palm Sunday* (New York: Delacorte/Lawrence, 1981) 296.

15. Reed 203.

Vonnegut as Messenger:
*Slaughterhouse-Five*_____

Donald E. Morse

> And I alone am escaped to tell you.
> —The Messenger to Job

Vonnegut wrote *Slaughterhouse-Five* as Joseph Heller wrote *Catch-22*, looking back on the Second World War from a vantage point of twenty to twenty-five years. Unlike Heller, however, what he found to criticize was not "everyone cashing in"—in an ironic moment he even admitted that "one way or another, I got two or three dollars for every person killed [in Dresden]. Some business I'm in" (*Palm Sunday*, p. 302)—but rather chose to focus on the brutal, excessive destruction done in the name of goodness, justice, and Mom's apple pie.

In his introduction to the novel, Vonnegut applauds Lot's wife, who in the Old Testament was turned into a pillar of salt for daring to witness the destruction of Sodom and Gomorah, the infamous cities on the plain. "I love her for that," says Vonnegut, "because it was so human" (*Slaughterhouse-Five*, p. 19). By looking back at the destruction of Dresden, Vonnegut reminds readers that, even in the best of causes against the worst of enemies, human beings have done and apparently will continue to commit the most unimaginable of atrocities. Why? In the Book of Job in the Old Testament, Job long ago found the answer to that question and Vonnegut repeats it for today's readers: "Why?" Why not? Because a person is good does not mean that he or she will escape evil or that he or she is incapable of doing evil. Job's expectation, that evil would not be visited upon a good or an innocent person, was as ill-founded a belief as Vonnegut's or anyone's might be. *Slaughterhouse-Five* suggests, therefore, that evil is beyond human understanding and that the destruction of the innocent and undefended is as common now as when Job bewailed his fate.

For much of his career as a writer and for half of his career as a novelist, Kurt Vonnegut wrestled with the terrible moral issue of surviving the destruction of the unarmed city of Dresden in a firestorm in which "The city appeared to boil" (PS, p. 302), leaving 135,000 dead in one night. Such massive destruction is almost beyond human imagining and certainly mind-numbing. About such devastation in *Slaughterhouse-Five*, Vonnegut says:

> . . . I felt the need to say this every time a character died: 'So it goes.' This exasperated many critics, and it seemed fancy and tiresome to me, too. But it somehow had to be said.
>
> It was a clumsy way of saying what Céline managed to imply so much more naturally in everything he wrote, in effect: "Death and suffering can't matter nearly as much as I think they do. Since they are so common, my taking them so seriously must mean that I am insane. I must try to be saner." (PS, p. 296)

But how? Having survived the firebombing and what may well be the largest single massacre of a European civilian population ever, he returned home after being repatriated as a prisoner of war. Like many of his contemporaries, he had interesting stories to tell of the war and the camaraderie he experienced, but again and again he failed to find the right medium for his message about the massacre and whatever it might mean. Unable to passively accept the destruction, he asked the questions all survivors ask, "Why me?" "Why was I allowed to survive?" And parallel to that question, there were all the others: "How could this terrible destruction have been allowed to happen?" "How could human beings do such awful things to one another?" In novel after novel, Vonnegut tries to deal with these questions directly or indirectly. In *The Sirens of Titan*, for example, he probes into history for the answers but finds there nothing but absurdity. In *Mother Night* he examines the possibility of good collaborating with the forces of evil to subvert and ultimately destroy such forces but has to conclude that this kind of naïveté is no match for a truly powerful evil force, such as Fascism. In *Cat's Cradle*, on the other hand, he explores the possibility of stoic cynicism as an answer to the moral dilemma through his splendid creation of Bokonon and Bokononism. Diogenes, the patron saint of cynics, would warmly approve of Bokonon and his view of life as given in the *Books of Bokonon*. If human beings are so hell-bent on their own destruction, then, suggests *Cat's Cradle*, no one or nothing can stop them, and all the novelist can do is warn against the impending disaster.

In *God Bless You, Mr. Rosewater*, Vonnegut tries the opposite tack by examining the effect of doing good works as a way of stopping or at least slowing down the forces of evil. "Sell all you have and give it to the poor" was Jesus' admonition in the first century, so Eliot Rosewater establishes his foundation to give money away. When the phone rings, he answers: "Rosewater Foundation, how may we help you?" and hopes that money may indeed help the person on the other end of the line. But good works ultimately do not appear to really slow evil down. Instead, they actually may encourage it to greater extravagances of connivance and fraud. Evil itself worms its way into the heart of good works and so threatens to destroy the Rosewater Foundation itself until Eliot thwarts it with his preemptive strike by giving away all he has.

In *Slaughterhouse-Five*, Vonnegut at last discovers a way of dealing artistically and personally with "death and suffering" by shifting his perspective from that of human beings to that of God or, in this instance, to that of the Tralfamadorians. When Billy Pilgrim finds himself in the Tralfamadorian zoo, he asks: "Why me?" The answer he receives both puzzles and instructs him:

> "That is a very *Earthling* question to ask, Mr. Pilgrim. Why *you*? . . .
> Why *anything*? Because this moment simply *is*. . . .
> Well, here we are, Mr. Pilgrim trapped in . . . this moment. There is no
> *why*." (SH, p. 66)

This Tralfamadorian perspective, which Vonnegut adopts, is very similar to God's as pictured in the Book of Job. In the prologue to the Book of Job, messengers come to Job bringing news of horrendous destruction. The first one reveals that all his servants have been killed; the second that his sheep have been destroyed by fire from heaven; the third that nomads have carried off his camels and killed his herdsmen; and the fourth brings the worst news of all: a hurricane suddenly killed all his sons and daughters. Naturally Job is heart-stricken. He rends his clothes and goes and sits on the village dunghill in deep mourning. While there, he receives visits from three friends who attempt to comfort him with conventional wisdom arguing that evil occurs because a person has done evil. Job claims, rightly, that he is innocent, God-fearing, and has done only good. The second friend contends that evil occurs because a person neglects to perform certain required ceremonies or religious duties, and if Job will repent and perform them, all will be well. But again Job says that he is a model of piety and has left no ceremony unobserved nor any duty unperformed. The third friend then argues that evil never occurs without a reason, and, therefore, if destruction has been visited upon Job, then, that is ipso facto proof that Job is indeed guilty of something. If he will but "search his heart" to discover his mistake and repent of it, then, all will be well. But Job has done nothing wrong. As Jesus was to say a few centuries later, "The rain falls on the just and the unjust," and because a hurricane destroys people or property is no reason to believe such people were guilty of any wrong-doing. Nature is notoriously neutral and is, therefore, an unreliable guide to human goodness or evil. Writing "A Letter to the Next Generation" in an "Open Forum" series of advertisements sponsored by Volkswagen, Vonnegut concludes by giving a lengthy list of natural disasters and saying: "If people think Nature is their friend, then they sure don't need an enemy." In other words, do not look to Nature for moral guidance.

Job's tragedy is that he is a good man who experienced great evil— exactly as Dresden was a "good" city, an "open," unarmed civilian city whose architectural beauty was legendary. Yet Dresden was destroyed though undefended to "hasten the end of the war" (SH, p. 155), as Job's innocent sons and daughters were destroyed to "teach Job a lesson." By the end of the book, Job accepts the imperfection of the world and his inability to account for the evil in it. As the man of faith, he also comes to accept the goodness of his Creator, although that goodness may not always be apparent in the less than perfect world in which he must live. He states simply, "I believe; help Thou mine unbelief," which is the heartfelt cry of all believers in a Deity.

Vonnegut, as a rational atheist, can find none of the consolation that Job found in the answers of traditional faith. He can and does find some consolation, however, in accepting an imperfect world where the power of evil to destroy is real and often terrifying, but where the power of reason and goodness is also real and occasionally even wins out over evil. As a character in a Bertolt Brecht play says, "In the worst of times, there are good people." So Eliot Rosewater gives all he has away, and Malachi Constant at long last learns "to love whoever is around to be loved." In *Slaughterhouse-Five*, Billy Pilgrim becomes the chief attraction in a zoo on another planet in another galaxy where he and Montana Wildhack are put on exhibit as interesting specimens of an endangered species. Although their captors have long ago concluded, based upon thousands of years of observation, that the most prominent characteristic of humans appears to be their ability to self-destruct, these two copulate and produce an off-spring while in the zoo, thus illustrating humanity's drive to continue the race, which may help to counterbalance its drive to destroy it. (Compare *Deadeye Dick*, p. 185.) This modest hopefulness is a far cry from the total despair experienced by Mona, the incredibly beautiful woman of the Sunday supplements who, as the world ends in *Cat's Cradle*, refuses to make love to Jonah-John because "that's how babies are made" and no sane person would want to have a child as the world ends. But Montana Wildhack and Billy Pilgrim, less worldly-wise and far more childlike, under much less favorable conditions in the Tralfamadorian zoo, amidst their

Sears Roebuck furnishings, copulate and reproduce to the delight and glee of their audience. Perhaps that suggests Earth's ultimate function in the universe: to puzzle and delight extraterrestrial on-lookers who visit this planet with the paradox of humans who both reproduce—that is, give life—and destroy themselves—that is, take life—at one and the same time. So it goes.

In his role as the "messenger to Job," besides dealing with the "commonness" of death, Vonnegut also attempts to account for unmotivated human suffering, such as that caused by the incineration of 135,000 people in Dresden, by pointing to the accidental nature of life. Some of this reasoning will be familiar from *The Sirens of Titan* in which the Space Traveller maintains that "I was the victim of a series of accidents. . . . As are we all," but here there is an important difference: in *The Sirens of Titan* the accidents are actually caused by visitors from Tralfamadore who manipulated all human history for their own ends. Worse, as Salo, the messenger, points out, these visitors are not even human beings or sentient creatures, but are machines. In contrast, in *Slaughterhouse-Five* there is no one using or abusing human history for any purpose whatsoever nor is anything or anyone in control. Rather than wrestle further with the issue of "purpose" or lack of it, Vonnegut replaces the question, "Why me?" with its twin question to which there is no reply: "Why not you?" Questions also posed in the conclusion of the Book of Job first by Elihu, then by God, as each asks Job in turn: "Why did you expect that your goodness would give you immunity from the effects of evil or from accidents of nature?" There is no such immunity for human beings. Good people suffer and bad people suffer since "The rain falls on the just and the unjust." Suffering, by itself, is no measure either of a person's evil—as Job's three friends had mistakenly maintained—nor of a person's goodness—as Job had assumed. Suffering simply is a part of this world and all human experience, and no divine force will interfere in human history to stop it: ". . . the little Lord Jesus/ No crying He makes" (SH epigraph, n.p.).

The thought behind Vonnegut's novel could, therefore, be called a challenging, if fairly orthodox, form of Judeo-Christian theology. No wonder school boards and other official bodies whose members rarely read, much less comprehend, the books which they ban or burn, have attacked it, and once, at least, in Drake, North Dakota, "*Slaughterhouse-Five* was actually burned in a furnace by a school janitor . . . on instructions from the school committee"![1] It threatened their comfortable view of the world and religion exactly as the Book of Job, the Old Testament Prophets, and Jesus's Sermon on the Mount did hundreds of years ago. In all these books, as in *Slaughterhouse-Five*, the terms "punishment" and "reward" it turns out, do not make a lot of sense from the human, but only from the divine perspective. In such a world, why would anyone do good rather than evil? A good person, according to the Book of Job and Judeo-Christian belief, is simply a good person and the only reason for being good rather than evil is because that is who and what a good person is; thus, a good person is someone who does good, which is its own reward. Someone who is evil, on the other hand, is simply someone who does evil, which is its own punishment.

None of Vonnegut's characters, including those in *Slaughterhouse-Five*, are evil, but they are rather human beings to whom accidents happen. Most are innocent. Vonnegut's father once said to him, ". . . you never wrote a story with a villain in it" (SH, p. 7). Billy Pilgrim is neither John Wayne, riding into the sunset to save Western civilization from the Fascists, nor Jesus preaching the necessity of "doing good to those who do evil to you." Instead he is a soldier in war and a child in peace, who neatly illustrates Céline's observation that "When not actually killing, your soldier's a child." The identity of soldiers as children is also reflected in the subtitle of *Slaughterhouse-Five: or The Children's Crusade*, which links the great war to end all wars with one of the most futile, exploitative, cynical events in all of western European history: the Children's Crusade—a crusade that never went anywhere and never accomplished anything, except to provide ample prey upon which all kinds of human vultures fed.

In *Slaughterhouse-Five* the soldiers in World War II, like the children on the crusade, had little or no idea about what they were doing and often did not know even where they were. It was the generals who planned such glorious operations as the destruction of Dresden (see SH, pp. 161-62). The reduction of a monument of human civilization, such as the city on the Elbe, to a pile of rubble overnight or the metamorphosis of hundreds of thousands of unarmed people into a "corpse factory" can, and, indeed, has happened in "a world where 'everything is permitted.'" In such a world, says Ivan Karamozov in *The Brothers Karamozov*, the issue is not whether to believe in God or not; it is the horror of the power of evil. Yet, as Eliot Rosewater, who also "found life meaningless, partly because of what [he] . . . had seen in war," says to Billy Pilgrim: "everything there was to know about life was in *The Brothers Karamazov*. . . . 'But that isn't *enough* any more' . . ." (SH, p. 87). And so perhaps all we can do is follow Theodore Roethke's advice, which Vonnegut quotes with approval, to "learn by going where [we] . . . have to go" (SH, p. 18). Dresden, one of the most beautiful of all the German, of all the European cities, was obliterated in one night with virtually all the people living there:

> When the Americans and their guards did come out [next noontime after the firestorm], the sky was black with smoke. The sun was an angry little pinhead. Dresden was like the moon now, nothing but minerals. The stones were hot. Everybody else in the neighborhood was dead. (SH, p. 153)

What do you say after a massacre? "Everything is supposed to be very quiet after a massacre, and it always is, except for the birds. And what do the birds say? All there is to say about a massacre, things like '*Poo-tee-weet?*'" (SH, p. 17).

If the slaughterhouse itself, from which the novel takes its title, was once a house of death, it became, paradoxically during the inferno of the Dresden firebombing, a house of salvation when it gave oxygen to its occupants rather than to the firestorm. Similarly, while Vonnegut's novel is an account of the worst massacre of unarmed civilians in modern Europe, it is also a plea for a change in values and attitudes which would make other such massacres impossible. One way it accomplishes this task is by making the massacre itself public knowledge, for the novel brought it back into living memory in a way that could not be ignored, a portion of American history which had never officially been acknowledged, and which had been either inadvertently or deliberately concealed. According to Vonnegut in the "twenty-seven-volume *Official History of the Army Air Force in World War Two* . . . there was almost nothing . . . about the Dresden raid, even though it had been such a howling success. The extent of the success had been kept a secret for many years after the war—a secret from the American people" (SH, p. 165).

William Butler Yeats, the Nobel Prize winning poet, once said that "a poet writes out of his personal life [and] in his finest work out of its tragedy, whatever it be. . . ." Vonnegut implies that *Slaughterhouse-Five* is the result of his "dance with death" without which he says, quoting Céline with approval, "no art is possible" (SH, p. 18). Thus he writes out of the "tragedy" he experienced, which raised acutely the profound moral issues with which he has had to wrestle as an adult human being and as a writer. Perhaps that also helps account for the relief he felt in finishing it: "I felt," he says, "after I finished *Slaughterhouse-Five* that I didn't have to write at all anymore if I didn't want to. It was the end of some sort of career" (WF&G, p. 280).

Clearly Vonnegut has written movingly, compellingly out of the tragedy he experienced in Dresden and for many—perhaps, for most—of his readers, *Slaughterhouse-Five* remains his finest work: an impressive achievement whether looked at as a human document or as a work of art. Robert Scholes sums up the qualities of the novel that contribute to its success:

> It is funny, compassionate, and wise. The humor in Vonnegut's fiction is what enables us to contemplate the horror that he finds in contemporary existence. It does not disguise the awful things perceived; it merely

strengthens and comforts us to the point where such perception is bearable. Comedy can look into depths which tragedy dares not acknowledge. (204)

After wrestling with some of the most profound and some of the most difficult human questions in *Slaughterhouse-Five*, Vonnegut promised himself: "The next one I write is going to be fun" (SH, p. 19), which certainly proved true in the wild comedy of *Breakfast of Champions*. It would be almost twenty years before he would return to these issues raised for him by World War II and, in *Bluebeard*, present a picture of the end of the war in Europe as a field crowded with people: the lunatics, the refugees, the war prisoners, the concentration camp victims— all the ragged remnants of an exhausted world, but more important: all survivors—and living human beings, rather than the stacked corpses of the Hospital of Hope and Mercy in *Cat's Cradle* or the "corpse mine" found in the desolate Dresden landscape of *Slaughterhouse-Five*. But that novel is another twenty years in the future after this one. For now it is enough that Vonnegut—the messenger—could bring news of the disaster together with the resulting examination of issues central to all human experience: the question of the power of evil, the awareness of inhuman destruction, and the omnipresence of human suffering.

Note

1. PS, p. 4. See also PS, pp. 3-17. In a "Dear Friend" letter written to solicit funds for the ACLU (The American Civil Liberties Union), Vonnegut reveals that *Slaughterhouse-Five* is among the ten "most frequently censored [and banned] books" in public schools and libraries. Others in the top ten include John Steinbeck, *The Grapes of Wrath* and *Of Mice and Men*, Judy Blume, *Forever*, and Mark Twain, *Huckleberry Finn*. "Kurt Vonnegut," undated letter, pp. 2-3.

Works Cited

Scholes, Robert. *Fabulation and Metafiction*. Urbana: University of Illinois Press, 1979.

Vonnegut, Kurt. *Palm Sunday: An Autobiographical Collage*. New York: Delacorte Press, 1981.

_____. *Slaughterhouse-Five*. New York: Dell, 1969.

_____. *Wampeters, Foma & Granfalloons (Opinions)*. New York: Dell, 1974.

Slaughterhouse-Five:
Existentialist Themes Elaborated in a Postmodernist Way_____

Hans van Stralen

Slaughterhouse-Five (1969) is a novel about war and the inability to understand or prevent it. In particular it is the description of an erratic reality forcefully disrupting the consciousness-controlled reality, which, I think, justifies calling Vonnegut's novel postmodern.[1] Fokkema considers the permutation of text and social context as one of this movement's major characteristics that can be related to *Slaughterhouse-Five* (Fokkema and Bertens 1986; 94). McHale points to the postmodern procedure of the 'dead author': "The writer does not *originate his* discourse, but mixes already extant discourses" (McHale 1989; 200). Bertens and D'haen consider the absence of a beginning, middle or ending, as well as the lack of any moral, sufficient grounds to conclude that Vonnegut's text belongs to Postmodernism. In addition they point to the use of pop elements and to the intentional sentimentalism (Bertens and D'haen 1988; 130, 164, 165, cf. also Brocher 1981; 132-133). Elsewhere Bertens and D'haen distinguish a number of American authors (including Vonnegut) who want to rewrite reality and history from an idiosyncratic viewpoint (Bertens and D'haen 1983; 236). *Slaughterhouse-Five* can be said to be existentialist in tendency since it thematizes the Second World War and its absurdities.

Quite a few studies have been devoted to the relations between Modernism and Postmodernism and the Historical Avantgarde and Postmodernism.[2] This cannot be said of the relation between Postmodernism and Existentialism. It seems that critics no longer wish to distinguish between these two movements and consider Postmodernism to be a radicalization of Sartre's view of the contingent world. This outlook has its limitations. Firstly, in *Quest-ce que la littérature?* Sartre reacts against both Modernism and Surrealism and Sartre's concept of literature in its turn is later rejected by Robbe-Grillet in his *Pour un*

Existentialist Themes Elaborated in a Postmodernist Way   **279** *nouveau roman*. In this collection of essays he particularly contests the anthropomorphizations of the reality of the être-en-soi (the being-in-it-self), by which Sartre is said to implicitly involve this fully autonomous reality in a subjectivizing domain. Also, he considers Sartre's concept of 'commitment' (Fr. 'engagement') to be obsolete. These reactions, reappearing to some extent in the debates surrounding Postmodernism, seem to provide a reason to give Existentialism its own place in the twentieth-century canon.

The differences between Sartre's Existentialism and Postmodernism are considerable. Particularly his ethics and the idea of an autonomous, free subject, struggling—although afraid of the consequences—with orderly problems no longer dominate the debate about Postmodernism. Today's conflict is not fear but its absence, D. Barthelme states in an allusion to Kierkegaard and Sartre (see G. Hoffmann in Fokkema and Bertens 1986; 198-199). I get the impression that a number of authors who are called postmodernist think that reality is unknowable and therefore not susceptible to change. I also discern this mentality in Vonnegut's *Slaughterhouse-Five*.

Sartre, however, is not the only representative of Existentialism. Elsewhere I have attempted to indicate that this movement encompasses two mainstreams of thought. On the one hand there are authors such as Kafka and Camus, on the other hand one can recognize a certain ethical variant of Existentialism in the work of Sartre and de Beauvoir (Van Stralen 1992; 4 ff). Camus may be distinguished from Sartre particularly by his rejection of every ethical and metaphysical frame of reference with which we would be able to judge the reality surrounding us. The idea in *Le Mythe de Sisyphe* is that existence (experienced as laborious by the Existentialists) with all its absurdities, but also with all its positive aspects, cannot be fundamentally changed and that one is right fully to accept earthly reality.

I think that *Slaughterhouse-Five*, as an exemplary novel among a number of other postmodernist texts, can very well be seen in relation to Camus' Existentialism. Let me elaborate on this point.

Vonnegut's novel is about war, more specifically about the bombing of Dresden on February 13, 1945. This military action has always raised a lot of questions. After all, the city could hardly be said to have been of any strategic value for the Nazi regime. This seems to justify the assumption that the destruction of the city only served to break the morale of the population, since it was first and foremost innocent civilians who became the victims of the Allied actions. Recent estimates of the number of dead range from 35,000 to 400,000. The atmosphere of pointlessness surrounding this bombardment is reinforced by the consideration that the pilots who had been given the assignment to drop the bombs were told that the transport links had to be destroyed, although these networks proved to have remained virtually intact after the attack.

These statements on the Second World War lead us to the existentialist notion of 'borderline situations': those situations in which the individual is confronted by a difficult decision with far-reaching consequences for the rest of his life. Take for instance the decision whether to break off a relationship, the decision concerning the life and death of a patient, the conversion to faith in God, and so on. Generally the Second World War is seen by the Existentialists as the borderline situation par excellence; many of their novels therefore deal explicitly with this universal and historical threat to human freedom. While in Sartrian texts, however, this borderline situation seems to invite a change of attitude in favour of commitment, in *Slaughterhouse-Five* the concept of a 'borderline situation' is elaborated, as regards its content, in the spirit of Camus, be it through the use of postmodernist techniques. I will first deal with this relationship.

Slaughterhouse-Five suggests that the Second World War brought about an absurd situation, but the implication is in the spirit of Camus—that one cannot come to grips with this chaos, let alone eliminate it. The narrator puts much emphasis on the unknowability of what he has been through. The first sentence of Vonnegut's novel is: 'All this happened, more or less' (*Slaughterhouse-Five*; 9). The unreliability of the message is further reinforced when we read that the narrator and an ex-buddy of his are visiting Dresden many years later and both are unable to match their observations with their memories. In this way *Slaughterhouse-Five* presents the reader with a borderline situation, but one which, in contrast to existentialist situations, is both incomprehensible and apparently irremediable. From the extraterrestrials from Tralfamadore, with whom Billy comes into contact through reading science fiction, he learns that "*Everything* is all right, and everybody has to do exactly what he does" (*Slaughterhouse-Five*; 132). From them Billy also learns that the universe will be destroyed again and again, "The moment is *structured* that way" (*Slaughterhouse-Five*; 80). The relation with Nietzsche's 'ewige Widerkehr' [eternal recurrence] and Camus' Sisyphus seems evident here. Like the French philosopher, who had studied Nietzsche thoroughly, Billy opts for enduring life with all the bad as well as the good sides that this involves (*Slaughterhouse-Five*; 81, 129, 140). In *Slaughterhouse-Five* the irony that can sprout from an absurd situation is even more clearly present than in the work of Camus. Instead of an ethical reversal—as envisaged by Sartre—it is made clear through Pilgrim that only by *flight*, particularly in the shape of time-travelling and reading science fiction, can the individual survive the sadistic universe (*Slaughterhouse-Five*; 70). The morals on the planet Tralfamadore, with which Billy is acquainted in the course of his time travels, are totally at odds with Sartrian ethics. There is a clear contrast between the philosophy of Sartre in *L'être et le néant* in 1943 and the philosophy of the inhabitants of Tralfamadore. The former postulates an absolute freedom, whereas the inhabitants of Tralfamadore believe that man is a will-less machine. The French philosopher speaks of an authentic 'project' of the individual to improve the situation. In contrast Billy stipulates, in imitation of the Tralfamadorians, that: "One of the main effects of war, after all, is that people are discouraged from being characters" (*Slaughterhouse-Five*; 110). The allusions to the AA motto, likewise amounting to a high degree of acceptance of human limitations, can also be seen in this light (*Slaughterhouse-Five*; 110). Although Camus does not propagate a flight from the borderline situation, the affirmation of the 'condition humaine' in *Slaughterhouse-Five* can very well be related to his Existentialism.

Contrasted with the borderline situation is the state of alienation, manifesting itself in many an existentialist work in the guise of 'mauvaise foi', 'Seinsvergessenheit'.[3] In each case it is inauthenticity flowing from the subject's failure to appreciate a number of essential structures at the ontological or mental level. In Sartre's literary work this inauthenticity is often described elaborately in order to make the reader reject it. More often even—as titles like *Les chemins de la liberté* suggest—Sartre shows the way to a positive attitude to life by way of a liberation from this 'mauvaise foi' or by depicting 'projects' of good faith contrary to it.

Conversely in his gloomiest work, *La chute*, Camus postulates the idea that a certain measure of inauthenticity is unavoidable, particularly because the margins of human abilities are limited. With some justification it can be said that apart from his time-travelling Billy Pilgrim lives the languid life of 'das Man' (Heidegger's term). His is the monotonous existence of the well-to-do bourgeois who properly observes social conventions. Pilgrim has nothing of the existential hero who in the spirit of Sartre revolts to improve the situation, like Orestes from *Les Mouches*, who obliterates people's guilt and restores them to freedom. More than once the narrator draws our attention to Pilgrim's sheepish appearance and his bourgeois character. Vonnegut even seems to have left behind him Camus' option for the heroism of enduring the situation, when we read that Billy does not like life and appears to be kept alive rather by circumstances than by his personal effort (*Slaughterhouse-Five*; 71). The frequent 'why me' utterances can be seen in this light. The answer to those utterances seems to have got stuck in the chaotic web of reality. It is remarkable that the same question rebounds to Billy both from 'above' and from 'below': "Why anybody, why anything", Nazis as well as Tralfamadorians coolly remark

(*Slaughterhouse-Five*; 56, 64).[4] The pressure of this view practically reduces Pilgrim's freedom of action to zero. An identical passage can be found in Camus' *La chute* where a camp guard explains the inevitability of fate to an inmate of a concentration camp (Camus 1956; 86). In this novel though, the emphasis is still very much on the guilt of the individual, a status which turns out to be inseparably linked to the human limitation. In *Slaughterhouse-Five*, hardly a word is devoted to this.

After this discussion of the borderline situation as an important topos, a second existentialist topos must now be discussed: the other person. Time and time again fellow humans, often responsible for the borderline situation, coerce the subject into a confrontation. In Existentialism the other is often an anonymous force (such as God) who keeps the situation under control. In *Slaughterhouse-Five* the other appears on three levels. First there is the relation between the anonymous narrator and his character, Pilgrim. The former appears to manipulate Billy like a puppet and occasionally steps out of his powerful domain when he enters Billy's storyline. A second level has already been mentioned; I am referring to the relation between the German enemy and Pilgrim. Although there are obvious confrontations, the Nazis are represented as (products of) anonymous forces. Finally there is the situation in modern American society, where Pilgrim attempts to lead a bourgeois life among bourgeois people. The problems he has with his wartime experiences lead to escapism, in particular into flight into the world of science fiction. Nonetheless his behaviour is experienced as 'shocking' by the [Heideggerian] 'das Man' surrounding Billy.

Sartre claims that the individual, upon confrontation with the other, may be caught out by authentic feelings of shame, fear or revulsion. These emotions are scarcely perceptible in *Slaughterhouse-Five*, firstly because it is not so much the subject as the 'world' that is speaking, secondly because the individual never appears able to achieve the status of authenticity.[5] Again I refer to the central idea of the absence in postmodernist texts of a metaphysical frame of reference to which one could relate feelings of shame, fear and the like. Kierkegaard, the precursor of Existentialism, distinguished fear—which is object-directed—from the 'Angst' that ultimately thematizes the contingency of existence. Although Billy has a concrete fear of war, he hardly appears to know any terror (in Kierkegaard's sense), just like the characters in Camus' work.

To sum up, it can be stated that *Slaughterhouse-Five* presents a Camusean vision of reality. Only the tendency to show that insight still reminds us of Sartre's ethical aims. The tenor of *Slaughterhouse-Five* is mainly that one has to resign oneself to the grief of the world and that humour and science fiction can pull you through. One can explain the presentation of the anguished character, Pilgrim, as an implicit protest against the forces experienced as anonymous that are held responsible for his perilous situation. Nevertheless it would be going too far to connect the central semantic topos of Existentialism—commitment ['engagement']—with Vonnegut's novel. The emphasis in *Slaughterhouse-Five* is rather on survival, even more than on Camus' honourable endurance of existence. There is no political involvement whatsoever, let alone a reorientation with respect to the borderline situation, although we must realize that Vonnegut's novel was published in 1969 against the backdrop of the Vietnam problems of the time.[6]

Apart from the implicit criticism of the forces depicted as anonymous, the differences with Sartre's Existentialism are considerable, particularly where the technical means are concerned which can be related to Postmodernism. Sartre, in an essay on Camus' *L'étranger*, comments on his style, that is to say the description of events, without establishing interrelationships between them. In his debut novel Camus is said to postulate events as 'islands' (Sartre 1947; 92-113). In *Slaughterhouse-Five* this method is radicalized. First of all I point to the narrative sequence, which is not chronological and moreover has more than one beginning and end. In this connection Meeter speaks of a "schizophrenic manner of narration" (in: Klinkowitz and Somer 1973; 230). This narrative technique may be seen as an analogue of Pilgrim's inner confusion.[7] At another level the text can also be seen as the reflection of the Tralfamadorian view of time and space; many events are described simultaneously from various perspectives, disrupting the linear notion of time.

The actual text of *Slaughterhouse-Five* is preceded by a triplet of titles, followed by the name of the author with some information about his person and his novel. Prior to the beginning of the text three works from which the author has quoted are mentioned. Apart from these sources, it turns out that quotations from Roosevelt, Horace, Goethe, Blake and Céline, among others, have been used. These statements have the same function as the reproduced notes, drawings and so on, i.e. the intermingling of fact and fiction. This permutation underlines the chaotic atmosphere surrounding Vonnegut's novel.

One can separate the autobiographically tinged beginning and end of *Slaughterhouse-Five* on the one hand and the adventures of Pilgrim, taking up the middle part, on the other. Protagonist and narrator have been situated in different temporal dimensions, which creates a great distance between the two. The comparison with a God manipulating his creation as a puppet suggests itself here. At the same time this distance is occasionally transcended by 'intrusions' by the narrator (every time related intentionally with the author) in the form of phrases like 'I was there' and 'That was me', creating the suggestion that he fought alongside Billy during the Second World War. This method heightens the realistic content of the novel. In the central section three narrative levels can be distinguished: first, the reality of Second World War; secondly, the highly fictionalized report of Billy's ups and downs in this situation and thirdly, the narrator's interventions mentioned above, "the author as a guest in his own test" (McHale 1989; 205). Loeb speaks of a "technique of intrusion" here, namely between Vonnegut [sic] and "another impersonal, seemingly omniscient narrator" (Loeb 1979; 7). Its aim, I think, is the introduction of the silent witness who was not merely a victim like Pilgrim. This figure is after all better suited—considering his distance to the past—to judge the total character of Billy's experiences. The consequence is a permutation of text and social context; the reader is given the impression that intra- and extra-literary reality are inseparable. Another form of merging is the intrusion of the science fiction world into everyday American reality.

Closely connected to these mixtures is the postmodernist 'zone' also called 'heterotopia' where "worlds of incompatible structure" are postulated alongside one another (McHale 1989; 44). Tralfamadore can be considered such a zone; it is a place where all kinds of systems and structures have been brought together which are mutually exclusive on earth, thereby suggesting to the reader an atmosphere of incongruence. Think for instance of the principle of total insight, coupled with the principle of the selectivity of every perception (the Tralfamadorians are able to have a total view of everything) and their conviction that organisms are machines.

Apart from this postmodernist juxtaposition of worlds one can also discern in *Slaughterhouse-Five* the typically postmodernist procedure of metafiction. What I mean is the embedding of certain narrative levels by means of commentary on the narration itself. The result is that the story told appears more fictional, while the commentary gains a realistic effect.[8]

The first pages of the novel deal with the nature and the progress of the actual novel, which is embedded as follows:

> It [the book, HvS] begins like this:
> *Listen*:
> *Billy Pilgrim has come unstuck in time.*
> It ends like this:
> *Poo-tee-weet*? (*Slaughterhouse-Five*; 22)

Because these metalinguistic utterances are ultimately placed within the fictional framework of the novel, *Slaughterhouse-Five* can be seen as a text in which the permutation of fact and fiction has been strongly thematized. Related to this is the passage in Vonnegut's novel where a rather pretentious academic discussion on the death of the novel is parodied by the presentation of an incoherent story by Billy about flying saucers. Within the fictional frame of the text as a whole this discussion about the novel has been described quite realistically, but it is reduced at the same time to a meaningless discourse as a result of Billy's stammering. During the reading of *Slaughterhouse-Five*, the possibility forces itself upon the reader that he or she might be reading an example of a dead genre, one which manages to merge fact with fiction.

These procedures serve to show the chaos that the war has produced in the narrator and to communicate this to the reader.

Although Camus did not use these techniques as radically, we can very well relate them to his philosophy, if we realize that the world view established by these procedures is along the lines of Camus' views. Both *Slaughterhouse-Five* and the French author's work are dominated by the idea of the limits that condemn man to eternal repetition.[9] Evil is not vanquished and therefore continues to exist. The individual who recognizes this begins to feel some discomfort. While Camus thematizes this crisis, the emphasis in Vonnegut's work is more on the status after this phase, which is typified by irony, compulsive escapism and resignation.

From *Neophilologus* 79, no. 1 (January 1995): 3-12. Copyright © 1995 by Springer Science and Business Media. Reprinted with permission of Springer Science and Business Media.

Notes

I would like to thank D. W. Fokkema, A. M. Iken and A. Rigney for their critical attention to draft versions of this essay. [Translation: Rob Kievit.]

1. Although I am using the designation of Postmodernism here, I do not consider myself able to unequivocally define the movement to which the term refers. This inability also has to do with the fact that the debate on the nature of Postmodernism is still going on. I am aware that in this essay I am using postmodernist concepts which are mutually contradictory. Nonetheless I think that a certain coherence may be discerned in the body of statements concerning *Slaughterhouse-Five*. It is in terms of this coherence that I want to talk about *Slaughterhouse-Five* as a postmodernist novel, and

about its relations with other texts to which this coherence is applicable.

2. Particularly H. Lethen's essay on the relationship between the Historical Avant-garde and Postmodernism deserves attention (in: Fokkema and Bertens 1986). I would like to comment on this. Lethen points to a number of similarities: the destruction of the idea that art could produce meanings, the disintegration of the subject, the dominance of coincidence and the emphasis on the contingency of history. I think that these relations are correct. On the other hand I feel that the term 'deconstruction' is more useful in the discussion of Postmodernism than 'destruction'. Many postmodernist authors are not—as the Surrealists were—out to dethrone the bourgeoisie, by confronting the establishment with its repressed urges. Rather they attempt, in Derrida's spirit, to demonstrate the untenability of any (ideological) statement.

It seems that the attacks of postmodernist authors usually are not aimed—as with the Surrealists—at the bourgeoisie, but at the upholders of traditional academic views. Read for instance the parody of professor Uzzi-Tuzzii in Calvino's *If on a winter's night a traveller*. These allusions, often incomprehensible to laymen, might explain why some postmodern novelists have failed in their attempts to reach a wider audience.

3. Herzog, in Saul Bellow's novel of the same name, parodies this 'Seins-vergessenheit', according to Heidegger the consequence of the fall from 'das Sein', as follows: "Dear Doktor Professor Heidegger, I should like to know what you mean by the expression 'the fall into the quotidian'. When did this fall occur? Where were we standing when it happened?" (Bellow 1965; 55).

4. This existential oppression is closely related to the experiences of man in the Old Testament, hence the references to this in many postmodernist texts. The 'wildly transcendental God' (Hegel's term) from the Old Testament, arbitrarily imposing his laws on the Jewish people, has been replaced in many postmodernist texts by an anonymous system tyrannizing the powerless individual. In this respect I would like to point to the relation between Lot/Sodom and Billy/Dresden; death awaits both characters if they dare look back to the gruesome reality that is behind them. In addition I want to mention Pilgrim's reversal of the bombardment, by which he transfers the New Testament-coloured apocalypse to the peaceful harmony as described in the book of Genesis.

5. Particularly by accentuating that which escapes perception, by presenting magic, coincidence and absurdity, the postmodernist novel conveys the impression that the world is revealed in all its autonomy. In *Slaughterhouse-Five* the characteristic of the world presenting itself can be perceived in the sometimes completely 'unpreferential' description of events, which is reminiscent of Camus' *L'étranger*. Bombardments and singing parrots are described quite apart from any ethical or emotional hierarchy. In other words Pilgrim, the protagonist, is unable or unwilling to place the events within a meaningful whole.

6. The absence of any ethical norms has received a lot of emphasis in the criticism of Vonnegut (cf. Ruiter 1991; 98). Hawinkels, referring to *Slaughterhouse-Five*, speaks of a "bourgeois, nihilist view of the war problem: war is a moment in history, which you undergo, which you cannot do anything about as an individual" (quoted in Ruiter 1991; 225).

7. Interesting in this respect is D. Fokkema's following conclusion: "(. . .) the Post-

modernist writer may, quite deliberately, produce texts which have the appearance of being built on the principal of non-selection" (Fokkema and Bertens 1986; 84). The principle of non-selection, according to which a number of postmodernist texts might be structured, is occasionally confirmed by its authors. In those instances they refer to their intentions with respect to the text. I can only see the presentation of these testimonies in this post-positivist era as a peculiar atavism. The reader is asked repeatedly not to read any deeper meanings into the text, thus naively ignoring the existence of accepted conventions *which the principle of non-selection is in fact referring to.* The statement to the effect that the text presents an autonomous-impossible reality lends little support to this request, because this view of the work as being semantically incoherent firstly elevates a subjective experience (viz. that of the author) into a norm. Secondly the presentation of an impossible universe does not imply that of an inconceivable world. Glossing over the fact that every novel is always within the limits of the thinkable leads, I think, in fact to an underestimation of the reader's imagination, to which many postmodernist texts specifically refer. Finally one should not exclude the possibility that the reader may indeed fail to construct a coherent semantic network on the intra-literary level, but that after reading he can operationalize this inability either positively or negatively in concrete reality, for instance along the principle of recognizing or contrasting.

8. The following song reproduced in *Slaughterhouse-Five* provides a 'mise en abyme' of the problem sensed by the narrator in recounting his experiences:

> *My name is Yon Yonson,*
> *I work in Wisconsin,*
> *I work in a lumbermill there,*
> *The people I meet when I walk down the street,*
> *They say, 'What's your name?'*
> *And I say,*
> *'My name is Yon Yonson,*
> *I work in Wisconsin . . .'*

And so on to infinity. (*Slaughterhouse-Five*; 10)

Particularly the last sentence, commenting in its turn on the repetitive structure of the song, emphasizes the postmodernist process of repetition.

9. The theme of eternal repetition manifests itself in Vonnegut's novel when Billy's son, Robert, turns out to be a pugnacious soldier, and all over the globe the killing of innocent people and various wars keep going on.

Works Cited

Alphen, Ernst van. "The Heterotopian Space in the Discussions on Postmodernism." In: *Poetics Today* 10 (Winter 1989) 4, pp. 819-839.

Bellow, Saul. *Herzog*. Middlesex. 1964.

Bertens, Hans en D'haen, Theo. *Het postmodernisme in de literatuur*. Amsterdam. 1988.

Blanken, Henk. "Langs de Lijnbaan van Dresden". In: *De Volkskrant* 2-3-1991.

Brocher, Sabine. *Abenteuerliche Elemente im modernen Roman*. München, Wien. 1981.

Calinescu, Matei. *Five Faces of Modernity, Modernism, Avant-garde, Decadence, Kitsch, Postmodernism*. Durham. 1987.

Camus, Albert. *Le mythe de Sisyphe, essai sur l'absurde*. Paris. 1942.

_____. *L'homme révolté*. Paris. 1951.

_____. *La Chute*. Paris. 1956.

Fokkema, Douwe W. *Literary History, Modernism, and Post-Modernism*. Amsterdam/Philadelphia. 1984.

Fokkema, D. and Bertens, H. (ed) *Approaching Postmodernism*. Amsterdam, Philadelphia. 1986.

Gianonne, Richard. *Vonnegut, a Preface to his Novels*. London. 1977.

Goldsmith, David H. *Kurt Vonnegut, Fantasist of Fire and Ice*. Ohio. 1972.

Ibsch, Elrud. "Postmoderne (on) mogelijkheden in de nederlandse literatuur". In: *De achtervolging voortgezet* by Breekveldt, Van Halsema, Ibsch en Strengholt (ed). Amsterdam. 1989. pp. 346-373.

Klinkowitz, J. & Somer, J. *The Vonnegut Statement*. New York. 1973.

Loeb, Monica. *Vonnegut's Duty-Dance With Death—Theme and Structure in Slaughterhouse-Five*. Örnsköldvik. 1979.

McHale, Brian. *Postmodernist Fiction*. London and New York. 1989.

Reed, Peter J. *Kurt Vonnegut Jr*. New York. 1972.

Robbe-Grillet, Alain. *Pour un nouveau roman*. Paris. 1963.

Ruiter, Frans. *De receptie van het Amerikaanse Postmodernisme in Duitsland en Nederland*. Leuven/Apeldoorn.1991.

Sartre, Jean-Paul. "Explication de L'étranger", In: *Situations I*. Paris. 1947.

_____. *Qu'est-ce que la littérature?* Paris. 1948.

Schatt, Stanley. *Kurt Vonnegut Jr*. Boston. 1976.

Silverman, Hugh J. and Welton, Donn (ed) *Postmodernism and Continental Philosophy*. New York. 1988.

Stralen, Hans van. "Vestdijk en het existentialisme." In: *Vestdijkkroniek* 74-75 (March/June 1992), pp. 1-27.

Vonnegut, Kurt. *Slaughterhouse-Five*. Glasgow. 1987 (1969).

Diagnosing Billy Pilgrim:
A Psychiatric Approach to Kurt Vonnegut's
*Slaughterhouse-Five*_____

Susanne Vees-Gulani

> "That's the attractive thing about war," said Rosewater. "Absolutely ev-
> erybody gets a little something."
>
> —*Slaughterhouse-Five* 111

Kurt Vonnegut's *Slaughterhouse-Five* has been widely discussed as an antiwar novel based on the author's own experiences in World War II. As a German POW, Vonnegut witnessed the bombing and complete destruction of Dresden, and *Slaughterhouse-Five* is the author's mani-festation of what he called "a process of twenty years [. . .] of living with Dresden and the aftermath" (Allen 163). Indeed, the words that describe the war, the Dresden events, and their effect on the people who experienced them did not come easily to Vonnegut. In an inter-view in 1974, he commented on the difficulties of articulating his ex-periences: "I came home in 1945, started writing about it, and *wrote about it*, and wrote about it, and WROTE ABOUT IT" (Allen 163). This agony is echoed in the first chapter of the novel:

> When I got home from the Second World War twenty-three years ago, I thought it would be easy for me to write about the destruction of Dresden, since all I would have to do would be to report what I had seen [. . .].
>
> But not many words about Dresden came from my mind then. [. . .] And not many words come now, either. [. . .] (2)

Vonnegut's problems with articulation are evidence of the long-term consequences of his witnessing those events. Although critics gener-ally recognize that the war, and particularly the destruction of Dresden, had a traumatizing effect on Vonnegut, the nature of that trauma and how it manifests itself in the novel have yet to be explored in a systematic manner. A fresh look at *Slaughterhouse-Five* using psychiatric theory not only offers new insight into the work but also opens a window on the author himself. Vonnegut's writing of *Slaughterhouse-Five* can be seen as a therapeutic process that allows him to uncover and deal with his trauma. By using creative means to overcome his distress, Vonnegut makes it possible for us to trace his path to recovery. We slowly narrow in on his condition using the novel as a conduit first to the protagonist, Billy Pilgrim, then to the narrator, and finally to the author himself.

Lawrence Broer has suggested that "[p]robably no characters in contemporary fiction are more traumatized and emotionally damaged than those of Kurt Vonnegut" (3). Billy Pilgrim in *Slaughterhouse-Five* certainly supports Broer's observation. Even his wife, Valencia, who is unaware of Billy's psychological turmoil, gets "a funny feeling" that he is "just full of secrets" (121). Attempting to define Billy's psychological state more precisely, critics have frequently associated *Slaughterhouse-Five* and its protagonist with schizophrenia, most likely inspired by the author's own comments on the title page characterizing the novel as "somewhat in the telegraphic schizophrenic manner of tales of the planet Tralfamadore."[1] Yet even some of the critics who describe Billy as schizophrenic seem uneasy with that assessment. In the introduction to a recent collection of essays on Vonnegut, for example, Harold Bloom qualifies his description of Billy as suffering from schizophrenia with the parenthetical comment, "(to call it that)" (1). Symptoms of schizophrenia have to be present for at least six months before the disease can be diagnosed, and it is not caused by an external event. Schizophrenics usually suffer from hallucinations,[2] in most cases hearing voices, and from social and occupational dysfunction (*Diagnostic and Statistical Manual of Mental Disorders* 285). Those criteria do not apply to Billy. His problems are directly related to his war experiences. Furthermore, after he returns home from the war, he manages to lead, at least externally, a very functional life—having a family, running a business, and being a respected member of society. He does not suffer from hallucinations. Rather, Billy's fantasies seem

portant insight is that PTSD is believed to be caused not only by the traumatizing events themselves; the "psychosocial atmosphere in a society is clearly a factor that facilitates or hinders the process of coping with stressful life events" (Kleber, Figley, and Gersons 2). This can also be observed in the novel. When Billy returns home, America does not provide him with the possibility of working through his war experiences, particularly the bombing of Dresden, and thus occasions Billy's chronic suffering. The most striking symptom of Billy's condition is his altered perception of time. He sees himself as having "come unstuck in time":

> Billy has gone to sleep a senile widower and awakened on his wedding day. He has walked through a door in 1955 and come out another one in 1941. He has gone back through that door to find himself in 1963. He has seen his birth and death many times, he says, and pays random visits to all the events in between.
>
> He says.
>
> Billy is spastic in time, has no control over where he is going next, and the trips aren't necessarily fun. (23)

Being "spastic in time" thus is a metaphor for Billy's repeatedly re-experiencing the traumatic events he went through in the war, particularly as a POW during the Dresden bombings. Psychologically, Billy has never fully left World War II; instead, in Jerome Klinkowitz's words, he lives in a "continual present" (55). In *Trauma and Recovery*, Judith Herman describes a similar situation with regard to former captives suffering from PTSD. While imprisoned, they "are eventually reduced to living in an endless present" (89). After their release, they "may give the appearance of returning to ordinary time, while psychologically remaining bound in the timelessness of the prison" (89). It has also been observed that a former prisoner "even years after liberation, [. . .] continues to practice doublethink and to exist simultaneously in two realities, two points in time" (89-90).

Billy's situation is comparable to that of the soldiers Herman describes. Although he is "outwardly normal" (175), the traumatic memories persistently intrude on him in forms typical to people suffering from PTSD. At times Billy also finds himself simultaneously at two different points of his life, for example, "simultaneously on foot in Germany in 1944 and riding his Cadillac in 1967" (58). Billy frequently relives the past through his dreams, distressing recollections, and flashback episodes. Often certain "internal or external cues that symbolize or resemble an aspect of the traumatic event" (*DSM* 428) trigger painful memories or cause Billy to re-live the war episodes. Psychiatrists note specifically that "sensory phenomena, such as sights, sounds, and smell that are circumstantially related to the traumatic event [. . .] reactivate traumatic memories and flashbacks" in PTSD sufferers (Miller 18). This symptom is readily observed in the protagonist and explains the novel's abundance of both psychological and structural "linking devices" between different scenes of Billy's life (Klinkowitz 78). For instance, the novel repeatedly mentions certain colors ("ivory and blue," "orange and black") or smells ("mustard gas and roses") that carry significance in Billy's past.[4] Other triggers include sounds, such as a siren (57, 164), which Billy associates with the Dresden air raid alarms: It "scared the hell out of him" (57) and "he was expecting World War Three at any time" (57). Not surprisingly, seconds later he is "back in World War Two again" (58). In another episode, the sight of men physically crippled by war going from door to door selling magazines immediately causes great distress to Billy, himself mentally crippled by the war:

> Billy went on weeping as he contemplated the cripples and their boss. His doorchimes clanged hellishly.
>
> He closed his eyes, and opened them again. He was still weeping, but he was back in Luxembourg again. He was marching with a lot of other prisoners. It was a winter wind that was bringing tears to his eyes. (63)

A barbershop quartet that performs at his anniversary party causes a strong response in Billy because they remind him of the four German guards in Dresden who, when they saw the destruction of their hometown, "in their astonishment and grief, resembled a barbershop quartet" (179). The memory of the German guards lies at the center of Billy's trauma, the destruction of Dresden. In this case Billy first responds with physical symptoms, looking as if "he might have been having a heart attack" (173). Finally, away from the guests, Billy "remembered it shimmeringly" (177) but does not revisit that event. The Dresden bombings and their effect are too painful to relive and at first even too frightening to remember. Thus the strong physical and psychological reaction to the barbershop quartet, which even disturbs Billy's usually normal outward appearance, shows how deeply Billy has buried his Dresden memories.

Suppression of parts of the trauma goes hand-in-hand with other techniques of evading the trauma, such as avoiding "thoughts, feelings, or conversations associated with [it]," as well as "activities, places, or people that arouse recollections" (*DSM* 428). Billy displays all of these symptoms prominently. He hardly ever talks about his experiences in the war, even eluding the topic when his wife questions him about it (121-23). This behavior accords with studies of prisoners of war that "report with astonishment that the men never discussed their experiences with anyone. Often those who married after liberation never told even their wives or children that they had been prisoners" (Herman 89).

Another striking feature of Billy's behavior that connects with the symptom of avoidance and also is among the criteria for PTSD is his diminished responsiveness to the world around him. He is described as one who "never got mad at anything" (30) and bears everything without reaction, because "[e]verything was pretty much all right with Billy" (157). Throughout the novel Billy's range of affect is severely restricted, shown most prominently in the much repeated phrase "So it goes," his passive and emotionless reaction to tragedy and death. Robert J. Lifton observed similar reactions toward death in survivors of the Hiroshima bombing, reactions he labeled "psychic numbing" (115) or "psychic closing-off" (125).[5] For Billy, avoidance and "psychic numbing" are protective shields, offering him the possibility to live an "outwardly normal" (175) life.

However, it is impossible for Billy to stop the intrusion of his memories completely because the events have destroyed him inside, which now mirrors the ruins he saw in Dresden. At first he seeks help by committing himself to a mental hospital because he felt "that he was going crazy" (100). Yet just as mainstream American society does not provide an atmosphere conducive to recovery from the horrors of war, the psychiatric establishment also fails Billy. By neither providing an accurate diagnosis nor offering any coping mechanisms, it proves itself completely separated from true world experience. When Billy checks himself in, "the doctors agreed: He *was* going crazy" (100), but "[t]hey didn't think it had anything to do with the war. They were sure Billy was going to pieces because his father had thrown him into the deep end of the Y.M.C.A. swimming pool when he was a little boy and had then taken him to the rim of the Grand Canyon" (100). Billy thus falls victim to the previous tendency in psychiatry to underestimate the role of "an external factor, something outside the person" in causing trauma and to focus instead only on "individual vulnerability as the reason for people's suffering" (Kleber, Figley, and Gersons 11, 13).

Billy and his roommate, fellow war veteran Rosewater, thus embark on their own path of "trying to re-invent themselves and their universe" (101) in order to cope with the war events. In what has been referred to as "a desperate attempt to rationalize chaos" (Merrill and Scholl 69), they resort to science fiction. Billy claims that he was kidnapped by aliens from the planet Tralfamadore and displayed there in a zoo. Tralfamadorian philosophy, which opposes trying to make sense out of occurrences, helps Billy deal with the horrible events and their consequences by reinterpreting their meaning. When he asks the Tralfamadorians why they chose to abduct him, they tell him: "'Why *you*?

Why *us* for that matter? Why *anything*? Because this moment simply *is*. [. . .] There is no *why*'" (76-77). These beliefs enable Billy to avoid some of the distress he feels when facing death:

> "When a Tralfamadorian sees a corpse, all he thinks is that the dead person is in bad condition in that particular moment, but that the same person is just fine in plenty of other moments. Now, when I myself hear that somebody is dead, I simply shrug and say what the Tralfamadorians say about dead people, which is 'So it goes.'" (27)

Although the idea of Tralfamadore as a coping mechanism may strike one as bizarre, it seems to Billy the only option in a world that fails to provide him with a different path. As Leonard Mustazza points out, Vonnegut, by indirectly identifying Kilgore Trout's science fiction novels as the source of Billy's ideas, "takes pains to show whence Billy's fantasy derives, and, in this regard, the novel proves to be quite realistic, a portrait of one of life's (especially war's) victims" (302). With the help of his Tralfamadorian fantasy and his idea of time travel, Billy conquers his trauma in a way that enables him to function. He controls his anxiety, so that nothing can surprise or scare him; and his symptoms of arousal are confined to his trouble sleeping and his occasional bouts of weeping (61). However, Herman points out that "the appearance of normal functioning [. . .] should not be mistaken for full recovery, for the integration of the trauma has not been accomplished" (165). The price Billy pays for appearing normal is high. Not only is he bound to a life of indifference, passivity, and a science fiction fantasy, but also he can never fully escape from the trauma that continues to intrude into his life.

The story of Billy's trauma is not the only one in the novel; it is framed by that of the narrator, who is a fictionalized version of Vonnegut himself. Although separated from Billy's story, some of the "linking devices" (Klinkowitz 78) found there, the Tralfamadorian "so it goes," the smell of "mustard gas and roses" (4, 7), and even a "Three

Musketeers Candy Bar" (9), also appear in the first chapter.[6] At the same time, the narrator interrupts Billy's story on several occasions to authenticate the events. The text implies that because the horrible consequences of the bombing of Dresden truly happened but are too far removed from normal experience to be easily reported, they can neither be completely fictionalized nor simply repeated through an eyewitness account. The novel thus becomes a mixture of autobiography and fiction that simultaneously binds Vonnegut to and distances him from the text and its implications.

Traumatic memories are usually not verbal, but surface as visual images (de Silva and Marks 166). Before they can be shared with others, they first have to be translated into language—a task that, difficult in itself, is complicated by avoidance and denial. PTSD sufferers are often unable to recall important aspects of the trauma (*DSM* 428). This is a problem the narrator faces when he simply cannot remember much about the war (14). Even though he continually tries to write the novel, he feels unable to do so. On finishing the book after nearly a quarter of a century, he considers it "a failure" (22). In fact, as Peter Freese points out, "the thematic center of his novel [Dresden] is endlessly circumnavigated but never fully encountered" (221). This aspect of the novel is what Herman calls "the central dialectic of psychological trauma": "the conflict between the will to deny horrible events and the will to proclaim them aloud" (1).

This difficulty of expressing the events is enhanced by the political and societal denial surrounding them. The narrator shares Billy's experience that America does not offer an atmosphere that easily allows recovery. Because there is no forum for a discussion of the events, "I wrote the Air Force back then, asking for details about the raid on Dresden, who ordered it, how many planes did it, why they did it, what desirable results there had been and so on. I was answered by a man who [. . .] said that he was sorry, but that the information was top secret still" (11). Just as there is no public discussion of the events, there is also no discussion of them in private conversation. Most of the victims of the air raids were Germans, the aggressors and major victimizers of the war. Therefore, the question of whether it is even legitimate to talk about the horrible and traumatizing aspects of the bombings is part of every discussion of the bombings:

> I happened to tell a University of Chicago professor at a cocktail party about the raid as I had seen it, about the book I would write. He was a member of a thing called The Committee on Social Thought. And he told me about the concentration camps, and about how the Germans had made soap and candles out of the fat of dead Jews and so on.
> All I could say was, "I know, I know. *I know.*" (10)

The desperate "'I know, I know. *I know*'" seems by no means Vonnegut's "expression of his exasperation at having to hear, once again, about the horror of the death camps" (275), as Philip Watts contends. Rather it is an acknowledgment of the difficulty and inability to talk or write about a topic that deeply affected one's psychology, but which at the same time cannot be separated from questions of guilt, because it necessarily includes portraying the victimizers of the war, the Germans, as suffering during the bombings. Consequently one needs to design one's own coping strategies and path of healing to deal with the horror of the Dresden air raids.

For Vonnegut, the recovery process is bound to literary production, so he understands his works as "therapy" (Allen 109). His war and particularly his Dresden experience have not left him scarless. What we learn in the novel is corroborated by comments that the author has made in interviews; the two together point to an underlying trauma. Vonnegut especially emphasizes his amnesia about Dresden:

> [T]he book was largely a found object. It was what was in my head, and I was able to get it out, but one of the characteristics about this object was that there was a complete blank where the bombing of Dresden took place, because I don't remember. And I looked up several of my war buddies and

---

they didn't remember, either. They didn't want to talk about it. There was a complete forgetting of what it was like. There were all kinds of information surrounding the event, but as far as my memory bank was concerned, the center had been pulled right out of the story. (Allen 94)

Writing *Slaughterhouse-Five* meant the long and painful process of uncovering what Vonnegut had pushed out of his consciousness. Even though it is painful, psychiatrists see the telling of the story of one's trauma as an important step in the recovery from PTSD (Herman 177). Herman stresses how difficult it is "to come face-to-face with the horrors on the other side of the amnesiac barrier" (184). Successful therapy requires a balancing act, because "[a]voiding the traumatic memories leads to stagnation in the recovery process, while approaching them too precipitately leads to a fruitless and damaging reliving of the trauma" (Herman 176). Vonnegut tries not to face his suppressed memories directly but to get to the core by slowly uncovering layer after layer. The novel reflects this process of narrowing in on himself through the two trauma stories. Billy's story allows an indirect and detached exploration of the effects of the Dresden bombing because the character is mostly fictional. The narrator's story parallels Vonnegut's on one level, but on another level, it is an integral part of a work of fiction. Removing himself from the factual to the fictional plane by creating the narrator allows Vonnegut a degree of distance from himself and his experiences. Consequently, the final point of recovery in this process of self-therapy is not achieved in the novel but rather comes with its completion:

I felt after I finished *Slaughterhouse-Five* that I didn't have to write at all anymore if I didn't want to. It was the end of some sort of career. I don't know why, exactly. I suppose that flowers, when they're through blooming, have some sort of awareness of some purpose having been served. Flowers didn't ask to be flowers and I didn't ask to be me. At the end of *Slaughterhouse-Five*, [. . .] I had a shutting-off feeling, [. . .] that I had done what I was supposed to do and everything was OK. (Allen 107)

However, although *Slaughterhouse-Five* is the result of a successful self-treatment, telling the story does not mean that the trauma can then be forgotten. As in psychotherapy, which aims at "integration, not exorcism" (Herman 181) of trauma, the Dresden experience does not lose its important position in Vonnegut's life after he completes the novel; but it can now be adequately integrated into the author's past. The events may no longer paralyze the writer, but they are still available for further creative exploration, thus continuing as "the informing structure of all his novels" (Leeds 92). Yet Vonnegut has done more than cure himself. As Herman points out:

> In the telling, the trauma story becomes a testimony. [. . .] Testimony has both a private dimension, which is confessional and spiritual, and a public aspect, which is political and judicial. The use of the word testimony links both meanings, giving a new and larger dimension to the patient's individual experience. (181)

By publishing *Slaughterhouse-Five*, which draws the reader into the path of healing, the stories of Billy, the narrator, and consequently Vonnegut take on public dimension. They draw attention to something that we often prefer to suppress and deny although it is important to remember, namely, the crippling nature of war and the terrible toll that modern warfare extracts from those forced to live through it.

From *Critique* 44, no. 2 (Winter 2003): 175-184. Copyright © 2003 by Heldref Publications. Reprinted with permission of Heldref Publications.

Notes

The author would like to thank Prof. Sari Gilman Aronson, M.D., and Vikas Gulani, M.D., Ph.D., University of Illinois, College of Medicine at Urbana, for their insightful comments and encouragement in the preparation of this manuscript.

1. A few of the many examples include Leonard Mustazza ("Vonnegut's Tralfamadore and Milton's Eden"), who refers to Billy as "schizophrenic" (302); Lawrence R.

Broer (*Sanity Plea*), who characterizes Billy's state as "schizophrenic deterioration" (91); Peter Freese ("*Slaughterhouse-Five* or, How to Storify an Atrocity"), who describes Billy's story as sounding "suspiciously like the biography of a man who develops schizophrenia" (212).

2. Hallucinations are defined as "a *sensory* perception that has the compelling sense of reality of a true perception but that occurs without external stimulation of the relevant sensory organ" (*DSM* 767, emphasis added).

3. Billy's more externally observable erratic behavior after the plane crash and his wife's death by carbon-monoxide poisoning also does not comply with the criteria for the diagnosis of schizophrenia. Rather, it seems consistent with the consequences of a head trauma he might have suffered in the crash, adding to Billy's traumatized state by worsening his psychic condition even further.

4. The combination "ivory and blue" appears throughout the novel, usually as a reference to bare feet and implying cold or death. The image originates in the war when Billy sees "corpses with bare feet that were blue and ivory" (65). The significance of the colors "orange and black," which reappear in the striped pattern of a tent put up for his daughter's wedding (72), is connected to the POW train Billy rides during the war, which was "marked with a striped banner of orange and black" (69). The recurring smell of "mustard gas and roses" is also connected to death. Its significance arises from Billy's experience of having to dig out victims from under the Dresden ruins after the raids: "They didn't smell bad at first, were wax museums. But then the bodies rotted and liquefied, and the stink was like roses and mustard gas" (214).

5. Donald Greiner was the first to note the applicability of Lifton's ideas to Vonnegut's text. For further detail see Donald Greiner's 1973 essay "Vonnegut's *Slaughterhouse-Five* and the Fiction of Atrocity."

6. The "Three Musketeers Candy Bar" is directly related to a scene in which Billy's wife Valencia visits Billy in the mental hospital a few years after the war and eats a "Three Musketeers Candy Bar" (107). The significance of the image, however, lies in the time of the war. After the Battle of the Bulge, Billy is part of a group of soldiers, called by one of them, Weary, "the Three Musketeers" (48). Weary later blames Billy for breaking up the (completely imagined) great union of the Three Musketeers and becomes obsessed with wanting Billy dead.

Works Cited

Allen, William Rodney, ed. *Conversations with Kurt Vonnegut*. Literary Conversations Series. Jackson: UP of Mississippi, 1988.

Bloom, Harold. Introduction. *Kurt Vonnegut*. Ed. Harold Bloom. Modern Critical Views. Broomall: Chelsea, 2000. 1-2.

Broer, Lawrence R. *Sanity Plea: Schizophrenia in the Novels of Kurt Vonnegut*. Rev. ed. Tuscaloosa: U of Alabama P, 1994.

Diagnostic and Statistical Manual of Mental Disorders. 4th ed. Washington: American Psychiatric Association, 1994. 209-22.

Freese, Peter. "Kurt Vonnegut's *Slaughterhouse-Five* or, How to Storify an Atrocity." *Historiographic Metafiction in Modern American and Canadian Literature*. Ed. Bernd Engler and Kurt Muller. Beiträge zur englischen und amerikanischen Literatur 13. Paderborn: Schöningh, 1994.

Greiner, Donald. "Vonnegut's *Slaughterhouse-Five* and the Fiction of Atrocity." *Critique* 14 (1973): 38-51.

Herman, Judith. *Trauma and Recovery*. 2nd ed. New York: Basic, 1997.

Kaplan, Harold, and Benjamin J. Sadock, eds. *Comprehensive Textbook of Psychiatry/VI*. 6th ed. 2 vols. Baltimore: Williams and Wilkins, 1995.

Kleber Rolf J., Charles R. Figley, and Berthold P. R. Gersons, eds. *Beyond Trauma: Cultural and Societal Dynamics*. The Plenum Series on Stress and Coping. New York: Plenum, 1995.

Klinkowitz, Jerome. *Slaughterhouse-Five: Reinventing the Novel and the World*. Twayne's Masterworks Studies 37. Boston: Twayne, 1990.

Leeds, Marc. "Beyond the Slaughterhouse: Tralfamadorian Reading Theory in the Novels of Kurt Vonnegut." *The Vonnegut Chronicles: Interviews and Essays*. Eds. Peter J. Reed and Marc Leeds. Contributions to the Study of World Literature 65. Westport: Greenwood, 1996. 91-102.

Lifton, Robert J. *History and Human Survival: Essays on the Young and the Old, Survivors and the Dead, Peace and War, and on Contemporary Psychohistory*. New York: Random House, 1971.

Merrill, Robert, and Peter A. Scholl. "Vonnegut's *Slaughterhouse-Five*: The Requirements of Chaos." *Studies in American Fiction* 6 (1978): 65-76.

Miller, Laurence. *Shocks to the System: Psychotherapy of Traumatic Disability Syndromes*. New York: Norton, 1998.

Mustazza, Leonard. "Vonnegut's Tralfamadore and Milton's Eden." *Essays in Literature* 13 (1986): 299-312.

Saigh, Philip A. and J. Douglas Bremner. *Posttraumatic Stress Disorder: A Comprehensive Text*. Boston: Allyn and Bacon, 1999.

Silva, Padmal de and Melanie Marks. "Intrusive Thinking in Post-Traumatic Stress Disorder." *Post-Traumatic Stress Disorders: Concepts and Therapy*. Ed. William Yule. Wiley Series in Clinical Psychology. New York: Wiley, 1999. 161-175.

Vonnegut, Kurt. *Slaughterhouse-Five*. New York: Laurel, 1969.

Watts, Philip. "Rewriting History: Céline and Kurt Vonnegut." *The South Atlantic Quarterly* 93 (1994): 265-78.

Speaking Personally:
Slaughterhouse-Five and the Essays_____
Jerome Klinkowitz

"The Hyannis Port Story" is more than Kurt Vonnegut's last piece of fiction for the *Saturday Evening Post*. That it never appeared there, waiting for publication five years later in *Welcome to the Monkey House*, makes it fit into the author's canon all the more comfortably, for in this narrative he looks forward to the next stage in his career. As a short story it uses a formula Vonnegut had exploited from his start with the family magazines, the theme of homely simplicity triumphing over wealth and pretension. But the device is played out with several major differences. The wealth and fame are immensely greater than in "Custom-Made Bride" and any of the other earlier tales. As well they should be, for these trappings belong not to fictive creations but to actual people, the family of President John F. Kennedy living in Hyannis Port. It is the third distinguishing element of this story that shows the method Vonnegut began using at that time and which would bring him his greatest success: the story's events, as richly fabulous yet historically true as they are, get measured from the narrator's highly personal point of view. In "The Hyannis Port Story" President Kennedy is much like the actual sitting president, and the narrator is much like Kurt Vonnegut. In bringing the two together a refreshing perspective is gained, one that the author would exploit for the rest of his career, propelling himself to great fame with *Slaughterhouse-Five* and sustaining his role of public spokesmanship ever after.

In terms of short-story salesmanship this Kennedy piece was surely a last-gasp effort. Already having reduced its fiction, the *Post* would soon go the way of *Collier's*, Vonnegut's other big market, and cease publication. To fill this gap in his income the author turned to something new, writing highly personal essays on current topics for other popular magazines, among them *Esquire*, *McCall's*, and *Life*. In need of money, he took on book reviews, especially tough ones such as covering the new *Random House Dictionary*, personalizing the experience as best he could. This personalization drew the notice of publisher Seymour Lawrence, who figured that anyone who could write so engagingly about a dictionary would surely be interesting as a novelist. In the meantime Vonnegut had taken an instructorship in creative writing at the University of Iowa, earning less than eight thousand dollars per year. A twenty-five-thousand-dollar advance from Lawrence let him quit and work full time on *Slaughterhouse-Five*, a novel whose structure shows the effects of all this personal essay writing. Yet before the novel and before the first essay stands "The Hyannis Port Story," evidence that Vonnegut was developing in this direction well in advance of economic need. If as a *Saturday Evening Post* story it marked the end of one road, its narrative method signposted a grand new avenue toward the ultimate Vonnegut effect.

The current events of this piece are as solid and as necessary as those in any essay. Its readership in 1963 would not just remember Dwight D. Eisenhower's recent presidency but would also know that this two-time winner had never been accepted by the Republican Right, which made a conservative hero of Sen. Robert Taft from Ohio. They would also know more about Walter Reuther than that he was president of the United Auto Workers, for at the time this man was even more important for his involvement with Kennedy politics. Because the Kennedys had such starlike popularity even *Post* readers could be trusted to know such particulars as the fate of Adlai Stevenson, beaten out for the nomination and given an awkward ambassadorship to the United Nations instead. All of this information would be crucial for an essay, but for his special purposes Vonnegut uses them as key elements in his fiction. Why fiction? Because he has noted that by 1963 the Kennedy fame has become as fabulative as any piece of creative writing, with both legendary narratives and literary references—the PT-109 war story, for example, and the constant comparisons of the Kennedy style to life in King Arthur's Camelot. Why not mix in some fiction of his own, particularly from the plain and simple world outside? This was the world, after all, that was real. The Kennedy hysteria was something else indeed.

"The farthest away from home I ever sold a storm window was in Hyannis Port, Massachusetts, practically in the front yard of President Kennedy's summer home" (*WMH*, 133)—these opening words make reference to the famous scene but measure things from a much more humble source, the narrator's own. Everything in the narrative will be valued from this point of view, which spans the simple and the fabulous. In the process *Post* readers are brought into the equation, for the storyteller's perspective is much closer to their own than to that of the Kennedys. The posture is really Vonnegut's own. The North Crawford, New Hampshire, from which the narrator travels is as homely a place as West Barnstable, Massachusetts, seven miles away from Hyannis Port but light years in distance from the Kennedy glamour. On his humbler part of Cape Cod, Kurt Vonnegut has run his short-story business in the same style as this narrator's trade in storm windows and bathtub enclosures, so it is appropriate that the Kennedy business takes less prominence in his life than simply getting the job done. Having a business matter confused with politics has prompted a Kennedy neighbor, Commodore Rumfoord, to order a full set of storms and screens, rewarding the narrator for right-wing sentiments the man does not have—he has already wisely advised his magazine readers that he has yet to decide between Kennedy and Goldwater for the next year's election. But a sale's a sale, and taking it gets him caught up in the Hyannis Port turmoil.

Dealing with this turmoil constitutes the story's action. For all the Kennedy notoriety, this simple tradesman is the person who faces most of it, but in his reaction is a clue for understanding the president. It is summer 1963, and the Cape is awash with gawkers drawn by the Kennedy fame. In a traffic jam, the narrator finds himself stalled next to Ambassador Stevenson. The two get out and walk around a bit. "I took the opportunity to ask him how the United Nations was getting along. He told me they were getting along about as well as could be expected.

That wasn't anything I didn't already know" (*WMH*, 136), readers learn. If this sounds like a good-natured but banal exchange between neighbors, so be it; in the ultimate democracy of a traffic jam the Ambassador's limousine is getting no farther than the narrator's van. For the second time now the standard is affirmed: a job is a job.

When UN ambassador and storm-window salesman meet, it is on the level of the latter. In a similar way Vonnegut's narrator brings the whole Kennedy hullabaloo to his own level, where he can deal with it as an honest workman. He will have to do this to survive the installation, given the determination of these rich folks to drag him into their own stories. But the pattern is clear just from his drive into town. Unsnared from traffic, he finds himself on the commercial strip where everything has become thematic, from the Presidential Motor Inn and the First Family Waffle Shop to the PT-109 Cocktail Lounge and a miniature golf course called the New Frontier. Needing lunch, he stops for a waffle, but he is faced with an equally corny menu with entrees named after Kennedys and their entourage. "A waffle with strawberries and cream was a *Jackie*," he reports, and "a waffle with a scoop of ice cream was a *Caroline*" (*WMH*, 136). And so forth? No, it is even worse, for "they even had a waffle named Arthur Schlesinger, Jr." But here is how he not only makes the best of it but also brings the whole affair into a more reasonable orbit: "I had a thing called a *Teddy*," which mercifully is left undescribed, "and a cup of *Joe*" (137).

The *Post* readership of 1963 could be expected to know how appropriate these menu names were and even that the Harvard historian was a top administration adviser. Such identifications were signs of Kennedy notoriety—everyone at the time knew them, and as a writer Vonnegut was able to manipulate them in narrative play. In a few years literary critics would begin using such terminology, finding that such cultural signs worked together like syntactic forms in a generative grammar—*semiotics* will become fashionable in America about the same time as Kurt Vonnegut's fiction. And popular readers certainly knew what a sign was—perhaps not in deconstructive terms but definitely in the way this story uses the device. For as he approaches his customer's property the narrator notices something to the Rumfoord house besides its towers and parapets. "On a second-floor balcony was a huge portrait of Barry Goldwater" (*WMH*, 137), the conservative Republican likely to face Kennedy in the 1964 election. "It had bicycle reflectors in the pupils of its eyes." Is this not odd for a property right next door to the president's home? Such is the point: "Those eyes stared right through the Kennedy gate. There were floodlights all around, so I could tell it was lit up at night. And the floodlights were rigged with blinkers."

This remarkable line is followed by one in which the narrator pauses to draw a breath. "A man who sells storm windows can never really be sure about what class he belongs to," he tells his readers and reminds himself, "especially if he installs the windows too" (*WMH*, 137). Given the crazy semiology at hand, he judges it best to keep out of the way, getting the job done quickly so that he can return to the calmer world of North Crawford. But his customer, Commodore Rumfoord, insists on chatting with him through the job, in the process drawing the poor man into the rarefied world of presidential politics. In the process there is much fun with the contrasts between the old money style of Rumfoord's Republicanism and the Kennedy ambience—one wonders which is worse, their liberal politics or nouveau status in this yacht club community. But a serious theme emerges. Mocked by a guide on a sight-seeing boat as an unproductive member of the idle rich, the commodore begins doubting himself; after all, with the tradesman quietly observing, he has seen his beloved son fall in love with a Kennedy cousin and plan for marriage into the clan.

Has the old man's life amounted to nothing? Here is where the story begins resembling a classic Vonnegut *Post* composition, as the narrator's quiet example of steady work provides an antidotal example for Rumfoord. He can redeem himself, his wife points out, by simply doing something *useful* (his commodore's title dates from having captained the Hyannis Port yacht club for one year a generation earlier).

The entire atmosphere becomes nicer as the house quiets down and everyone can enjoy the peace that lies beyond blustering politics and the pretensions of old money.

But Vonnegut cannot let his story end just yet. This is, after all, his new style of work, in which historical reality becomes integrated with the structure of fiction—and the narrative's most famous figure, President John Fitzgerald Kennedy, has yet to appear. One guesses that he would like to keep out of it, given his neighbor's adversarial politics and flamboyant habits of self-expression. But in the quiet of the story's nightfall a familiar voice comes across the lawn: that of the president asking the commodore why his Goldwater sign is dark—the son-in-law of Soviet premier Nikita Khrushchev is visiting and would like to see it. Khrushchev? Half a day earlier this name would have sent Commodore Rumfoord into fits, but in his new mood he just complies respectfully. "He turned it on," the narrator reports, and "the whole neighborhood was bathed in flashing lights." Especially in the visitor's presence, and right in the president's face, is this not the greatest insult of all? These have been the reader's worries all along, but now the homely truth is revealed. Would the commodore please leave the sign on? the president requests. "That way I can find my way home" (*WMH*, 145). Far from taking it as a sign of political animosity, President Kennedy has been using the display for what it is literally: a sign marking the way to where he lives. What could be more neighborly?

Turning the great and the famous into the comfortably familiar and ordinary would be Kurt Vonnegut's method for the personal essays he would begin writing about this time. With a method much like that of "The Hyannis Port Story," the narratives of these pieces—and they were heavily anecdotal—would approach some currently challenging event and, by measuring it against the author's experience, reduce it to manageable size. A mass murderer on Cape Cod, the Maharishi Mahesh Yogi, genocidal warfare in Biafra, the extravagances of America's space program—these and other topics generated a steady stream of essays that replaced Vonnegut's lost short-story income. More importantly, they deepened an autobiographical strain that began appearing in his fiction at this same time, typified by the prefaces he wrote for the 1966 hardcover edition of *Mother Night* and the 1968 collection of his short stories, *Welcome to the Monkey House*, that implicated his own life in his otherwise creative writing. At this point the Vonnegut effect seems to be as much "Vonnegut" as "effect," especially when integrated into such a major work as *Slaughterhouse-Five*. For the previously unwriteable material of the author's World War II experience at Dresden this new manner proves critically helpful; if there is indeed nothing to say about a massacre, the author would have to talk about something else—namely himself. This is precisely what he does in a book review sufficiently anecdotal to merit inclusion in his short-story collection. What does one say about a dictionary? Lexicology defies popular comment, even when there is a conflict to its story, as Vonnegut finds in the debate between prescriptive and descriptive linguistics. And so he characterizes the argument as it seems to him: "Prescriptive, as nearly as I could tell, was like an honest cop, and descriptive was like a boozed-up war buddy from Mobile, Ala." (*WMH*, 108). This is the style that would not just get the hungry writer more assignments but would also draw publisher Seymour Lawrence to his work.

There is more to this method than the inclusion of self as a point of reference. The nature of Vonnegut's personality also generates a unique structure, one that would be instrumental in getting the difficult matter of Dresden expressed. Here too the essays are a helpful guide for seeing the methodology take shape. "Science Fiction" is an essay written for the *New York Times Book Review* of 5 September 1965 and collected as the lead piece in *Wampeters, Foma & Granfalloons*. Its message is a serious one: that Vonnegut has never liked being called a science-fiction writer because such categorization relegates his work to triviality. For this, science-fiction buffs are partly to blame, given their insistence that everything they like be qualified as sci-fi. More important than this complaint, however, is the way Vonnegut structures it, taking off from readers who find futuristic tendencies in *1984*, *Invisible*

Man, and even *Madame Bovary*: "They are particularly hot for Kafka. Boomers of science fiction might reply, 'Ha! Orwell and Ellison and Flaubert and Kafka are science-fiction writers, too!' They often say things like that. Some are crazy enough to try to capture Tolstoy. It is as though I were to claim that everybody of note belonged fundamentally to Delta Upsilon, my own lodge, incidentally, whether he knew it or not. Kafka would have been a desperately unhappy D.U." (*WFG*, 4). Franz Kafka in a fraternity rush at Cornell University? The image is preposterous—and funny because of that. But most effective is the way Vonnegut gets such diverse terms together, using the rhetorical fallacy of the excluded middle to suggest that if science fiction is to Franz Kafka as Franz Kafka is to Delta Upsilon fraternity life, then Herr Kafka is suffering as a D.U. brother. Yes, he surely would have. But allowing such an image to discredit the claims of science-fiction buffs involves a deliberate misuse of rhetoric, thus getting Vonnegut's narrative to a point it might not otherwise be able to reach.

This and almost every other essay Kurt Vonnegut would publish in the late 1960s uses his own personality to force a comic issue that seals his otherwise conventionally expressed argument. These instances usually are positioned like a punch line in a joke: after a serious question has been posed, and after the listener has made some serious mental effort to answer it, at which point the joker springs the trap, providing the relief of laughter that comes with the happy dismissal from hard, serious thought. In the science-fiction essay the author has made his point by the time Franz Kafka comes along; the D.U. story is just some icing on the cake, letting readers leave with a happily complicit attitude—they have gotten the joke. Vonnegut's essay on the Maharishi, who was all the rage at the time as a guru to the stars who preached a self-improvement doctrine so easy that anyone could master it in a few quick lessons, forecasts its joke in the title! "Yes, We Have No Nirvanas," a play on the old novelty song "Yes, We Have No Bananas" that joked with linguistic patterns of reason (and of nonreason!). The writer starts off by making fun of himself, mocking his own irritation that his wife and daughter have invested seventy dollars of his money in the Maharishi's program. But the punch line comes when Vonnegut, supposedly a religious skeptic, leaves the *flimflam* of a transcendental meditation session in search of something quite surprising: "I went outside the hotel after that, liking Jesus better than I had ever before liked Him. I wanted to see a crucifix, so I could say to it, 'You know why You're up there? It's Your own fault. You should have practiced Transcendental Meditation, which is easy as pie. You would also have been a better carpenter'" (*WFG*, 39-40). Appraising the U.S. space program, Vonnegut plays the same trick he does for explaining astrophysics in *The Sirens of Titan*, quoting a children's book on the subject but using the device to make fun of himself. "'We are flying through space. Our craft is the earth, which orbits the sun at a speed of 67,000 miles an hour. As it orbits the sun, it spins on its axis. The sun is a star.' If I were drunk, I might cry about that" (78). The message is that to ignore human needs on earth while wasting billions on space is even more irresponsible than alcoholism. "Earth is a pretty blue and pink and white pearl in the pictures NASA sent me," he writes, adding that on his way down to Cape Canaveral he flew over Appalachia. "Life is said to be horrible down there in many places, but it looked like the Garden of Eden to me," he confesses. "I was a rich guy, way up in the sky, munching dry-roasted peanuts and sipping gin" (84).

The space program as a drinker's buzz, the Maharishi teaching transcendental meditation to Christ crucified, Franz Kafka as a terribly unhappy D.U.—these are jokes against logic, using logic's own terms, that help Kurt Vonnegut find ways to articulate the otherwise unspeakable aspects of a massacre. Attempting to write a book about Dresden coincides with the great critical debate over whether a novel could be "about" anything. The 1960s had begun with novelists such as Philip Roth and Stanley Elkin worrying that the personal extravagances and public idiocies of current life were eclipsing even satirists' abilities to make fun of the American scene—the scene was simply doing too good a job of it itself. At the same time theorists debated the referentiality of fictive language, or of any language at all; deconstruction-ists argued that any linguistic system operated not on identities but on differences.

The currency of these debates registers within *Slaughterhouse-Five* when during his trip to New York City, Vonnegut's protagonist, Billy Pilgrim, gets himself involved with a radio show's panel discussion of the presumed death of the novel. For all of his trouble at making a liv-ing with the genre Kurt Vonnegut might well have agreed; but when Billy ignores the critical dialogue taking place and just launches into his explanation of life on Tralfamadore, he is giving hints at how, in the author's hands, the form has been reinvented. Tralfamadore—the dis-tant world several galaxies away from which the flying-saucer pilot Salo had come in *The Sirens of Titan* to determine (through no fault or effort of his own) several thousand years of world history—is for Billy a parallel universe, where the problematic aspects of his earthly exis-tence are all nicely resolved. When considered as a creation of science-fiction writer Kilgore Trout, a significant character in this novel as well as in *God Bless You, Mr. Rosewater* (and in other Vonnegut narratives afterward), Tralfamadore becomes just as much a resolution of human problems as Trout's social philosophies are in the previous work. And so it stands to reason that in the Tralfamadorians' world, which re-solves so much trouble, there would be a solution to the death of the novel.

What are the problems with fiction in Billy Pilgrim's earthly world? Probably the same ones that have frustrated Kurt Vonnegut in his at-tempt to write the book he has wanted to write since coming home from the war. It is the limitation of temporal and spatial causality that makes it so hard to wrestle the matter of Dresden into the conventional format of a novel, one observing the traditional unities of time, space, and action and the consequences that result when insisting a story have a beginning, a middle, and an end. On Tralfamadore novels have none of these. In fact they do not look like novels at all, as Billy observes to the disembodied voice that is his mentor on the distant planet:

Billy couldn't read Tralfamadorian, of course, but he could at least see how the books were laid out—in brief clumps of symbols separated by stars. Billy commented that the clumps might be telegrams. "Exactly," said the voice.

"They *are* telegrams?"

"There are no telegrams on Tralfamadore. But you're right: each clump of symbols is a brief, urgent message—describing a situation, a scene. We Tralfamadorians read them all at once, not one after the other. There isn't any particular relationship between all the messages, except that the author has chosen them carefully, so that, when seen all at one time, they produce an image of life that is beautiful and surprising and deep. There is no beginning, no middle, no end, no suspense, no moral, no causes, no effects. What we love in our books are the depths of many marvelous moments seen all at one time." (*SF*, 76)

It is not surprising that Tralfamadorian fiction answers objections from deconstructionists and death-of-the-novel critics alike. There is nothing here of conventional fiction's attempt at a totalizing effect, a fraudulent impression that life is orderly and that unities of character and idea will, by virtue of systematic study, accrete themselves into some conclusive meaning. It is the false rhetoric of such practices, critics argue, that lets the truly important products of fiction—those "marvelous moments" seen in all their depths—slip away, never to be articulated. It is the reason why, in other words, there is nothing intelligent to say about a massacre, just when a witness of such an event is struggling to say everything: to say everything *all at once* because imposing conditions of time and space steal meaning from the event.

In earthly terms, of course, there are reasons why the depths of many moments cannot be seen all at one time. Even single words must be read, and sentences must be read in sequence for them to make sense. Linearity forces its demands on the reader in just one line of print; expand this demand to the length of a page, let alone that of a chapter or several chapters, and the material confines of a printed novel are obvious. But what if an author could devise a way of writing that did not depend on the reader's steady accumulation of data in any progressive sense, a way that instead let items be noted and then held in abeyance from any need for meaning, until one came to the book's end—and at that point everything suddenly became meaningful all at once? This is the strategy Vonnegut uses for *Slaughterhouse-Five*. Similar to what he is accomplishing at this time in his personal essays, the method involves interposing himself between the troublesome nature of his material and the reader's need to have that material explained. There is, of course, no logical reason for such involvement. That is why the images of Kurt Vonnegut's relation to the Maharishi (seventy dollars of his hard-earned money that his wife and daughter have blown on transcendental meditation sessions) and to the space program (with references to his own inebriation) are so funny. They simply do not belong with the otherwise serious subject matter. But by putting himself in, the author at once upsets the logical structure that keeps things so serious (and so unsolvable) and introduces a comic element that yields the relief of a solution. Vonnegut, and his way of making matters humorous, thus opens a crack in the confinements of convention that have withheld the liberating knowledge he and his readers can now celebrate.

"All this happened, more or less"—so begins this novel that really does not look like one. Fiction traditionally asks its readers to suspend their disbelief, but here they are not required to make such a willing act. There is no reason to, as the story to come is factual with no need to pretend that it is real because it actually is. That is the first rule to be broken. The second is that the author identifies himself with the "I" doing the narration—just as the events of this World War II story truly happened, the person talking about them is the real Kurt Vonnegut. A lifetime of instruction that the narrator of a novel is not the author thus flies out the window. But there is more. Just as in his Maharishi and U.S. space program essays, Vonnegut does something else unconventional: he talks about his writing even as he does it. Thus all the objections that might be raised about the novel in the discussion session

storm. "So it goes," the author notes, the first of one hundred times that he says this in the novel, spoken each time someone or something dies. Afterward, Müller commemorates their meeting with a Christmas card that Vonnegut quotes in full: "I wish you and your family also as to your friend Merry Christmas and a Happy New Year and I hope that we'll meet again in a world of peace and freedom in the taxi cab if the accident will" (*SF*, 2). The grammar is comically if understandably fractured, which Vonnegut appreciates for the way it runs everything together in serial manner, the only qualifier being an open-ended aside, "if the accident will." Müller's syntax is just what the author of this novel needs, for it throws what others try to discern as history's grand plan into undiscriminating chaos so random that the only principle of order is the fact of no order at all.

The text of this postcard is one of several in chapter 1 that argue against conclusive narrative structure. A limerick turns back on itself, mocking any hopes the author has of benefiting from long experience; a song progresses to a last line that is a repeat of its first, generating repetition after repetition with no advancement. Professionals in the entertainment business warn Vonnegut that writing an antiwar book is about as effective as authoring an antiglacier book or as resisting death itself. Yet resisting death is what every living organism does every day right up to the end. And so like life, *Slaughterhouse-Five* goes on, detailing how hard it has been to write *Slaughterhouse-Five*.

The quarter century it took to produce this book had given Vonnegut plenty of stories to tell in this first chapter. There is his experience as a graduate student at the University of Chicago, where any reports about the Dresden atrocity pale in comparison to news of the Holocaust. At the same time in these immediately postwar years the author also works as a pool reporter for Chicago's City News Bureau, where he is confronted with more death and more dispassionate ways of handling it. Readers hear about his attempts to gather facts about the raid and the frustration that it is still considered secret, and they hear also about how detours in his writing career have taken him to the University of

Iowa, where as a teacher in the Writers' Workshop he is no better able to get his war book written. Then publisher Seymour Lawrence comes through with a generous contract, Vonnegut takes off for Dresden with Bernie O'Hare, and the novel gets written—but it is such a short and jumbled and jangled affair that the author is apologetic when he turns it in for publication. Why? Because there is nothing intelligent to say about a massacre, at least nothing that adds up in a coherent, conclusive sense of order. That has been the coherent, conclusive message Vonnegut has broken all the rules of novel writing to clarify in this first, atypical chapter.

Yet looking back on it, chapter 1 of *Slaughterhouse-Five* is as jumbled and as jangled as anything that follows in the book, though readers must have their attention called to all the structural deviations to see it because for two dozen pages they have been carried along quite comfortably. Carried by an orderly chronology? Not at all. From a starting point in 1967, when Vonnegut and O'Hare meet Müller, the action jumps back to 1964, when Vonnegut tracks down his old friend via long distance telephone. Their conversation takes the narrative back to 1945 and from there to the author's various postwar experiences. Readers eventually learn about the publishing contract and the fact that the novel has been written, but only to jump back two years to the 1967 Dresden trip—and not even to Dresden but rather to the night before in a fog-bound Boston airport, where the author puts his sleeplessness to use by reading two more texts, a collection of poetry by Theodore Roethke and a critical study of the French novelist Louis-Ferdinand Céline. If time travel becomes a theme later in the novel and if spatial jumps serve as Vonnegut's way of propelling his narrative across such vast distances, the method for each has been demonstrated right off in chapter 1, a chapter that any reader can follow with ease. Why so? Because the organizing principle has not been spatial unity or temporal progression but rather the inviting presence of Kurt Vonnegut.

Any human being is more interesting than physical models. The story

Vonnegut tells in his "Address to the American Physical Society," collected in *Wampeters, Foma & Granfalloons*, is about how concerns of humanism overpower all the interests of a zoo, even for the author's pet dog. In this first chapter of *Slaughterhouse-Five*, Kurt Vonnegut has managed to make *himself* more interesting to readers than any compensatory satisfactions with unities of time and space would be, particularly because his own problems with these unities have made his life this past quarter century such an intriguing adventure. Having tried without success to map out a chronological story line, he turns to a different line, that of the long distance telephone, to prompt some action—and from there it weaves in and out, backward and forward, until the novel he wants to write gets written. Along the way readers learn many things about the author that will help shape their understanding of his narrative to come. He is a veteran of the war, a POW at Dresden who saw the city destroyed in a firestorm. But that alone cannot generate a novel. For *Slaughterhouse-Five* to be written, much more must take place in this man's life, from studying anthropology and reporting small tragedies in Chicago to working for GE in the 1940s, living on Cape Cod in the 1950s, and teaching in Iowa for two academic years a decade later. All that will figure in the novel Vonnegut writes, as will the texts he and the reader peruse in this same first chapter: Gerhard Müller's Christmas card, the limerick about the young man from Stamboul, Yon Yonson's song from Wisconsin, Mary O'Hare's synopses of war movies, Charles Mackay's account of the Crusades, a history of Dresden, Ted Roethke's poem, and Erika Ostrovsky's book on Céline.

Thus in the first chapter of *Slaughterhouse-Five*, Kurt Vonnegut manipulates the structure that will let his protagonist, Billy Pilgrim, understand what life means. Trying to write his novel the conventional way has brought the author nowhere, just as Billy's attempts to bring the world into focus fail. To be successful each must find a different way of transcending the limits of conventional time and space in order to comprehend what these factors hide. Just sitting at his writer's desk on Cape Cod using the techniques that the tradition of the novel make available to him is not productive for Vonnegut, just as trying to do his duty in the army (as a hapless chaplain's assistant) and follow a worthwhile profession back home (as an optometrist married to the boss's daughter) has not given poor Billy much of a clue to existence. Granted, Billy's salvation will be a deus ex machina of sorts, a raisonneur's explanation of things delivered from outside the action and above the intelligence of those taking part in it. But Vonnegut has used such devices before—each of his previous novels has them in one form or another—and always with a double proof worked into the narrative. In *Slaughterhouse-Five* the correlation to Billy's time travel and adventures on Tralfamadore is Vonnegut's own experience in wishing to write about his Dresden experience, being frustrated in trying to do so the conventional way and finally breaking those conventions in order to get the job done. For this, chapter 1 is the model as the author transcends time and space with the long distance telephone calls to old friends, transatlantic travel to places from the past, and a library of reading that makes the temporal and spatial leaps of phones and jet seem child's play.

The author ends chapter 1 with another breaking of conventions, telling readers not just how the story begins but also how it ends. Why then should anyone spend time with the book's many pages knowing how things will turn out? The answer lies in the description of a Tralfamadorian novel Billy's mentor provides: not for any sense of progressive, accumulating knowledge (less at the beginning, more in the middle, and complete at the end) but rather for the depth of many beautiful moments seen all at the same time. Throughout the novel Vonnegut will arrange his narrative to provide this sensation; Billy's time travel lets the author juxtapose elements from different times and places in a way that creates the sense of a third time, the reader's, existing independently from the march of events and the confinements of space. Doing so solves Vonnegut's problems as a writer and Billy's as a human being. In structuring his novel the author emphasizes how he and his character are not the same person. Three times within the novel as Billy goes about his own business Vonnegut distinguishes himself as a different person in the scene: climbing aboard the POW train, relieving himself in the British prisoners' latrine, and remarking on Dresden's architectural beauty as the prison train rolls in. Note how Billy and Kurt are thus different persons but occupying the same time and place. The two are also sympathetic to each other's aims. Billy's response to Dresden is not to write a novel, but he does type letters to the newspaper and speak his piece on talk radio. His subject is Tralfamadore and its different way of viewing reality, a disposition quite similar to the invention of novelistic form; and of course the Tralfamadorian novel Billy Pilgrim is shown appears to be a structural equivalent to the book Kurt Vonnegut is writing and which his readers now read.

Above all, Vonnegut and his protagonist find themselves conventionally speechless in the face of ultimate but unanswerable questions, unanswerable at least within the limits working to confine them. Here is where the frequently cited novels of Kilgore Trout join the two quests together. One of Trout's works, *Maniacs in the Fourth Dimension*, takes the familiar sci-fi theme of an added level of existence to pose a medical possibility: perhaps supposedly incurable diseases are cases of being sick in a fourth dimension where treatments must wait until physicians from our own 3-D world can cross the barrier and do their work to make the patients better. As a sci-fi device this fourth-dimensionality might bring to mind Vonnegut's similar use of time travel. But in fact it pertains even more closely to an experience Billy has had: getting drunk at a party and being unable to find the steering wheel in his car when he tries to drive home. Vonnegut takes pleasure in letting Billy run through every style of test, from randomly windmilling his arms to starting on the left side and working carefully, inch by inch, all the way over to the right. When no steering wheel is discovered anywhere, the poor drunk assumes that someone has stolen it. Is this true? No, the steering wheel exists but in a different dimension; Billy is sitting in the back seat of his car.

A more important question both Kurt and Billy struggle to answer involves death. Billy faces it when visiting his mother in a nursing home. The woman suffers from pneumonia and can speak only with difficulty, but she struggles with a question. Billy is just as eager to answer it until after several promptings she finally gets it out, leaving her son with nothing to say. Her question is, "How did I get so *old*?" (*SF*, 38). How does someone answer a question like this? It poses the same difficulty that Vonnegut, as author of the novel, must face when trying to write about Dresden: what do you say about a massacre? Billy's example dramatizes this problem, letting readers share the frustration. But being unable to answer it does not discredit the query or lessen the need to respond. That there is no possible answer produces the empty feeling Vonnegut confronts with Dresden, a narrative strategy that manages to articulate an absence without attempting to fill it, as conventional fiction might. Silence is thus empowered with a voice beyond the talents of physical articulation.

In this way author, character, and reader share the same experience. None of it is exotic. Kurt Vonnegut is as simple and straightforward a person as can be: chapter I makes his efforts to write a novel as familiar as the task of anyone trying to get a job done. Billy Pilgrim, as almost every critic studying the novel says, is a virtual Everyman; with nothing heroic about him, his fate is simply to have survived World War II and the Dresden firebombing—and to wonder why. As far as what's required of the reader, no more is demanded than the humanism Kurt Vonnegut has found in his pet dog: a simple interest in people and their doings. Readers of this novel do not need the knowledge of science that Thomas Pynchon demands in *Gravity's Rainbow*, the facility with interweaving plots from world mythology that John Barth expects in *Giles Goat-Boy*, or the mastery of stylistics that William H. Gass requires for an appreciation of any of his works. Kurt Vonnegut is not one of critic Tom LeClair's self-confident practitioners of fictive mastery, a writer of the novel of excess that intentionally smothers the reader in intellectual overkill. Far from it—*Slaughterhouse-Five* reads at times with the simplicity of a primer for early grades' reading. Everything, from the way Billy searches for the steering wheel in the back seat of his car to how American prisoners of war react to their captivity, is explained in simple, follow-the-instructions form. As well these events should be because their author considers them ungraspable in any conventional way and falsified by the earlier attempts of conventional fiction to do the job. Avoiding deep thought and fancy style in favor of speaking plainly is for Vonnegut at least a way to begin.

This simplicity is not a dumbing down or in any sense a pandering to vulgar tastes. Instead there is a common dignity to what author, character, and reader do. Vonnegut portrays himself not as a precious or precocious writer but rather as a familiar, middle-class American with habits no more extreme than any other married men his age (and likely to get in the same type of trouble with his wife when he makes such typical mistakes as staying up too late and drinking too much). In similar manner Billy Pilgrim is a simple, familiar type: no war hero (lest Mary O'Hare object), just as Vonnegut is seen as no great towering success as a writer (something reputationally true at the moment though soon to be remedied by high sales and critical acclaim for the first time in his twenty years in the business). Of equal importance, the novel's readers are not expected to share the mastery needed to fully appreciate something by Pynchon, Barth, or Gass. But neither is their intelligence insulted. Any space opera present comes in the guise of fiction by Kilgore Trout, whom Vonnegut does not have to characterize as a pathetic failure—Trout does so himself. These sci-fi plots can be taken for what they are, oddball but usually insightful musings that are trapped in the humiliating form of science-fiction pulp. No reader is expected to believe in any of Trout's preposterous fictive situations, but everyone sees them played out—not as the novel itself but as part of its larger ongoing action, ways that the readers can be informed of things as if flipping through a magazine or skimming items on a newsstand. Meanwhile, as Vonnegut and Pilgrim do their sincere best to perform their tasks as novelist and soldier respectively, the reader is asked to do no more than can be reasonably expected: to watch the author struggling with the material of Dresden and witness Billy reduced to muteness at his dying mother's bedside, appreciating how no one is immune to such trauma, given how death, whether on a grand scale or so closely personal, is an inevitable fact of life.

As for Billy Pilgrim's situation, it is much more than having witnessed the destruction of Dresden and survived the event. At the beginning of chapter 2 when he is introduced, we learn that he has become "unstuck in time," living in a "constant state of stage fright" because "he never knows what part of his life he is going to have to act in next" (*SF*, 20). Readers of *Cat's Cradle* will recognize Billy's condition as an inversion of the happy state provided by Bokononism, in which the people of San Lorenzo, otherwise so deprived, were given easily performed roles to play in a drama whose purposes they understood. He would seem a perfect candidate for the teachings of the Caribbean holy man, but by this point there are alternatives: not just the Tralfamadorian ethic from *The Sirens of Titan* but Eliot Rosewater and his favorite writer, Kilgore Trout, still in residence from Vonnegut's previous novel. For Eliot, traumatized by World War II, science fiction makes better sense of the world than do either the higher arts or science, and Trout is the perfect source for articulating his problems—and Billy's, too, once the two men meet. To this system of beliefs Billy becomes a convert and acts energetically to proselytize the world. Time, he teaches (in letters to newspaper editors and ramblings to his concerned family), is a spatial, not temporal entity, it exists not from one moment to the next but in a solid continuum, like the full stretch of the Rocky Mountains visible from on high, with the observer able to look at this or that peak at will. Bad moments that cause people so much trouble are just like one particular segment of the mountain range. "When a Tralfamadorian sees a corpse," Billy explains, "all he thinks is that the dead person is in a bad condition in that particular moment, but that the same person is just fine in plenty of other moments" (23). Therefore he can say something about death while other people remain speechless: "I simply shrug and say what the Tralfamadorians say about dead people, which is 'So it goes.'"

The ethic Billy adopts, of course, is one of simple perspective. Ignore the bad moments and concentrate on the good ones—by itself so banal but when voiced as Tralfamadorian physics having the dignity of the anthropological relativism Vonnegut employs in most of his work. As a cultural description these words beg to be taken seriously, just as in their science-fiction trappings they provide entertainment. In Billy's hands these sentiments become a metaphorical extension of his optometrist's work, letting him do "nothing less, now, he thought, than prescribing corrective lenses for Earthling souls. Many of those souls were lost and wretched, Billy believed, because they could not see as well as his little green friends on Tralfamadore" (*SF*, 25). Time, readers may come to believe, is not a physical absolute but just a cultural description. Regarding it as an absolute can be just as self-destructive as regarding religion that way, a point Kilgore Trout makes in one of his many novels quoted as the narrative proceeds. Trout's *The Gospel from Outer Space*, for example, suggests that in Christian liturgy the Crucifixion story is not properly an absolute axiom of belief but rather is something that can be improved on—the notion that gets Kurt Vonnegut in much trouble with religious fundamentalists who have lobbied that *Slaughterhouse-Five* be banned from libraries and school curricula. For Trout the story of Christ's death as presently told is ineffective because all it teaches is that great trouble will result if the person crucified has big-time connections. Far better, the writer suggests, to reshape the tale so that the crucifiers are condemned for having killed a perfectly average guy. If this were the case, Christianity would be more humanely beneficial.

As teachers, however, Billy and Trout are considered laughable (as is Vonnegut at times) and are scorned (as happens with Vonnegut among the fundamentalists). But this is the way they can make their corrections to impaired vision: not as authorities against whom a wary culture's guard will be up but rather as trickster figures who beguile their readers with entertainments that quietly subvert the standards of belief. Vonnegut had introduced this subliminal technique in *Mother Night*, in which absurdities rebound in multiples of three and names of otherwise exotic characters have a kitchen-cupboard familiarity to them, all of which help make an apparently disorganized novel seem to cohere. In *Slaughterhouse-Five* the trick is clinically subliminal as the linkages are thematically unimportant and technically random. There is no reason, for example, why during Billy's childhood visit to Mammoth Cave the otherwise total darkness is pierced by the glowing face of his father's radium watch dial and that then as a POW in Germany the same young man sees Russian prisoners with faces glowing exactly this way. Nor is there a reason why Billy's POW train is painted with the same orange and black stripes that decorate the caterer's tent at a wedding reception. Many other correspondences can be found throughout the novel. Unrelated to plot or theme or character development, and in most cases not even noted consciously by the reader, they nevertheless pull an otherwise diverse narrative together, making discrete events from many different times and places appear unified. When they work best they allow the reader to time travel, the commonality of the stripes or the radium faces letting attention span the many pages in between—a typically Tralfamadorian effect.

Throughout all this Billy remains almost deadeningly simple. With his Ronald Reagan bumper sticker, big suburban house, and lucrative optometry practice (based less on genuine caregiving than on factory orders for safety glasses and overpriced frames), the man is as solidly middle class as can be imagined. He is not a science-fiction nut or an extraterrestrial enthusiast—Rosewater, Trout, and the Tralfamadorians are just new sources of information for him, practicalities that seem to help with his problems relating to life and finding meaning in it. Billy is, after all, an essentially passive person, and so he has been able to absorb all these new ideas without experiencing a violent change. In this same way the novel in which he is the protagonist manages to be thoroughly postmodern while never putting popular readers off, as works by Ronald Sukenick, Steve Katz, or others of the radical experimentalists might do. Like his outer-space creatures who look like plain old plumbers' helpers, Vonnegut's innovative techniques are drawn from common enough sources so that the book he writes seems more a part of everyday life than a revolt against it.

Revolt against convention, especially in terms of commonly over-worked themes, is left to Kilgore Trout, a character easily distanced from Billy's guy-next-door familiarity. As Billy's time travels bring readers to a new awareness by forcing juxtapositions of incidents that would otherwise remain safely insulated from each other by conventions of time and space, Trout's somewhat madcap fictive materials expand Vonnegut's narrative from within. Citations of his many books, undertaken in the manner of Jorge Luis Borges drawing on an imaginary library, make *Slaughterhouse-Five* read like something much greater than the sum of its parts. The great Argentine fictionist had fashioned a rich strategy of imagining all of the books he would like to have written and then quoting them as if they existed. This is precisely what Vonnegut does with Kilgore Trout, with the added benefit of putting in some stinkers he would never dream of writing yet that can be cited for the fun of it. Vonnegut's own sentences and paragraphs are disarmingly simple, but when he is quoting Trout an entire universe of references is provided for readers.

Trout's flesh-and-blood appearance in the novel—after all the flashbacks and flashforwards in Billy's life over the five decades of action scrambled together in its time-travel plot—is itself a matter of fictive structure. It comes in chapter 8, which begins with another character from Vonnegut's earlier fiction: Howard W. Campbell, Jr., who visits Billy's POW camp to recruit American volunteers for the war against Russia. That night Dresden is firebombed and Billy (time traveling) dreams of Kilgore Trout. The next scenes, which in a conventional novel would happen in the immediate aftermath of the bombing, take place in 1964, when Billy talks with Trout in Ilium, New York. Thus the sci-fi writer appears within the context of what would be a conventional novel's climax: the bombing of Dresden. His behavior here accomplishes in structural terms what a realistic account of the bombing (not a part of *Slaughterhouse-Five*) would otherwise provide: a portrayal of conclusive theme. How does he behave? For the first time in his life he acts like a novelist, having learned something he had never before known or even imagined: that his work, written for next to nothing and published as pulp, has a reader.

At the anniversary party to which Billy invites him Trout is so giddy with success that he parodies what fictionists do. The guests are gullible, and so he pours it on, suggesting that all the things that happen in novels are omnisciently true, just as at this very minute "God is listening, too. And on Judgment Day he's going to tell you all the things you said and did" (*SF*, 147), followed by severe punishments for bad actions. This, of course, is a preposterous view of fiction, but it in fact exaggerates the type of readings given so naively to traditional novels whose conventions are never questioned. Trout's listener is terrified by this news and becomes "petrified" (148), the way Vonnegut has described himself at the end of chapter 1, becoming (like Lot's wife) a pillar of salt for looking back at the destruction of Dresden. It also looks forward to Billy's posture on the next page when, after listening to a barbershop quartet singing at his party, he nearly collapses, having been turned as rigid as a ghost. What has happened is that in Trout's presence Billy has finally been put in touch with the heart of his Dresden experience, the truth of which has been eluding him for this whole novel that Kurt Vonnegut, for similar reasons, has been having a hard time writing. As the quartet pulls together for some close harmony about "that old gang of mine," Billy suddenly sees four of his guards at Dresden grouped tightly with their mouths similarly open—except in their case it is with the speechless horror of having witnessed the apocalyptic destruction of all they have ever known. It is Trout's presence that for the first time articulates this connection and confirms the meaning of connections between disparate points in time. As with his parody of fiction's truthful nature, Trout's description of looking through a time window to see the past comes across as hokey space opera, something only true gulls would believe in. Yet it is just the space opera and not the notion of time that Billy denies, for the same reason he can deny that he has seen a ghost. What *has* happened to him is that by virtue of this specific temporal relation he is able to tell a story, the same talent Vonnegut's efforts with the structure of *Slaughterhouse-Five* have enabled him to do. In this context Trout's own works are given new dignity. He is a fitting guest at the occasion, which now celebrates not just Billy's eighteen years of marriage but also his newfound ability to put together the truth of his life in 1964 and 1945, the two events combining to produce a meaningfulness that it is storytelling's task to accomplish.

Through it all Billy remains thoroughly normal. The device of time travel (which by this point appears nothing more exotic than an ability to adjust one's self to the multidimensionality of life) lets him live on Tralfamadore (with a kidnapped pornographic movie starlet, no less) while still fulfilling his duties as husband, father, civic figure, and optometrist on Earth. In becoming a storyteller of his own life Billy is no more removed from normality than is Kurt Vonnegut, who takes center stage once more in chapter 10 to conclude the novel. Here readers learn that *Slaughterhouse-Five* is being completed at a point in time they have shared: when newscasts announce the assassination of Sen. Robert Kennedy, one of those occurrences that people customarily can associate with where they were when they heard the news. His attempt has paralleled Billy's, and the words for it have come in a similar way. The Dresden book, like Billy's Dresden experience, is articulated by an intimately expressed characterization of silence, the testimony of four prison guards "who, in their astonishment and grief, resembled a barbershop quartet" (*SF*, 154). Like Vonnegut at the start of this book and like Billy Pilgrim through all of it to this point, they are speechless in the face of such enormity. But now the temporal and spatial juxtapositions of the human mind provide the words. Yes, they are sung decades later in a completely different context. But Billy's imagination helps the language of 1964 articulate the meaning of 1945. Imagination is what novels are made of, Vonnegut knows. But he also recognizes the more important fact that imagination is one of the talents that distinguish human beings from other living creatures.

There are good structures that the human imagination can devise and also structures that work less effectively. Mary O'Hare has warned Vonnegut against the ones that falsify, and in the course of his narrative he finds characters facing the war's events who do the same thing. On the one hand, Paul Lazzaro, for example, is an American POW who interprets everything that happens as a call for personal revenge, to the point that his being is consumed by it. On the other hand, British POWs have turned their camp into a fairyland that denies the war's reality—which is fine for them personally but a great cruelty for their neighboring Russian prisoners, whose starvation they ignore. Yet the imagination shows promise for making things better, even wars. At one point long after the events of Dresden, Billy watches a World War II movie on television, his technical abilities with time and space letting it run backward. It is a simple enough procedure, one that the most basic home movie projector of the era could provide; yet it is replete with such wondrous effects that Vonnegut devotes nearly a page to the happy result:

American planes, full of holes and wounded men and corpses, took off backwards from an airfield in England. Over France, a few German fighter planes flew at them backwards, sucked bullets and shell fragments from some of the planes and crewmen. They did the same for wrecked American bombers on the ground, and those planes flew up backwards to join the formation.

The formation flew backwards over a German city that was in flames. The bombers opened their bomb bay doors, exerted a miraculous magnetism which shrunk the fires, gathered them into cylindrical steel containers, and lifted the containers into the bellies of the planes. The Germans below had miraculous devices of their own, which were long steel tubes. They used them to suck more fragments from the crewmen and planes. But there were still a few wounded Americans, though, and some of the bombers were in bad repair. Over France, though, German fighters came up again, made everything and everybody as good as new.

When the bombers got back to their bases, the steel cylinders were taken from the racks and shipped back to the United States of America, where factories were operating night and day, dismantling the cylinders, separating the dangerous contents into minerals. Touchingly, it was mainly women who did this work. The minerals were then shipped to specialists in remote areas. It was their business to put them into the ground, to hide them cleverly, so they would never hurt anybody ever again. (*SF*, 63)

Impractical for real life? Certainly, but this is not Vonnegut's point. The idea of bombing raids going the other way, the usual way, is something that had to be devised at some point. The challenge is motivating the human imagination to work in a more beneficial manner. In *Slaughterhouse-Five* this is what the author's method does. As an effect it is as improvisatory as running a war movie backward, yet as practical as the act of the mechanical handyman who first tried reversing the processes of furnaces and air conditioners to produce the heat pump. There are always temptations to be meanly selfish (Paul Lazzaro) and blithely unaware (the British POWs), and there are also easier ways to write war novels (the examples Mary O'Hare abhors). *Slaughterhouse-Five* does not ignore these possibilities. Instead it engages them as models to demonstrate their ineffectiveness. Their failures contrast with Billy's success in life and Vonnegut's achievement in portraying it, a way of articulating the unspeakable by letting silence have its proper voice.

Works Cited

Vonnegut, Kurt. *Slaughterhouse-Five, or The Children's Crusade*. New York: Delacorte Press/Seymour Lawrence, 1969. Abbreviated as *SF*.

_____. *Wampeters, Foma & Granfalloons*. New York: Delacorte Press/ Seymour Lawrence, 1969. Abbreviated as *WFG*.

_____. *Welcome to the Monkey House*. New York: Delacorte Press/ Seymour Lawrence, 1969. Abbreviated as *WMH*.

RESOURCES

1922	Kurt Vonnegut is born on November 11 in Indianapolis, Indiana, to Kurt and Edith Vonnegut. He is the youngest of three children.
1929	The Great Depression hits, and Edith Vonnegut's family fortune is lost. Vonnegut's father, an architect, finds himself out of work.
1936-1940	Vonnegut attends Shortridge High School and eventually becomes editor of the school paper, the *Shortridge Daily Echo*.
1940-1942	Vonnegut attends Cornell University as a biochemistry major. He writes for the school newspaper, the *Cornell Sun*, and eventually becomes the managing editor.
1943	On the brink of flunking out of Cornell, Vonnegut enlists in the U.S. Army in January. He attends the Carnegie Institute and the University of Tennessee for training.
1944	Edith commits suicide on Mother's Day, while Vonnegut is home on leave. Shortly after, the Army deploys Vonnegut to Europe as a scout with the 106th Infantry Division. On December 19, he is captured during the Battle of the Bulge; he is sent to Dresden as a prisoner of war.
1945	Vonnegut witnesses the firebombing of Dresden on February 13. He is repatriated on May 22 and marries Jane Marie Cox, a childhood friend, on September 1. The couple moves to Chicago in December, and Vonnegut begins studying for a master's degree in anthropology at the University of Chicago and working as a police reporter for the Chicago City News Bureau.
1947	When the University of Chicago rejects his master's thesis, Vonnegut moves with Jane to Schenectady, New York, where his brother, Bernard, is working as a physicist for General Electric (GE). Vonnegut works as a writer for the public relations department of the GE Research Laboratory. His son Mark is born.
1950	Vonnegut's first published short story, "Report on the Barnhouse Effect," appears in *Collier's* in February.

1951	With a good income from short-story writing, Vonnegut quits GE and moves to West Barnstable, Massachusetts. His daughter Edith is born.
1952	Vonnegut's first novel, *Player Piano*, is published.
1955	Vonnegut's daughter Nanette is born.
1957	Kurt Vonnegut, Sr., dies on October 1.
1958	Vonnegut's brother-in-law, James Carmalt Adams, is killed in a commuter train accident on September 15, and Vonnegut's sister, Alice, dies from cancer soon after. Vonnegut adopts three of Alice's four children.
1959	*The Sirens of Titan* is published.
1961	*Canary in a Cat House*, a short-story collection, and *Mother Night*, a novel, are published.
1963	*Cat's Cradle* is published.
1965	*God Bless You, Mr. Rosewater: Or, Pearls Before Swine* is published to good reviews. Vonnegut begins a two-year teaching residency at the Writers' Workshop at the University of Iowa. He begins publishing essays in the *New York Times Book Review*, *Esquire*, and *Harper's*.
1967	Vonnegut is awarded a Guggenheim Fellowship, which enables him to travel to Dresden to conduct research for *Slaughterhouse-Five*.
1968	*Welcome to the Monkey House*, a short-story collection, is published.
1969	*Slaughterhouse-Five: Or, The Children's Crusade, a Duty-Dance with Death* is published and climbs to the top of the *New York Times* best-seller list.
1970	*Happy Birthday, Wanda June* is produced. Vonnegut travels to Biafra and receives a National Institute of Arts and Letters grant. He is appointed to teach creative writing at Harvard University.

1971	The University of Chicago awards Vonnegut a master's degree in anthropology for *Cat's Cradle*. Vonnegut separates from Jane and moves to New York.
1972	*Between Time and Timbuktu: Or, Prometheus-5, a Space Fantasy* is published. A film adaptation of *Slaughterhouse-Five* is released by Universal Pictures. Vonnegut becomes a member of the National Institute of Arts and Letters. His son Mark suffers a mental breakdown and enters a Vancouver psychiatric hospital.
1973	*Breakfast of Champions: Or, Goodbye Blue Monday* is published. Vonnegut is appointed Distinguished Professor of English Prose at City University of New York (CUNY).
1974	*Wampeters, Foma, and Granfalloons (Opinions)*, an essay collection, is published. Vonnegut resigns his position at CUNY.
1975	Vonnegut is elected vice president of the National Institute of Arts and Letters.
1976	*Slapstick: Or, Lonesome No More!* is published and receives poor reviews.
1979	*Jailbird* is published. Vonnegut divorces Jane and marries photographer Jill Krementz, with whom he had been living for several years.
1980	*Sun Moon Star*, a children's book, is published.
1981	*Palm Sunday: An Autobiographical Collage*, an essay collection, is published.
1982	*Deadeye Dick* is published. Vonnegut adopts a daughter, Lily.
1985	*Galápagos* is published.
1987	*Bluebeard* is published.
1990	*Hocus Pocus* is published.
1991	*Fates Worse than Death: An Autobiographical Collage of the 1980s* is published.

1997	*Timequake* is published. Vonnegut's brother Bernard dies.
1999	*God Bless You, Dr. Kevorkian*; *Like Shaking Hands with God: A Conversation About Writing*; and *Bagombo Snuff Box: Uncollected Short Fiction* are published.
2000	Vonnegut's New York townhouse catches fire in January, and the author is hospitalized for treatment of smoke inhalation.
2005	*A Man Without a Country* is published.
2007	Vonnegut dies in New York on April 11 after suffering brain damage from a fall.
2008	*Armageddon in Retrospect: And Other New and Unpublished Writings on War and Peace* is published.

Long Fiction

Player Piano, 1952
The Sirens of Titan, 1959
Mother Night, 1961
Cat's Cradle, 1963
God Bless You, Mr. Rosewater: Or, Pearls Before Swine, 1965
Slaughterhouse-Five: Or, The Children's Crusade, a Duty-Dance with Death, 1969
Breakfast of Champions: Or, Goodbye Blue Monday, 1973
Slapstick: Or, Lonesome No More!, 1976
Jailbird, 1979
Deadeye Dick, 1982
Galápagos, 1985
Bluebeard, 1987
Hocus Pocus, 1990
Timequake, 1997
God Bless You, Dr. Kevorkian, 1999 (novella)

Short Fiction

Canary in a Cat House, 1961
Welcome to the Monkey House, 1968
Bagombo Snuff Box: Uncollected Short Fiction, 1999
Look at the Birdie: Unpublished Short Fiction, 2009

Nonfiction

Wampeters, Foma, and Granfalloons (Opinions), 1974
Palm Sunday: An Autobiographical Collage, 1981
Conversations with Kurt Vonnegut, 1988
Fates Worse than Death: An Autobiographical Collage of the 1980s, 1991
Like Shaking Hands with God: A Conversation About Writing, 1999 (with Lee Stringer)
A Man Without a Country, 2005
Armageddon in Retrospect: And Other New and Unpublished Writings on War and Peace, 2008

Drama

Penelope, pr. 1960 (revised pr., pb. 1970 as *Happy Birthday, Wanda June*)

Teleplay

Between Time and Timbuktu: Or, Prometheus-5, a Space Fantasy, 1972

Children's Literature

Sun Moon Star, 1980 (with Ivan Chermayeff)

Allen, William Rodney. *Understanding Kurt Vonnegut*. Columbia: University of South Carolina Press, 1991.

_____, ed. *Conversations with Kurt Vonnegut*. Jackson: University Press of Mississippi, 1988.

Boon, Kevin A. *Chaos Theory and the Interpretation of Literary Texts: The Case of Kurt Vonnegut*. Lewiston, NY: Edwin Mellen Press, 1997.

_____, ed. *At Millennium's End: New Essays on the Work of Kurt Vonnegut*. Albany: State University of New York Press, 2001.

Broer, Lawrence R. *Sanity Plea: Schizophrenia in the Novels of Kurt Vonnegut*. Rev. ed. Tuscaloosa: University of Alabama Press, 1994.

Coleman, Martin. "The Meaninglessness of Coming Unstuck in Time." *Transactions of the Charles S. Pierce Society* 44.4 (2008): 681-98.

Crichton, Michael. "Sci-Fi and Vonnegut." *The New Republic* 26 Apr. 1969: 33-35.

Davis, Todd F. *Kurt Vonnegut's Crusade: Or, How a Postmodern Harlequin Preached a New Kind of Humanism*. Albany: State University of New York Press, 2006.

Giannone, Richard. *Vonnegut: A Preface to His Novels*. Port Washington, NY: Kennikat Press, 1977.

Klinkowitz, Jerome. *Kurt Vonnegut*. London: Methuen, 1982.

_____. *Kurt Vonnegut's America*. Columbia: University of South Carolina Press, 2009.

_____. *Literary Disruptions: The Making of a Post-contemporary American Fiction*. Urbana: University of Illinois Press, 1975.

_____. *"Slaughterhouse-Five": Reforming the Novel and the World*. Boston: Twayne, 1990.

_____. *The Vonnegut Effect*. Columbia: University of South Carolina Press, 2004.

_____. *Vonnegut in Fact: The Public Spokesmanship of Personal Fiction*. Columbia: University of South Carolina Press, 1998.

Klinkowitz, Jerome, and Donald L. Lawler, eds. *Vonnegut in America: An Introduction to the Life and Work of Kurt Vonnegut*. New York: Delacorte Press, 1977.

Klinkowitz, Jerome, and John Somer, eds. *The Vonnegut Statement*. New York: Delacorte Press, 1973.

Leeds, Marc. *The Vonnegut Encyclopedia: An Authorized Compendium*. Westport, CT: Greenwood Press, 1995.

Lundquist, James. *Kurt Vonnegut*. New York: Frederick Ungar, 1977.

Merrill, Robert, ed. *Critical Essays on Kurt Vonnegut*. Boston: G. K. Hall, 1990.

Merrill, Robert, and Peter A. Scholl. "Vonnegut's *Slaughterhouse-Five*: The Requirements of Chaos." *Studies in American Fiction* 6 (1978): 65-76.

Morse, Donald E. *The Novels of Kurt Vonnegut: Imagining Being an American*. Westport, CT: Praeger, 2003.

Mustazza, Leonard. *Forever Pursuing Genesis: The Myth of Eden in the Novels of Kurt Vonnegut*. Lewisburg, PA: Bucknell University Press, 1990.

_____, ed. *The Critical Response to Kurt Vonnegut*. Westport, CT: Greenwood Press, 1994.

Pieratt, Asa B., Jr., Julie Huffman-Klinkowitz, and Jerome Klinkowitz. *Kurt Vonnegut: A Comprehensive Bibliography*. Hamden, CT: Archon Books, 1987.

Rackstraw, Loree. *Love as Always, Kurt: Vonnegut as I Knew Him*. Cambridge, MA: Da Capo Press, 2009.

Reed, Peter J. *Kurt Vonnegut, Jr*. New York: Warner Books, 1972.

_____. *The Short Fiction of Kurt Vonnegut*. Westport, CT: Greenwood Press, 1997.

Reed, Peter J., and Marc Leeds, eds. *The Vonnegut Chronicles: Interviews and Essays*. Westport, CT: Greenwood Press, 1996.

Schatt, Stanley. *Kurt Vonnegut, Jr*. Boston: Twayne, 1976.

Simmons, David. *The Anti-Hero in the American Novel: From Joseph Heller to Kurt Vonnegut*. New York: Palgrave, 2008.

_____, ed. *New Critical Essays on Kurt Vonnegut*. New York: Palgrave, 2009.

CRITICAL INSIGHTS

About the Editor

Leonard Mustazza is Distinguished Professor of English and American Studies at Penn State Abington in suburban Philadelphia. He is the author of more than forty scholarly articles and nine books on a diverse range of literary and cultural topics. Among his publications are studies of English poet John Milton, singers Frank Sinatra and Johnny Hartman, dramatists Sam Shepard and Peter Shaffer, cultural critic Tom Wolfe, and popular writers Stephen King and Michael Crichton. His most recent book is a two-volume reference work on film adaptations of fictional stories titled *The Literary Filmography: 6,200 Adaptations of Books, Short Stories, and Other Nondramatic Works* (2006). He has written extensively on the fiction of Kurt Vonnegut. He is the author of *Forever Pursuing Genesis: The Myth of Eden in the Novels of Kurt Vonnegut* (1990) and the editor of *The Critical Response to Kurt Vonnegut* (1994). In addition, his biographical essay on Vonnegut, written after the author's death in 2007, appears in *The Scribner Encyclopedia of American Lives*, volume 8.

About *The Paris Review*

The Paris Review is America's preeminent literary quarterly, dedicated to discovering and publishing the best new voices in fiction, nonfiction, and poetry. The magazine was founded in Paris in 1953 by the young American writers Peter Matthiessen and Doc Humes, and edited there and in New York for its first fifty years by George Plimpton. Over the decades, the *Review* has introduced readers to the earliest writings of Jack Kerouac, Philip Roth, T. C. Boyle, V. S. Naipaul, Ha Jin, Ann Patchett, Jay McInerney, Mona Simpson, and Edward P. Jones, and published numerous now classic works, including Roth's *Goodbye, Columbus*, Donald Barthelme's *Alice*, Jim Carroll's *Basketball Diaries*, and selections from Samuel Beckett's *Molloy* (his first publication in English). The first chapter of Jeffrey Eugenides's *The Virgin Suicides* appeared in the *Review*'s pages, as well as stories by Rick Moody, David Foster Wallace, Denis Johnson, Jim Crace, Lorrie Moore, and Jeanette Winterson.

The Paris Review's renowned Writers at Work series of interviews, whose early installments include legendary conversations with E. M. Forster, William Faulkner, and Ernest Hemingway, is one of the landmarks of world literature. The interviews received a George Polk Award and were nominated for a Pulitzer Prize. Among the more than three hundred interviewees are Robert Frost, Marianne Moore, W. H. Auden, Elizabeth Bishop, Susan Sontag, and Toni Morrison. Recent issues feature conversations with Salman Rushdie, Joan Didion, Norman Mailer, Kazuo Ishiguro, Marilynne Robinson, Umberto Eco, Annie Proulx, and Gay Talese. In November 2009, Picador published the final volume of a four-volume series of anthologies of *Paris Review* interviews. *The New York Times* called the Writers at Work series "the most remarkable and extensive interviewing project we possess."

The Paris Review is edited by Philip Gourevitch, who was named to the post in 2005, following the death of George Plimpton two years earlier. A new editorial team has published fiction by André Aciman, Colum McCann, Damon Galgut, Mohsin Hamid, Uzodinma Iweala, Gish Jen, Stephen King, James Lasdun, Padgett Powell, Richard Price, and Sam Shepard. Poetry editors Charles Simic, Meghan O'Rourke, and Dan Chiasson have selected works by John Ashbery, Kay Ryan, Billy Collins, Tomaž Šalamun, Mary Jo Bang, Sharon Olds, Charles Wright, and Mary Karr. Writing published in the magazine has been anthologized in *Best American Short Stories* (2006, 2007, and 2008), *Best American Poetry, Best Creative Non-Fiction*, the Pushcart Prize anthology, and *O. Henry Prize Stories*.

The magazine presents two annual awards. The Hadada Award for lifelong contribution to literature has recently been given to Joan Didion, Norman Mailer, Peter Matthiessen, and, in 2009, John Ashbery. The Plimpton Prize for Fiction, awarded to a debut or emerging writer brought to national attention in the pages of *The Paris Review*, was presented in 2007 to Benjamin Percy, to Jesse Ball in 2008, and to Alistair Morgan in 2009.

The Paris Review was a finalist for the 2008 and 2009 National Magazine Awards in fiction, and it won the 2007 National Magazine Award in photojournalism. The *Los Angeles Times* recently called *The Paris Review* "an American treasure with true international reach."

Since 1999 *The Paris Review* has been published by The Paris Review Foundation, Inc., a not-for-profit 501(c)(3) organization.

The Paris Review is available in digital form to libraries worldwide in selected academic databases exclusively from EBSCO Publishing. Libraries can contact EBSCO at 1-800-653-2726 for details. For more information on *The Paris Review* or to subscribe, please visit: www.theparisreview.org.

Contributors

Leonard Mustazza is Distinguished Professor of English and American Studies at Penn State Abington. The author of numerous scholarly articles and nine books, he has written extensively on the fiction of Kurt Vonnegut. He is the author of *Forever Pursuing Genesis: The Myth of Eden in the Novels of Kurt Vonnegut* (1990) and editor of *The Critical Response to Kurt Vonnegut* (1994).

Peter J. Reed is Professor Emeritus of English Language and Literature at the University of Minnesota. He is the author of *The Short Fiction of Kurt Vonnegut* (1997) and coeditor of *The Vonnegut Chronicles: Interviews and Essays* (1996) and *Kurt Vonnegut: Images and Representations* (2000).

Sarah Fay is an advisory editor of *The Paris Review.* Her writing has appeared in the *New York Times Book Review, Bookforum,* and *The American Scholar.*

Jerome Klinkowitz is Professor of English at the University of Northern Iowa and is the author of several books on Kurt Vonnegut, including *Vonnegut in Fact: The Public Spokesmanship of Personal Fiction* (1998), *The Vonnegut Effect* (2004), and *Kurt Vonnegut's America* (2009).

Kevin Alexander Boon is the author and editor of eleven books, including three books on Kurt Vonnegut. He is Associate Professor at Penn State University, where he teaches writing, film, and literature and coordinates the English program for the Mont Alto campus. His Web site is Kevin.Boon.us.

David Simmons is a lecturer in American literature, film, and television studies at the University of Northampton. He has published extensively in the areas of American literature and media, including a monograph titled *The Anti-Hero in the American Novel: From Joseph Heller to Kurt Vonnegut* (2008) and the edited collection *New Critical Essays on Kurt Vonnegut* (2009). He is also coeditor (with Nicola Allen) of *Reassessing the Contemporary Canon: From Joseph Conrad to Zadie Smith* (2010), a collection of essays concerned with reevaluating the contemporary novel.

Christina Jarvis is Associate Professor and Director of American Studies at the State University of New York at Fredonia. Her lectures focus on American literature, feminist theory, and gender studies. She is currently working on a book that will investigate post-1970 cultural representations of fatherhood in America. She is the author of *The Male Body at War: American Masculinity During World War II* (2004).

Donald J. Greiner is retired Distinguished Professor of English and Dean of Undergraduate Studies at the University of South Carolina, where he worked for nearly forty years. He is editor of *Dictionary of Literary Biography: American Poets Since World War II* (1980) and *The Notebook of Stephen Crane* (1969). His authored books include *Comic Terror: The Novels of John Hawkes* (1978) and *Robert Frost: The Poet and His Critics* (1976).

Joyce Nelson was Director of English Education at Brigham Young University, where she taught for seventeen years before retiring in 2007. She was the recipient of the 2007 Benjamin Cluff Jr. Award as Distinguished Teacher Educator.

Arnold Edelstein was Professor of English at the University of Hawaii. He is the author of "*Slaughterhouse-Five*: Time Out of Joint," which was featured in the popular literary magazine *College Literature*.

Wayne D. McGinnis is Professor of English at Henderson State University. He has written critical essays on such works as *The Canterbury Tales* and *Slaughterhouse-Five*.

Dolores K. Gros Louis was Associate Professor of English in the Honors Division of Indiana University. Her work has appeared in *Biblical Images in Literature* (1975).

Maurice J. O'Sullivan, Jr., is Kenneth Curry Professor of English at Rollins College. He is codirector of the Florida Center for Shakespeare Studies and codirector of the Drey Summer Shakespeare Institute. His literary contributions are extensive; he is editor of *Shakespeare's Other Lives* (1997) and *Elizabeth Smith's Book of Job* (1996) and coeditor of *Orange Pulp* (2000) and *Florida in Poetry* (1995). His essays have appeared in *Philological Quarterly, Shakespeare Quarterly*, and *Dutch Quarterly Review*. He served as President of the College English Association in 2006-2007.

James Lundquist was Professor of English at St. Cloud College. He has edited several critical works on such great American authors as J. D. Salinger, Sinclair Lewis, Theodore Dreiser, Jack London, and Kurt Vonnegut.

C. Barry Chabot is Associate Professor of Literature at the American University. His literary criticism has been published in such journals as *Critique*, the *Georgia Review*, and *Diacritics*.

T. J. Matheson is Professor of English at the University of Saskatchewan. His research interests include American literature and modern satire. He is the author of numerous articles that concentrate on Canadian, American, and British writers.

William Rodney Allen is Professor of English at the Louisiana School for Math, Science, and the Arts. As a close friend of Kurt Vonnegut, he has published several works that center on the famous author and his writings, including *Understanding Kurt Vonnegut* (1991) and *Conversations with Kurt Vonnegut* (1988).

Donald E. Morse is Visiting Professor of American, Irish, and English Literature at the University of Debrecen in Hungary. He is also Professor Emeritus of English and Rhetoric at Oakland University. In addition to his numerous contributions to literary magazines and publications, he is the author of *The Celebration of the Fantastic* (1992), *More Real than Reality: The Fantastic in Irish Literature and the Arts* (1991), and *The Fantastic in World Literature and the Arts* (1987).

Hans van Stralen is Professor of Literature at Utrecht University in the Netherlands. Focusing primarily on modernist, existentialist, and historical literature, he has contributed critical essays to literary magazines such as *Vestdijk Chronicle*, *Meridians*, and *Vooys*. He is currently working on an essay detailing existentialism and a book on hermeneutics.

Susanne Vees-Gulani is Assistant Professor of Modern Languages and Literatures at Case Western Reserve University. Her research interests include German literature and culture, World War II, postwar reconstruction, and literature in relation to medicine and science. She is the author of *Trauma and Guilt: Literature of Wartime Bombing in Germany* (2003), which examines post-World War II literature.

Acknowledgments

"Kurt Vonnegut" by Peter J. Reed. From *Magill's Survey of American Literature*. Copyright © 2007 by Salem Press, Inc. Reprinted with permission of Salem Press.

"The *Paris Review* Perspective" by Sarah Fay. Copyright © 2011 by Sarah Fay. Special appreciation goes to Christopher Cox, Nathaniel Rich, and David Wallace-Wells, editors at *The Paris Review*.

"The Vietnamization of World War II in *Slaughterhouse-Five* and *Gravity's Rainbow*" by Christina Jarvis. From *War, Literature & the Arts* 15, nos. 1-2 (2003): 95-117. Copyright © 2003 by the U.S. Air Force Academy. Reprinted with permission of the U.S. Air Force Academy.

"*Slaughterhouse-Five* and the Fiction of Atrocity" by Donald J. Greiner. From *Critique* 14, no. 3 (1973): 38-51. Copyright © 1973 by Heldref Publications. Reprinted with permission of Heldref Publications.

"*Slaughterhouse-Five*: Novel and Film" by Joyce Nelson. From *Literature/Film Quarterly* 1, no. 2 (April 1973): 149-153. Copyright © 1973 by Salisbury University. Reprinted with permission of Salisbury University.

"*Slaughterhouse-Five*: Time Out of Joint" by Arnold Edelstein. From *College Literature* 1, no. 2 (Spring 1974): 128-139. Copyright © 1974 by *College Literature*. Reprinted with permission of *College Literature*.

"The Arbitrary Cycle of *Slaughterhouse-Five*: A Relation of Form to Theme" by Wayne D. McGinnis. From *Critique* 17, no. 1 (1975): 55-68. Copyright © 1975 by Heldref Publications. Reprinted with permission of Heldref Publications.

"The Ironic Christ Figure in *Slaughterhouse-Five*" by Dolores K. Gros Louis. From *Biblical Images in Literature*, edited by Roland Bartel, with James S. Ackerman and Thayer S. Warshaw (1975), pp. 161-175. Copyright © 1975 by Abingdon Press. Reprinted with permission of Abingdon Press and Donald C. Farber. Quotations from *Slaughterhouse-Five* taken from *Slaughterhouse-Five* by Kurt Vonnegut, Jr. Copyright © 1968, 1969 by Kurt Vonnegut, Jr. Used by permission of Dell Publishing, a division of Random House, Inc.

"*Slaughterhouse-Five*: Kurt Vonnegut's Anti-Memoirs" by Maurice J. O'Sullivan, Jr. From *Essays in Literature* 3, no. 2 (Fall 1976): 244-250. Copyright © 1976 by Western Illinois University. Reprinted with permission of Western Illinois University.

"The 'New Reality' of *Slaughterhouse-Five*" by James Lundquist. From *Kurt Vonnegut* (1977), pp. 69-84, 108-109. Copyright © 1977 by Continuum International Publishing Group, Inc. Reprinted with permission of Continuum International Publishing Group, Inc.

"*Slaughterhouse-Five* and the Comforts of Indifference" by C. Barry Chabot. From *Essays in Literature* 8, no. 1 (Spring 1981): 45-51. Copyright © 1981 by Western Illinois University. Reprinted with permission of Western Illinois University.

"'This Lousy Little Book': The Genesis and Development of *Slaughterhouse-Five* as Revealed in Chapter One" by T. J. Matheson. From *Studies in the Novel* 16, no. 2 (1984): 228-240. Copyright © 1984 by the University of North Texas. Reprinted with permission of the University of North Texas.

"Adam and Eve in the Golden Depths: Edenic Madness in *Slaughterhouse-Five*" by Leonard Mustazza. From *Forever Pursuing Genesis: The Myth of Eden in the Novels of Kurt Vonnegut* (1990), pp. 102-115, 205-207. Copyright © 1990 by Associated University Presses. Reprinted with permission of Associated University Presses.

"*Slaughterhouse-Five*" by William Rodney Allen. From *Understanding Kurt Vonnegut* (1991), pp. 77-100. Copyright © 1991 by University of South Carolina Press. Reprinted with permission of University of South Carolina Press.

"Vonnegut as Messenger: *Slaughterhouse-Five*" by Donald E. Morse. From *Kurt Vonnegut* (1992), pp. 22-30. Copyright © 1992 by Starmont House. Reprinted with permission of Wildside Press.

"*Slaughterhouse-Five*: Existentialist Themes Elaborated in a Postmodern Way" by Hans van Stralen. From *Neophilologus* 79, no. 1 (January 1995): 3-12. Copyright © 1995 by Springer Science and Business Media. Reprinted with permission of Springer Science and Business Media.

"Diagnosing Billy Pilgrim: A Psychiatric Approach to Kurt Vonnegut's *Slaughterhouse-Five*" by Susanne Vees-Gulani. From *Critique* 44, no. 2 (Winter 2003): 175-184. Copyright © 2003 by Heldref Publications. Reprinted with permission of Heldref Publications.

"Speaking Personally: *Slaughterhouse-Five* and the Essays" by Jerome Klinkowitz. From *The Vonnegut Effect* (2004), pp. 75-97. Copyright © 2004 by University of South Carolina Press. Reprinted with permission of University of South Carolina Press.

Marling, Karal Ann, 82
Mary O'Hare. *See* O'Hare, Mary
McHale, Brian, 279
Meeter, Glenn, 232
Merrill, Robert, 215, 232, 248
Metafiction, 287
Meyer, Eric, 92
Milton, John, 232
Modernism, 53, 279
Montana Wildhack. *See* Wildhack, Montana
Morse, Donald E., 31
Mother Night (Vonnegut), 9, 111, 158, 174, 186, 196, 255, 269, 312, 328
Murchie, Guy, 153
Mustazza, Leonard, 29, 299

Names and naming, 95, 180, 194, 197, 237, 309, 328
Narration and narrators, 5, 15, 26, 83, 133, 149, 181, 216, 220, 224, 254, 260, 284, 286, 299, 308, 317
Nealon, Jeffrey T., 104
Nixon, Richard, 80, 96, 105

O'Hare, Bernard V. (*Slaughterhouse-Five*), 15, 38, 67, 72, 144, 220, 227, 255, 318
O'Hare, Mary (*Slaughterhouse-Five*), 5, 15, 67, 83, 125, 144-145, 213, 224, 265, 318, 332
O'Sullivan, Maurice, 215-216

Pacifism, 61, 68, 175-176, 215
Palm Sunday (Vonnegut), 11, 23, 265
Paradise Lost (Milton), 232
Patch, Jerry, 75
Paul Lazzaro. *See* Lazzaro, Paul
Pilgrim, Billy (*Slaughterhouse-Five*), 5, 29, 36, 67, 85, 114, 126, 132, 149, 160, 180, 192, 198, 205, 232, 257,

270, 282, 293, 315; as Christ figure, 164, 199, 258; innocence of, 68, 130, 235, 274; and schizophrenia, 22, 233, 286, 293, 303
Player Piano (Vonnegut), 4, 9, 190
Postmodernism, 72, 77, 83, 91, 103, 279, 288, 290, 328
Post-traumatic stress disorder, 261, 294
Prescott, P. S., 191
Pynchon, Thomas, 77, 81, 92, 191, 324

Rackstraw, Loree, 34
Reed, Peter J., 26, 88, 255, 266
"Report on the Barnhouse Effect" (Vonnegut), 9
Richard M. Zhlubb. *See* Zhlubb, Richard M.
Roethke Theodore, 198, 228, 275, 320
Ronald Weary. *See* Weary, Ronald
Rosewater, Eliot (*Slaughterhouse-Five*), 112, 123, 153, 233, 275, 298, 326
Rubens, Philip M., 219
Rubin, Louis D., Jr., 65
Rumfoord, Bertram (*Slaughterhouse-Five*), 91, 127, 136, 310
Russell, Bertrand, 193

Sacks, Sheldon, 179, 188
Sartre, Jean-Paul, 279
Satire, 65, 76, 84, 132, 317
Schatt, Stanley, 248
Schickel, Richard, 158
Scholes, Robert, 23, 26, 111, 191, 276
Scholl, Peter, 215, 232, 248
Schriber, Mary Sue, 249
"Science Fiction" (Vonnegut), 312
Scoggins, Michael C., 65
Scott, Nathan A., Jr., 25, 32
Shaw, Patrick, 215
Sheed, Wilfred, 248
Silverstein, Norman, 40

"Yon Yonson," 146, 150, 196, 218, 223, 230, 290

Yossarian, John Joseph (*Catch-22*), 68; sanity of, 69

Zhlubb, Richard M. (*Gravity's Rainbow*), 96

Ziolkowski, Theodore, 165